Leading Change in Healthcare

Leading Change in Healthcare

TRANSFORMING ORGANIZATIONS USING COMPLEXITY, POSITIVE PSYCHOLOGY AND RELATIONSHIP-CENTERED CARE

Edited by

ANTHONY L SUCHMAN, MD, MA

Senior Consultant, Healthcare Consultancy
McArdle Ramerman & Company
Rochester, NY, USA

DAVID J SLUYTER, EdD

Fetzer Institute
Kalamazoo, MI, USA

PENELOPE R WILLIAMSON, ScD

Senior Consultant
Relationship Centered Health Care
Baltimore, MD, USA

Forewords by

PETER BLOCK

Author and Citizen
Cincinnati, OH, USA

CAROL A ASCHENBRENER, MD

Executive Vice President and Chief Strategy Officer
Association of American Medical Colleges
Washington, DC, USA

RALPH STACEY

Professor of Management and Director
Complexity and Management Centre
Business School
University of Hertfordshire, UK

Radcliffe Publishing
London • New York

Radcliffe Publishing Ltd
33–41 Dallington Street
London
EC1V 0BB
United Kingdom

www.radcliffepublishing.com
Electronic catalogue and worldwide online ordering facility.

British Library Cataloguing in Publication Data

A catalogue record for this book is available from the British Library.

ISBN-13: 978 184619 448 1

Typeset by Pindar NZ, Auckland, New Zealand
Printed and bound by Cadmus Communications, USA

Contents

Foreword by Peter Block

There is no industry encountering rougher seas than healthcare. In the last 20 years or so every industry has gone through its own private hell, but few have been so politicized and moralized as medical institutions and healthcare professionals for the way they do their business. Most of this "reform" conversation is about cost and ideology. The cost burden in companies is shifting to the employee; fewer people can afford healthcare; the total cost of healthcare is consuming an increasing amount of our national wealth. The debate also focuses on questions of whether every citizen has a right to healthcare and whether services should be privatized or single payer. Add to these issues the argument about what procedures and research are morally right or wrong and you have a lot on your hands.

All of this conversation is commonly called "healthcare reform," but it is not really about that. It is essentially about the distribution of money and which ideology wins. Little of it has to do with the essence of care, which is the day-to-day way healthcare professionals actually work with each other and with patients to reduce human suffering. This is the playing field where real reform will be played out, or not. Reform is about shifting our thinking and our practices, often in radical and previously unthinkable ways.

The good news is that most people in healthcare are longing for change or even transformation. They know the system could be much better, and yet most people in healthcare feel a sense of helplessness about what they can do to make the shift happen. That is where this book, *Leading Change in Healthcare*, makes a contribution. It offers new ways of thinking and doing that local institutions and units within those institutions can implement today, often at very little cost.

This new way of thinking is being developed in a context where for the last three decades every executive has given ten talks a year about the need for change. A whole industry has arisen out of the anxiety that the future seems increasingly uncertain, and that industry is called "change management." Most every large and small consulting firm now makes a living from the need for adaptable, agile, lean, resilient, thriving organizations. Not a bad thing, except that most of the efforts to produce these kinds of organizations have not worked. The reason is that all the methodologies have several things working against them: They believe that the future can be managed, engineered and blueprinted; they start with a vision, a plan and strategy to enroll people; they talk about getting people "on board;" they begin to train people in the new requirements and then measure them more closely. These strategies think change starts at the top and needs to be defined from the beginning and then rolled out like a new marketing strategy.

These are the hallmarks of conventional thinking about reform. If so many in healthcare want it to change, but have little hope that it will, holding on to these conventions is a good part of the reason why nothing will change. If we truly want a future distinct from the past, better planning, better design, more measurement, and tighter management cannot get us there. What is needed is more open-hearted leadership and more open-ended, relational and deeply democratic ways of thinking.

This is where this book begins and why the book is important.

Leading Change in Healthcare is an ambitious undertaking in several ways. For one, it attempts to combine theory and practice. It begins with some core theories that have been developing in the leadership and organizational change world and tells us, in effect, if you get a basic grasp of these ideas, you are well equipped to discover new ways of bringing powerful outcomes into the life of large systems. Then come the stories of people using these ideas and making a big difference in communities and healthcare institutions. Bringing together these theories and practical applications in and of itself is a big step forward. There is a serious attempt here to bring together disciplines in change management that usually only meet each other in passing when presented at the same conference.

Each of the theories is worth careful attention. Complexity theory here is enriched by the focus on relationships, rather than the more traditional reference to science. "Relationship-centered Care" is a way of thinking that brings love and all that is personal into a world, the world of healthcare, that is mostly interested in more control and more data-based, evidence-based practices.

In a world that is primarily interested in disease and problem-based practice, this book talks about ways to change institutions by focusing on people's strengths and on the times in an institution's life where something worked well. These disciplines from positive psychology bring something relatively fresh and new to the change-management world. Included among them is perhaps the most innovative recent thinking about how social systems transform themselves: the discipline of Positive Deviance. In this work, whole villages and large systems have produced stunning outcomes by believing that whatever the problem, the answer lies with the community and its members.

These disciplines from positive psychology are organized around what is possible in the world, rather than what is wrong with it. You may notice that this worldview is radically different from what drives the ongoing healthcare debate. Healthcare is a sector where everyone thinks there is something wrong and the way to improve it is to focus even more on what is wrong. This is tantamount to not liking what is playing on a radio station and reacting by turning up the volume. So to present theory and practice that focus on gifts and what is working is an important step. In fact this may be the key to real reform in healthcare.

The final invitation in this book is to bring what we know about being an authentic, grounded, spiritual human being into the mix. The timeless ideas of self-acceptance, listening, silence, reflection, and self-awareness are offered as serious practices to be carried into what is probably one of the most stressful, high-tension work environments we know. The point is made throughout that administrators cannot bring real change into their healthcare institutions without going through change themselves. We are familiar with the admonition to physicians to first heal themselves, and so too must administrators.

Finally, how the book speaks to administrators is in itself significant. In most industries, the executives, the managers, the bosses are fully honored, blessed and made heroes. Bill Gates, Steve Jobs, Lee Iacocca, Rupert Murdoch, Jack Welch and Donald Trump are folk heroes. Administrators and executives in healthcare do not enjoy such privilege. In this industry, all the romance surrounds the physician and the nurse. They have been eulogized and publicized into noble warriors. Administrators live in their shadow.

This book speaks to administrators in that way honors the importance of this job. Rightfully so. We need to be grateful for people who take on this work. It takes a special kind of patience and commitment to lead a business that has a cost structure that no reasonable person would invent if starting today. It takes a special kind of wisdom to lead a culture where there is inherent tension between nurses, physicians, and the functions that support them. Then add the reality that every interest group and organized entity in the world—government, business, unions, associations, and professional guilds—have a hand in controlling practices, finding fault when bad things happen and setting guidelines in the name of safety and cost. They all have a piece of the action and, given the huge money involved, want their way.

In the midst of this, somebody has to manage the store and seek new ways to create institutions that can deliver on the promise of giving healing and compassionate service to the community. The work itself, the work of healing, is a sacred and caring vocation. It succeeds when every participant, both service provider and patient, is treated in a unique and generous way. There is a level of vulnerability in the customer and service provider that exists in few other industries. Creating systems that make this relationship easier and build enough common purpose and cooperation to succeed is quite a challenge. Systems are not designed for care; they are designed for control, efficiency and predictability. This is the paradox facing every administrator.

The real promise of this book is that it offers a way of thinking about administration that enables it to create humane systems that can also operate effectively in a control- and predictability-mad culture. The change efforts chronicled in this book demonstrate that when you focus on relationships you can produce amazing outcomes. That when you listen deeply to your own soul speaking and also listen deeply to people at the lower levels of a system, something important starts to shift and the culture becomes more human and capable of authentic care. You discover that the huge class system that exists in most institutions can be transcended and people begin to function more as equals and partners. This book gives examples where this occurs. The examples also show that a more organic and emergent way of thinking about change can produce surprising results beyond what might have been predicted by a more planned and engineered approach.

So in the end, what is of great value in this book is the useful questioning of the beliefs about leadership and control and outcomes that we hold dear. The system world in general, putting healthcare aside for the moment, is in dire need of fresh air and new beginnings. The care and thoughtfulness that went into creating *Leading Change in Healthcare* gives some wonderful clues that can eventually restore some humanity to all systems in their effort to make each of our contacts with them a little more humane, and a little better for the health of all of us, insiders and outsiders alike.

Peter Block
Author and Citizen
Cincinnati, OH
USA
November 2010

Foreword by Carol A Aschenbrener

Legend has it that Pearl Bailey—famed entertainer, humanitarian and former US Goodwill Ambassador to the United Nations—when asked to speak at a gala dinner about the secret of her remarkable life rose to the dais and said, "Life is so daily." Then she returned to her seat.

Life *is* so daily and so is the path to any meaningful change.

In healthcare, the calls for change come daily—from policy makers, payers, media, and patients frustrated in their search for coordinated care. Many physicians and healthcare leaders dismiss the doom-and-gloom rhetoric because they have heard it all before; the more seasoned among us have heard similar cries in several previous decades. We can argue that the crisis is different this time because the federal debt defies imagination, the recovery from the latest economic crisis is so far a jobless one, and the rate of growth in healthcare costs is unsustainable. Those arguments still may meet with disbelief or a resolution to "wait it out" until the next leadership change or retirement. But these times are different in a more compelling way. Amid the storms of economic crisis and the storming of partisan politics, there is an unprecedented opportunity for the healthcare professions to take a dominant role in reshaping, indeed transforming, healthcare in America. There *is* the possibility that, together, we could create a system that would, some day, meet the needs of all for safe, current, competent, compassionate, accessible and patient-centered care, the system that many of us dreamed of as naïve but hope-filled health professions students.

Such transformative change will mean leaving behind old and comfortable views about professional and leadership roles, organizational responsibilities and relationships between providers of care and their patients. It will mean taking our commitments to high quality care, accountability, life-long learning and cost-effectiveness to deeper levels and designing systems with the patient at the center. And it will mean developing and sustaining leaders who guide change and bring out the best in people at all levels in the healthcare system. We cannot create a new, responsive system with old hierarchical, mechanistic approaches. We need a new way of seeing, a new way of leading—and the authors provide a clear guide and resources for the path ahead.

It is my privilege to work at the Association of American Medical Colleges (AAMC), a not-for-profit association representing all 133 accredited US and 17 accredited Canadian medical schools; nearly 400 major teaching hospitals and health systems including 62 Department of Veterans Affairs medical centers; and nearly 90 academic and scientific societies. Through these institutions and organizations, the AAMC represents 128 000 faculty members, 75 000 medical students, and 110 000 resident physicians. The AAMC is deeply committed to serving and leading the academic medicine community to improve the health of all. We *do* believe that a better, more responsive healthcare system is possible. And we are convinced that the academic medicine community—which prepares the physician workforce, provides 41% of the charity care in the US, and receives more than 40% of all transferred patients whose illnesses or injuries require a sophisticated level of technology and expertise not available at a community hospital—can offer much to create such a system.

Four years ago, with the guidance of newly arrived AAMC President and CEO Darrell G Kirch, MD, the AAMC embarked on an ambitious agenda of change to develop the organizational competencies that seem essential for the future. We were already a highly regarded organization, valued by our member institutions, respected as a credible source of data in our community and among policy-makers, and financially sound. There was no burning platform, no specter of pain to escape. There was, instead, the belief that the AAMC could do much more to help its member institutions adapt themselves for a very different future and take a significant role in shaping a new healthcare system. We sought first to make change in our own organizational capacities—to become more focused, aligned, accountable, inclusive, agile, innovative and constantly improving—and to enhance our change management expertise in the process. This agenda would require changes in process, patterns of relationships and organizational culture.

Early in this change process, I learned of the culture change work that Tony Suchman and Penny Williamson were doing at the Indiana University School of Medicine. A year later, I and two of my AAMC colleagues signed up for the year-long course, Leading Organizations to Health, led by Tony, Penny and their colleague Diane Rawlins. As a serious student of organizational change for two decades, I was dubious about learning anything new. Was I wrong! Over four long week-ends at a Colorado dude ranch, we spent mornings discussing the theories and afternoons practicing the skills included in *Leading Change in Healthcare*. We returned to Washington with a deeper understanding of the importance of the conversations and relationship-building that are essential to organizational transformation and an array of tactics to engage staff. And it is working. In less than five years, we have:

➤ developed clear strategic priorities and integrated them with the budget process
➤ supplemented the decision-making structure with strategic and operational teams
➤ integrated behaviorally specific values and functional competencies with the performance management process
➤ implemented a competitive compensation system linked to employee development
➤ embedded intentional culture-shaping in our daily work
➤ increased transparency, flow of information and collaboration across the organization and
➤ partnered with our governing board to design and implement a new governance process that takes fiduciary, strategic and generative roles to a higher level.

The work of transformation is far from finished but much of the foundation has been laid. As we move to the next stage—developing more interventional initiatives that could have transformational impact, while maintaining a high level of service to members—we do so in the conviction that the future is, indeed, created in the present, in our daily conversations and actions. The principles and practices illustrated in *Leading Change in Healthcare* will continue to be a guide for action.

No one knows the shape or arrival time of health system reform. We do know some of the essential elements of a system that could meet the needs of all: new delivery models that are patient-centered and cost effective; communication strategies to reach an increasingly diverse population; emphasis on maintenance of health as well as treatment of disease; behavioral change strategies to help patients optimize their genetic endowment and health professionals integrate new knowledge; quality improvement practices to rapidly identify and mitigate sources of unacceptable variation in care; integration of the full cycle of science to bring the new knowledge of basic research to rapid fruition through clinical, translational and community research; and incorporation of implementation science to assess impact and guide us to optimal strategies for making individual behavioral change, as well as organizational change. Most of these needed changes run counter to the current culture of healthcare, to our cherished mental images of who and what is important and how the work should be done. We need new eyes to leverage the opportunities and meet the current challenges in healthcare.

This foreword is written on the eve of the AAMC's 2010 annual meeting, a gathering of more than 4000 leaders in academic medicine. The book is some months from publication but I have already begun alerting colleagues to its message. *Leading Change in Healthcare* offers hope—and a method. A daily dose is just what the change doctor ordered.

Carol A Aschenbrener, MD
Executive Vice President and Chief Strategy Officer
Association of American Medical Colleges, Washington, DC, USA
November 2010

Foreword by Ralph Stacey

Leading Change in Healthcare takes up a matter of great importance not just in the United States but also here in the United Kingdom and the rest of Europe.

Over the past two decades, increased investment, amounting to billions of pounds, has been made in the health sector in the United Kingdom. There has also been a marked change in patterns of power relations with control of the National Health Service shifting decisively away from the front lines of patient care and towards central government, accompanied by a shift in power relations in hospitals with physicians losing control and the new managerial class becoming more powerful. Control has been increasingly exerted through detailed target setting and performance monitoring by central government, enforced by hospital management.

Despite the enormous investment and detailed centralized control, however, reports on progress still conclude that the improvements have been modest at best. Some of the targets have not been met; others have, but often in rather dubious ways that distort clinical decision making. The eager media reporting on all this has created an impression in the wider public that the National Health Service is in decline. Amongst medical professionals of all disciplines there is widespread dissatisfaction with the subordination of their leadership and judgment to the whole "target" culture.

Now the new coalition government has started dismantling the many targets and intends to replace them with a specification of outcomes to be achieved. This sounds like a change in name to me but not a change in the underlying strategy and I am rather pessimistic that continuing efforts to improve healthcare through top-down design and control will make much difference.

A very different picture emerges when you focus instead on the day-to-day care provided by the many dedicated and competent professionals of the National Health Service. Down at the working level, the NHS delivers a very high standard of care to people of all races, classes and ages and is certainly not in decline.

The longstanding patterns of professionalism and service persist despite the distraction and frustration around the rapid succession of macro "improvement" policies.

I think this discrepancy between the perceived macro picture of unsuccessful centralized controls and the actual micro experience of successful healthcare makes a very important point. What we need is not a change in the nomenclature of centralized control but a total change in strategy, shifting the focus of attention from national policies and controls to the local interactions that actually constitute healthcare. Rather than imposing endless, disruptive, top-down policy and structural changes, we need to trust the professionals we rely on for our care, and to engage them in reflecting on and modifying the local patterns of their day-to-day work.

Leading Change in Healthcare makes just this shift in focus—from top-down control to mindful bottom-up participation. It offers a critique of the prevailing management metaphor of organization-as-machine with its linear logic and unrealistic expectations of control, and then elaborates an alternative approach—organization-as-conversation—that is more psychologically sophisticated and recognizes the non-linear, emergent nature of all human undertakings, including organizations. In the theories and illustrative case studies it presents, this book makes an important contribution to thinking about the transformation of healthcare in the UK and everywhere.

Ralph Stacey
Professor of Management
Director, Complexity and Management Centre Business School
University of Hertfordshire, UK
November 2010

List of contributors

DeWitt C Baldwin Jr
Scholar-in-Residence
ACGME
Chicago, IL
USA

Joe Carthy
University College Dublin
Dublin
Ireland

Joanne Cohen-Katz
Director, Behavioral Sciences
Lehigh Valley Health Network Department of Family Medicine
Allentown, PA
USA

Ann H Cottingham
Director of Special Programs
Deans Office of Medical Education and Curricular Affairs
Indiana University School of Medicine
Indianapolis, IN
USA

Alison Donaldson
A Working Alliance
Kingston upon Thames
UK

Julie A Dostal
Vice Chair of Education
Department of Family Medicine
Program Director, Family Medicine Residency Program
Lehigh Valley Health Network
Department of Family Medicine
Allentown, PA
USA

Richard Frankel
Professor of Medicine and Geriatrics (with tenure)
Senior Research Scientist Regenstrief Institute
Indiana University School of Medicine
Indianapolis, IN
USA

Lana Funkhouser
Vice President, Human Resource/Education
Clarian West Medical Center
Avon, IN
USA

Al Gatmaitan
President and CEO
Clarian Arnett Health, Inc.
Lafayette, IN
USA

James L Greene
Retired Medical Anthropologist
West Jefferson, NC
USA

Karen Greiner
Doctoral Student
Communication Studies
Scripps College of Communication
Ohio University
Athens, OH
USA

Thomas S Inui
President and CEO
Sam Regenstrief Professor of Health Services Research
Associate Dean for Health Care Research
Professor of Medicine, Indiana University School of Medicine
Indianapolis, IN
USA

Debra K Litzelman
Richard Powell Professor of Medicine
Associate Dean for Medical Education and Curricular Affairs
Indiana University School of Medicine
Indianapolis, IN
USA

Jane Maher
Consultant Oncologist, Mount Vernon Cancer Centre
Chief Medical Officer, Macmillan Cancer Support
Visiting Professor, Business School, University of Hertfordshire
London
UK

William L Miller
Leonard Parker Pool Chair
Professor of Family Medicine
University of South Florida College of Medicine
Lehigh Valley Health Network
Department of Family Medicine
Allentown, PA
USA

Michael Monaghan
Project Director, UCD Science District Development
University College Dublin
Dublin
Ireland

David L Mossbarger
Manager, Training and Development
Indiana Professional Management Group (IPMG)
Indianapolis, IN
USA

Gopal Naidoo
RKD Architects
Dublin
Ireland

Zeev Neuwirth
Chief of Clinical Effectiveness and Innovation
Harvard Vanguard Medical Associates/Atrius Health
Newton, MA
USA

Beth Newton Watson
Director, Chaplaincy Services
Clinical Pastoral Educator, ACPE and Pastoral Education
Clarian Health
Indianapolis, IN
USA

Kathy O'Boyle
University College Dublin
Dublin
Ireland

Patricia Shaw
Visiting Professor
Business School, University of Hertfordshire
London
UK

Arvind Singhal
Samuel Shirley and Edna Holt Marston Endowed Professor
Department of Communication
University of Texas at El Paso
El Paso, TX
USA

David J Sluyter
Fetzer Institute
Kalamazoo, MI
USA

Emma Sokell
University College Dublin
Dublin
Ireland

Cathy Stoll
Marketing Communications and PR Director
Clarian West Medical Center
Avon, IN
USA

Anthony L Suchman
Senior Consultant, Healthcare Consultancy
McArdle Ramerman & Company
Rochester, NY
USA

Penelope R Williamson
Senior Consultant
Relationship Centered Health Care
Baltimore, MD
USA

William Wilson
Wilson Architects
Boston, MA
USA

Acknowledgments

We are indebted, each in different ways, to the Fetzer Institute for its pioneering work in developing the idea of Relationship-centered Care. This book originated in the work of the Relationship-centered Care Network, a group convened by Fetzer and comprised of innovative health professions educators, researchers and practitioners who implemented Relationship-centered Care in diverse institutions around the United States. We particularly want to acknowledge the work of three people at Fetzer. Rob Lehman initiated the work even before the notion of Relationship-centered Care emerged. Tracy Wimberly, along with one of us (DS) expanded and facilitated the network and, in collaboration with Tom Gillette and John Cronin, created for the other two of us (AS and PW) our first consulting opportunities on Relationship-centered Administration. Mickey Olivanti carried out the organizational work that kept the network vibrant.

We are grateful to the following people for feedback and other forms of help with various parts of the text: Alasdair Honeyman, Diane Rawlins, Larry Belle, Janet Bickel, Chris Callahan, Barry Egener, Brian Justice, Jerry Kaiser, Fay Krawchick, Curt Lindberg, Deb Litzelman, Dan Pesut, David Raymond, Jane Spinner, Ralph Stacey, David Ullman, and Daniel Wolfson.

We offer deep appreciation to Peter Block, Carol Aschenbrener and Ralph Stacey for their thoughtful and thought-provoking forewords.

Many thanks to the editors and staff at Radcliffe Publishing and Pindar NZ for their encouragement, patience, and capable assistance.

Finally, we offer our most profound thanks to the many people who contributed their stories to this book. We appreciate their courage to walk the talk, their efforts to share the wisdom of their experience with others, and their passion to make the world a better place.

Anthony L Suchman
David J Sluyter
Penelope R Williamson
November 2010

In addition to these shared acknowledgments, we'd also like to offer the following personal notes of thanks:

With deep gratitude, I would like to acknowledge my father, J Richard Suchman, for teaching me to think about thinking; Brian Justice for prodding me with his enthusiasm and sense of urgency about this project; my consulting clients for inviting me into their worlds so we could learn together; and the friends and colleagues (more than I can list) in the following organizations from and with whom I have learned so much: Leading Organizations to Health; the American Academy on Communication in Healthcare; the Plexus Institute; the Complexity and Management Centre of the University of Hertfordshire; the Division of Behavioral and Psychosocial Medicine and the Department of Family Medicine at the University of Rochester; and the Department of Medicine at Highland Hospital, Rochester, New York.

My deepest thanks go to my family, the ultimate source of my learning about relationship and authenticity, and especially to my wife, Lynne Feldman. Your love, support and belief in me make everything possible.

Anthony L Suchman

Thank you first to my wife, Jill, who not only offered encouragement and support, but also put on her English teacher hat when I prevailed upon her to review parts of the manuscript. Thank you also to my friend and former associate, Cheri Dundon, who was invaluable in the early stages of the project, and to Mark Nepo, a writer and friend who was always generous with his guidance.

I will also mention our grandchildren, Koby and McKenna Stewart (ages 6 and 8), who let me work even though they would have preferred to use the computer themselves, and who, when asked what advice they had for healthcare professionals and administrators, offered this wise counsel: wash your hands and don't kill your patients.

David J Sluyter

I have learned so much from mentors, friends, and colleagues along the way who have informed my thinking and being. In particular I want to acknowledge George Engel and Parker Palmer who have been key influences in my life. I thank my two co-authors Tony and Dave for inviting me to join them in co-authoring this book and for the profound experience of our thoughtful, fiercely honest and mutually supportive "relationship-centered" collaboration in producing this book. I thank my husband, Jim Dilts, for his love and support, always, and in particular during the writing of this book.

Penelope R Williamson

CHAPTER 1

Introduction

David J Sluyter

HOW THIS BOOK CAME TO BE

As do many great projects, this book began with a chance encounter. The encounter was between two of the authors, Tony Suchman and me (David Sluyter). Tony had come to the Fetzer Institute to participate in a program at its retreat center, Seasons. I had just returned to my office at Fetzer after completing a heavy schedule of travel. During a break in the retreat proceedings, Tony walked over to the administration building to see if I was available for a brief hello and check-in. I was, and as always, was glad to see him. But the brief check-in became an earnest discussion that ended with an idea and a mutual commitment to create this book. Here is how that happened.

Tony had recently completed a graduate degree at the University of Hertfordshire in organizational change with a particular emphasis on *complexity theory*. He was transitioning his career from medical practice, teaching and healthcare administration, to consulting to delivery systems on leadership development and organizational culture change. He was especially interested in applying the concept of *Relationship-centered Care*, a partnership-based clinical philosophy that is gaining prominence in the healthcare sector, in the administrative realm.

As Tony began to talk enthusiastically about his work, especially about the interaction between complexity theory and building relational organizations, I became excited. One of the themes of my work at the Fetzer Institute had been the development and promotion of the concept of Relationship-centered Care. For several years, the Norman Cousins Award, named after the accomplished writer and iconic proponent of humor as an aid to healing, had been presented by the Fetzer Institute to organizations that epitomized Relationship-centered Care in action. Through the nomination process, I knew there were organizations practicing relational models and that many of their stories matched well the concepts which Tony was discussing. Tony, of course, knew of other organizations through his consulting work.

Both of us realized that the organization itself can often be one of the impediments to implementing Relationship-centered Care. It is difficult to be relationship-centered or to practice relational healthcare with integrity in an organization that is not itself relational; an organization, for example, which is excessively budget-driven with profit as the highest value, or in which a strict command and control hierarchy is the dominant leadership style.

As we talked, I said at one point, "We should write a book about this." It was an exclamation more than a suggestion, but by the end of our brief encounter, we had made a commitment to seriously explore the idea of this book.

This book is the very embodiment of one of its core themes from complexity theory—that a small perturbation like a chance meeting and conversation can grow into a large effect over time. This pattern is recapitulated in the stories that illustrate the concepts presented in this book. The addition of Penny Williamson as a co-author is another example that will play out often, that of a person "showing up" who has the skills and ability needed at the time. In this case, Penny, who had worked closely with both of us, was highly skilled at working in healthcare organizations in a relational way and in leading these organizations towards the processes in which we were most interested. She appeared on the scene at a time when Tony and I had reached a bit of a plateau on the project, and her infusion of enthusiasm and energy helped re-energize us and bring the project to a successful conclusion.

THE NEED FOR *LEADING CHANGE IN HEALTHCARE*

Why bring forward yet another book in the already crowded field of leadership and management? The short answer is that you cannot look anywhere in healthcare today without confronting the need for major organizational change. It might be transforming roles and processes to improve patient safety and customer service, reducing health disparities, or increasing access to care. It might be changing the patterns of interaction among basic scientists, clinical researchers, policy makers, industry, and the public so that research findings translate more directly into better care and better health. It might be fostering interprofessional health professions education or improving the learning environment for students—the "informal curriculum" that shapes their emerging professional identities. Or it might be restructuring healthcare delivery to provide better service at a lower cost.

Success in addressing every type of strategic organizational initiative depends upon changing the way people work together. For-profit, non-profit and public sector organizations alike are seeking to unleash the full wisdom, creativity and initiative of their work forces by changing the workplace environment and changing the traditional top-down relationships between managers and staff.

In the face of these and so many other changes, most healthcare leaders find themselves thrust into the responsibility for leading change without the benefit of adequate preparation for this work. Few have undertaken formal study or had skilled role models. But, arguably, the biggest barrier to effective organizational change is the persistent and widespread use of an outdated and psychologically unsophisticated theory—Frederick Taylor's 19th century model of Scientific Management. The top-down redesign and re-education initiatives it engenders fail to harness the wisdom of front-line workers or win their commitment. These workers are further antagonized when the failure of change programs is attributed disparagingly to their "resistance" or the difficulty of "herding cats." All this leads to ineffective action, the waste of scarce resources and widespread cynicism. Frustration abounds.

Fortunately many exciting and effective new approaches are emerging from a variety of disciplines. *Leading Change in Healthcare* will introduce you to practical and proven new approaches from complexity science, positive psychology and Relationship-centered Care, all of which converge on the idea of leading by participating mindfully and authentically in each moment. This new integrated approach, which we call *Relationship-centered Administration*, offers an evidence-based alternative to traditional organizational change methodologies—one that is far more effective.

Leading Change in Healthcare will be a resource for executives, managers and team leaders in every kind of healthcare organization: hospitals, group practices, home care, research institutes, health professions schools, insurers, regulatory organizations, for-profits, non-profits, and governmental organizations. The principles in this book apply equally well to organizations outside of healthcare and are also relevant for students and teachers of management and leadership. Readers of all types will hone their leadership skills by:

➤ appreciating Relationship-centered Administration as an effective new approach to the work of organizational change and management;
➤ learning to apply principles of complexity theory, positive psychology and Relationship centered Care to organizational behavior and culture change and performance improvement;
➤ seeing that an organization-wide focus on "right relationships" can result in excellent performance on financial, quality and other measures;
➤ recognizing the importance of the leader's authenticity and personal presence, and how these qualities can be developed by deeper engagement and reflection; and
➤ restoring hope by reinforcing their belief in the possibility of positive and comprehensive organizational change and the creation of collaborative and respectful work environments for employees, patients, families, customers, students and other stakeholders.

These are ambitious goals. As in any work that is breaking new ground, this book represents our best contribution to what we hope will become a growing body of literature fostering the development of compassionate organizations that focus on people, not at the expense of but as means to economic viability. We believe, and the case studies presented here confirm, that you can be relational and profitable at the same time.

A BRIEF OVERVIEW

Leading Change in Healthcare is written in two parts plus three appendices. Part 1 contains four chapters that put forth the theories that serve as the conceptual foundation of Relationship-centered Administration. These are practical theories. In the midst of uncertain and complicated organizational situations, they offer guidance in making sense of what's going on and figuring out what to do. Part 2 contains eight case studies that show these theories in action. We hear the voices of the people who lived the stories telling us what they did and what it felt like to work in this way—what to expect. They are written informally as narratives about what happened, not as an instruction manual or recipe book. (Indeed, one of the main points of the book is that there are no recipes, no standard solutions that can be known in advance and imposed on organizations.) Each case study is accompanied by a commentary that links it to the principles of Relationship-centered Administration. A brief overview of the chapters follows.

The theory section (Part 1) begins with Chapter 2, which contrasts the traditional view of organizations as machines with a more dynamic perspective that integrates principles from complexity science: organizations as conversations. This perspective shows how organizational identity and culture are patterns of thinking and relating, respectively, that are being created continuously in the course of moment-to-moment human interaction. These patterns are self-sustaining, but sometimes small disturbances in the patterns can spread rapidly to become large transformational patterns. For change agents, this perspective redirects efforts away from elaborately planned top-down projects and moves towards a more spontaneous, participative, emergent approach that helps groups reflect on how they are working together—what patterns they are creating in each moment—and fosters more mindfulness and authentic participation.

Chapter 3 introduces several relevant theories from the domain of positive psychology, and grounds them in recent research on brain function. *Self-Determination Theory* is a rigorous, practical theory of human motivation. Well proven in workplace, educational and healthcare settings, it describes factors that help individuals voluntarily adopt and maintain new behaviors. *Appreciative Inquiry* is a well-established method that turns the logic of problem solving upside down. Instead of looking for what is wrong in an organization and trying to fix it, Appreciative Inquiry looks for what is right, discovering and disseminating the root causes of success. It presumes and calls forth the competence of each individual. Because it is a highly social process based on sharing and exploring success stories, it also builds community as it unfolds. *Positive Deviance* also presumes and calls forth the capacity of an entire organization. It features an internally facilitated search for innovative solutions and best practices within the organization and constant rapid-cycle experimentation.

Chapter 4 presents the history and core concepts of Relationship-centered Care, a clinical philosophy that features robust partnership and respect for personhood at every level of healthcare: between patients, family members and clinicians; between members of the healthcare team; and between healthcare organizations and their communities. Underlying and supporting these levels of partnership is one's relationship with self. The goal of Relationship-centered Administration, the focus of this book, is to bring the same qualities of partnership and respect from the clinical to the organization realm—to treat clinical staff members in the same way that we want them to treat their patients. The case studies in Part 2 demonstrate the power of this approach.

The notion of "relationship with self" that is highlighted in Relationship-centered Care is more fully developed in Chapter 5. This chapter explores the importance of *self–awareness, self-acceptance,* and *awareness and acceptance of others* as the foundation of effective leadership. These are the core capacities that enable one to participate mindfully in the pattern-making here and now, to call forth the best capacities of others, and to form trustworthy relationships. This chapter shows that Relationship-centered Administration is more than a set of theories and skills; it is a way of being.

Part 2 contains eight case studies, representing a range of organizational and geographic settings. Each illustrates in detail the application of the principles of Relationship-centered Administration that were described in Part 1. In keeping with one of the core principles of relationship-centered process—valuing diversity—we have respected the unique language and narrative styles of each of the authors and have not imposed a standard format. Instead, we offer a commentary on each case study to point out the various theories at work and to highlight connections and comparisons with other cases.

Part 2 begins with two stories about systematic, organization-wide implementations of Relationship-centered Care. Chapter 6 tells the story of Clarian West Medical Center, a new for-profit community hospital that made Relationship-centered Care one of its core operating principles. The story describes the hiring and orientation of the staff and the opening of the hospital. At every step, the management team tried to treat the staff in the same relationship-centered way that they hoped the staff would treat patients and families. The result was top hospital performance in every category.

In Chapter 7, we find the story of the Department of Family Medicine at Lehigh Valley Health Network, a large academic community hospital. It describes the establishment and growth of a new academic department and an associated residency program within a large traditional medical center. As with Clarian West, the Department strove to mindfully live the values of Relationship-centered Care in every aspect of its function. This involved experimenting with various governance models, organizational rituals, selection and recruitment methods and assessment processes. Throughout the story, we see the organizational leaders struggle to hold fast to the vision while remaining open to negotiating the details of implementation. The Clarian West and Lehigh Valley stories both demonstrate that Relationship-centered Administration can have a very positive impact on professional and organizational performance.

Chapter 8 takes us to Kenya and the emergence of a multifaceted organization to fight the HIV/AIDS epidemic in that country. The dramatic story describes a regional system of treatment and care, the Academic Model for Prevention and Treatment of HIV/AIDS (AMPATH), that transcends traditional medical management and begins to actively address a variety of social issues. The program has grown to include provision of maintenance medications, prevention initiatives, food production and distribution for patients who need it, outreach and support services and more. It offers an outstanding example of *emergent design*.

Fostering organizational change almost always begins by gathering a group of like-minded people and helping them become a community of change with a shared identity, a common purpose and an agenda for collective action. The case study in Chapter 9 describes the convening of 12 nurses and allied health professionals to change the thinking in the United Kingdom on how to deal with the short- and long-term effects of cancer treatment in community settings. The group is composed of senior health professionals who are active both in academic/research and clinical venues. The story describes in detail how the group formed, established its purpose and culture and began to work, and how these processes were helped, though never controlled, by skilled facilitation and careful attention to communication process.

Positive Deviance, an organizational change methodology introduced in Chapter 3, is described in greater detail in Chapter 10. This absorbing story describes the effort of a large Veterans Administration healthcare system to eliminate MRSA, a dangerous hospital-acquired bacterial infection. The project leaders engaged the entire staff and also patients in a creative process to accomplish behavior change on a large scale. The change process both presumed and called forth the wisdom and leadership of everyone in the organization. The story challenges traditional views about the need for and role of outside expertise and shows how staff, patients and families are ultimately the best source of solutions.

The redesign of medical facilities requires the integration of diverse perspectives and the anticipation of practice models that aren't yet in place. Chapter 11 describes a redesign process not in healthcare but in university science education where there are also independent-minded professionals reluctant to depart from the status quo. The story describes the work of a faculty design team charged with building a new science center at the University College Dublin, the largest university in Ireland. The team needed to design a new, more flexible building which would be conducive to modern teaching modalities. The project leaders hoped to disturb standing patterns of thinking about teaching, learning and instructional space. Using site visits to other universities, novel conversational formats and even, at one point, an impassioned personal story, they set in motion a wave of transformational change. The story affords us the opportunity to get inside the minds of the project leaders, understanding what they observed and felt, how they made sense of what was happening and how they decided what to do.

Demoralization is widespread in primary care, as is the need for a more efficient and effective practice model (with the "medical home" being the latest new solution). In Chapter 12, we read about a remarkable turnaround in a large primary care practice within Harvard Vanguard Medical Associates that was beset with internal conflict and low morale. In that state, it was utterly incapable of fulfilling its part in an organization-wide initiative to introduce a new patient-centered model of care. The first step taken by the new practice leader was to inaugurate a process of listening, healing and relationship building that succeeded enormously in just a few months. It also positioned the practice to implement the Toyota Production System, or Lean, resulting in the massive redesign of work processes and job roles, all undertaken enthusiastically by the staff and resulting in dramatic improvements in practice performance. This one dysfunctional site quickly became the innovation leader for the whole system. Their work instigated a change process that spread throughout the entire multispecialty group practice. This chapter and its commentary describe in depth the relationship-centered social dynamics that are at the heart of Lean and a major source of this method's success. Unfortunately, these social dynamics are overshadowed or even displaced by the analytic technique in some Lean implementations, compromising results.

The last case study, Chapter 13, describes a far-reaching initiative taken on by the second largest medical school in the US, the Indiana University School of Medicine (IUSM). A new competency-based curriculum had been introduced that included such relationship-centered competencies as professionalism, ethics, self-awareness and communication. The story describes the application of *emergent design* and *Appreciative Inquiry* in a four year project focused on changing the "informal curriculum" of medical education—the organizational culture, which is the most powerful influence on students' emerging sense of professionalism.

Following some summative comments in the Conclusion (Chapter 14) are three appendices describing specific methods to support the implementation of Relationship-centered Administration. Appendix 1 describes specific communication techniques that build the partnerships that are the hallmark of relationship-centered process in both clinical and administrative settings. It also includes descriptions of exercises you can use to teach these techniques to others. Appendix 2 describes conversational formats and facilitation techniques you can use to make meetings more relational, and thus use meetings to help create a more relationship-centered organizational culture. Appendix 3 applies the principles of relationship-centered process to the crucial administrative practices of delegating authority and maintaining accountability. The latter is often problematic in that critical feedback is widely believed to pose a threat to relationships. Managers often avoid giving important feedback for just this reason. This chapter offers practice guidance and shows how even a dismissal from a job can be accomplished in a relational fashion.

Taken together, these theories, case studies, and practical methods offer a transformative new approach to organizational change, one that integrates the best new thinking from complexity, positive psychology, Relationship-centered

Care and authentic presence. We have adopted the term Relationship-centered Administration to emphasize that Relationship-centered Care can only be provided by an organization that holds strongly to relational principles and values in all of its activities, onstage and off. We hope you will see that these principles and values are based on rigorous theories and that introducing them into your organization can result in both a better workplace culture and better performance and business success. We also hope that this book will contribute to a broader movement already in progress to make the organizational world a more relational place, which will make it a healthier place for us all.

PART I

Practical Theories

CHAPTER 2

How we think about organizations: a complexity perspective

Anthony L Suchman

The way we think about organizational change makes a big difference in the way we approach the work and, ultimately, how successful we are. In Part 1, we offer the foundations of a new way of thinking that we call Relationship-centered Administration. It integrates a variety of theories and perspectives including complexity science, positive psychology, Relationship-centered Care, authentic presence and others.

This chapter compares two ways of thinking about organizations. The first is a mechanistic perspective that has been around for a hundred years and is still the basis for most managerial thinking and action. We contend that it is psychologically unsophisticated and creates expectations of control that are unrealistic and get us into trouble. The newer perspective is based on principles of complexity—the spontaneous emergence and evolution (self-organization) of patterns that occurs everywhere in nature.[1] It weans us off our unrealistic expectations of control and focuses our attention instead on the continuous, unpredictable pattern-making of human interaction.

With this complexity perspective on organizations as a foundation, the following three chapters of Part 1 further develop the concept of Relationship-centered Administration adding principles of individual and group behavior change, relationship process and personal presence and authenticity. This new theory is better suited to the world of human interaction than a theory about machines. It will show us that to change big patterns of organizational culture and behavior we have to start with the small patterns of how we are working together in each moment. It will lead us to be more mindful of and intentional about how we relate to others and the patterns we are creating with our every act. And it will show us that our capacity to be authentically present and to value the differences of others is the ultimate source of organizational creativity and resourcefulness.

Before we begin to build the theory of Relationship-centered Administration, it would be helpful to reflect for a moment on theories in general and how it is that they exert such a powerful influence on our day-to-day lives.

NOTICING THEORIES IN ACTION

A theory is not a truth; it is a story we invent to explain how and why things happen and to help us figure out what to do. It may be formal or informal; expressed in the dense language of scientific prose or the imaginative and ambiguous language of mythology. It may be rigorously tested and refined by researchers or invented on-the-spot by people who are working on a task. And it may be transmitted in any number of ways: by means of an oral folk-tradition, a scholarly book or a set of operating instructions.

Theories do their work by helping us focus our attention. In the midst of any given activity, there are an infinite number of internal and external stimuli that impinge on us and are available for our attention—everything that we can see, hear, touch, smell or taste; every emotional sensation; every memory and thought that could potentially come into awareness. There are also an infinite number of actions we could take. Theories help us by filtering our perceptions, sorting out what deserves attention and what to ignore, and reducing to a manageable number the choices of action we should consider. Without them we would be overwhelmed and paralyzed.

> Theories help us by filtering our perceptions, sorting out what deserves attention and what to ignore, and reducing to a manageable number the choices of action we should consider. Without them we would be overwhelmed and paralyzed.

Here's an example of theories at work. Imagine that we're sitting before a hearth enjoying a fire that has burned low and is in need of rejuvenation. If our theory of fire is "in order to burn, a fire needs wood" we'll look for more wood and won't pay any attention to the dishes, bottles or light bulbs that are within view. If our theory describes the essential roles of fuel, oxygen and concentrated heat, we'll pay attention not only to the wood, but also to the space between the logs and the proximity of the coals to the new logs we're hoping to ignite. The second theory directs our attention to important observations (air and heat) and potential actions (spread the logs just a little, pile up the coals) that we would miss using the first theory; under its guidance we are more likely to successfully rekindle the fire. This example shows us how theories help us by filtering perceptions, focusing attention, and guiding action.

But theories can also get in our way and limit us. They may be incomplete, failing to direct our attention to important observations, as we saw in the first fire building example. Theories can also be self-fulfilling and self-reinforcing. By focusing our attention, they determine what we perceive. Our perceptions then constitute the body of data from which we create an interpretation—a story we tell ourselves about what's happening around us. That story then shapes our expectations, intentions and behaviors. In a circular fashion, our stories and expectations can then go back and influence how we focus our attention. (We know from many studies of expectancy bias, the Hawthorne effect, how powerfully expectations shape perceptions.) Thus a theory can perpetuate itself by making it harder for us to perceive data that are inconsistent with it and might prove it wrong.

An example may be helpful here.[2] Suppose I am giving a talk and you are in the audience. As my talk proceeds, I notice that you are nodding off to sleep intermittently. From that data, I form an interpretation, a theory about you, namely, that you are not interested in my ideas. At the end of my talk, when you ask me a question, the story I've started to tell myself about you leads me to expect that you will be dismissive of what I'm about to say, so I respond in a somewhat hostile and arrogant fashion, which not surprisingly elicits a hostile response from you. I see this and think, "Aha! I knew you were against me!" and from that moment on I will be on the lookout for further evidence of your hostility, so much so that I could easily miss cues that you are actually very interested in what I'm saying. Now the truth might be that you were so interested in my talk that you attended even though your 14-month-old kept you up all night, and you felt badly that you couldn't stay awake. But my brusque response to your question might lead you to think, "What a jerk! Why did I bother coming to this talk?" My erroneous theory about your sleeping set in motion a self-fulfilling and self-reinforcing pattern of hostility.

Our theories tend to operate subliminally. We often forget that they are theories; we forget that we are seeing selectively filtered information and presume that we are simply seeing "reality." (This was the case when I mistook my theory about your falling asleep as a fact; I started to climb a "ladder of inference."[3]) So it's important for us pause from time to time to think about how we think, and to pay attention to how we pay attention. Often this will reveal limiting assumptions that we have been making and allow new ways of thinking and acting to emerge. In this spirit, then, let's proceed to examine how we think about organizations.

CONVENTIONAL MANAGEMENT THEORY: AN ORGANIZATION IS A MACHINE

Current management practice has its origins in a theory called Scientific Management that was published by Frederick Taylor a hundred years ago.[4] It invites us to look at an organization as a machine. A machine is designed with a specific purpose in mind, each part moving precisely and reliably to serve its function in the larger process of turning the "input" into the desired "output." A machine can be fully specified in a blueprint which is the end product of a design process. If the design is sound and the blueprint and operating instructions are faithfully executed, the machine will fulfill the designer's exact intentions. If a machine does not perform as expected, the engineers try to improve its performance by either correcting errors in how the blueprint was executed or by "going back to the drawing board" to come up with a better design.

The machine metaphor leads us to view an organization as a group of workers carrying out their assigned tasks exactly as instructed, precisely and without variation, to achieve the desired outcomes (objects manufactured, services provided, revenue generated, etc.). The organization's blueprints include its mission statement, bylaws, organizational chart, budget, strategic plan, and policy and procedure manuals. When something about the organization needs to change, the managers sequester themselves someplace and return with a new blueprint for everyone to follow.

The machine metaphor for managing organizations has been remarkably successful in the evolution of industrialization and mass production. But there are at least three major problems in using it as a framework for management and leading change.[5] The first is that it creates expectations of control that are unrealistic and cause anxiety. Machines are supposed do exactly what we want them to do. They obey the logic of linear causality: A causes B; if you know A you can predict B; if you can control A you can control B. Everything in the organization should be subject to prediction and control.[6] When unexpected things happen or things don't go according to plan, someone must be at fault. Either the plan wasn't good enough or the employees did not execute it properly. This generates anxiety and defensiveness; nobody likes to be at fault. It makes people reluctant to talk about errors and waste. A considerable amount of attention and activity gets diverted towards self-justification and self-protection and away from doing the work at hand. And anxiety actually alters brain function, rendering people less capable of thinking creatively (*see* Interpersonal Neurobiology in Chapter 3).

The second problem with the machine model is that it puts all the responsibility for designing and operating the machine on the engineer. Machine parts don't think or come up with new ideas. It's the engineer's job to do that. So when we view an organization as a machine we assume that it's the manager who is supposed to be creating the plans. In so doing, we fail to avail ourselves of a vast resource—the creativity of the workers—and we diminish their motivation (*see* Self-Determination Theory in Chapter 3). In healthcare, where the opportunities for standardization are limited, most care plans must be individualized and cannot be specified in generic plans or treatment guidelines. The front line staff members, who are in closest contact with patients and families, must exercise considerable independent judgment, which is incompatible with the machine model.

The third problem is that the machine model is not psychologically sophisticated. By predisposing us to see people as machine parts, it leads us to approach organizational change as if it is a purely technical matter—getting the design right—without attending to all the human dimensions of change such as fears, losses, and changes of identity and loyalties.[7]

To summarize, traditional management theory focuses attention on the manager's intended outcomes and the creation of blueprints. It likens the manager to an engineer, and thus fosters expectations of control and responsibility. This way of thinking can be very useful; it has given rise to technological breakthroughs and analytic methods such as process mapping and statistical process control that can lead to substantial improvements in quality and efficiency in processes for which standardization is desirable. However, standardization is neither desirable nor possible in most circumstances given the enormous amount of individualization and shared decision making needed in the activities of a healthcare organization. And unlike machine parts, human beings are not amenable to having their behavior designed and specified by others. Thus the machine metaphor is ill-suited to most management tasks and to the work of organizational change.

RELATIONSHIP-CENTERED ADMINISTRATION: AN ORGANIZATION IS A CONVERSATION

A very different image lies at the heart of Relationship-centered Administration: the organization as a conversation.[8] Not just a metaphor, this is actually the case. An organization is a conversation before it is anything else: it begins with people talking together about something they would like to do that is beyond their capacity to do as individuals. At some point, their shared idea gains sufficient coherence—there is sufficient similarity in what each of the individuals is understanding—that they can begin to coordinate their actions effectively. That's when the organization begins to function. As the themes in the conversation change, so will the more tangible aspects of an organization: buildings get torn down; organizational charts are modified; budgets are revised; people are hired, fired, promoted and so forth. The organizational conversation is at the core of everything.

> An organization is a conversation before it is anything else: it begins with people talking together about something they would like to do that is beyond their capacity to do as individuals.

We can perceive a healthcare organization as a gigantic complicated conversation involving its staff, patients (and their families), payers, regulators, neighbors, competitors, and anyone else who interacts with or is affected by it. Within this gigantic conversation, there are, of course, myriad sub-conversations. Some are formal and ongoing, such as regularly recurring board meetings. Others are informal and sporadic, such as chance conversations at the water cooler or in the hallway. They may be face-to-face or in virtual space, and they may be in the language of spoken or written words or of symbolic gestures. The conversations may be between individuals or in the private space of each person's thinking. All these sub-conversations are weaving through each other simultaneously, infecting each other with ideas and emotions rather like the spread of an epidemic.

Thinking of an organization as a conversation rather than a machine leads us to approach the work of organizational change in a very different way. We understand that we can influence but not control what goes on, and that we do so more by the way in which we participate than by the plans we make.

CURIOUS PROPERTIES OF CONVERSATIONS

There are several curious and important properties of conversations that are relevant to our understanding of organizations and organizational change. Conversations are comprised of two types of patterns—patterns of meaning (themes) and patterns of relating (how people interact). Important patterns of meaning in an organizational conversation include the organization's identity (its mission, vision and values), its intellectual capital (knowledge about how to do the work), and its strategy (a plan for how to succeed). The patterns of relating in an organization are its culture: for instance, what people say or don't say, how people behave at meetings, the way decisions are made, and all the dynamics of power and authority.

Unlike a material object that is static—once you create it, it remains just as it is—patterns of meaning and patterns of relating are ephemeral; they must be recreated moment by moment or they cease to be. If we say that an organization has a friendly culture, it means that people keep on interacting in a friendly way from one moment to another. To say that we have some bit of knowledge—say, knowing how to remove an inflamed appendix—means that we keep thinking about it in the same way from one time to the next. These patterns of meaning and patterns of relating are continuously under creation. The patterns being created in any one moment tend to carry forward those that were created the moment before, but that's not immutable. New patterns can be created at any time.

> Conversations are comprised of two types of patterns—patterns of meaning (themes) and patterns of relating (how people interact).

Patterns of meaning and patterns of relating are self-organizing. They can form spontaneously, evolve, or perpetuate themselves, all without anyone's intentional direction or control. At first glance, this may seem puzzling, but self-organizing patterns of meaning and relating are actually very common experiences.

For instance, think of a time when you were a newcomer in an existing group of people. Without necessarily being conscious of it, you probably paid close attention to how the other people were acting so you could figure out how to fit in. This powerful, highly developed social dynamic has its basis in brain chemistry. Brain levels of opioids—naturally occurring molecules similar in structure and effect to opiate drugs like morphine—increase or decrease based on how much interpersonal connection or attachment we are experiencing at the moment.[9] In a situation of low attachment, the drop in brain opioid levels causes anxiety and other distress similar to drug withdrawal. To avoid this unpleasant state, we have a strong tendency to try to fit in with the others around us.

So there you were observing the others and gradually taking on their behaviors; you began to participate in their patterns of relating. At a subsequent meeting of that group, another person joined the group and that person looked to you to see what behaviors were expected. As people kept joining and leaving the group over the course of time, the group's composition might have changed completely—none of the original people were still present—yet the patterns of behavior remained the same. No one directed, planned or controlled this process; it was self-organizing. This same dynamic can apply to patterns of meaning such as a personal story, an organizational identity, or the identity of a people or culture; beliefs, practices, even patterns of conflict can propagate themselves across many generations.

Self-organization can produce change as well as stability. For instance, think of a time when you were talking with some friends or colleagues, and someone made a chance remark that sparked a new thought for you. You described your new thought and then someone else took it further, and that stimulated you or a third person to add something more, and on it grew to become a major new idea or plan. This new idea emerged spontaneously in the course of the back-and-forth interactions of the conversation. It was not the result of anyone's intentional planning, direction or control. No one announced, "In this conversation today we are going to create a transformative new idea." It just happened, a new self-organizing pattern of meaning.

We can see similar self-organization in patterns of relating when children spontaneously make up a game, or when a social order starts to emerge within a group of people who have never been together before. Patterns of power, leadership, and inclusion/exclusion inevitably and necessarily arise when new groups form, sometimes influenced by people's intentions but not subject to their direction or control.[10]

COMPLEXITY PRINCIPLES AND THEIR IMPLICATIONS FOR ACTION

The self-organization of new patterns in conversations is an example of a principle from complexity science (the study of self-organizing processes) known as Critical Dependence on Initial Conditions, or more popularly, the "Butterfly Effect." It describes how immeasurably small differences or disturbances that are present at the beginning of an interaction can be enough to drastically change the outcome. In the course of back-and-forth interactions, those tiny differences can become amplified rapidly into large differences or even into transformative new patterns. For example, the tiny air currents associated with the beating of a butterfly's wings can affect nearby air currents, creating a larger disturbance that then affects an even wider circle of adjacent air currents. The pattern keeps growing and spreading, ultimately resulting in a tornado halfway around the world.[11]

A second and closely related principle is the Inverse Power Law, known more popularly as the "Sand Pile Model." Imagine that we're at the beach, dropping grains of sand on top of a sand pile. What happens when each grain lands will depend on characteristics of the grain and how it's falling and on the structure of the sand pile. Most grains will stick where they land and will cause no disturbance. Occasionally a grain will dislodge a few other grains and they all will tumble down a bit. And once in a great while, the way that one grain lands and the structure of sand pile will combine to result in an avalanche. (The mathematical term for this is a "catastrophe.") The name "Inverse Power Law" refers to the mathematical relationship between the size of the disturbance and its frequency. Minimal disturbances happen nearly all the time. Catastrophes occur rarely. Even so, they are not aberrant; they are a normal and expected part of the system.

Returning to the sand pile, we can never know in advance what the effect of any one grain of sand will be. We cannot accurately predict the avalanches. No matter how precisely we can measure a sand grain's mass and momentum, air movements and the sand pile's structure, even smaller differences can cascade to radically alter the outcome. The best we can do is to learn to recognize the conditions that make catastrophes more likely (for instance, when a lot of sand has accumulated and the slope of the sand pile is getting steep) and try to modify those conditions (spreading out the sand to decrease its slope), but we cannot predict or control individual events.

The Butterfly Effect and Sand Pile Model show why the machine model's goal of control is impossible. Unpredictability is built in to every complex system, including organizations. When we hold ourselves and others to impossible expectations of control, we may be instigating patterns of anxiety and frustration that can grow and spread, impairing organizational function. An excessive effort to control can actually make things go farther out of control. But the fact that we can't be in control doesn't mean we're helpless. There are many things we can do. We just have to go about our work differently, and with different expectations. Let's see how.

> Unpredictability is built in to every complex system, including organizations. When we hold ourselves and others to impossible expectations of control, we may be instigating patterns of anxiety and frustration that can grow and spread, impairing organizational function.

Emergent design

One thing we can do is to adopt a mindset of emergent design. Rather than planning a long series of steps in advance and getting anxious when things start to go off course, we can just plan one step at a time and pause after each one to notice what's happened, and only then plan the next step. The plan emerges as we go. Planning is necessary to decide upon each step, but no sooner is that step taken than something unexpected happens that calls for a change in subsequent steps. When our attention is focused too narrowly on our original plan, we may fail to notice other circumstances or opportunities that are arising. So we hold our plans lightly; we think of them not as finished blueprints to be followed exactly but as transitory descriptions of what we happen to be thinking right now about the future and how to prepare for it.

> Rather than planning a long series of steps in advance and getting anxious when things start to go off course, we can just plan one step at a time and pause after each one to notice what's happened and only then plan the next step. The plan emerges as we go.

Unlike the machine model in which "not knowing" is seen as a deficiency, the organization-as-conversation perspective shows us that "not knowing" can be a virtue. Without the burden of having to have the answers (or pretending we do for the sake of appearances), we can be more curious and less anxious. We can observe and experiment more and we don't have to feel threatened when things don't go as expected. And we can have more realistic expectations about how change happens: we know from the Sand Pile Model that we may have to cause a large number of disturbances—drop many grains of sand—before we get a response.

Chapter 8 offers an outstanding example of emergent design. It describes the development of a comprehensive program for the care of people living with HIV/AIDS in Eldoret, Kenya. There was no grand plan. Instead, efforts to address an initial need—antiretroviral therapy to treat the AIDS virus—led to the recognition of another need—adequate nutrition without which the antiviral treatment doesn't work. Finding a sustainable solution to nutritional needs of patients, in turn, led to the establishment of farms, which then led to the introduction of new methods of sustainable farming and the teaching of these methods to HIV-infected individuals so they could earn a livelihood. In this manner of making-it-up-as-you-go, a remarkable program emerged.

Reflecting on pattern-making and acting differently

Another thing we can do is to shift our attention from the future and how we want it to be to the present and what we actually are doing right here, right now. We can notice what patterns we are creating in the way we are behaving together. For the patterns that seem undesirable, we can ask questions like, "What am I doing—how am I participating—that contributes to the propagation of this pattern?" (it could be something as simple as not speaking up) and, "What can I do differently that might disrupt this pattern and start a new one?" We can also ask ourselves what we can do to reinforce desirable patterns to help them grow and spread. Even as we take these actions, we recognize that we can't know in advance what effects our actions will have. We just make our best guess and see what happens. We hope that as we start to act differently it might invite someone else to do so, and then another, in a spreading wave of change. Every large pattern in human activity—in economics, politics, fashion, science, everywhere!—started as a small local disturbance that then amplified and spread. There is nowhere else to start a change process but with what we are doing here and now.

> Every large pattern in human activity—in economics, politics, fashion, science, everywhere!—started as a small local disturbance that then amplified and spread. There is nowhere else to start a change process but with what we are doing here and now.

We can also invite others to join us in reflecting on our pattern-making in the moment, trying to start an epidemic of mindfulness. Chapter 13 describes such an epidemic in a very large institution, the Indiana University School of Medicine, that wanted to change its culture so it could do a better job of teaching professionalism. The heart of the initiative, and the key to its success, was engaging an ever-widening circle of individuals and committees in reflecting on the values they were exhibiting in their everyday behavior and the extent to which those values were the ones they wished to pass on to their medical students. They discovered countless ways in which their longstanding habits of organizational behavior were reinforcing values of impersonal hierarchical control, exactly the opposite of what they intended. They were able to stop doing these things and invent more relational ways to accomplish the same tasks, and as a result the culture began to change. Reflecting collectively on "what are we doing together right here, right now" was the key.

Identifying and modifying constraints

Complexity science tells us that self-organization requires the simultaneous presence of order and disorder, of freedom and constraint. So as we are trying to understand and influence emerging patterns of thinking and behavior, we can think about what constraints are shaping them and how those constraints might be modified. Some constraints on behavior are unalterable, like the need for oxygen. (Whatever patterns of relating might emerge, they will necessarily allow for the participants to continue breathing!) But other constraints are more flexible, and as they change, behaviors might change: for example, financial incentives, regulatory requirements, or themes of identity (points of pride).

Chapter 6 describes the start-up of Clarian West Medical Center, a hospital in Avon, Indiana, with a founding vision of being a sanctuary of healing. Its leaders hired staff members based not only on their technical competence but also on their relationship skills and attitudes. This was a powerful constraint that influenced the kind of people who worked there and how they related to each other. (Imagine the patterns that might have ensued had they established a different constraint, say, who will work for the least amount of pay!)

We cannot design and control the behavior of others. Their behavior in each moment emerges spontaneously. Instead we can try to understand the constraints that influence these self-organizing patterns and to introduce constraints that make it more likely that desirable patterns will emerge.

> We cannot design and control the behavior of others. Their behavior in each moment emerges spontaneously. Instead we can try to understand the constraints that influence these self-organizing patterns and to introduce constraints that make it more likely that desirable patterns will emerge.

Fostering (or inhibiting) innovation

A fourth kind of action follows from our understanding of how new patterns emerge in conversation. A group's capacity to innovate, to produce new ideas, depends upon two key factors: diversity and responsiveness. We can try to enhance these factors if we want new ideas to emerge, and to inhibit them if we don't. Differences within a group are the seed crystals for creativity. We saw earlier how a serendipitous comment—a small spark of difference—could initiate an amplifying cascade that gives rise to a transformative new idea. The more difference and diversity there is with regard to work roles, personal experiences, demographics, and so on, and the more willing people are to express their differences, the greater the opportunity for serendipitous sparks to happen.

> A group's capacity to innovate, to produce new ideas, depends upon two key factors: diversity and responsiveness.

But differences alone are not enough. The people in the group also have to be responsive, that is, open to hearing and being changed by each other's differences. If people are holding rigidly to their own perspectives and plans, or are not even listening to each other, the richest sparks of diversity won't have an opportunity to seed and grow.

The implication for us as leaders is that if we want innovation, we can invite people into responsive conversations in which we call forth differences and help people feel comfortable expressing them (*see* Appendices 1 and 2 for specific methods).

In overseeing the design of a new science building at University College of Dublin, the project leaders wanted to engage the faculty in the design process and not impose a new solution in a top-down manner (*see* Chapter 11). At the same time, they wanted to encourage the faculty to let go of their traditional views of teaching and reconceptualize both the learning process and the new kind of instructional space that would support it. They convened conversations and used a variety of creative formats to get everyone involved. Though initially unruly, the conversation ultimately produced a coherent and exciting new vision that surprised everyone.

Sometimes we do *not* want new patterns to emerge. In aviation, cockpit conversation is severely restricted during takeoff and approach, times when it is most critical for the pilots to be focused on following standard procedures and distracting new patterns are undesirable. In healthcare, too, there are situations in which the safety of patients and/or staff members calls for high reliability, carrying out well-established procedures precisely and without variation. Checklists, protocols and highly structured formats for communication inhibit the expression of diversity and reduce responsiveness, making it harder for new patterns (variability) to emerge.

The task for leaders is to distinguish between situations with known solutions in which people need to follow orders faithfully and those without known solutions, which require the creative engagement of everyone doing the work. Heifetz has named these situations "technical" and "adaptive" challenges, respectively, and has observed that one of the most common errors in management is to treat adaptive challenges as if they are technical—that is, leaders attempt to provide solutions (blueprints, from the machine metaphor) instead of engaging the team in creating them (fostering conversation).[12]

SUMMARY AND CONCLUSIONS

We've now had a chance to compare two very different perspectives on organizations. When we look at an organization as a machine, it leads us to think of leaders as engineers, planning and operating the organization with great precision and control, and to see workers as machine parts who are supposed to perform their work consistently and do just what they're told. From our exploration of self-organization in human interaction, we know that this degree of control is impossible. So these unrealistic expectations of control result in anxiety, blame and defensiveness, which distract attention and energy away from doing the work.

In contrast to this static view of an organization as an object upon which we can act, we've considered an alternative view—the organization as conversation. It's a more dynamic view, more focused on process. It shows us how we are creating the organization anew in each moment by what we are saying about it and how we are relating to each other as we carry out its work. In this view, there is still a role for planning, but we hold the plans lightly, remaining curious, flexible and responsive to what is emerging around us.

> We are creating the organization anew in each moment by what we are saying about it and how we are relating to each other as we carry out its work.

An important task for leaders is to participate mindfully in the organizational conversation and encourage others to do likewise. This involves reflecting on what we are doing together, what ideas and culture we are creating or perpetuating in each moment, and when new patterns are needed, to live them, to create a disturbance in the existing pattern in the hope that others will join in. We can also try to notice and modify constraints that influence self-organizing patterns of behavior.

There are circumscribed situations in which solutions are known, and control and consistency are desirable, if not essential. In these situations we seek to inhibit the expression of diversity and responsiveness, the key factors that favor the emergence of new patterns. But in most situations, where solutions are not known and innovation and adaptability are desirable, we try to foster these factors.

The organization-as-conversation perspective and its underlying principles from complexity science expand the focus of our attention beyond our goals and plans to also encompass the self-organizing pattern-making that is taking place in the here and now. The next chapter, which describes several theories from positive psychology, involves another shift in attention, from focusing exclusively on problems and problem-solving to also notice successes so we can enhance the human capabilities and other enabling factors that make them possible.

NOTES

1 The complexity perspective that we use throughout this book derives from a new theory, Complex Responsive Processes of Relating, developed by Ralph Stacey and his colleagues at the University of Hertfordshire. This theory, which is based in social constructionism, is better suited for describing human interaction than the more popular theory, Complex Adaptive Systems, which has its origins in the natural sciences and computer simulations. More information is available in Stacey R. *Complex Responsive Process in Organizations: learning and knowledge creation.* London: Routledge; 2001, and Stacey R, Griffin D, Shaw P. *Complexity and Management: fad or radical challenge to systems thinking?* London: Routledge; 2000.

2 Thanks to Penny Williamson for this example.

3 A "ladder of inference" begins with an observation on which we all would agree, but then we begin to make up our own interpretations as to the meaning, significance or cause of what we have just observed, and we begin to act upon that assumption as if it's a fact. When we aren't careful to distinguish between the observation and the assumption we get caught in a self-fulfilling dynamic of expectations, behaviors and responses. From Ross R. The ladder of inference. In: Senge P, Kleiner A, Roberts C, *et al. The Fifth Discipline Fieldbook*. New York: Doubleday; 1994. p. 243. *See* Appendix 1 for a more extensive description of this dynamic.

4 Taylor F. *Scientific Management*. New York: Harper Brothers; 1911.

5 A detailed critique of classical management theories can be found in Stacey R. *Strategic Management and Organisational Dynamics: the challenge of complexity*. 3rd ed. Harlow, England: Pearson Education Ltd; 2000.

6 Predictability and control were the aspirations of classical physics, and while they have now been supplanted in physics by the unpredictable world of relativity and quantum mechanics, they continue to hold sway in modern management, and in most social sciences, for that matter. *See* Flyvbjerg B. *Making Social Science Matter.* Cambridge, England: Cambridge University Press; 2001.

7 Heifetz R. *Leadership Without Easy Answers*. Cambridge, MA: Harvard University Press; 1994.

8 Broekstra G. An organization is a conversation. In: Grant D, Keenoy T, Swick C, editors. *Discourse and Organization*. London: Sage; 1998.

9 Smith TS, Stevens GT, Caldwell S. The familiar and the strange: Hopfield network models for prototype-entrained attachment-mediated neurophysiology. *Soc Perspect Emot*. 1999; **5**: 213–45. See the section on interpersonal neurobiology in Chapter 3 for a more extensive description of the relationship between interpersonal interactions and brain activity.

10 See the groundbreaking work of Thomas S Smith and colleagues on the self-organization of social patterns, for instance: Smith TS, Stevens GT. Hyperstructures and the biology of interpersonal dependence: rethinking reciprocity and altruism. *Sociological Theory*. 2002; **20**(1): 106–30.

11 Lorenz E. *The Essence of Chaos*. Seattle: The University of Washington Press; 1993.

12 Heifetz R, op. cit.

CHAPTER 3

Positive psychology and interpersonal neurobiology

Anthony L Suchman

Positive psychology is a movement to widen the focus of psychology that came to prominence in the late 1990s. Traditional psychology concerned itself with human development and function, with a particular emphasis on the abnormal—the causes and treatment of mental illness and dysfunction. The aim of positive psychology is to call attention to human strengths, virtues and optimal experience; the factors that give rise to them; and how to foster the highest human capacities. In this chapter, we will consider three specific theories and approaches from positive psychology that are of particular practical value in fostering organizational change: Self-Determination Theory, Appreciative Inquiry and Positive Deviance.

> The aim of positive psychology is to call attention to human strengths, virtues and optimal experience; the factors that give rise to them; and how to foster the highest human capacities.

Before we visit these theories, we'll first have a look at some recent discoveries from neuroscience. It turns out that the way we interact with each other affects and is affected by how our brains are working in each moment. Putting that into the language of complexity and pattern-making, the patterns of relating constrain and are constrained by patterns of brain activity. Understanding these constraints will help us better understand the practical applications of positive psychology.

INTERPERSONAL NEUROBIOLOGY
Attachment and opioids
We've already encountered in Chapter 2 a powerful socio-biological constraint on human behavior—the association between interpersonal attachment (the

sense of being connected to others) and opioid levels in the brain. Recall that when we are feeling close and well-connected to others, brain opioid levels are elevated, which we experience as a state of contentment, well-being or even bliss—a natural "high." Conversely, a state of low attachment lowers brain opioid levels producing an anxious, unpleasant experience similar to drug withdrawal. All this constrains how we behave in each moment, making it more likely that we will seek a greater degree of connection with others to enhance our comfort and minimize our distress.

This hardwiring of social behavior goes even deeper. Another circumstance in which our brain opioid levels drop is when we witness another person's suffering.[1] (Think of what you experience when you hear a baby crying on an airplane flight. The baby's distress is replicated in you.) When we comfort suffering people, our actions cause opioid levels in their brains to rise and in our brains as well; we and they end up feeling better. This is another neurobiological constraint on emerging patterns of behavior: our discomfort when we see people in distress inclines us towards comforting them.

If avoiding the discomfort of opioid withdrawal is such a strong constraint, how is it that people engage in conflict or, worse, inflict suffering on others? There are several possible explanations. First, other constraints may also be present—fear and a need for safety, for instance—that take precedence over attachment needs. Second, there is natural variability in people's capacity to attune to others. There are rare individuals who are completely unaffected by the suffering of others. (This is, essentially, the defining characteristic of a psychopath.) Third, for some groups a central theme of group identity—and therefore the key to belonging—is a shared antipathy towards certain others. Members of hate groups or of groups with long histories of reciprocal violent acts meet their own attachment needs by means of their shared hatred. It brings them together—a harsh paradox, indeed.

A milder version of this paradox is common to many workplaces. It happens when a group of people maintains an impersonal pattern of interacting—nobody saying what they're really thinking, no one disclosing any emotion, people not offering each other praise or support. Each person who joins such a group quickly adopts these unspoken rules (the self-organizing perpetuation of a pattern that we saw in Chapter 2). The force or constraint that sustains this unsatisfying pattern is the fear of rejection people imagine they would experience (opioid withdrawal) were they to say something personal or "soft." In fact, nearly everyone in the room might prefer a more relational environment, but when they don't see anyone else acting that way they each think that they are the only one. Fearing ridicule, they refrain from any personal engagement and perpetuate the impersonal pattern. So we have a persistent lack of attachment behavior that is driven, paradoxically, by a fear of losing attachment.

One further variation on the theme of attachment and opioids deserves our attention, namely our ability to meet our own attachment needs and maintain our own brain opioid levels. As we grow through childhood, we each develop a self-image, that is, we learn to see ourselves as we imagine others are seeing us. To the extent that we see ourselves as acting in a skillful or virtuous way, we experience the approval of this "imagined other" and derive from that a feeling of attachment. But in a situation in which we are not skillful, in which we feel incompetent, we imagine the criticism or even ridicule of others and actually experience physical distress.[2] Thus feelings of competence and incompetence constrain our emerging patterns of behavior in a similar way as actual acceptance or rejection by others.[3] This constraint is of particular importance in situations that call for us to learn a new skill. The initial sense of incompetence that inevitably accompanies learning something new can be enough to make us avoid the learning situation altogether—opioid dynamics constraining behavior yet again.

Fear and brain activation

Another socio-biological constraint on patterns of interaction and behavior involves the association between perceived threats and brain function.[4] In a setting of safety or comfort, incoming sensory information (what we see, hear, touch and so forth) activates portions of the cerebral cortex—the most recently and highly evolved part of the human brain that performs creative and analytic thinking. But in the presence of a perceived threat, something altogether different happens. There is a small area deep in the center of the brain called the amygdala which constantly scans incoming information for signs of danger. When it senses a potential threat, it activates not the cortex but an evolutionarily older and more primitive part of the brain (sometimes referred to as the "reptilian" brain) that triggers the fight-or-flight response. Our perception and thinking become much narrower; we assume a more defensive and reactive stance. This is not a brain state that is conducive to forming creative new associations and ideas.

Organizational change creates a social climate in which threats abound. Roles and relationships may be disrupted, people may have to learn new skills and work-processes, their jobs may even be at risk. If left untempered, all these threats that accompany organizational change shift people's brain function from the newer, higher-functioning parts of the brain to the older, more-primitive parts. Their capacity for creative thinking diminishes and their fight-or-flight reflex is activated, leading to reactive, self-protective behavior: hardly the setting for innovative thinking. The quality pioneer W Edwards Deming understood this dynamic when he wrote 50 years ago that one has to "drive out fear" from the workplace to engage workers constructively in quality improvement.[5] (Now we know the underlying brain function that accounts for this.) How can we drive out fear and call forth people's highest level of brain function and their most creative thinking? This is where positive psychology comes in.

SELF-DETERMINATION THEORY

The first positive psychology theory we'll examine is Self-Determination Theory (SDT). It is a theory of intrinsic-motivation, i.e. motivation that is sustained without any specific external rewards or punishments. Developed by Richard Ryan and Edward Deci and verified by extensive research in workplace, education and clinical settings,[6] SDT identifies three factors that make people more likely to embrace and maintain new behaviors:

➤ competence—feeling skilled and comfortable with the new behavior, knowing what to do and how to do it
➤ autonomy support—being involved in determining how and when the new behavior will be introduced (in contrast to being told what to do)
➤ relatedness—feeling known, cared about and personally supported in undertaking the new behavior.

We can readily see the influence of interpersonal neurobiology here. Learning a new behavior involves a temporary period of feeling incompetent, dropping brain opioid levels. But feeling cared about and being treated by others as competent (having your autonomy supported rather than being controlled) counteracts this, raising opioid levels through the transitional period of incompetence, reducing fear and distress, and activating the higher levels of brain function needed for learning. Once you have gained competence, it is then easier to maintain the new behavior.

SDT is quite practical; it offers a checklist for reviewing the design of change projects and assessing their likelihood of success. Do people have an adequate opportunity to develop competence? Do they have a meaningful role in planning the change? Are they feeling personally supported and connected? In launching "Relationship-centered Lean" at the Harvard Vanguard Medical Group (*see* Chapter 12), there was an initial learning phase with education and mentoring to help the practice staff become comfortable with the process. The staff members were then engaged in observing their own work flow and designing and testing changes; their autonomy was not only supported but taken to a new level. The program leaders paid scrupulous attention to the relational environment: one of the three core principles of the program was "respect your clinicians and staff" and the Lean work had been preceded by a major team-building initiative. All three factors from SDT were fully realized, and the program was dramatically successful.

> SDT is quite practical; it offers a checklist for reviewing the design of change projects and assessing their likelihood of success. Do people have an adequate opportunity to develop competence? Are they involved in planning the change? Are they feeling personally supported and connected?

Contrast the Harvard Vanguard experience with typical physician pay-for-performance programs. Physicians receive feedback reports tied to financial incentives, but get no specific help gaining competence in the new processes or behaviors needed to improve their scores. They rarely participate in designing the programs or selecting performance standards; they often feel manipulated and controlled.[7] And with rare exceptions,[8] the programs are impersonal and bureaucratic. Little wonder that the value and effectiveness of such programs remain in question.[9] They are the embodiment of non-relational machine metaphor thinking (*see* Chapter 2).[10]

APPRECIATIVE INQUIRY

We turn next to Appreciative Inquiry (AI), which can be regarded as both a theory and a methodology of organizational change. Developed by David Cooperrider, AI is based on a deceptively simple premise, namely, that people are more motivated to change when they focus on what they are doing well and how to do more of it, than when they focus on what's not working and how to do less of it.[11] AI is the converse of problem solving; it begins with a root-cause analysis of *successes* rather than failures or errors and then envisions and moves towards a future in which those success factors are present in full abundance.

> Appreciative Inquiry is the converse of problem solving; it begins with a root-cause analysis of *successes* rather than failures or errors and then envisions and moves towards a future in which those success factors are present in full abundance.

As an example, suppose the Chief Operating Officer (COO) of a hospital wants to launch an initiative to reduce tensions and improve the working relationships between physicians and clinical service managers. The most common approach would be to identify what's wrong and then try to fix it. Gathering a group of physicians and managers to conduct a root-cause analysis of the problem, she is likely to hear each group assign blame to the other—physicians' arrogance and indifference to cost on one hand and the "bean counters'" insensitivity to patients' needs on the other. Such attributions and blame quite predictably evoke defensiveness and thwart constructive conversation. They drop opioid levels and shift the meeting participants into their reptilian brains. We've all experienced conversations like this; they make limited progress at best, with much waste of time and potential.

Using an AI approach, the COO sets out in the opposite direction by inviting the physicians and managers to explore instances, however infrequent, when they collaborated well to achieve a good result. She might have the participants divide into pairs, each taking the role of storyteller and interviewer by turns. Then several pairs would combine into groups of six, with each person summarizing their partner's story. The small group's task would be to harvest and share back to the whole group (in the form of a big drawing on a flip chart page) the wisdom from the six stories: what were the key factors that made these successes possible.

Perhaps it was having a strong shared vision or goal, or facing an external threat, or having a personal relationship from some social activity outside of work (e.g. being in the same cycling club or having children on the same soccer team), or making an extra effort to fully understand each other's needs and perspectives. Having discovered in this fashion the success factors in their own stories—the best of *what is*—the group might then envision a future in which these factors are fully present, articulating a vivid and compelling vision of *what might be*, and then move to planning specific steps to get there—*what will be*.

AI is a richly nuanced approach that we cannot fully describe here.[12] For our present purposes, we need only notice how AI focuses our attention differently than problem solving and with what consequences. The way we focus our attention—what we choose to look for—determines what we perceive. Our perceptions get woven together as an interpretation, an emerging pattern of meaning, a story about what kind of people or organization we're dealing with. That story then determines how we act, which affects how others act back to us. The story also filters our perceptions, predisposing us towards observations that reinforce the story and making it harder to notice contradictory data. It is all very circular and self-fulfilling.

The critical choice is the one we make at the very start—the choice of where to focus our attention; everything else follows in a self-organizing cascade. Problem solving, focusing on what's wrong, leads us to perceive deficiencies and formulate a story about how messed up this place is, resulting in lower expectations for the future which become self-fulfilling. AI focuses attention on stories of success, setting us up to perceive our own and others' best qualities. It highlights our competence, showing us that we already have the ability to make the desired change. It creates hopeful expectations, grounded in actual experience, which we are then more likely to enact.

There is a moment in the case study from the Indiana University School of Medicine (IUSM) that captures this positive cascade just starting to take hold (*see* Chapter 13). Recognizing that it is the organizational culture—how people are relating to each other in each moment—that teaches professionalism to medical students, IUSM set out to establish a relationship-centered culture based on core values of respect and partnership. The first step in the change process was to conduct a round of appreciative interviews, gathering stories about moments when the school's culture was at its best. Hearing the themes from these stories at a presentation, one audience member responded,

> I never realized how good we are. When I see what we're capable of, I can no longer be silent when I see someone throw something in the operating room, or humiliate a student. We're too good for that.

The perceptions gleaned from the appreciative interviews led her to construct a new, more positive story about IUSM, which altered her expectations and, subsequently, her behavior. Many others got caught up in that cascade, too, ultimately resulting in measureable change in the culture as perceived by the students. One of many changes that rippled through the organization was the use of appreciative storytelling, which helped to propel the process of reflection that contributed to culture change.

AI is commonly misunderstood as only talking about the positive and never talking about the negative, an approach that could only lead to superficial and ineffective conversation. AI doesn't seek to restrict conversation; rather, having found a problem, it begins the conversation at a more favorable starting point and approaches change from a different direction. AI ends up addressing exactly the same behaviors that a problem-solving approach would point to, but with an opposite emotional valence—capability rather than blame, and hope grounded in actual experience rather than fear and hopelessness. In the example of physicians and managers, the conversation about action steps might focus on "strengthening our ability to understand each other's needs and perspectives" rather than "not interrupting and arguing anymore." Both phrases point to exactly the same desired behavior, better listening, but the associated emotions are different, with very different consequences for brain function, relationship patterns and the likelihood of success in changing behaviors.

We can also compare AI to problem solving from the perspective of Self Determination Theory. AI presumes and strengthens the people's competence. It respects their autonomy by entrusting to them the responsibility for identifying success factors, articulating a vision for the future, and planning subsequent action steps towards that future. And through the community-weaving dynamics of sharing stories, AI creates a strong relational environment. In contrast, problem-solving approaches can easily threaten feelings of competence, reduce perceptions of autonomy and foster antagonism, thus reducing the likelihood of intrinsically motivated behavior change.

POSITIVE DEVIANCE

Positive Deviance (PD), a close cousin of AI, also begins with a belief in the capacity of people to find their own solutions. It rejects the idea that organizations or communities need experts to provide them with answers to their problems. It proposes instead that in every group there are people who have already figured out the answers for themselves and that solutions that arise within the community have much greater traction than ones imparted from without.[13]

> Positive Deviance rejects the idea that organizations or communities need experts to provide them with answers to their problems. It proposes instead that in every group there are people who have already figured out the answers for themselves and that solutions that arise within the community have much greater traction than ones imparted from without.

In a typical PD project, someone within an organization or community, perhaps with unobtrusive coaching from a consultant, gathers a group of people who share a common interest in bringing about a beneficial change. For Jerry and Monique Sternin, who helped to popularize PD, the change was improving child nutrition in Vietnam. For Dr Jon Lloyd, the change was to stop the spread of drug-resistant bacteria in healthcare institutions (*see* Chapter 10).

Workgroup members then talk with their peers to discover unique solutions created within the community or organization, and to identify people within the local context who have consistently achieved superior results (the "positive deviants" for whom the method is named). After sorting through and testing the various ideas they gather, the work groups devise ways to engage their peers in trying out these new approaches. The fact that the innovations are already in use by peers enhances their credibility and hastens dissemination.

Like AI, PD focuses attention on competence within the group, organization or community. It supports the group's autonomy and is highly relational. So, with the help of Self-Determination Theory and interpersonal neurobiology, we find the reasons for its success as a methodology for organizational change. Chapter 10 provides a detailed account of a successful institution-wide project that used a PD approach to reduce the incidence of a serious hospital-acquired infection.

In the previous chapter on complexity we considered the self-organization of patterns of meaning and patterns of relating in the course of human interaction. In this chapter, we have looked at neurobiological constraints on what kinds of patterns can emerge, and approaches from positive psychology that utilize these constraints to foster patterns of enhanced motivation, collaboration and creativity. This is the essence of Relationship-centered Administration—a culture of partnership in the workplace to maximize performance and meaning. We turn next to a closer examination of Relationship-centered Administration and its precursor, Relationship-centered Care.

NOTES

1 Smith TS, Stevens GT, Caldwell S. The familiar and the strange: Hopfield network models for prototype-entrained attachment-mediated neurophysiology. *Soc Perspect Emot.* 1999; **5**: 213–45.

2 Although I'm not aware of any empirical research on opioid levels under these circumstances, the discomfort associated with the feeling of incompetence is similar in quality and intensity to that of social rejection and the attachment dynamics are similar, so it stands to reason that the opioid response would be similar as well.

3 Suchman AL. Uncertainty, competence and opioids [editorial]. *J Gen Intern Med.* 2005; **20**: 554–5.

4 A very readable summary of this research for non-neuroscientists can be found in Zull J. *The Art of Changing the Brain: enriching the practice of teaching by exploring the biology of learning.* Sterling, VA: Stylus Publishing; 2002.

5 Deming WE. *Out of the Crisis*. Cambridge, MA: Massachusetts Institute of Technology, Center for Advanced Engineering Study; 1986.

6 Ryan RM, Deci EL. Self-determination theory and the facilitation of intrinsic motivation, social development, and well-being. *Am Psychol*. 2000; **55**: 68–78.

7 Beckman H, Suchman AL, Curtin K, *et al*. Physician reactions to quantitative individual performance reports. *Am J Med Qual*. 2006; **21**(3): 192–9.

8 Francis DO, Beckman H, Chamberlain J, *et al*. Introducing a multifaceted intervention to improve the management of otitis media: how do pediatricians, internists, and family physicians respond? *Am J Med Qual*. 2006; **21**(2): 134–43.

9 Petersen LA, Woodard LD, Urech T, *et al*. Does pay-for-performance improve the quality of healthcare? *Ann Intern Med*. 2006; **145**(4): 265–72. McDonald R, White J, Marmor TR. Paying for performance in primary medical care: learning about and learning from "success" and "failure" in England and California. *J Health Polit Policy Law*. 2009; **34**(5): 747–76.

10 This is not to say that feedback reports and incentives have no role; they can be very useful tools. It's more a matter of the way they are being implemented and used, the relational quality and autonomy supportiveness of the work environment.

11 Cooperrider DL. Positive image, positive action: the affirmative basis of organizing. In: Srivastva S, Cooperrider DL. *Appreciative Management and Leadership*. Revised ed. Euclid, OH: Williams Custom Publishing; 1999. pp. 91–125.

12 For more complete descriptions see Watkins JM, Mohr BJ. *Appreciative Inquiry: change at the speed of imagination*. San Francisco: Jossey-Bass/Pfeiffer; 2001 or visit http://appreciativeinquiry.case.edu (accessed November 11, 2010).

13 Singhal A, Buscell P, Lindberg C. *Inviting Everyone: healing healthcare through positive deviance*. Bordentown, NJ: PlexusPress; 2010.

CHAPTER 4

Relationship-centered Care and Administration

Anthony L Suchman

The central concept of this book, Relationship-centered Administration (RCA), has its roots in a clinical approach called Relationship-centered Care (RCC). The original objective of RCA was to support and enhance the practice of RCC, although it's now clear that it can do so much more, as we'll see. In this chapter we explore the origin and meaning of the term "Relationship-centered Care," and consider how this approach can be transposed from clinical to administrative work.

DOCTOR-CENTERED CARE

The term "Relationship-centered Care" was introduced in 1994 in a report by the Pew–Fetzer Task Force.[1] We can appreciate the full significance of this term by tracing the history of the patient–doctor relationship. We begin by going back to the 1950s and 60s when the modern biomedical era was in strong ascendancy. It was the start of a boom time for biomedical research, with massive growth in funding and facilities. All the new knowledge that was emerging led to new medicines, procedures and devices, and also to increasing specialization among health professionals. Thanks to the rapid spread of employer-, union- and government-based programs in the United States (especially Medicare and Medicaid) and national health programs everywhere else in the developed world, a rapidly growing number of people had access to the latest specialty care and the newest technology, so many more specialists were trained.

> Medical decision-making was viewed as an exclusively professional prerogative, with doctors having the greatest authority of any of the health professions.

This era was the age of the expert. It was also the beginning of the age of depersonalization; as the experts had more and more scientific detail on which to focus their attention, they began to lose sight of the life stories and circumstances of their patients. Technological prowess took priority over "bedside" skills in both professional education and fee schedules. Most physicians at this time were white men; white and male privilege was not yet being challenged. Trust in and obedience to authority were the norm. For all these reasons, medical decision making was viewed as an exclusively professional prerogative, with medicine having the greatest authority of any of the health professionals. Although the term was never actually used at the time, we could easily characterize this as the age of "doctor-centered" care.

PATIENT-CENTERED CARE

The political and social movements of the late 1960s and 1970s challenged hierarchical authority and the privileging of experts' knowledge. Instead, they advocated for more participatory decision-making processes and valued the wisdom of individuals regarding their own local needs and circumstances. These trends affected all social institutions; healthcare was no exception. A response emerged simultaneously from many quarters against the unilateral authority of the physician and the depersonalization of care.[2]

New integrative disciplines arose—family medicine, general pediatrics and general internal medicine—to reverse the fragmentation of care that resulted from specialization. These primary care disciplines would foster continuity of relationships and the coordination of care, and restore a balance of attention between the reductionist perspective of biomedical science and the lifeworld of the patient. (This was not without some irony—the cure for excessive specialization was the creation of new specialties . . .) George Engel issued his now-famous call for a new integrative medical paradigm, the "biopsychosocial model."[3] But for the purposes of our story, another name for the same movement, championed by Ian McWhinney, helps us recognize the trend more clearly: "Patient-centered care."[4]

> Patient-centered care called for care to be organized around the patient's goals and values, with patients as active participants in, if not the ultimate makers of, treatment decisions.

From the late 1970s into the early 1990s, even as biomedicine continued to advance, there was a growing parallel interest in the patient's experience of illness and care.[5] Part of the clinician's task was to explore and understand the patient's subjective experience of illness. Principles and language from phenomenology found their way into the medical mainstream[6] and the fields of medical anthropology and case-based medical ethics flourished.[7] Patient-centered care called for care to be organized around the patient's goals and values, with patients as active participants in, if not the ultimate makers of, treatment decisions. Instruction in medical interviewing and relationship skills was becoming more commonplace in both undergraduate and graduate medical education. However, the debate still raged about the basic identity and role of the physician; strong polemics in defense of the biomedical tradition continued to appear.[8]

RELATIONSHIP-CENTERED CARE

In 1994, the Pew Charitable Trusts' Health Professions Commission and the Fetzer Institute convened an interprofessional task force to make recommendations about health professions education.[9] This thoughtful group of clinicians, researchers and educators recognized that while the *purpose* of healthcare is to respond to the needs of the patient, the *process* of care can be successfully understood from neither a doctor-centered nor a patient-centered perspective alone. Instead, it required an explicit focus on the *relationship* between them, hence the term "relationship-centered." The personhood of the clinician matters as much as that of the patient with regard to how successfully they can work together, and there are attributes and qualities of the relationship that deserve consideration that are distinct from those of either the patient or the clinician alone. The whole of the patient–clinician system is a different entity than either of its parts.

The Task Force identified four important levels of relationship in healthcare. Beyond the traditional relationship between patient and clinician (and family, which they omitted, curiously), they also called attention to relationships between the various members of the healthcare team, relationships between the healthcare system and the community, and underlying all other levels of relationship, the practitioner's relationship with her- or himself. The term "Relationship-centered Care" calls attention to the communication and relationship dynamics, self-awareness and specific partnership behaviors on which every collaboration depends, even those of a highly technical and scientific nature.[10]

Twelve years after the initial monograph on RCC appeared, Mary Catherine Beach and Tom Inui expanded upon these ideas by articulating four principles of RCC.[11]

1 "Relationships in healthcare ought to include the personhood of participants." This principle recognizes the patient's and clinician's unique experiences, values and perspectives and emphasizes the importance of the clinician's authenticity in interacting with patients.
2 "Affect and emotion are important components of relationships in healthcare." There is always an emotional dimension of the patient's illness experience. The emotional availability of the clinician and the expression of support and empathy for patients are essential to good care.
3 "All healthcare relationships occur in the context of reciprocal influence." While patient's goals take priority, both the clinician and the patient influence each other and benefit from the relationship.

4 "RCC has a moral foundation." Personal relationships allow clinicians to develop the interest and investment needed to serve others, and to be morally committed to and renewed by those they serve.

The components and principles of RCC thus include and expand on patient-centered care by reintegrating the clinician's perspective and adding the perspective of the relationship itself.

More than anything, RCC is about partnership at every level and the respect, mutual understanding and shared decision making of which partnership is comprised. It involves the ability to be genuinely present in an interaction and at the same time to be aware of what we are experiencing, how the others are responding and what patterns of interaction are unfolding. The domain of RCC includes an extensive body of research on relationship process and a rich set of communication, relationship and self-awareness skills that we can use to create patterns of partnership moment by moment as we work (*see* Appendix 1).[12]

> More than anything, RCC is about partnership at every level and the respect, mutual understanding and shared decision making of which partnership is comprised.

Relationship-centered Care resonates with the theories we've considered previously. Both RCC and the complexity perspective (organizations as conversations) foster an awareness of how people are interacting here and now, what patterns of relating they are enacting together, and what other ways of behaving towards each other might change those patterns (*see* Chapter 2).

The complexity perspective points to diversity and responsiveness as crucial factors for innovation and adaptation. To be willing to reveal our differences and open our minds to being changed by each other we must be experiencing a sufficient quality of relationship characterized by respectful listening, mutuality and trust.

There are also points of convergence between RCC and positive psychology. When we looked at Self-Determination Theory (*see* Chapter 3) we saw that a caring relationship was a critical success factor in fostering behavior change. We also saw how the storytelling of Appreciative Inquiry and the active engagement of Positive Deviance helped to build community, that is, a network of relationships.

RELATIONSHIP-CENTERED ADMINISTRATION

Relationship-centered Administration brings the same quality of partnership and the same attentiveness to relational process to organizational work, that Relationship-centered Care brings to clinical work.[13] You'd think it would be obvious: for staff members to treat patients and their family members compassionately and to engage them respectfully as partners in decision making, they need to be treated the same way in the workplace. You can't beat people into being compassionate; you can't mandate partnership. Yet impersonal, hierarchically controlling workplaces abound in healthcare. Too often we find organizations with toxic cultures trying to help people be healthier—a sad irony. It doesn't work and it results in enormous waste.

> You can't beat people into being compassionate; you can't mandate partnership. Yet impersonal, hierarchically controlling workplaces abound in healthcare. Too often we find organizations with toxic cultures trying to help people be healthier—a sad irony.

The goal of Relationship-centered Administration is to create a workplace environment that engages the staff deeply and calls out their commitment and creativity. A large and growing literature shows that the relational quality of the healthcare workplace affects virtually every dimension of organizational performance. For example, Gittell and colleagues, studying joint replacement surgery at specialized orthopedic hospitals for patients with severe osteoarthritis, found a strong association between the quality of teamwork and clinical outcomes—patients' pain and functional status six weeks after discharge.[14] Shortell and colleagues found similar associations for coronary artery bypass grafting.[15]

Staff relationships are also associated with quality and safety. Nurse–physician collaboration is the strongest predictor of ICU mortality rates.[16] Aiken and colleagues found that hospital-wide mortality rates were lower in hospitals with collaborative workplace cultures.[17] The findings were similar in studies of staff satisfaction and resilience,[18] staff retention,[19] patient satisfaction and retention,[20] and cost.[21] Even the capacity to master new technology depends on the quality of team relationships.[22]

These data and the case studies in Part 2 of this book show that all kinds of benefits can result when leaders pay attention to the quality of relationships in their organizations. Behavioral patterns spread from the senior leaders to everyone else. Front-line care and the patient experience are affected by everything we do behind the scenes—the way we conduct staff recruitment and development, resource allocation, performance measurement, strategic planning and every other aspect of administrative work. By undertaking these and every other administrative activity in a relational way and inviting greater engagement, we can build high-performance organizations. Relationship-centered Administration is not only a moral imperative; it is also a successful business strategy.

> Relationship-centered Administration is not only a moral imperative; it is also a successful business strategy.

What we do in every moment matters. Executives and managers can learn to refine their awareness of themselves and others, enhance their capacity to reflect on group dynamics and strengthen their listening and communication skills (*see* Chapter 5 and Appendix 1). They can use a variety of techniques to make meetings more relational, building an organizational culture of respect and collaboration (*see* Appendix 2). They can be clearer about behavioral expectations and more rigorous about maintaining accountability (*see* Appendix 3).

This is what we mean by Relationship-centered Administration. It all comes down to how we lead in each moment—our mindfulness, skills, knowledge and personal presence—and how we participate in and influence the pattern-making.

Even as we note the important *parallels* between clinical and administrative work, we should also note an important difference, one that frequently trips up clinicians as they step into administrative roles. The traditional focus of clinical work is on the well-being of *individuals*; above all else, it is about relieving suffering. Administrative work focuses on the successful function of *groups* in service of customers, external or internal. There is often a tension between the individual and group perspectives. Sometimes what is needed for the good of the group (and the good of patients) can cause suffering for an individual employee: for example, delivering specific feedback regarding poor performance. Clinician-administrators seem to have particular difficulty with this, tolerating poor performance or making do with cumbersome work-arounds rather than confronting individuals with their need to improve, and thereby causing suffering. It may help them to reframe feedback as a service, a form of caring, that helps individuals and organizations fulfill their best potential. It may also help to be mindful of the less-visible but greater suffering of patients and colleagues that results from problem behaviors. And it certainly helps to recognize that problem behaviors can be addressed in a relationship-centered manner (*see* Appendix 3). Chapter 6 includes a story about a relationship-centered approach to removing someone from a job she could not perform, and in Chapter 13 we read about a relationship-centered layoff.

CONCLUSION

In this chapter, we have reviewed the history and principles of Relationship-centered Care. We have traced the evolution of the patient-clinician relationship from hierarchy to partnership. We have seen how the expertise and power of patients have become recognized and how the subjective experience of both patients and clinicians has come to be valued and integrated into the realm of legitimate clinical work. We have explored the four levels of relationship encompassed by RCC: patient–clinician, healthcare team, healthcare system–community and relationship with self. And finally, we have considered the relevance of this partnership-based approach to the realm of administration.

In Part II of this book we will consider many examples of relationship-centered approaches to administration and organizational change. The case studies will show how the dynamics of partnership, emergence and shared decision making are as powerful in administrative work as in patient care. But first we need to add one more ingredient to our theory mix, the one that brings it all together and makes it work: authentic presence.

NOTES

1 Tresolini CP, Pew–Fetzer Task Force. *Health Professions Education and Relationship-centered Care* [monograph]. San Francisco, CA: Pew Health Professions Commission; 1994.

2 Elkes J. Presidential address: Word fallout: or, on the hazards of explanation. *Proc Annual Meeting Am Psychopathol Assoc.* 1970; **59**: 118–37. Engel GL. The need for a new medical model: a challenge for biomedicine. *Science.* 1977; **196**: 129–136. McWhinney IR. Beyond diagnosis: An approach to the integration of behavioral science and clinical medicine. *N Engl J Med.* 1972; **287**: 384–7.

3 Engel GL, op. cit.

4 McWhinney IR, op. cit.

5 For example, *see* Kleinman A. *The Illness Narratives: suffering, healing and the human condition.* New York: Basic Books; 1988, and Sontag S. *Illness as Metaphor.* Harmondsworth, Middlesex, England: Penguin Books; 1987.

6 Baron RJ. An introduction to medical phenomenology: I can't hear you while I'm listening. *Ann Intern Med.* 1985; **103**: 606–11.

7 Kleinman A, op. cit. Hunter K. Overview: "the whole story" [comment]. *Second Opinion.* 1993; **19**: 97–103.

8 Seldin DW. The boundaries of medicine. *Trans Assoc Am Physicians.* 1981; **94**: 75–84.

9 Tresolini CP, Pew–Fetzer Task Force, op. cit.

10 Kahn RL. *An Experiment in Scientific Organization [monograph].* Chicago, IL: The MacArthur Foundation; 1993.

11 Beach MC, Inui TS. Relationship-centered Care Research Network. Relationship-centered care: a constructive reframing. *J Gen Intern Med.* 2006; **21**(Suppl. 1): S3–8.

12 Silverman J, Kurtz SM, Draper J. *Skills for Communicating with Patients.* 2nd ed. Abingdon, UK: Radcliffe Publishing; 2005. Novack D, Daetwyler C, Clark W, *et al.* doc.com Version 4.0. Available at: http://webcampus. drexelmed.edu/doccom (accessed August 10, 2010).

13 Suchman AL, Deci EL, McDaniel SH, *et al.* Relationship-centered administration. In: Frankel RM, Quill TE, McDaniel SH, editors. *The Biopsychosocial Approach: past, present and future.* Rochester, NY: University of Rochester Press; 2003: pp. 180–95.

14 Gittell JH, Fairfield KM, Bierbaum B, *et al.* Impact of relational coordination on quality of care, postoperative pain and functioning and length

of stay: a nine-hospital study of surgical patients. *Med Care.* 2000; **38**: 807–19.

15 Shortell SM, Jones RH, Rademaker AW, *et al.* Assessing the impact of total quality management and organizational culture on multiple outcomes of care for coronary artery bypass graft surgery patients. *Med Care.* 2000; **38**: 207–17.

16 Baggs JG, Schmitt MH, Mushlin AI, *et al.* The association between nurse-physician collaboration and patient outcomes in three intensive care units. *Crit Care Med.* 1999; **27**: 1991–8. Knaus WA, Draper EA, Wagner DP, Zimmerman JE. An evaluation of outcome from intensive care in major medical centers. *Ann Intern Med.* 1986; **104**: 410–8.

17 Aiken LH, Smith HL, Lake ET. Lower Medicare mortality among a set of hospitals known for good nursing care. *Med Care.* 1994; **32**: 771–87.

18 Baggs JG, Ryan SA. ICU nurse-physician collaboration and nurse satisfaction. *Nurs Econ.* 1990; **8**: 386–92. Spickard A, Gabbe SG, Christensen JF. Mid-career burnout in generalist and specialist physicians. *JAMA.* 2002; **288**: 1447–50. Hoffer Gittell J. Relationships and resilience: care provider responses to pressures from managed care. *J Applied Behav Sci.* 2008; **44**: 25–47.

19 Ulrich BT, Buerhaus PI, Donelan K, *et al.* How RNs view the work environment: results of a national survey of registered nurses. *J Nurs Adm.* 2005; **35**: 389–96.

20 Hoffer Gittell J, Weinberg D, Pfefferle S, *et al.* Impact of relational coordination on job satisfaction and quality outcomes: a study of nursing homes. *Hum Resource Manag J.* 2008; **18**: 154–70. Safran DG, Montgomery JE, Chang H, *et al.* Switching doctors: predictors of voluntary disenrollment from a primary physician's practice. *J Fam Pract.* 2001; **50**: 130–6.

21 Ashmos DP, Huonker JW, McDaniel RR. Participation as a complicating mechanism: the effect of clinical professional and middle manager participation on hospital performance. *Healthcare Manage Rev.* 1998; **23**: 7–20. Anderson RA, McDaniel RR. RN participation in organizational decision making and improvements in resident outcomes. *Healthcare Manage Rev.* 1999; **24**(1): 7–16.

22 Edmondson A, Bohmer R, Pisano G. Speeding up team learning. *Harvard Bus Rev.* 2001; Oct: 125–32.

CHAPTER 5

Authentic, affirmative and courageous presence

Penelope R Williamson

In this chapter, we look at how the theories we have described thus far depend for their optimal realization on the "authentic, affirmative and courageous presence" of leaders.[1] (By leaders we mean all persons who influence others and help shape the environments in which they work, not simply those with positional authority. Every member of an organization is a potential leader.) Relationship-centered Care points to the importance of authenticity for trust-worthy interactions and believable leadership. Positive psychology demonstrates the power and efficacy of an appreciative stance. Interpersonal neurobiology helps us understand at a physiological level the risks of rejection associated with acting outside the norm and highlights the courage that is needed to hold true to ourselves and to lead change.

AUTHENTICITY AND THE MOMENT BY MOMENT SHAPING OF CULTURE

In Chapter 2, we saw that one of the implications of a complexity perspective for leadership is to notice the patterns we are making together moment by moment. We have nowhere else to work but here in the moment we are in, and the only way we can influence those patterns is by the way we show up. We may have theories and skills to contribute, but they will just be seen as gimmicks unless people trust us and believe in us. A leader's influence resides in his or her *personal* power as much if not more than his positional power. And personal power comes from an individual's authenticity and integrity.

When Al Gatmaitan became the founding CEO of Clarian West Medical Center, a new hospital with a vision to be a "sanctuary of healing" (*see* Chapter 6), he shared with his new staff that his physician father's home office was his first experience of a sanctuary of healing. He believed it was possible to realize this vision because he had experienced it. His genuineness opened others to be real in turn and gave credibility and weight to this idea and to the relational culture that he intended to create to support it.

> A leader's influence resides in his or her personal power as much if not more than his positional power. And personal power comes from an individual's authenticity and integrity.

It seems ironic that being authentic is challenging for many of us. You would think that "being yourself" would be natural. However, our personal and professional experiences all too often actively discourage us from being genuine, especially in our work roles. The implicit and often explicit message is to be "professional" (expert and skilled, but also detached) rather than real—as if that was a useful choice. Objectivity is prized. The prevailing culture in many healthcare settings defines norms of professional behavior that create distance between how one acts with colleagues, patients, and staff and how one truly feels or thinks.

Our own internal dialogue may also contribute to our hiding our true selves and, in Parker Palmer's words, "living a divided life" where what we show to the outside world is separate from what we experience on the inside. (*A top administrator at a large teaching hospital once shared with me that she felt like she became her real self again as she drove out of the parking lot at the end of each day.*) Leaders may ask themselves, "Can I be myself here? Is being different worth risking a negative response?" This is an understandable question. Feeling rejected lowers brain opioid levels resulting in an unpleasant anxious state that is the internal equivalent of drug withdrawal (*see* Interpersonal Neurobiology in Chapter 3).

Hard as it may seem to do, making the choice to be real can have a profound impact. When leaders are authentic it invites others to be courageous and authentic. The courage to speak our truth and to hear the truths of others increases the diversity of experience and views available to the organization, which, as we've seen, is a valuable natural resource. It sets the stage for creating a trustworthy and resilient culture.

SELF-AWARENESS, REFLECTION AND EMOTIONAL SELF-MANAGEMENT

Because leaders are visible role models (people look to them to learn how they are supposed to act) and because they have the authority to reward and sanction, they have a disproportionate impact on patterns of relating. Therefore they have an important responsibility to be mindful of their emotions, assumptions and habits of thinking. What they bring to each moment is consequential—fear, generosity, blame, belief in the capacity of others, defensiveness, hope. They have the power to impose their negative and positive projections onto others. Their assumptions can become everyone else's reality,[2] and their fears can become constraints around which other peoples' emotions and behaviors organize. (*The COO of a hospital revealed that he always made sure to size up the mood of the CEO before asking him a question, as his boss had a volatile temper which often erupted when he felt overloaded or stressed.)* All too easily, people can end up being responsible for managing their bosses' anxieties. This is emotionally draining, time consuming, and unfair.

In his provocative essay, *Leading from Within*, Parker Palmer speaks about five basic human fears: of not being good enough, of being able to count only on oneself, of the world's hostility and cruelty, of not being in control, and that the losses that lie ahead will be overwhelming.[3] Only as we become aware that one of these fears has us in its grip can we release its hold on us so that we neither are captive to it nor inflict it on others.

> Beth had risen through the ranks of a large hospital, and after 25 years was now the head of Human Resources. Although the hospital was known for its service orientation, there had been serious complaints from patients and staff about the decline in a culture of compassion and service excellence. Beth was asked to organize and lead a culture-change initiative.
>
> At the start of this initiative, she participated in a leadership program that allowed her to reconnect with her passion to make a difference, and to learn new tools for how to implement a relational approach to this important initiative. In the supportive environment of this learning group Beth acknowledged experiencing the fear that she couldn't count on anyone else and that only she could do the job right. She recognized that this fear had long held her in a stance of "command and control" and that she could only change the hospital culture by unleashing the motivation and participation of many others. She felt ready to try a more collaborative approach.
>
> With trepidation and great courage, Beth led a day-long retreat for a 30-person culture-change leadership team from across all sectors and positions of the hospital. The day was interactive, built relationships and dreams, and began a successful process of fostering shared responsibility for the work ahead.

We come to know ourselves accurately through an ongoing practice of reflection, and through the feedback of others. Learning to reflect means listening inwardly for what is true for us, taking into account our own views as well as others' observations. When we develop the capacity to reflect and the discipline to do so regularly, we become aware of our innate gifts and limits (those qualities we were born with that no one can take away). In this way we may come to understand and embrace what we shine at, to discover where we are vulnerable, and to learn how to protect ourselves from and compensate for what we are not good at. Thomas Merton put it this way: *"If we attempt to act and do things for others or for the world without deepening our own self-understanding, our own freedom, integrity, and capacity to love, we will not have anything to give to others."*

> We come to know ourselves accurately through an ongoing practice of reflection, and through the feedback of others.

Developing the discipline to discern what is happening internally before responding opens a vital space between what we experience and what we do, so we can respond mindfully rather than just reactively. This is particularly important for leaders who often face complex, emotion-laden situations. In the heat of tough moments, dissociating from or ignoring inner feelings may cause leaders to fool or deceive themselves and take ill-considered actions or cause relational problems. It takes discipline to develop a regular practice of self-reflection; yet it is only in this way that we can recognize the patterns we are helping to create in the moment and to be intentional about how we sustain or alter them.

> Jack was the COO of a large hospital. He was deeply thoughtful and very much an introvert. He learned that he did his best work when he took the time he needed to observe and explore a complex situation, make sense of what he was seeing and hearing, connect his observations (his mind) with his native capacity to empathize (his heart), and then to act. His boss was a brilliant, fast-paced, extrovert who believed that rapid diagnosis of a problem followed quickly by action was best. He did not always take time to understand or empathize with others. Jack admired his boss, and for several years he tried to follow his boss's directives and to emulate him, assuming his boss's way must be right and denying his own gifts. At length, he recognized the cost to himself and to the organization. He couldn't be his boss. He had to be himself. And faster wasn't always better. Jack spoke to his boss about the complementarity of their strengths and claimed the power of his own gifts. This courageous act of authenticity turned the tide of his leadership with positive impact on the organization and his relationships therein.

In addition to reflection as an individual act, leaders can also cultivate this practice among colleagues. When groups regularly reflect together on their interpersonal interactions, they have the opportunity to be more intentional about how they are relating to each other and to self-correct. This marks the difference between mindless, automatic continuation of existing patterns (what Otto Scharmer calls "downloading"[4]) and mindful participation—intentionally reinforcing desirable patterns and seeking to disrupt undesirable ones. At both a personal and collective level, reflection may prompt us to ask, "What can I/we do that might instigate a different, better pattern?" Such a discipline of reflective practice distinguishes relationship-centered from non-relationship-centered groups and organizations.

Beyond reflection, leaders need skills to manage their emotions. Individual practices such as yoga, meditation or meditative activities such as running, swimming, gardening or cooking may help to settle anxiety and create space for exploring one's experience. Coaching by an individual or in a community of trusted and mutually supportive peers can provide support and a safe space for grappling with challenges.[5] Leaders can convene their own peer-coaching groups or find them through existing leadership-education programs that emphasize reflection and discernment.[6]

CLARIFYING ONE'S CORE BELIEFS

Each of us operates from a world view (mental model, grounding belief) which guides our actions, consciously or unconsciously, and which offers us very different sources of existential security. So another dimension of self-awareness is to know the core beliefs that shape our thinking and action.

Tony Suchman has compared two foundational worldviews, based on core values of control on the one hand and relation on the other.[7] Working under a paradigm of control means needing to be in charge, to predict and control outcomes. The major questions for the control-oriented leader are, "What do I want to happen here? What is wrong? How do I fix it?" The modus operandi is mastery and vigilance (believing that "if something bad happens I am at fault"). As we saw in Beth's story above, this is a fear-based paradigm in which one trusts oneself more than others and holds tightly to power. The control paradigm focuses attention on the realization of our will, on outcomes and objective phenomena. It predisposes leaders towards dominance, distracts them from cultivating relationships and leads them to set unrealistic expectations of control (*see* Chapter 2).

Working under a paradigm of relation means recognizing that one is connected and belongs to a larger whole. In this world view, the best outcomes are realized by attending to relationships and maximizing the quality of interactional processes. The major question for the relation-oriented leader is, "What is trying to happen here?" This leader recognizes the interdependence of self and others in the larger order of things. She seeks to shape others and the world while remaining open to being shaped, holding a balance between control and receptivity. Diversity is welcomed as a resource. The modus operandi is self-awareness, acting in accordance with one's feelings and cultivating relationships of respect and genuineness. This is a trust-based paradigm, anchored in the belief that the sources of order, goodness and meaning lie beyond one's own creation. It predisposes leaders to do their best in partnership with others, to attend to the process of relating and to personal experience (their own and others') and to remain open to possibility.

ACCEPTING ONESELF

Our self-acceptance influences how we view the world and how we relate to others. We have already considered the importance of being aware of our strengths and limitations and the impact of various life experiences on what drives us or holds us back. It serves us even more profoundly, particularly as leaders, when we accept ourselves with all of our capacities and frailties. Accepting yourself doesn't mean that you stop learning or continuing to grow. It does mean that you hold yourself in hope, in the belief that you *can* grow and learn, and also in the conviction that you are valuable just as you are.

Accepting oneself increases one's capacity for equanimity with the ups and downs of organizational life, both for leaders and those they serve. There is less likelihood of taking oneself too seriously or relentlessly blaming oneself or others for every missed step. This is beautifully illustrated in Chapter 8, where senior leaders of an international program to prevent and treat HIV/AIDS in Kenya encouraged staff to create new approaches to issues and to treat mistakes as valuable learning opportunities. As one example, Caroline Opiyo, Head of Human Resources recounts how she felt empowered to develop new rural clinics through the encouragement of her boss:

> Joe's word to me always was, "Do what you can to make this thing work!" None of us really knew how to approach it, but by making constant mistakes and correcting ourselves along the way I managed to get four centers up and running within two months.

> Accepting oneself increases one's capacity for equanimity with the ups and downs of organizational life, both for leaders and those they serve. There is less likelihood of taking oneself too seriously or relentlessly blaming oneself or others for every missed step.

Many great poets, writers and thinkers from all wisdom and faith traditions have expressed similar beliefs over the ages. To name two, an ancient Spanish proverb says, *"If you are not good for yourself, how can you be good for others?"* The practice of "Metta" in Buddhist philosophy teaches self-acceptance and self-well-wishing as the ground from which true empathy, hope and love for others spring.[8]

When leaders genuinely accept themselves they model humility, humanity, and healthy confidence for those they serve. Self-acceptance is closely aligned with self-trust, which in turn opens the possibility of being trusted by and trusting others. When self-trust is lacking, much as described above about leading from fear, subordinates have to manage the leader's insecurities, distorting communication processes and making work more inefficient. Moreover, as long as we cannot trust or accept ourselves, no amount of external validation will make a difference. Yet there is always possibility. The Trinidadian poet Derek Walcott holds out the universal hope for self-acceptance in the lines from his poem "Love After Love":

> The time will come
> when, with elation
> you will greet yourself arriving
> at your own door . . .[9]

We are social beings. Others play a vital role in helping us know and accept ourselves. Friends and colleagues may name and affirm our gifts in ways we don't recognize; they may point out our limitations in ways we might not see or acknowledge for ourselves. Some find individual or group therapy helpful in learning where habits of self-criticism originate and discovering other ways to look at things. Such practices allow for the development of healthy self-confidence seasoned by thoughtful challenges as well as affirmation of our ideas. African Bushmen have a centuries-old greeting when two people meet: The first says, "I See You." The other responds, "I Am Here."[10] Being seen allows us to claim our own presence. As social beings, knowing and being known, affirmed and believed in by others is vital and essential to our sense of well-being (harking back to attachment theory, *see* Chapter 3).

ACCEPTING OTHERS

In our consideration of positive psychology in Chapter 3 we saw the power of identifying existing capabilities and of learning from success. This is more than just a technique; it requires a genuine belief in the capacity and potential of others. Seeing, believing in, and affirming the capabilities of others are major determinants of their growth and effectiveness. When we can let go of the need to control and instead support the autonomy and competence of the people we lead, we call out their best (*see* Self-Determination Theory, Chapter 3). This belief in self and others is rooted in a deeper belief in possibility—that the world can be a better place and that we can each contribute by showing up authentically and doing our best, by calling out the best in others, and by respecting the mystery of what we can't know. The power of looking for what is working and what is possible (the life-giving core) in self, others and organizations is illustrated in many of the case studies, in particular Chapters 6, 10 and 13. For example, the first intervention in the initiative to change the culture at Indiana University School of Medicine (described in Chapter 13) was to interview 80 faculty about the culture when it was at its best. In hearing these stories, one faculty member said, "When I see what we're capable of, I can no longer be silent when I see someone throw something in the operating room, or humiliate a student. We're too good for that."

> The ability to accept others and value their ideas and life-worlds is at the heart of our ability to form healthy partnerships—open to influence and co-creation. This is the essence of welcoming diversity and fostering responsiveness, the crucial ingredients for innovation.

In the complex issues that leaders face, each person has a unique and important perspective to bring; none is wise enough to have all perspectives. The ability to accept others and value their ideas and life-worlds is at the heart of our ability to form healthy partnerships—open to influence and co-creation. This is the essence of welcoming diversity and fostering responsiveness, the crucial ingredients for innovation (*see* Chapter 2 and Appendix 1). Letting go of the desire to control the thinking of a group, we can create a trustworthy partnership process, thereby accessing the group's best potential. Ways will open that we couldn't have imagined or created by ourselves. In daunting situations, recognizing that we are not alone and that we can turn to and count on others can be a deep source of solace and hope.

HOLDING THE PARADOX OF SELF-DIFFERENTIATION AND ATTUNEMENT

Being an effective leader requires managing the dynamic tension between self-differentiation and attunement.[11] When we are self-differentiated we are clear about our own beliefs, values and opinions, even in the face of others' anxiety and opposition. When we are attuned, we strive to understand and be responsive to others' beliefs and opinions. It takes courage to stand by what one believes in the face of challenges. Yet this act of self-differentiation may enhance trustworthiness.

> One night, Joe, a junior surgery resident, was preparing to assist his attending physician with a complex surgery that he had never performed before. Everything was in readiness, the patient was anesthetized, but the supervising primary surgeon had not arrived. The nurses urged Joe to get started with the operation but he refused, knowing that he was not competent to do so. Twenty minutes late, the attending surgeon rushed into the operating room, gowned and ready, and when he found that the procedure had not been started he screamed at the resident in abusive terms, calling him unprofessional and lazy. Joe said in a calm but firm voice that he would not perform a surgery for which he had no experience without the presence and help of his supervising physician. Later the attending physician apologized to Joe and to the team. He admitted that he had been embarrassed at being late and that the junior resident was right not to begin.

It also takes courage to invite others' views, especially in the midst of a charged situation. Yet leaders call out the best in others when they are genuinely curious to understand their perspectives, balancing their own "knowing" with inquiry and listening for diverse truths (*see* Appendix 1). The quality of deep attentiveness has profound capacity to open hearts (the seat of empathy) and to soften a rigid stance, allowing for the building of mutual trust and meaningful collaboration.

> Lisa had recently started her tenure as the Executive Director of a non-profit healthcare advocacy organization when she was invited to meet with a small group of the members. The person who invited her said they were eager to share some of their views about the organization. Readily agreeing, Lisa expected to have a fruitful dialogue with these long standing supporters. Much to her surprise, when she entered the meeting room, she was handed a "manifesto" and told in an angry voice that the members were no longer willing to be treated badly; they had drawn up a list of demands. After taking a moment to collect herself (during which time she reasoned that this could not be a personal attack as no one yet knew her) Lisa said in an empathic way, "Things must feel pretty hard for you to have taken the time and effort to write this list. I am very interested in hearing your views." Immediately the tension in the room lessened. One person said, "We're so glad you really want to understand us." An honest, respectful conversation ensued.

Being human, we are not always able to rise to each occasion with grace and skill. We each tend more naturally towards either self-differentiation or attunement, especially under pressure. Honing the capacity to reflect on what causes us to move away from attending to self *and* others and what allows us to re-equilibrate serves us well in the hurly burly of daily challenges. For instance, you may have experienced yourself digging in steadfastly to one point of view in the face of divergent opinions, or conversely, under stress, agreeing too quickly with a prevailing view, and giving up your own opinion to keep the peace. When our default stance under pressure is holding on to control without staying connected to others we risk isolation. When we default to over-attuning to others, we risk losing our voice for the sake of togetherness. Becoming aware of our propensities, we can learn to compensate and to better manage this paradox. The capacity to hold this dynamic tension resides in our capacity to simultaneously accept ourselves and others.

LEADING WITH COURAGE AND LOVE

It takes courage and heart to be a leader. Bolstered by the practices of partnership described above, leaders may more consistently choose an authentic and courageous path in their moment-to-moment actions. Courageous leaders are often the first to name a difficult issue, or to create a disturbance (step outside a norm) that opens up a new or broader way of seeing, hearing and responding. And by doing so, they model these possibilities and foster the same in others. Wise and courageous leaders connect their minds and their hearts.

> Courageous leaders are often the first to name a difficult issue, or to create a disturbance (step outside a norm) that opens up a new or broader way of seeing, hearing and responding. And by doing so, they model these possibilities and foster the same in others.

The poet and philosopher Mark Nepo talks about knowing whether your heart serves your mind or your mind serves your heart, of discerning in any situation which is foreground and which is background. Nepo says:

> The mind works best as a tool of the heart. Given the chance, the mind will take over. We can get so task driven that we forget our connections. We make plans and checklists and then they take over and we forget the heart of what we're serving.[12]

In our results-driven world, this can be hard to remember.

> Meredith, a senior physician-leader, was committed to creating a relational culture in her clinic as a means of enhancing quality and safety. She developed a proposal to provide training for leaders of healthcare teams to enhance their communication and collaborative skills with patients, family members, colleagues and staff. After many months of laying the groundwork, she was invited to present her ideas and proposal to her Board of Directors. She asked a small group of trusted peers to listen to a dry run of her presentation. In her informal conversations with peers, Meredith was compelling— her passion, knowledge and dedication were evident. But when she gave her practice talk all the life was gone. The data were there but Meredith had disappeared. One of the group asked, "What would you say if you let yourself speak from your heart?" This question allowed Meredith to reconnect with her deeper purpose and to speak simply and with great conviction. Her presentation to the Board was a tour de force and Meredith has since shared that she never forgot that lesson and now regularly asks herself, "What would I say if I were speaking from my heart?"

Martin Luther King, Jr named similar ideas in the language of power and love:

Power properly understood is nothing but the ability to achieve purpose. It is the strength to bring about social, political, and economic change. . . . And one of the great problems of history is that the concepts of love and power have usually been contrasted as opposites—polar opposites—so that love is identified with the resignation of power, and power with the denial of love. Now we've got to get this thing right. What [we need to realize is] that power without love is reckless and abusive, and love without power is sentimental and anemic. . . . It is precisely this collision of immoral power with powerless morality which constitutes the major crisis of our time.[13]

It takes courage to act. It takes courage to love. When both are held in balance, we recognize leadership at its best.

THE ONGOING JOURNEY TO AUTHENTIC, AFFIRMATIVE AND COURAGEOUS PRESENCE

We return once again to re-emphasize how the personhood of the leader brings to life the lessons from complexity, positive psychology, and Relationship-centered Care. Relationship-centered Administration is more than a set of theories and skills; it is a way of being.

Complexity science shows how organizational culture is being created continuously in the course of moment-to-moment human interactions. By the ways in which they behave and interact with others, leaders have particular power to perpetuate cultural patterns or to create disturbances that may change and even transform the status quo. They do this by modeling and fostering in others the qualities of mindfulness, regular reflection, and authentic participation in the work rather than imposing top-down, predetermined plans.

It is a leader's authentic and positive stance, bolstered by methodologies from positive psychology, that can unleash creative potential and the realization of a vision. Appreciative Inquiry points to discovering the root causes of success rather than of failure as a more powerful motivator of desired change. Positive Deviance calls forth the capacity of a group to identify its own solutions by seeking out the innovators within its own ranks. Self-Determination Theory demonstrates the efficacy of specific leadership behaviors to effect change: providing people with opportunities to develop competence, supporting their autonomy, and fostering respectful and caring relationships. Embracing a positive stance rests on a leader's capacity to believe in self and others.

The philosophy of Relationship-centered Care features robust partnerships and respect for persons at every level of healthcare. One's relationship with self and core recognition of interdependence with others are grounding conditions for building effective collaborative relationships.

Being authentic, courageous and affirmative is a lifetime journey. It is a commitment to living with integrity and wholeness, not a fixed destination. This is hopeful and challenging—hopeful because there is always opportunity for us to learn and deepen into the people we aspire to be; challenging because the work is never done! We can only do our best, faithful to reliable processes built on trustworthy relationships, knowing that in the largest sense it is out of our hands. That is the beauty and the mystery of life.

NOTES

1 Suchman A, Williamson P, Rawlins D. Core concepts of relationship-centered administration [presentation]. Leading Organizations to Health. Allenspark, CO. April 6, 2006.

2 *See* the Ladder of Inference in Chapter 2, note 3.

3 Palmer P. Leading from within. In Palmer P. *Let Your Life Speak: listening for the voice of vocation.* San Francisco, CA: Jossey Bass; 2000. pp. 73–94.

4 Scharmer CO. *Theory U: leading from the future as it emerges.* Cambridge, MA: Society for Organizational Learning; 2007: pp. 119–28.

5 Diana Chapman Walsh, past President of Wellesley College, talks of this as a core condition for developing trustworthy leadership. Walsh DC. *Trustworthy Leadership: can we be the leaders we need our students to become?* Kalamazoo, MI: Fetzer Institute; 2006.

6 Examples of such programs include those presented by the Center for Courage and Renewal and the Center for Creative Leadership, and also the program Leading Organizations to Health.

7 Suchman AL. Control and relation: two foundational values and their consequences. *J Interprofessional Care* 2006; **20**(1): 3–11.

8 Brach T. *Radical Acceptance: embracing your life with the heart of a Buddha.* New York: Bantam Books; 2003.

9 Walcott D. "Love After Love." In Walcott D. *Collected Poems 1948–1984.* New York: Farrar, Straus & Giroux; 1986: p. 328.

10 Nepo M. "December 31st." In: Nepo M. *Book of Awakening: having the life you want by being present to the life you have.* Berkeley, CA: Conari Press; 2000: p. 428.

11 I thank Diane (Robbins) Rawlins for her clear articulation of the concepts of self-differentiation and attunement. Diane in turn credits her mentors Donald Williamson and Edward Friedman for informing her thinking on these concepts.

12 Nepo M. The exquisite risk: daring to live an authentic life [presentation]. Annapolis, MD: March 26–28, 2010.

13 Quoted in Kahane A. *The Language of Power and the Language of Love: solving tough problems in practice.* Shambala Institute for Authentic Leadership: Fieldnotes, December 2007.

PART II

Case Studies

CHAPTER 6

Clarian West Medical Center: creating a sanctuary of healing

Al Gatmaitan, Beth Newton Watson, Lana Funkhouser, Cathy Stoll,
Anthony L Suchman and Penelope R Williamson

SYNOPSIS

Clarian West Medical Center in Avon, Indiana opened in December 2004. From the very start, its owners and administrative leaders were intent on building not just a hospital but also a healing culture. Their vision of clinical excellence and their business plan were based on the idea of creating a "Healing Sanctuary" combining the practice of Relationship-centered Care with the best traditions of patient safety, knowledge-based care and continuous quality improvement to achieve outstanding organizational results. This chapter describes a relationship-centered approach to the hiring, orientation and ongoing management of a new hospital staff. Hospital performance measures over the first two years showed consistently high levels of quality, safety, satisfaction (both patient and staff) and financial performance, validating the effectiveness of Relationship-centered Administration and a hospital strategy based on Relationship-centered Care.

BACKGROUND

This is the story about opening a new community hospital with dreams of changing the nature of hospital care in central Indiana.

In 2002, Clarian Health Partners, a multi-hospital health system in Indianapolis, Indiana, charged a development and design team with the task of planning, building and activating Clarian West Medical Center (CWMC). Clarian West was created as a for-profit hospital, owned jointly by the non-profit Clarian Health System and by a number of its physicians. Its design was to be a suburban community hospital in Avon, Indiana, opening with 76 beds and over 500 employees and eventually expanding to 400 beds. It also was to be a sanctuary of healing.

An executive member of that development and design team participated in one of the Center for Health Design's first "Pebble Projects"[1]: the redesign of a cardiac critical care unit in one of Clarian's downtown hospitals. It was the first project at Clarian Health Partners to focus explicitly on the design of a healing environment. The result was a truly revolutionary approach for thoughtfully addressing the needs of the patients, families and caregivers. Building on that success, the team was given the responsibility of designing an entire hospital where every aspect of the patient's experience—from architecture and environment to medical and nursing care—would enhance healing.

The design team was also influenced by the experience of three senior vice-presidents of Clarian Health Partners, Steve Ivy, Steve Wantz, and Karlene Kerfoot, who had undertaken a series of pilot culture-change initiatives within the downtown parent hospitals, nurturing healthy staff relationships and self-care. These initiatives, named "Sanctuary for Healing," provided language for the vision of CWMC as a "Healing Sanctuary."

GETTING STARTED

Al W Gatmaitan, FACHE, was hired as CWMC's first Chief Executive Officer for his specific expertise in establishing relationships with physicians and employees and his past success in the community hospital setting. He was excited by the role the building's architecture would play in creating a sanctuary of healing. Yet he sensed from past experience that the building alone would not be enough. The quality of relationships would be essential.

> When I reflect on my career in healthcare on the moments when patients felt most cared for, I realize that those moments were in the most modest of settings. The latest technology or trend in building designs was not present. My father opened a solo general practice in small town Indiana at the age of 53 as a foreign medical school graduate with a strong accent. Twenty-five years after the end of his ten-year practice and sudden death, I would return to that small town and always be approached by some patients who expressed what my father had meant to them as their physician. He has literally been irreplaceable. My father's Sanctuary of Healing was a modest, small house on the square, remodeled to accommodate his patients. This was just as much a sanctuary as the beautiful campus of Clarian West Medical Center. Since then, in my professional life, I have witnessed other Sanctuaries of Healing, in which the relationship between caregivers and their patients is nurturing and intimate, regardless of the setting.
>
> Al Gatmaitan, CEO, Clarian West Hospital

Gatmaitan wanted to create a workplace that would improve on prevailing industry trends of high burnout and staff turnover, excessive medical errors, and financial inefficiency. He was committed to achieving a hospital-wide performance level of unsurpassed service and excellence in step with the vision of the hospital's owners. His resolve was reinforced by external factors. The parent system was investing considerable capital and other resources in a new suburban growth strategy. All investors had specific expectations relative to a return on their investment.

In addition, the hospital would be opening in an era of unprecedented transparency about quality and consumer pricing, as well as increasing work-force pressures and shortages. Shortly after opening, two clicks of a "mouse" would show any consumer comparative hospital performance information relative to medical errors and patient perception via federal and state quality initiatives.

Gatmaitan and his CWMC executive team assumed responsibility for bringing the vision for the hospital to life. They were guided by the newly drafted Operating Principles for the hospital: 1) Healing Sanctuary; 2) Patient Safety; 3) Knowledge-Driven Care; 4) Service Excellence; and 5) Measured Performance/Accountability. The senior leaders further articulated the three essential components of Sanctuary of Healing upon which Clarian West Medical Center would be built: 1) healing environment, 2) enabling technology, and 3) Relationship-centered Care. The healing environment would establish a setting that complemented and promoted excellent medical and nursing care as well as inviting patients' own healing resources. Enabling technology would make communication between patient and caregiver and among caregivers themselves more efficient and effective, reducing the major cause of medical errors. The philosophy of Relationship-centered Care would inform the crea-tion and maintenance of a healing workplace culture that promoted caring, respectful relationships among staff, patients, family and the broader commu-nity, enabling crucial conversations, and inviting the well-being of everyone involved

> Relationship-centered Care became Clarian West's guiding management philosophy by both intention and serendipity.

Relationship-centered Care became Clarian West's guiding management philosophy by both intention and serendipity. Based on his own experience and a study of lasting and distinctive organizations, Gatmaitan believed that for Clarian West to be successful "in providing preeminent and remarkable care for its patients," attention to relationships and the workplace culture must be at the core of every aspect of its business and marketing activities. He began looking for ways to actualize these beliefs. Julie Long, Director of Service Excellence, discovered the Pew–Fetzer Task Force Report on Health Professions Education and Relationship-centered Care[2] in a literature search on new directions in care, and brought it to the table. Both Gatmaitan and Long agreed that this report articulated the philosophy they had been seeking.

Serendipitously, Tom Inui, Chair of the Pew–Fetzer Task Force, was just across town at the Indiana University School of Medicine. Conversation with him led Gatmaitan to Penny Williamson and Tony Suchman, consultants with expertise in Relationship-centered Care, who were working with Inui on a medical school initiative to promote relational competence in graduating physicians (*see* Chapter 13). Conversations with Inui, Williamson and Suchman convinced Gatmaitan and Long that Relationship-centered Care needed to be the third essential component in the Sanctuary of Healing and that they had found their mentors for the process of building a culture.

The executive team began the daunting tasks of overseeing the equipping and activation of the hospital, hiring the full management team, and conceptualizing and creating a new culture for Clarian West. Gatmaitan invited the team to consult constantly, to listen intentionally to one another, and to consider the impact of every key choice on the health and well-being of all involved. No issue was too small. As they made detailed decisions about the layout and decor of the hospital, they discussed such matters as the interrelationships between landscaped gardens and private rooms, the effect of bed height on the view out the window, and the color and style of staff uniforms. Team members asked themselves such questions as, "Does this room layout enable or inhibit healing relationships?" and, "Does this space foster crucial conversations?"

During the months of hospital construction, the management team developed the use of enabling technology. They laid out workflows for every imaginable process in a patient's journey and what it would take to make that journey possible. They asked questions such as, "Will this computer program enhance clinician–patient relationships? Can this technology make information sharing easy? Are we telling each other what we have learned?"

Gatmaitan and members of his team explored the personal, professional and organizational steps needed to implement a relationship-centered management philosophy. They found they had reliable processes as they considered the myriad aspects of the built environment and the parameters of enabling technology. Now, with every step they added questions such as, "Is there a way to make this more relationship-centered?" and "Are we contributing to the Healing Sanctuary by this action? Can we be intentional in the way workplace culture is developed?" The senior team, in consultation with Williamson and Suchman, grew in its understanding and kept its focus on Relationship-centered Care in a Sanctuary of Healing.

> With every step they added questions such as, "Is there a way to make this more relationship-centered?" and "Are we contributing to the Healing Sanctuary by this action? Can we be intentional in the way workplace culture is developed?"

Gatmaitan was convinced that excelling in the current healthcare environment would require building on the energy and passion of management and line staff alike.

> We held a retreat with future physician leaders, in which they were invited to identify their hopes and expectations for Clarian West Medical Center. They were asked to identify moments in their careers when their vision of medicine actually became reality, if only for a moment. This Appreciative Inquiry helped the physician leaders identify members of their groups who would thrive in CWMC's Sanctuary of Healing, and helped Executive Administration understand what physicians needed and valued in order to practice medicine in ways they had only dreamed of previously.
>
> Al Gatmaitan

The senior team brought into consciousness how relationships could enable healing: relationships between managers and staff persons, between patients and caregivers, between patients and their families. The management team was building a relationship-centered culture even as the physical plant took shape.

STORIES ALONG THE WAY
Hiring and orientation

As opening day approached, new members of the physician leadership and management team joined the CEO and senior leadership, expanding the commitment to build a distinctive model for hospital management, workplace culture and patient care.

As a group, we brought proven expertise, creativity, and a willingness to try new things. Each of the senior leaders and managers was responsible for hiring our respective staff. We used a variety of methods to recruit, assess and hire, recognizing that it is the staff that would ultimately have to create and maintain the Clarian West culture. For example, Human Resources introduced behavioral assessment to accompany the interviewing process, and managers were trained to interview prospective hires by soliciting stories about prior successful experiences and listening carefully to those stories to assess reflective and relational capacity. Interviews became a process of finding "good fits"—people who were hoping for greater fulfillment in their work and for whom a relationship-centered culture was important. Interviewers asked prospective staff how they could imagine making healing relationships a central part of their daily work life with patients and colleagues and for their ideas about how to build a Sanctuary of Healing.

> Shortly after we began interviewing our prospective staffs we had a leadership retreat downtown with Penny and Tony about

interviewing using relationship skills. It made me look at the interview in a different way—I knew I could find out about an applicant's job skills via references and by asking pointed questions. What I recognized was that I needed a better idea of an applicant's people skills, basic nature and approach to life and work. I had asked several applicants to give me examples of work experiences, and using Penny and Tony's approach, I amended that question to the following: "Anyone who has worked in healthcare for any amount of time will develop a repertoire of stories . . . we tell them to each other when we gather informally. Would you tell me the story from your work in healthcare that you consider to be the best experience you have had or that is an example of why you work in healthcare—something that made you very proud to be where you were, doing what you do?" I have asked this question of every single applicant since—not just RNs but also our surgical techs and unit secretaries.

. . . the stories I heard were incredible tales of the caring and nurturing that humans are capable of. Most of them ended sadly, although some of them recounted patients returning for happier times or events that did end happily. Many of them resulted in both the applicant and the interviewer (me!) in tears.

I was so touched by these stories and felt they were windows into the hearts of the people who told them. When all our staff gathered together for the first time as a team, we met in a large area that would become our unit's Family Waiting Room. It had only a few chairs so many of us stood or sat on the floor. It was an informal time! As a "getting to know you" exercise that first morning, I told my own story and then asked each person to tell the story they had told me during their job interview. As I knew would happen, there were many tears and much bonding that took place that day . . . it helped take 25 assertive, experienced, confident women who didn't know one another and transformed them into a team. From that morning on, we all knew we had one purpose—to get the unit and ourselves ready to give excellent, safe, nurturing care to the women who entrusted themselves and their babies to our care!

I can't say there were no conflicts in the days that followed— there were many. I recall two nurses sitting in my office so mad they could hardly speak to one another. I reminded them of our one purpose, and it didn't take long to get them talking and resolving the issue. They left my office able to once again work together. They will never be best friends, but they continue to work well together over a year later. I had one of them bring this up the other day, stating she thought we ought to gather again as a staff "for another kum-ba-yah meeting" so we can all remember why we are here!

Barb Bertram, RN, BSN, Maternity Center Manager

> From that morning on, we all knew we had one purpose—to get the unit and ourselves ready to give excellent, safe, nurturing care to the women who entrusted themselves and their babies to our care!

Continuing the tone set by the recruitment process, our orientation process for new hires was relational from the very start; especially important because opening a hospital is very anxiety provoking. Management assisted new staff leaders in developing relational strategies for building their teams. Our process allowed participants to gather the essential information while having conversations with one another and with the orientation leaders.

> While many hospitals have emphasized computer-based orientation, we keep it "live" and real here. We take small groups of new employees to each presenter's office. This establishes relationships between new employees and key leaders/managers up front. (New employees often comment favorably on this out-of-the-ordinary investment of time and relationship-building.)
>
> In a Sanctuary of Healing, [sharing] food is sacramental. The new employees' managers meet their new staff members for lunch on the second day of orientation in order to provide a sociable working experience. Relationships that began in the hiring process are picked up in a casual context and a "second installment" of relationship building can occur. By meeting away from the department, the focus can be on building relationships over food and conversation.
>
> In planning the orientation, we worked hard to anticipate needs and fears and to provide assurances. Questions and fears are barriers to establishing relationships on the first day of a new job. Providing a "go-to" person who will meet individual concerns, answer questions up-front and demonstrate follow-through builds trusting relationships and helps people feel cared for in the new environment.
>
> Mary Beth Simon, Director of Education

We experienced an early test of relationship-centered practice because of unexpected construction delays. We had interviewed staff, offered positions, and given start dates; and then management learned that the building would not be ready as scheduled. This posed a real problem, because the temporary office space being utilized by the Clarian West Medical Center team could not house all those who had been hired. Worse, there was a possibility that we would not be able to honor hiring commitments. Gatmaitan and Vice President Lana Funkhouser devised a relationship-centered approach to the problem.

> When opening was delayed, Al and I prepared a carefully scripted message for managers to use in contacting their staff. We asked ourselves, "What is our obligation to those who have taken a leap of faith and consented to become a caregiver at Clarian West Medical Center and a partner in our future?" We wanted the staff both to hear the news and experience a communication that expressed the importance of our relationship with them. Managers personally contacted staff who had been hired, but had not yet started, and asked them if they could delay their arrival without too much difficulty, even though our orientation and opening dates remained a moving target. For those who had given notice or were now unemployed and needed to start as planned, we made arrangements to engage them and pay them, though perhaps not in the capacities in which they would ultimately serve. This was an extraordinary experience, for the managers making the calls, and for the staff members. Senior leadership and managers continued a constant dialog of updates and reassurances for weeks and months until opening day. Amidst the shock, fear and potential chaos of an unexpected construction delay, we created an opportunity to set the tone for how our organization would operate in crises and how much we really valued relationships. One-on-one, we asked these "pre-employees" (our life's blood for opening and beyond) to trust us long before they had a chance to know us as individuals or as an organization. The managers did a stellar job in establishing and maintaining crucial relationships. Ultimately we lost only a handful of the 250-plus people hired initially. This was truly a defining moment for our organization.
> Lana Funkhouser, Vice President, Human Relations

> Amidst the shock, fear and potential chaos of an unexpected construction delay, we created an opportunity to set the tone for how our organization would operate in crises and how much we really valued relationships.

All members of the staff were learning that the CWMC was not some monolithic machine, but a vulnerable, developing entity and that they could be of assistance to it. We were also learning that our leaders were authentic, trustworthy individuals, who advocated for all of us and would not let staff down even when circumstances were difficult.

Building trust

Managers tell many stories about experiencing the confidence and very real support of senior leadership. Because senior leaders were committed to relationships of curiosity, open communication and trust, they were able to challenge and educate as well as affirm their managers throughout the planning, opening and activation stages of the hospital. This Relationship-centered Administration approach assisted everyone in managing the unpredictable and anxiety-provoking journey of this time.

> I was told that I had to be in charge of the pediatric unit as well as the Emergency Department. I had never run an inpatient unit, and I had never worked in a pediatric unit, although I took care of pediatric patients in the ED. I looked at it as a challenge and learned from my experienced pediatrics' staff. Administration had the confidence that I could oversee this unit and I did accomplish getting it opened and running by believing in the experienced pediatrics' nurses that I hired. This is a case of someone believing in me and me believing in others.
>
> Jane Forni, Manager, Emergency Department

> I was asked to help with the development of the Cancer program, specifically to help interpret and implement the standards required for certification by the American College of Surgeons. This task required skill sets and knowledge I didn't have. The VP of Clinical Services encouraged me and showed confidence in my ability. She expressed her willingness and the willingness of the institution to provide avenues for my development that would help me to accomplish these tasks. The support continues . . .
>
> Denise Clark, Manager, Radiation
> Oncology and the Cancer Center

> After opening, our in- and outpatient departments grew quickly. My vice president had left and we were in transition with leadership. There was a lot of inner turmoil in trying to deal with the transition and growth, and everyone's different ideas of how things should be done. The new vice president joined our administrative team and helped reaffirm my confidence and belief in myself. She gave me free rein to reset the department goals, establish limits and focus on the primary goals to stay on track with the mission. I found I could truly do my job and now our department is filled with wonderful people believing in the West mission and vision.
>
> Cheri Wenger, Manager, Rehabilitation Services

> When opening the sleep lab I faced the choice to hire either a coordinator with a lot of supervisory experience who didn't believe in the West culture of Relationship-centered Care in a Sanctuary of Healing, or a person with no supervisory experience but a great attitude who was willing to try new things. I chose the person with the great attitude who worked to learn the needed skills and wasn't afraid to ask questions. Eighteen months later the lab is expanding and we had our national accreditation survey performed in record time. (She) is a great asset to me and to Clarian West.
>
> Wendy Lalone, Manager, Respiratory Therapy

> I have no story but it was more of a feeling, a knowing comfort that [my vice president] believed I could accomplish anything my job required. She had a gift for making you believe in yourself, even when I didn't have a clue as to what I was doing.
>
> Sally Butler, Manager, Diagnostic Imaging

Building the staff members' trust in themselves, in one another, and in the Senior Leadership team has been an incremental but essential process in the administration of the hospital. Our commitment to relationship has fostered trust, communication, and both understanding and acceptance of the strengths and limitations of colleagues. We don't expect that everything will go as planned. We do increasingly trust that each of us is making every effort to create the best possible healing experience for patients, families and staff.

The new normal

Our growing patient volumes and staffing policies (no use of temps and no cancellation of shifts when the patient census is low—see "Staffing Policies" section below) created challenges for staff and management. Just after we opened, when the census was low, patient-to-nurse ratios were also low. Patients and nurses felt great satisfaction at the spaciousness, but the hospital could not succeed financially were this pattern to continue. As the census increased, management needed to help staff to become accustomed to more consecutive days of work, longer hours and higher patient loads.

Senior leadership could sympathize with the stress experienced as volumes increased, and realized they needed to offer education and challenge. Enlisting the help of physician leaders they developed and communicated the concept of the "new normal" to explain the need for understanding and adjustment. In doing so, they acknowledged the staff's reaction to the increased workload while simultaneously reaffirming that higher workload was consistent with the original staffing plan, consistent with the provision of high-quality care, and necessary for financial viability. They also called for an examination of all supporting processes and systems to ensure that staff still had an efficient and well-designed workplace in which to function.

Reinforcing relationship and reflection

The development of a culture of Relationship-centered Care has proven to be an ongoing and incremental process, rippling outward through the organization with each new employee and each new challenge.

We've also made intentional efforts to keep the ripples forming. We instituted a bi-weekly Relationship-centered Care seminar for senior leadership. In these meetings members first "check in" with one another, becoming present in a different way than when they start with urgent business items. (*See* Appendix 2 on relational meeting practices and Appendix 3 on delegation and accountability.) They share stories of situations throughout the hospital in which relationships made a difference. They consult one another about situations in which work relationships are problematic. Finally, they pause to reflect on what they found useful during the meeting and to acknowledge it to one another.

As another example, the Relationship-centered Care culture of Clarian West has been a regular agenda item first at the Clinical Managers' Meeting since the opening of the hospital, and more recently at the Operations Managers' Meeting. At these meetings, managers regularly share concerns, get consultation about staff and relationship issues, and receive the gift of a few moments to be still and present with themselves. In these ways, meeting leaders invite participants to think and feel differently about themselves, one another and their work. They have built a community that is mindful of relationships and that has enhanced the working of the hospital as a whole.

> [At the Clinical Managers' Meeting] I hated it when we had to sit still for three minutes, though listening to the music was nice sometimes. It was hard to move past the list of things I had to get done, to a place where I could relax. Then one day when I came through the Pharmacy door, my staff met me in a kind of feeding frenzy, and I knew what I had to do. "Take three minutes," I urged them. "Sit down. Be still. Let the panic subside. And then let's talk." A time out like that can give perspective.
>
> Leaman Mosley, Manager, Pharmacy

We have also developed relationship-centered approaches to our annual budgeting and strategy processes that engage staff members deep into the organization. These processes benefit from having perspectives and expertise well beyond those of the management team; the broad participation affords many people the opportunity to see beyond their own departments to gain a whole organization perspective.

OUTCOMES

As of this writing, we have outcome measures in a number of domains for the first seven quarters of operation. While it's not possible to trace clear cause-and-effect relationships, we believe the overall pattern suggests that the relationship-centered approach is making a difference.

Clinical quality

In the first year of operation, CWMC demonstrated "good" to "excellent" performance on the quality scorecard published by the Center for Medicaid Medicare. Additionally, Clarian West had no significant medication error in its inpatient areas for the first seven consecutive quarters, according to a high-reliability system measure for medication administration, and has just finished a third quarter without significant errors in all areas including the Emergency Department, inpatient (medical-surgical, ICU, Pediatrics, Obstetrics) and outpatient arenas. To underscore this record, Clarian West received an award from Indiana Public Health Foundation for its medication administration process.

In 2005, the Indiana State Department of Health began to require hospitals to report major errors or adverse events using the national Quality Forum "27 Never Events" (those events that should never happen in any hospitals, e.g. retained sponges, wrong site surgeries, falls or medical errors resulting in death). Clarian West Medical Center had no major adverse events or major errors to report.

Patient perceptions

CWMC used the NRC Picker patient perception tool to survey patient perception on a quarterly basis and compare results with the other 900+ hospitals using that tool. This survey focuses on eight dimensions of patient-centered care deemed most important by patients and serves as the foundation of patients' overall evaluation of care. The eight dimensions are: 1) Information, education and communication, 2) Coordination and integration of care, 3) Physical comfort, 4) Continuity and transition, 5) Emotional support, 6) Patient safety, 7) Involvement of family and friends, and 8) Respect for patient preferences.

In the first and second quarters of 2006, CW scored in the top 10th or top 25th percentile on the global item "would definitely recommend the hospital" in all five major clinical areas—Adult Inpatient, Emergency Department, Outpatient Surgery, Maternity and Outpatient service.

The maternity center, despite unexpectedly large volumes and construction challenges, scored better than the NRC Picker top 10% in "would definitely recommend." Outpatient surgery scored better than the NRC Picker top 10% in "definitely recommend" and had a 0% problem score in the question "rate your hospital experience". Similarly, outpatient testing had a 0% problem score, and a "definitely recommend" score above the NRC Picker average. In the Emergency Department, adult population problem scores fell to 4.2%, which is better than the top 10%.

Physician perceptions

A survey of physicians practicing at CWMC paralleled the perception of patients.

With a response rate of 18% (45 of 250 physicians surveyed), 86% of the respondents agreed with the statement "my patients tell me that the experience at Clarian West is different than other places," and 89% of respondents "would recommend" family and friends to Clarian West. The comments of two physicians bear this out.

> With the large, all private patient rooms with planned space for a family presence, it is rare to enter a patient's room and not encounter a family member. It is impossible to round quickly here, and that's not a bad thing The comfortable accommodations, along with the design, décor and other amenities, speak clearly to patients and families that they are cared for, and cared about. There is an ease fostered by that feeling, and that helps the initial relationship-building process.
>
> If you are a caring physician who wants to help sick people, you understand that a good relationship is better; that communicating and listening are key; that trust, respect and understanding foster a good environment for working and for healing. If Relationship-centered Care leads to better diagnosis and treatment (the priority), then it is inherently a good thing. Is CWMC the relationship nirvana? No. Are we learning by trial and error, Yes.
>
> Brad Sutter, MD, Clinical Director Adult Inpatient Services

> I have developed relationships with a core group of nurses and nursing assistants with whom I work most closely . . . overall, the environment at CWMC is markedly different than in my past experience. I've been able to avoid caregiver-to-caregiver relationships that are hostile and adversarial.
>
> Even with decades of experience I am continuing to learn the value of seemingly small gestures, such as knocking on a patient's door before entering, or making more eye contact—and what a difference they can make. And I'm not just acknowledging their value, I'm doing them.
>
> Greg Spurgin, MD, Internist

Staff satisfaction and retention

Referrals by Clarian West employees have been the most common source of new staff recruits. From the outset, we have not needed to use a recruitment firm, excessive hiring bonuses or other specialty pay in hiring personnel. In 2006, we experienced a vacancy rate less than 3% for mission critical staff and never needed to use a temp agency or outside traveler staff.

These numbers are supported by the results of the NRC Picker Staff Perception of Workplace Survey, which showed that 73% felt a close alignment between their personal values and those of the organization and a similar percentage were proud to be part of the organization. Sixty-five percent of employees surveyed rated Clarian West either "Excellent" or "Very Good" as a place to work and 58% were "Very Likely" to recommend Clarian West to a family member or friend looking for employment. Each of these ratings is significantly better than national averages. Ninety-seven percent of employees valued their job security, while 95% valued the technology in and safety of the work environment. Ninety percent of employees surveyed valued their flexibility in scheduling. Fifty-four percent of employees surveyed said they utilized the Healing Sanctuary spaces.

One manager's comments convey a common theme:

> My two years at Clarian West have been an experience in someone believing in me. From my initial hire I don't believe that my resume or experience were quite what anyone was looking for. However, I think that the leaders saw the spirit and caring in me that represent what Clarian West is all about. They gave me a chance to be part of something that even from that initial contact felt very different and special. Because of that I remain committed to the organization and feel they are committed to my growth and development.
>
> Lisa Sparks, Manager of Quality and Risk Management

Clinical volumes and financial performance

Through the third quarter of its second year of existence, CWMC surpassed projections for inpatient and outpatient volume, up 17% and 19%, respectively. In addition, August 2006 showed actual profit, eight months ahead of schedule. Net income exceeded budget by $2.78 million.

KEY RELATIONSHIPS AND RELATIONAL STRATEGIES
Mindfulness of culture

We realized that a workplace culture would emerge with or without management's intentional involvement. We have had the opportunity to be mindful and intentional about how we might try to influence our cultural development; we are hoping that the elements, patterns, and themes that we introduce now will propagate. Workplace culture exists within and between each social and work group. Management transcends and penetrates these micro-cultures with the whole organization's celebrations, rituals and traditions. Every detail, no matter how small, communicates the culture.

We realized that a workplace culture would emerge with or without management's intentional involvement. We have had the opportunity to be mindful and intentional about how we might try to influence our cultural development; we are hoping that the elements, patterns, and themes that we introduce now will propagate.

With this in mind, the senior leadership team meets for an hour twice a month for the express purpose of reflecting on the messages conveyed by their actions, decisions and practices, and on how these messages affect the daily work of the staff. They choose a topic such as absenteeism, an upcoming performance improvement initiative or a particular change project in the organization, and ask, "Are we being relationship-centered in our awareness of how such a change will affect the staff—and ourselves?"

We also assembled a multi-disciplinary group of caregivers, the "Culture Club," to plan CWMC's employee recognition traditions and celebrations. The Culture Club gathers regularly to recognize important moments in the life of the hospital and has developed several celebratory rituals that acknowledge the importance of the culture.

> The Culture Club has embraced its role as a key player in the development of our culture, honoring the diverse perspective each member brings to that work. The group's first task was to create the inaugural celebration of "Founders Day", commemorating not only the year anniversary of the day that West opened its doors to patients, but also the incalculable work it took to make that happen and the daily effort required to maintain a remarkable care environment. The Founders Day celebration incorporates relationship-building into the proceedings through sharing stories, blessing hands (for those who wish to participate) and bringing caregivers together for a meal. So, too, does West's employee-recognition program, called the STAR Awards, which allow patients, families, peers and managers the opportunity to reach out to an individual, acknowledge excellence and celebrate the extraordinary. Even in times of hardship, when a loved one has passed away, the intentional, relationship-centered culture at West reaches out to people in a unique way. Personal letters of condolence, signed by our CEO, our Vice President of Human Resources and our chaplains are sent to every caregiver who experiences a loss. The letters are followed by an invitation to participate in one of two annual Memorial Tree Celebrations, when a tree on the campus is dedicated to the memories of loved ones who have died.
>
> Cathy Stoll, Manager of Marketing and Public Relations

Staffing policies

We try to make policy decisions with an awareness of their implications for relationship and organizational culture. For example, it is our policy not to use temporary agency staff for nursing care. Al Gatmaitan and the rest of the leadership team believed that such a practice would compromise the quality of relationships among the permanent staff and the resulting diminution of community would also affect healing potential. Along with that commitment was a commitment not to "call people off" when census was low. People need to be able to count on having steady and predictable work to be able to build balance into their lives.

Staff counselor

Another unique choice made by the leadership team, which has positively affected the relationship-centered culture, was the hiring of a staff counselor, Beth Newton Watson, who was then the Manager of Spiritual Care and Chaplaincy Services. Combined with Clarian West's approach to Human Resources, Employee Assistance Program and caregiver relations, this choice further underscores the Administration's commitment to staff self-care even as they care for others. The Staff Counselor has consulted with executives and managers, counseled individual staff, mediated conflictual relationships, and provided in-service education on communication and conflict resolution skills.

> The chaplain's role in Relationship-centered Care at Clarian West has become part of the fabric of the workday and plays a part in many of our interactions. When the bi-weekly patient conferences began it was Beth who challenged the group to dig below the patient's medical needs to discover what we might add that would care for the patient's spirit as well as their physical being. When staff members have disagreements with each other our chaplain offers to speak with them together, as a loving mediator, helping them to sort out their feelings and ask for what they need from each other. When a manager is ready to have a crucial conversation with an employee, whether it be an unfavorable review or a termination, the chaplain is ready to assist, to be present during, or to be with the employee and/or the manager after the event, to offer support and to weave threads of understanding about the process and its impact. Her invitation to both parties to question their automatic responses and to look at the situation from other perspectives often makes an enormous difference in the outcome. Beth challenges us to show up, pay attention, speak the truth, and accept the consequences of doing so. This, she teaches us, is love. Being a teller of the truth as we see it is not easy. Because she is there for us on a regular basis, thereby validating our existence and our worthiness, many of us are now able to speak our truths, have the difficult conversations, take actions upon our beliefs, and accept the consequences in our relationships with those with whom we work. This presence of a

spiritual dimension in the workplace, embodied by our chaplain and her focus on the deeper aspects of our work lives, changes the hospital workplace for many who walk into our building each day. It helps caregivers maintain a focus of care for the sick and the dying, while knowing that they too are being cared for spiritually.
Shelley Lancaster, Clinical Nurse Specialist

On several occasions, the staff counselor has been present to offer support at the time of an employment termination—both to the administrator and to the person being terminated. Both sides have commented about this out-of-the-ordinary, more relational experience. The employee is allowed time with the counselor to respond, and express feelings, to contact friends or family, to brainstorm about the future. The staff counselor can collect belongings if the employee wishes, and accompany the person on the walk to the car. This feels very different than an escort even by the kindest of security guards. Managers also appreciate the acknowledgment that disciplinary action is painful to execute and the time to reflect on the experience.

Disciplining an employee is one of the aspects of being a manager that I dislike the most. Even though it should be no surprise to employees that they are being brought in to discuss their actions, they often appear to be caught off guard and become very defensive. Clarian West has provided managers with a trained counselor and spiritual advisor that I have not had access to at other hospitals. When I had to fire an employee, Beth did not tell me whether she thought disciplinary action was appropriate but rather asked about the situation, how I thought the employee would respond, and what outcome I would like to see. Beth's presence helped to lower the tension in the room. Additionally, she supported the employee who was struggling to understand that her actions did not match the expectations of the organization. Beth was able to stay with the employee after our meeting to help her begin to reflect on how to move forward. The employee contacted the staff counselor several times in the following days as she struggled with decisions about her future. Having a person present during employee counseling, who is not a disciplinary figure, is a great asset to the manager and the employee.
Wendy Lalone Manager, Respiratory Therapy

Connecting across and within departments

In response to an early challenge the clinical managers elected to eat together regularly and talk without an agenda about the workings of the hospital. Each department hosted two meals a year for the rest of the management team. This "Patient Flow and Employee Satisfaction Committee" gathering was informal, but very productive. Managers received support and consultation as they shared the concerns uppermost on their minds. Often, some of the best advice came from unexpected places, and new alliances were strengthened. Managers discovered common issues and were able to make rapid and collaborative decisions about changing processes that did not work. Recently, the operations managers have elected to join this twice-monthly gathering. This is not simply a problem-solving group, but one that also proactively sees the future in a hopeful way.

Other departments have found creative ways of inviting healthy relationships among staff. For example, the Surgical Services Department encourages staff to communicate in a way that fosters clarity and community and prevents errors. The Medical Surgical Department Shift Coordinators pair up for daily consultation and support. The Environmental Services Department gathers monthly to celebrate staff birthdays. At every Leadership Forum meeting managers always take time to check in with both personal and departmental updates. At the end of the meeting one manager will give another, along with explicit compliments and a statement of appreciation, a "Divinity in Disguise" tee shirt and a CWMC Indy Car model created by the Security Department manager in recognition of the community's racing heritage.

> The culture of Relationship-centered Care and the training we have received has given me a new outlook, a new perspective on the way I manage. I have always been task oriented—a "get the job done, final results" type of manager. I've been blessed to learn that the "Control Paradigm" can be enhanced by an intentional effort to improve relationships, and to encourage my employees to put caring for others, including patients, visitors and fellow caregivers at the top of the list of priorities. Several months ago a major rift occurred between two members of my staff. I knew that only by talking, understanding, agreeing to keep working together, and forgiveness could the relationship be mended. Today, both of these employees are committed Clarian West caregivers as a result of an intentional effort to focus on ways to repair and improve relationships.
>
> Spencer Worth, Manager of Environmental Services

Developing skills for relational problem solving has had an important effect on staff retention. By helping employees talk with one another they have learned to resolve issues without either person needing to leave. We encourage honesty to build trust, and accountability to build excellence.

Promoting relationship with self
Another essential component of Relationship-centered Care is a healthy relationship with oneself. Honoring the sacred and acknowledging the potential for healing also moves the focus from self to relationship with the greater work.

On several occasions it seemed appropriate for a group of one sort or another to gather in thoughtful meditation, to reclaim the intention of the hospital as a healing sanctuary, in right relationship with its patients, staff and larger community.

> Another essential component of Relationship-centered Care is a healthy relationship with oneself. Honoring the sacred and acknowledging the potential for healing also moves the focus from self to relationship with the greater work.

On a weekly basis, a small group of staff gathers in the Interfaith Chapel, to pray for the health of patients, families, staff and administrators. The essential interrelatedness of caregivers and institution, the relationship of the different faith perspectives represented in the chapel, the prayer journal in which people offer into relationship with other believers and seekers, prayers for themselves, others and the world, are robust expressions of Relationship-centered Care in a Sanctuary of Healing.

Understanding what is good for patients is good for caregivers. In that spirit, West consciously "walks the walk" by leading the system and its community in a commitment to be a non-smoking campus, offering exercise classes and regularly reminding staff to take advantage of the gardens, walking trails and retreat spaces available to them. The patient handbook includes an invitation for patients to call the chaplain if they believe their caregiver needs a visit, and staff have contacted Spiritual Care when they have observed a manager in need of support. In New Employee Orientation, a key message is that our work may, at times, be as healing for us as for others.

HOLDING THE PARADOX OF PLANNING AND EMERGENCE

Some employees who thought an experience of Sanctuary would automatically be an experience of peace and union were surprised and even dismayed to find it otherwise. Instead of a fantasized "smooth ride," employees had to learn how to build trustworthy relationships in the face of uncertainty and the constant change that exists in any complex hospital environment, but which was accentuated by our "start-up" situation.

Managers found some staff members difficult to please and occasionally less than disciplined in their work habits. Some staff members assumed they would never feel anxious or afraid for their jobs, and that managers would never be petty or vindictive. Both managers and staff sometimes thought that senior leadership would know how to be relationship-centered already and all the time. Disgruntled patients sometimes focused on the breakdown of communication or systems, feeling they had been promised unparalleled and completely integrated healing of mind, body and spirit. New systems revealed new glitches.

New habits of communication did not necessarily mean unanimity of opinion. A very flat administrative structure meant that all were exploring new aspects of former roles.

Relationship-centered practices provided useful touchstones for thriving under these difficult circumstances. We developed the habits of inquiring appreciatively into what was working, telling stories of relationships that helped with healing, emphasizing the importance of having ongoing conversations and of deepening collegial relationships. These helped us to survive the real although natural challenges of "giving birth to" a hospital, and the real transition of living into a new paradigm.

Not all clinical care is perfect. Errors are made and personal pressures still exist in our Healing Sanctuary. But we share a vision and a commitment to work to understand each other and collaborate on improvements. When a breach occurs, where even the best efforts inevitably fall short, we neither give up on the legitimacy of the vision nor retreat into cynicism. We talk about our shortcomings and make efforts to repair relationships.

KEY RELATIONSHIPS AND RELATIONAL STRATEGIES

Soon after opening, the management team learned an important and difficult lesson. One of the senior leaders had developed caring relationships with staff but could not meet the task requirements within the essential period of time. Making the difficult decision to ask that person to leave Clarian West led the senior leadership team to explore and articulate a relationship-centered approach for maintaining accountability. They realized that being relationship-centered was not enough. They had to ensure competence in the performance and supervision of all the complex tasks of a growing hospital. And they discovered that these two principles were not in conflict with each other. It's possible to apply all the principles of relationship-centered process in conducting performance reviews, offering feedback, creating and monitoring remedial plans and even in removing someone from a position (*see* Chapter 4: An introduction to Relationship-centered Care, and Appendix 3: Relationship-centered approaches to delegation and accountability). We were developing the combined standards of inspired caregiving and competent professionalism.

The loss of a senior leader affected all of us. We learned important lessons about being relationship-centered as we dealt with the severing of a relationship. It was necessary for members of our community, line staff and leadership alike to acknowledge the impact of this event. We needed time to speak truth, examine mistakes, and re-weave a sense of community. This meant setting aside time for sharing appropriate information and inviting reflection and acknowledgment, in spite of the discomfort that some felt in talking about such things openly. It was not an option to "tiptoe" around this event as if it never happened. In parallel during this time, administration worked hard to meet the needs of the "leaderless" team and the needs of the patients and staff. In retrospect, many felt that this difficult event and the leadership's way of dealing with it was an important milestone in the effective formation of a meaningful relationship-centered culture—one that required accountability as well as caring.

In a parallel situation, it was determined that a clinical manager did not have the correct balance or fit for the combined requirements of excellence in clinical work, timeliness of administrative evaluation and reporting, and the fostering of healthy relationships among staff. Despite outstanding patient perception and quality performance scores, and the fact that by traditional measures the department was functioning quite well, the subtle deterioration of relationships in the department was leading to the loss of key personnel and declining quality of care. The decline in relationships was undermining the senior leadership's commitment to its philosophy of Relationship-centered Care within a Sanctuary of Healing. Care for culture could not be overlooked, nor could competent professionalism be developed at the cost of cultivating inspired caregiving. Therefore, based on an inability to maintain a collaborative and healing work environment, this manager was removed.

The interim manager invited all the staff to come together: those who rejoiced at the departure and those who grieved. In a completely impromptu fashion they took each other's hands and committed to rebuilding relationships for the good of the patients, family and staff.

CONCLUSIONS AND LESSONS LEARNED

Five years after opening, outcome measures in all domains at Clarian West Medical Center indicate that Relationship-centered Care is a viable core business strategy, not simply good practice. There are effective strategies to address the constant threat of staff turnover. We have experienced high levels of patient satisfaction, strong employee and physician commitment, and profitability ahead of projections. While these outcomes are the result of many factors, we believe that the emphasis on Relationship-centered Care is making an important contribution; this was an important proposition in the hospital's business plan from the very outset and experience is bearing it out.

> Five years after opening, outcome measures in all domains at Clarian West Medical Center indicate that Relationship-centered Care is a viable core business strategy, not simply good practice.

It is still early in the history of this new hospital. Can we manage our corporate and management anxiety enough to hold the space open for creative solutions to emerge spontaneously? Can we build the structures necessary for excellent patient care, putting work flows in place, and still allow the freedom necessary to invite evolving solutions to daily challenges? Can we inquire appreciatively and reinforce the behaviors we desire, or will problem solving as a thought-process be our fall-back position? Can we continue to build the culture and educate those involved as the organization moves from its fluid start-up processes to a more steady-state maintenance phase? Balancing time, money and personnel is a necessary process that can be done in relationship-centered ways. And sometimes that balance requires decisions that seem to move the organization more towards a control and hierarchical orientation and away from an emergent and relational approach. Nevertheless, decisions are data driven and the process is painstakingly organized, requiring detailed planning, control, *and* dialogical processes. We continue to do two seemingly opposite things at the same time, every day.

Clarian West Medical Center remains committed to Relationship-centered Care in a Sanctuary of Healing. Relationship-centered Care has proven to be a deeply challenging and deeply satisfying management philosophy. Its effects ripple through administrative decisions from the most critical to the seemingly least significant. It has not made Clarian West Medical Center into a relationship "nirvana," but those who have experienced it say there is nothing like it.

NOTES

1 For more information about the Pebble Project, see the Center for Health Design's website at www.healthdesign.org/pebble (accessed November 11, 2010).

2 Tresolini CP, The Pew–Fetzer Task Force. *Health Professions Education and Relationship-centered Care*. San Francisco, CA: Pew Health Professions Commission; 1994.

Commentary: Clarian West
Medical Center

Imagine for a moment what it would be like to have the challenge and the opportunity to create a new organization, a hospital, from the ground up. Buildings, grounds, staffing, patient flow, internal and external politics and the resources necessary to support them all need to be considered. How would you begin? What guiding principles would you use? And how would you engage those principles?

This was the challenge to the leadership team at Clarian West. This story follows that team through the complexity, joy and difficulty of bringing such a great dream to life. It is a story of paradox—between emergence and strong intentionality; of creating a relational culture using mindfulness and an appreciative approach, and offers proof of the concept of Relationship-centered Administration as a potent business strategy. It also shows that a relational organization is not always synonymous with a challenge-free or idyllic place to work. Issues of accountability, responsibility and human frailty still need to be handled as part of a relational environment, and they need to be handled in relational ways.

THE PARADOX OF EMERGENCE AND INTENTIONALITY

The paradox illustrated by the story of Clarian West is common when trying to engage in Relationship-centered Administration. We saw in Chapter 2 the importance of being open to what is emerging in the organization rather than just trying to control organizational processes. However, intentionality and planning are crucial to getting things done. At Clarian West, this paradox played itself out with a strong intention to be relational in all aspects of the organization and, based upon that guiding principle, to see where it took them. The leadership team embraced the concept of emergence from the outset when it began with the idea of a "healing sanctuary", defined quite broadly, then invited others to join in helping the thinking unfold and lead to its natural consequences.

Whether developing workflow for every process in the hospital or considering any weighty decision, they always asked what it might mean for the patients and for the relationships within the organization, allowing the structures and the patterns of the organization to emerge. They worked closely together as a team, listening and questioning each other rather than making unilateral decisions.

Concurrently, we can see the strong intentionality of the leadership team. For example, even in the face of severe crisis, as when the starting date for the new hospital was delayed, the team decided to bring many people on board before the organization needed them. They decided that relationships already developed with hired staff would be honored and they planned how to do this in practice. In this story, openness to emergence is supported by the strong intention to be relational no matter what, and vice-versa. This is also seen in the efforts and resources expended to create shared vision and in the relational practices used in hiring, orienting and managing the staff.

CREATING A RELATIONAL CULTURE

It took more than intention to create the relational culture that the Clarian West chapter describes. It also took hard work over a period of time. The intentionality was translated into action in a number of illustrative ways. One key is that senior leadership fully supported and lived the values of Relationship-centered Care from the outset. This important aspect of developing a relational culture is also seen in Chapter 7 (Lehigh Valley), and Chapter 13 (Indiana University School of Medicine). At Clarian West, recruiting and hiring new staff embodied Relationship-centered Administration so that at the outset there was a strong tendency to attract and retain those who were at least comfortable with, if not strongly attracted to the idea of working in a relational organization. Relational values are also deeply integrated into staff orientation, establishing policies and placing culture on the agenda of management meetings, the Culture Club, and the Staff Counselor. Relational principles are also compellingly evident when conflict arises with staff and disciplinary measures, including termination are necessary. The use of an appreciative approach to interviewing (see the story by Barb Bertram) is an intriguing application of one of the principles of positive psychology (Appreciative Inquiry) in order to make that process relational as well.

One more example of creating a relational culture, and perhaps the most radical example from a business perspective, is creating opportunities for relationship with self. Right relationship with self requires inner work, the work of self-knowledge and self-acceptance as noted in Chapter 5. It includes a sense of integrity and authenticity. You need to know who you are and where you stand in order to be truly grounded and to be able to move forward in holding the paradox of emergence and intentionality. To be comfortable with emergence requires the personal courage to make decisions without knowing where they might lead. To be intentional, especially when doing something countercultural—and Relationship-centered Care is in most places still countercultural—also requires personal courage. Recognizing all of this, Clarian West went far beyond providing for the health of its staff, as with exercise classes. The organization also created places that encourage reflection and contemplation, such as gardens and walking trails, and encouraged staff to use them.

OUTCOMES

One strength of the Clarian West story is the emphasis on outcomes and the use of Relationship-centered Administration as a business model. The focus of the leadership team on Relationship-centered Care was not only to do well, for the patients and the staff, but also to do well with respect to finances (they became profitable ahead of schedule), staff turnover (less than average), patient satisfaction (better than average), and occupancy (ahead of schedule). These accomplishments are not, of course, due solely to the relational approach, but they do provide proof of the principle that a primary emphasis on relationship is consistent with a thriving business model.

A REVOLUTIONARY MODEL

The business model described in this chapter is revolutionary in the business world, where rewards are usually received for setting and accomplishing goals. In this case study, relationship centeredness was established as a high value. But being relationship centered is not a goal that can be accomplished and checked from a list. Rather, it is a continuing process about which an organization is continually learning. Rewards, therefore, are received not for attaining a critical level of relationality, but for remaining true to a process. This was especially true in times of difficulty, for example when the start-up date was delayed and when terminations were necessary. Because of the integrity of the process these events could be dealt with in a compassionate way.

Relationship-centered Administration is not a panacea—difficult changes will always develop in organizations and, of course, people will always be people. But Relationship-centered Administration offers a different perspective from which to deal with changes and with people. The story of Clarian West is important for its lessons in creating a relational culture, for demonstrating unequivocally that relational principles can produce a highly successful business model that has measurable outcomes, and for its integrity in remaining true to a process that puts relationships first. And, last, the story clearly demonstrates that Relationship-centered Administration is an ongoing process, which, like any process, requires constant attention and care in order to succeed.

CHAPTER 7

Growing relationships on the turtle's back: Family Medicine at Lehigh Valley Health Network

Joanne Cohen-Katz, William L Miller and Julie A Dostal

SYNOPSIS

Healthy and healing relationships thrive in the nurturing and rich soil of humility. This is certainly true for the Department of Family Medicine at Lehigh Valley Health Network (LVHN). We began in a musty trailer in the back lot of the hospital. The lingering memory of a satisfying backache after carrying boxes to our trailer office through the late January snows of 1994 still brings a smile. The Department was founded with the mission of creating a "community of healing" for every partner it serves—patients, community, organization, students, residents, faculty, and staff members—and strives to embody principles of relationship centeredness at every level of the organization.

Fourteen years after the trailer, the Department is thriving and located in central office spaces. The LVHN family physician staff has grown from 94 to nearly 200. An innovative and successful family medicine residency program was established and has graduated eleven classes of family medicine residents (6 per class). The Department has an active research division, and has spawned many innovations within our network and community. These include a comprehensive inpatient and outpatient palliative care service run partly by family physicians; primary care practices founded by graduates based on the principles of Relationship-centered Care; a network-wide Family Violence Task Force that partners closely with the local domestic violence service provider; a network-wide Access-to-Care Task Force that addresses issues of barriers to care that partners with other hospital systems, local health agencies and school systems; community outreach satellites that are pioneering work on co-production of health; a community time bank fostering exchange of services; widespread cross-disciplinary collaboration; a Center for Mindfulness; and many other programs. And, two years ago our culture of innovation took another leap forward when we were designated a P4 (Preparing the Personal Physician for Practice) site by the American Academy of Family Practice's TransforMED

Residency Innovation initiative. But, like the growth of oak trees, our story is not a straight line to success but one of many twists and branches as we gained strength, robustness, and resilience through multiple surprises, challenges, upsets, and celebrations. We invite you to learn with us as we share part of our story.

THE ORGANIZATION

Our creation story as a department and organization nested within a large and complex organization begins at the confluence of several streams. The first of these streams was LVHN. Lehigh Valley Health Network is a regional academic tertiary care community hospital with 835 beds. General hospital services are augmented by a Level 1 Trauma Center, Burn Center, Cancer Center, Sleep Center, and Heart Care Program. Additional major clinical programs include comprehensive pediatric services with neonatal and pediatric intensive care units, an active obstetric service with more than 3200 deliveries annually, and a full spectrum of psychiatric services.

In the early 1990s, LVHN was specialty-dominated and comprised of silos. Surveying the rapidly changing landscape of healthcare at that time, including the rise of managed care, the Board of Trustees decided to commit the institution to add a Department of Family Practice that included a residency program. Coincidentally, a local foundation, the Dorothy Rider Pool Healthcare Trust had just funded a community health status survey that identified local needs and the Chief Medical Officer of LVHN, Dr Headley White, was one of their few family physicians.

Shortly thereafter, a new CEO, Elliot Sussman MD, a general internist, was hired. He set the goal for LVHN to become a premier academic community hospital with a more collaborative culture and a greater responsiveness to the health needs of the community. The new Department of Family Medicine was launched with Dr White serving as the first Chair.

IMPETUS FOR CHANGE

At this same time, Will Miller, a family physician/anthropologist, had been exploring the question of what a residency program, clinical practice, and department might look like if they really took the core values of primary care and family medicine to heart. He received a letter from Dr White inviting him to return to his family-of-origin community to become the Vice Chair and Program Director.

> Ever since graduate school, I knew I wanted to be in academic family medicine, and that I wanted to create a different kind of training program—one where residents grow and thrive both personally and professionally instead of being significantly wounded and disconnected from their own embodied experiences. This program would enable them to better handle the relational complexities and

stresses of medicine. As a child, I personally witnessed the impact of medical training in my own family. My father was, in so many ways, an exemplar family physician; yet he struggled to balance work and family life and handle the emotional needs of his family. These issues and traits were shared by nearly all of his physician friends. In fact, my own birth story is a terrible lesson in what happens when relationships are not central in medical care. In spite of my mother's desire to pursue natural birthing, she was coerced to accept "modern scientific" delivery methods and was induced, resulting in uterine atony, bleeding and near death. Several days later I was finally brought to her and she put me to her breast, but I was promptly removed by her pediatrician, who insisted that I be bottle fed.

Before pursuing medical training, I studied anthropology, and learned and thought a great deal about the socialization of physicians, and how much this process can work against healing relationships. I had a deep desire to develop a training program that was humane and healing for both the residents and the patients they treated, and the community in which they both lived. These personal experiences and stories have certainly contributed to my lifelong desire to help future healers be better listeners, critical thinkers, and more in touch with their own feelings and growth.

When the letter arrived about an opening at LVHN, it was at just the right time. I had completed a stint as program director at my former site and believed that if I was going to do something really innovative, it would require a brand new start. I was ready to take a leap of faith and try something totally different.

When I read the Pew–Fetzer monograph on Relationship-centered Care in 1994,[1] I immediately recognized the beautiful articulation of many of the principles I was striving to create in family medicine practice and education. I decided this would serve as an organizing framework for our new department and residency.

Will Miller, Chair

The confluence of Relationship-centered Care, Dr Miller's interests and visions, and the readiness of the hospital created the space, energy, and resources to build a new department based on relationship-centered principles.

The confluence of Relationship-centered Care, Dr Miller's interests and visions, and the readiness of the hospital created the space, energy, and resources to build a new department based on relationship-centered principles. One of the great benefits of coming to LVHN was that the department would be completely new. There would be no history of doing things the "way we've always done it," allowing for a great deal of creativity, innovation, and learning about what works and what doesn't. Headley White essentially offered Dr Miller an open invitation to create his ideal vision in this new department. Nevertheless, Will still recalls feeling some doubt about making the move.

> There were many attractors beckoning me to return to my family-of-origin home in the Lehigh Valley to begin a new residency program. I had been dreaming of what an ideal program might look like for more than twenty years. But it was a huge move for our family. I remember wondering, "Are they really helping me be innovative and create a different kind of department and residency program? Is this very traditional hospital system prepared to make some radical changes? What if they're not serious?" It was then that my wife, with her usual wisdom, said to me, "What if they are serious?" I decided to take the risk.
>
> Will Miller

GETTING STARTED

The Department of Family Medicine officially opened its administrative trailer doors on February 2, 1994 with three family physicians, an administrator, and an administrative assistant. This core group complemented each other and provided the fundamental components that were necessary to get the department off the ground. The first chair, Dr White, was a beloved family doctor who had practiced in the community for over 30 years, and a deeply respected and trusted administrator, Dr Miller brought creative vision and academic credentials. Brian Stello MD, a family physician, the first faculty hire, was and continues to be a pragmatic, front-line translator of the vision with a gift for presenting the most abstract, theoretical ideas in an easily understood, unpretentious manner. Barbara Salvadore RN, our first administrator, came with a nursing and a business background, a no-nonsense pragmatism, and a thick web of connections throughout the hospital system after 20+ years of service. Added to this group was an administrative assistant, Marcia Shaffer, who also had a long history of service in the hospital and with Dr White. Organized, calm, and always there, she provided and continues to provide the team with a steadying force and an undergirding of help.

While there was creative tension between Will's "visionary" style and the "let's get practical" approach favored by other team members, this confluence of personalities, with their shared vision, respect for each other, connections within the network, and pragmatic skill, made it possible to launch a visionary family medicine department within a large, traditional, hierarchically structured hospital system. And this system was changing.

Even before Will's start date, he was asked to meet with Dr Sussman to discuss the name of the department. Will was hired to be Vice Chair of the Department of Family and Community Medicine, but Elliot wanted to create a separate Department of Community Health and Health Studies. He wanted Family Medicine to be one of the core clinical departments and Community Health and Health Studies to bring the mission of community service and research to all of the departments as part of a long-term culture change towards greater collaboration and interdependence. Family Medicine it was, but it was also clear that the department and the home organization were on a common culture-change mission.

One final element of our early history that was essential to our development was the role played by the Dorothy Rider Pool Healthcare Trust. The Trust was established in the will of Leonard Parker Pool who upon his death in 1975 directed his estate to found the Trust in the name of his first wife. The mission of the Trust is to enable Lehigh Valley Health Network to be a superior regional hospital and improve the health of the region it serves. The Trust is committed to improving the health of the local community and has been instrumental in funding the growth and development of LVHN since its inception. In June 1996 we submitted a grant for over $1.5 million to the Pool Healthcare Trust titled "Initiatives in Family Practice: Community, Connections & Collaborations" that described our vision of a community of healing that would practice empowerment-based community-oriented primary care.[2]

As part of the preparation process for this grant, in the spring of 1995, we invited the chairs of every department in the hospital, as well as a number of key community stakeholders, to two collaborative grant planning sessions, one with and one without outside consultants. This type of openness was unusual in our organization at that time and allowed for initial experiences of developing trust.

It also was a key factor in attracting the Pool Trust to the work we were doing. Ed Meehan, who serves as Executive Director of the Trust and also has experience in community-based participatory research, was excited to see the hospital focusing on community-oriented healthcare. Equally impressive was the fact that our department conducted a planning session for a grant openly, inviting the chairs of all departments to participate. The Trust had expressed a desire to see synergy among Trust funded efforts both among clinical departments and extramurally with community agencies, in hope of having a greater impact and leveraging other extramural resources. This planning process signaled a different approach that was much more in keeping with the kind of collaborative care that the Pool Trust wished to support. This started new conversations across the network and between departments, priming the pump for relationship-centered strategies across the organization.

We received a substantial financial award that funded salaries for a multidisciplinary faculty, faculty development, innovative projects, and evaluation. The Pool Trust has continued to support the Department with more than 20 grants that total over $8.4 million, including an endowed chair for the department held by Will. Three of these grants were of significant size and were instrumental in supporting and disseminating our work.

> Relationships are fundamental for life and are the beating heart of healing. Our department has used the Relationship-centered Care Method as a guide for organizational structure, process, and curriculum, and as a filter for selecting administrative approaches from the literature throughout our history.

Relationships are fundamental for life and are the beating heart of healing. Our department has used the Relationship-centered Care Method as a guide for organizational structure, process, and curriculum, and as a filter for selecting administrative approaches from the literature throughout our history. Enabling theories for our understanding of Relationship-centered Care integrated theories such as complexity theory,[3] family systems theory,[4] evolution and ecology,[5] and social construction.[6] These theoretical perspectives led us to the literature on learning organizations,[7] stewardship,[8] and empowerment evaluation.[9]

I believed it was essential to address the culture of medical education itself, which is known for wounding physicians-in-training at the same time that it is supposed to be creating healers. I knew that shamanic healers also experienced wounding during their apprenticeship but, in their case, the wounding is explicitly named, supported, and used to teach personal healing.

In my own training, I actively sought out experiences that were more humane and tried to avoid the more toxic ones. I remember once, when interviewing for residency, I was speaking with the program director and asked, "How are the marriages of your residents?" His answer, without any look of distress, was direct and simple,"Not one marriage has survived the residency years!" I selected a different program.

Even though I chose a more humane program, I still felt that we were doing too much harm in the training process for future healers. A year after I completed residency, one of the residents still at the program, a sensitive and generous healer that I knew well, committed suicide. This further solidified my belief that residency training needed to change.

I proposed that a relationship-centered program has to acknowledge that physicians become wounded during training by the nature of the work itself, and then provide a culture that supports and nurtures them through this process—helping them be transformed and open rather than broken and cynical through denial. From a systemic perspective, the faculty and staff supporting the residents would also need to be nurtured and supported as they helped the residents with this process. We could become a "community of healing".

Will Miller

Drawing on the intellectual streams mentioned above, five core strategies have guided the department's development and growth:

1 All structures, processes, and people should support becoming a relationship-centered, stewardship-based learning organization.
2 Learn by doing, remembering that mistakes are for learning.
3 Always collaborate! In every activity and initiative, always involve someone outside the department.
4 Explicitly establish value to the larger organization through increasing referred admissions, educational innovation, enhancing community access, and facilitating vertical and horizontal integration of care.
5 Implement explicit culture-building strategies that support and nourish the above.

STORIES ALONG THE WAY
Gathering the right people

We have been gifted with the presence of many radiant and passionate colleagues throughout our 14 years of existence; sometimes they stayed for a few years, sometimes for more than ten, and some have stayed for the whole journey. Common to all of them is a strong alignment between their personal stories and the emerging departmental story. We offer two examples. Joanne Cohen-Katz came in early 1996 and was instrumental in helping to launch the behavioral science component of the new residency program.

> I was at a Society of Teachers of Family Medicine meeting in New Orleans and was introduced to Will by a mutual colleague. I remember going back to my room and telling my friend, I just met my new boss. I had been working at a very large residency that trained over 45 residents. While I had had the good fortune to start some new programs, I always seemed to be bumping up against "the way things have always been done." Will was essentially offering me an opportunity to start from scratch and do anything new, completely outside of any box. I have to admit I was almost stunned when Will described his vision of Relationship-centered Administration and relationship-centered medical education. I had never really heard anyone talk that way about medical education. For me, coming to LVHN was also a very personal, home-coming decision, because my family lives in Philadelphia, just an hour from the Lehigh Valley,

and I hoped to become a mother in the near future.

Joanne Cohen-Katz, Co-Director of Behavioral Sciences

Julie Dostal arrived in 1998 to be the Vice Chairperson of our department.

I first met Will when we both started as residency program directors in the late 80s. My own journey in medicine had led me to a
place of wanting to change residency education so that it supported
healthy people and relationships.

At the beginning of my third year of medical school I got mar-
ried. My first clinical rotation was an Internal Medicine hospital
rotation that first opened my eyes to the drive of Medicine to
consume a physician's life. I was working my way through medical school and struggling to balance those commitments with
frequently changing call schedules and weekend requirements.
The Chief Resident called me in to his office in the middle of the
rotation and told me that I needed to decide if I was going to be a
doctor, a wife, or gymnastics teacher. I struggled to continue being
all of these things and it only got more complex when I became
pregnant! I had some difficult conversations with the Dean of
Students as I tried to figure out how to finish my medical school
career successfully both professionally and as a parent and partner.
It became incredibly important for me to find training experiences
that supported my relationships. For my residency interviews, I
always brought my husband and my infant son with me and nursed
the baby or let him crawl around in the middle of the interview to
give the clear message; "I am a doctor, a partner to my husband,
and a mother! They all will need to co-exist!"

As I got more involved in working with domestic violence and
collaborating with women around the country who were investi-
gating bringing feminist principles into family medicine, I became
more interested in thinking about what an ideal training program
might look like. By ideal, I mean one that applied the principles of
Relationship-centered Care, and honored and nurtured physicians
in training. In 1988 I became program director at the residency
where I had trained and met Will at a conference for residency
program directors. We spent many a late afternoon and evening at
these conferences, over the next few years, talking about what a residency could be and how we could better prepare family physicians
for their roles as healers and to live their lives more fully.

When it became clear that the experiment in Allentown was
going to make it past its initial three years, I joined the Department
to help make real the dreams we had shared. But it was not without risk! Moving to Allentown was a huge deal for my family! My

children, husband, and I were very connected to our community, and my garden was thriving.

Will and I spent a weekend contemplating the work of the department and created a planned partnership with my focus tending to the internal work of a relationship-centered department and residency and his focus on our external work with the network.

After the move, one of my peak moments came when I was commuting with my son to his soccer game in Wilkes Barre (our former home), and he said: "Mom, I think I know why you wanted to move to Allentown to do this. I'm studying this guy Socrates, and he said, 'The unexamined life is not worth living.' That's why you moved to Allentown to work in this program, isn't it?"

Julie Dostal, Vice Chair, Department of Family Medicine

As we reflected on other people in our story, we became aware that our department cycles between stages of expansion in which there are creative bursts of energy and new activities, followed by stabilization during which our energies go into implementing and maintaining these changes on the ground. At the transition time between these two stages we have recognized the need for people with different skill sets, and people have chosen to leave the department. For example, we recruited a new residency director during a time of stabilization, when our developing culture seemed to be moving too far away from medicine's traditional core. Dr Pamela LeDeaux was hired in 1999 to assume this role at a time when we needed a very pragmatic person to provide clarity and stability in our day-to-day operation of the residency program while still keeping an eye on the vision. She in turn hired a team (residency coordinator, scheduler, residency secretary) with similar qualities. They helped navigate us towards full Residency Review Committee accreditation and to make some of our very innovative curricular programs, such as the longitudinal curriculum, work more effectively "on the ground."

More recently, as our program developed a successful submission to the American Academy of Family Physicians/TransforMEd P4 Residency Innovation initiative (Preparing the Personal Physician for Practice), most members of this team used this opportunity to change positions, and a new team was recruited to implement these new curricular innovations.

We have also learned that our department's culture is not for everyone at all times. While some people find the culture filled with possibility and excitement, others find it messy and chaotic. And still others find it just the right thing for a given time in their life, and too difficult at other times. We have learned to be flexible and adapt to the changing seasons of our department and the individuals in it, and the changes in personnel that have often accompanied them.

. . . our department's culture is not for everyone at all times. While some people find the culture filled with possibility and excitement, others find it messy and chaotic. And still others find it just the right thing for a given time in their life, and too difficult at other times. We have learned to be flexible and adapt to the changing seasons of our department and the individuals in it . . .

Throughout, we have promoted the growth and development of employees and encouraged additional training. The result is that many of those who leave are promoted into other positions in LVHN where they help spread the culture of relationship-centeredness. "Graduates" of our department now include key personnel in Internal Medicine, Information Systems, Interpreting Services, and the Lehigh Valley Physicians' Group. And high performers from other parts of the network seek to join the Department of Family Medicine.

Relationship-centered governance structure: learning from trouble

We have experimented with a variety of governance structures over the years in order to realize our vision of Relationship-centered Administration and education. This experiment is an ongoing one, though we believe we have learned a lot about what works and even more about what doesn't.

Our original structure was set up as a star, with a Commons Oversight Team in the center, and a number of other teams connecting to the star. This structure was intended to reflect a collaborative management style, with work groups reporting to a central team, comprised of representatives from each of these work groups. As we began to work with the original star diagram, it became clear to many of us that we had inadvertently confused the idea of a non-hierarchical system with one in which everyone has a say in everything! Teams would make decisions, only to be second guessed by everyone else in the department. This turned out to be a formula for frustrating everyone. Also, people within our department were repeatedly saying that they didn't know what their role was and that it was too confusing trying to figure out who was doing what.

Out of some exasperation, with some pressure and helpful assistance from senior hospital leaders, and with the guidance of a consultant used by senior management, Will developed an organizational structure that was more hierarchical and added clarity. This structure still included a Commons Oversight Team under the chair, just as the original diagram had. This team would allow key stakeholders in the organization to be involved with governance; however, the rest of the diagram was more traditional, designed to mirror the structure of the hospital.

Will and Julie recall a conversation they had at this time.

> When I saw this chart, my first reaction was, this is not in line
> with our vision. It is a reversion back to hierarchy because we are
> struggling with the messiness of this new way, but it isn't what we

want. Will and I had agreed that my job was to hold his feet to the fire around staying true to our vision. So, I went in to see him, and asked him, "Is this really what you want? Because it's not what you've been saying you wanted."

Julie Dostal

Will recalls that as a difficult conversation. In retrospect, he recognized that she was right, that in the chaos of that time period he had wanted something definitive and safe. This conversation allowed for more meetings and discussions, and several more attempts at defining organizational structure in a way that supports role clarity and effective decision making without reverting to hierarchy.

We began using our present organizational chart in late 2005 (*see* Figure 7.1). It has the patients and community of the Lehigh Valley at the top, and then

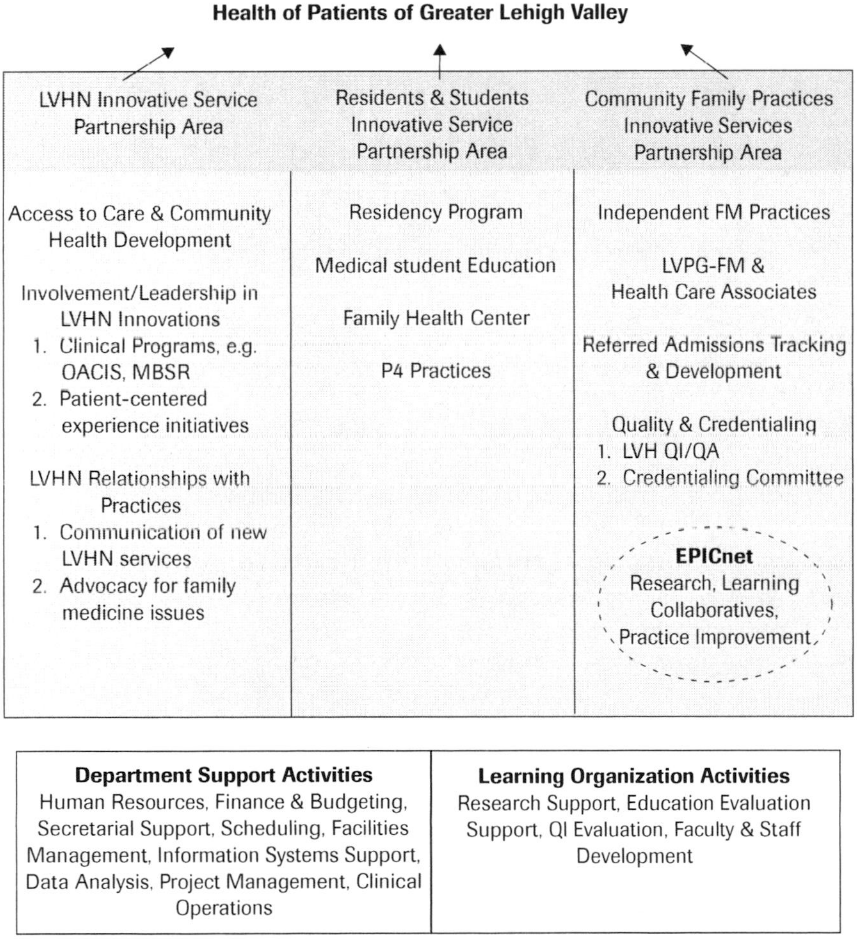

Health of Patients of Greater Lehigh Valley

LVHN Innovative Service Partnership Area	Residents & Students Innovative Service Partnership Area	Community Family Practices Innovative Services Partnership Area
Access to Care & Community Health Development Involvement/Leadership in LVHN Innovations 1. Clinical Programs, e.g. OACIS, MBSR 2. Patient-centered experience initiatives LVHN Relationships with Practices 1. Communication of new LVHN services 2. Advocacy for family medicine issues	Residency Program Medical student Education Family Health Center P4 Practices	Independent FM Practices LVPG-FM & Health Care Associates Referred Admissions Tracking & Development Quality & Credentialing 1. LVH QI/QA 2. Credentialing Committee **EPICnet** Research, Learning Collaboratives, Practice Improvement

Department Support Activities	Learning Organization Activities
Human Resources, Finance & Budgeting, Secretarial Support, Scheduling, Facilities Management, Information Systems Support, Data Analysis, Project Management, Clinical Operations	Research Support, Education Evaluation Support, QI Evaluation, Faculty & Staff Development

LVPR-FM: Lehigh Valley Practice Group-Family Medicine

FIGURE 7.1 The organizational structure for the Lehigh Valley Health Network Family Medicine Department.

three major areas of service partnership: Network (LVHN) Innovative Service Partnership Area, Residents and Students Innovative Service Partnership Area, and Community Family Practices Innovative Services Partnership Area. These service partnership areas are then supported by Department Support Activities (such as scheduling, secretarial support, etc.), and Learning Organization Activities (research support, education evaluation support, etc.).

Each department member now completes a stewardship contract that includes sections on the department's core mission, structure and constraints, basic governance strategy, accountability and results, and focusing attention (*see* Figure 7.2). The document on our basic governance strategy is titled: "Relationship-Centered Partnership (not parenting)," emphasizing this need for co-creation versus passively receiving dictates from management. At the end, department members sign the contract and complete the section that states, "My own Personal Vision within this contract is as follows . . ."

> Each department member now completes a stewardship contract that includes sections on the department's core mission, structure and constraints, basic governance strategy, accountability and results, and focusing attention. . . . At the end, department members sign the contract and complete the section that states: "My own Personal Vision within this contract is as follows . . ."

An ongoing challenge for us has been establishing clarity about roles. We frequently found ourselves resorting to the creation of boundaries between department leaders, staff, and various groups, thus recreating silos similar to those we were trying to overcome in the larger hospital system. But sometimes when working across boundaries with multiple stakeholders became especially difficult, messy, and time-consuming, we have found it helpful to convene conversations to clarify roles and decision-making processes. Even so, these conversations never seemed to happen often enough or clearly enough for everyone to be comfortable.

We have sometimes needed more hierarchy than we would like because, in spite of our successes at fostering personal mastery, many faculty and administrative staff personnel have had trouble advocating directly for the roles they want within the department. For example, in our annual evaluation sessions, we ask people to co-author their goals and adjust their job descriptions for the coming year, with an eye towards owning their role as stewards of the department. Some people find this especially challenging, and at times as administrators we have had to give them choices, rather than having the goals and changes come directly from them.

We are hopeful about our stewardship model, but aware that the same challenges are likely to emerge no matter what model we use. In a relationship-centered organization, it is critical that people grow into believing they can

STEWARDSHIP CONTRACT

Core Mission

The Department of Family Medicine for Lehigh Valley Health Network exists for the purpose of assuring that every person in the Lehigh Valley has a **relationship-centered personal healing home** with *optimal access* to the very **best quality primary medical care** that also **connects** them to whatever additional creativity and services contribute to their thriving and healing.

Focusing on **collaboration, service excellence,** and **clinical innovation,** the Department of Family Medicine will activate this mission for patients in our communities through direct creative service to **local and regional family physicians and their practices,** to **family medicine residents and medical students and other appropriate learners,** and to **Lehigh Valley Health Network** in its excellent and innovative service to the health of the community.

The unique qualities that we present to those we creatively serve are *relationship-centeredness,* a *generalist* and *whole system perspective,* and a *three circle model* emphasizing relationships, mindfulness, and knowledge at the point of care. These qualities are elaborated through the disciplines of fidelity, thought, and community, the practice of hospitality, and the celebration of abundance, mystery, and grace.

Structure & Constraints

The Department of Family Medicine's structure is designed to facilitate our mission of service to patients through our service and creativity in three communities: Community Family Practices, Residents and Students, and LVHN. These areas are supported by departmental support and learning organization resources.

See attached Organization Diagram.

Our collaborative, excellent, and innovative service must be offered within the following constraints:

➤ We cannot alter department mission without approval of Chair.
➤ We cannot exceed overall cost center budgets without approval of Chair.
➤ We must think & connect outside the confines of our area.
➤ We cannot ignore LVHN policies and procedures.

Basic Governance Strategy

Our basic governance strategy is founded upon **Relationship-Centered Partnership** (not parenting) and emphasizes *sharing power* (discipline of community), *sharing wealth* (discipline of fidelity), *growing wisdom* (discipline of thought), *rejoicing in the success of others* (practicing hospitality), and *enhancing relationships* (celebrating abundance, mystery, and grace).

See attached Basic Governance Strategy sheets.

Accountability & Results

Each creative service area will specifically define their expected goals and outcomes and be responsible for the implementation and assessment. This work is based upon the following three guidelines:

➤ Define measure(s) of activated partners in community of creative service (think mission, unique qualities & values). These measures become the basis for EIP/MIP goals, Annual Report, QI/QA Reports.
➤ Meet budget targets
➤ Meet scorecard requirements

Focusing Attention

We anticipate the following challenges in implementing our stewardship contract and will each pay special attention to them:

➤ The need to overcome doubt, distrust, and inertia
➤ The challenge of transparency and truthfulness
➤ The difficulty of cross-reporting, communication, and coordination between areas
➤ Making this structure and process work within the current structure and constraints of LVHN and the current dominant culture

My own **Personal Vision** within this Contract is as follows:

FIGURE 7.2 The stewardship contract signed by each staff member at the LVHN Family Medicine Department.

own their role as stewards of the organization. And it requires what we believe is the primary tool of relationship-centered work: learning to have difficult conversations while being honest and openhearted.

> We are hopeful about our stewardship model, but aware that the same challenges are likely to emerge no matter what model we use. In a relationship-centered organization, it is critical that people grow into believing they can own their role as stewards of the organization.

Culture building strategies

From the beginning, in keeping with our vision of creating a community of healing, we have intentionally used a variety of events and processes to encourage a collaborative, relationship-centered style of management and healthcare at every level of the organization. These strategies may be broadly thought of as culture-building strategies and include the intentional use of symbols and rituals, empowerment evaluations, and whole-system events that create spaces for conversations. In addition, our patient care and teaching are informed by relationship-centered clinical tools and a curricular model that emphasizes self-reflection and relationship skills and thus reinforces the culture-building strategies.

Symbols and rituals

The use of symbols helps to remind our community of its mission. A central symbol in our department is the turtle, which appears on our logo and on artifacts throughout the department. The turtle was chosen by Dr Miller for several reasons. In the Native American culture of our region (Leni Lenape) the creation story tells of a turtle offering its back so that life fallen into the mud can be lifted up. The Latin for patient is "patiens" which means reclined or flattened by life, i.e. fallen into the mud. The Greek for clinic is "clinikos" which means stood up, i.e. supported and returned into life. The turtle thus represents both our ancient western healing traditions and the ancient tradition of our home place in the Lehigh Valley. We practice "turtle craft." The willingness to get into the uncertain and ambiguous mud with a patient, family or colleague and deal with difficult issues is a hallmark of Relationship-centered Care. It often feels "cleaner" and easier to ignore relationship processes and resort to hierarchical or authoritarian ways of being. Also, the turtle, like the family physician, resides in multiple environments.

Our community has gone through a variety of cycles in its relationship to the turtle symbol. In our early years it almost seemed to become a flashpoint for whatever issues or difficulties people were experiencing. For example, for residents who thought the curriculum focused too much on relationships and not enough on biomedicine (described more fully below), "turtle" was synonymous with "not scientific, touchy feely, etc." Others saw it as being alienating because it set us apart as different or special (or weird). Some used it as a way of describing problems in the department with governance or role clarity. Still others loved the turtle symbol as a way of talking with pride about who we are. It was often challenging to discern what it was people were really talking about when they mentioned "the turtle!"

Nevertheless, the symbol still exists in our department. Many people have turtle pictures and objects all over their offices, and patients have also enjoyed giving "turtle" gifts to their doctors and nurses. Certainly, in more recent years, the intense feeling surrounding the turtle seems to have subsided, just as many of the issues surrounding our community's identity have become less intense as we matured from a new program to an established department. Also, to some extent, we toned down the use of the turtle symbol although we still do describe our clinical teaching tools as the "tools of turtle craft."

Two stories illustrate the evolution of this symbol in our community. In the late 1990s, one of our residents stated in a focus group:

> I find that every time I wear a turtle pin people make assumptions about the kinds of cases I want to see. They seem to give me patients who are emotionally distressed, automatically, and I feel like I'm missing out on other cases that I might want to see. So I decided not to wear my pin anymore.

By contrast, in the summer of 2008, one of our new first-year residents shared in support group the following story of the turtle pin from her time in the Emergency Department:

> I was assigned to see an acutely ill elderly man who had many chronic illnesses and was a frequent patient in the ER and the hospital. As I entered the room, his wife welcomed me with a smile and said, I'm so happy to see you. Whenever we see a doctor with a turtle pin, we know we are going to get the best care possible.

Like symbols, rituals were intended to build a sense of identity and community.[10] For resident physicians, the beginning of training, and the transition from one year to the next are all marked with a ritual called the "ceremony of passage." Initially, these rituals included many elements such as drumming, guided visualizations on learnings received in the past year, walking down a "turtle path" that has our core values written on it to symbolize passage into another stage of training, lighting a candle, and receiving a turtle pin that is worn daily at work.

Our earliest rituals were challenging for many members of our community; while some loved them, others found them objectionable. Some associated them with religion, which brought up a great deal of conflict and confusion. There was a delicate balancing act of working to preserve the intentionality behind the rituals: building culture and community, while also responding to the needs of everyone in the community. Will describes the difficulty of doing this work and a source of support:

> The use of earth-based rituals and symbols involved some real risk-taking for me. When initial resistance and some outright fear about the rituals surfaced, my family came through. . . . From the start, I had involved my wife and children in many of the group activities; they attended most of the early rituals themselves, and they loved them! So whenever I would come home discouraged about some people's reactions, they would give me the strength and perspective and observed evidence that these rituals were exciting and useful.
>
> Will Miller

Will charged our residency team, then headed by Pam LeDeaux, with the task of re-fashioning the rituals while keeping their purpose at the forefront. This team conducted an anonymous survey of our community members to determine what they found helpful and what was objectionable. They then worked on simplifying and streamlining the rituals, in a way that respected the feelings of all our colleagues. For example, some features of the earlier rituals such as incense burning and drumming were eliminated even as we kept others such as guided visualizations about one's hopes and dreams and walking down a path that illustrates the core values of the department (disciplines of fidelity, thought, and community, practice of hospitality, and celebration of abundance, mystery, and grace). The formal "ceremonial" part of the rituals are now a bit shorter, and are followed by a less structured time of celebration, including the sharing of a meal together: a universal ritual that seems to speak to everyone!

Empowerment evaluations

A major culture-building strategy within our department is the use of evaluation strategies to provide all members of the organization with ongoing feedback using processes that allow everyone to participate in and benefit from the feedback. One such strategy, called empowerment evaluation, is defined as "the use of evaluation concepts, techniques, and findings to foster improvement and self-determination." It is designed to help people help themselves and improve their programs using a form of self-evaluation and reflection.

Beginning in 1997, we conducted a series of nine empowerment evaluations. The first six were conducted by the same evaluator, allowing for the development of relationships over time. The evaluator immersed himself in our community for an intensive period of 2–4 weeks. He precepted residents, took call, and functioned as a temporary faculty member. At the same time, he conducted interviews with all residents, faculty, staff, and administrators in the department, some in group settings, and many individually. The transcripts of his interviews and his final report were shared with the entire department as well as with representatives from other departments, and from the Pool Trust. His reports addressed three areas:

➤ Vision: How are you being who you say you want to be? Where are you doing it well?

➤ Discrepancy: Where are the discrepancies between your vision and what you are actually doing?

➤ Discovery: What are the surprises (emergent data)?

These evaluations were enormously beneficial in our early years in helping us to see ourselves over time, and in pointing out recurrent themes. Probably the single most recurrent and powerful theme has been our difficulty saying "no" to new, innovative ideas. Our desire to think abundantly and to be on the cutting edge of new ideas and practices can easily override any awareness of where our resources may be limited. While this has caused us to accomplish many wonderful things, the shadow side of this tendency can be burnout or ignoring some more basic realities. Empowerment evaluations have helped us recognize this as a continuing issue, one that is intrinsic to working at the "growing edge" and which requires ongoing vigilance.

Empowerment evaluations have also served a unique purpose in giving people an opportunity not only to provide input and shape the direction of the organization, but also to take stock of themselves by speaking with an outside evaluator with whom they had developed a trusting relationship. Some people described these interviews as helpful "venting sessions" and interventions that helped them clarify personal and professional goals.

> I remember being in shock a few months after my first child was born—I felt so unproductive and so unable to accomplish professional goals at the same pace that I was used to before I became a mother. I recall telling Jeff Borkan, our evaluator, "I feel like I'm walking in molasses." He completely normalized my experience, and I still remember him saying that in Israel, where he was then working, people gave a lot of leeway to parents in the first year, not really expecting much from them. This was a huge relief for me to hear! I drew great strength from this conversation, and have returned to it many times over the past years of being a working mother!
>
> Joanne Cohen-Katz

Whole system events

From the start, we have regularly conducted participatory whole system events, both with our department and with other groups in our hospital and community system, in addition to our empowerment evaluation sessions. For example, within the department we hold retreats twice a year for the entire department.

A skeletal staff maintains the Family Health Center so that medical and administrative support staff, faculty, residents, and others can work together on exercises such as team building, developing communication skills, and learning to thrive through diversity.

Other whole group events include an annual Year-in-Review afternoon in which all members of the department participate and hear about the activities that the various subgroups within the department are engaged in, as well as the activities of the department within the larger network.

Subsystem events include regular resident retreats, faculty retreats, and monthly Family Health Center staff meetings. All of these events are designed to promote team learning and collaboration, to strengthen connections with a particular work group, and to break down barriers between the different work groups through conversations. While these events do not always run smoothly or easily, we describe below two of our more successful events and ways they have been modified over the years.

Year-in-Review Meetings: In our original Year-in-Review meeting, the chairman described the accomplishments within the network and department, followed by the sharing of a meal together. However, invariably some people or groups felt less acknowledged than others. Based on this input, this process has been completely revised in the past several years. Each work group now has a time slot for the afternoon, during which its members are encouraged to present poems, skits, songs, or anything else that highlights their team's major accomplishments of the year. The gatherings are now quite lively and creative, and provide people the opportunity to develop a deeper understanding of things going on in our large department of which they were not aware or fully appreciative.

Future Search Meetings: Another whole-system event that has been successful is our use of Future Search methodology.[11] In the spring of 2000, we conducted a Future Search process in preparation for the submission of our third large Pool Healthcare trust grant. A Future Search process invites key stakeholders at every level of an organization to gather together and help shape the future direction of the organization in a collaborative manner. Just as we had done in preparation for our first Pool Trust grant, we invited key community stakeholders and chairs, as well as other personnel from departments around the hospital. Faculty, administrators and staff members from our Family Health Center were freed up from other work responsibilities in order to attend the Future Search process. Residents and Family Health Center patients were also active participants.

This process was important to us internally in helping some of our Family Health Center staff recognize the importance of their roles as shapers of our department, and to develop their own professional skills to a greater degree. For example, one of the significant groups that grew out of this work was one looking at diversity issues. We have a significant Spanish-speaking population of patients and medical staff. The members of our medical staff at the Family

Health Center felt that we weren't adequately addressing the needs of these patients. This group worked actively for several years and produced significant changes in our health center and beyond.

Teaching Relationship-centered Care and searching for biomedicine

From the beginning, we have put Relationship-centered Care at the center of our teaching. We created a curriculum called "Turtle Craft" that integrates self-knowledge, reflection, and relationship process with traditional core medical content and skills (*see* Figure 7.3). We incorporated a variety of models to teach Relationship-centered Care: the Clinical Hand,[12] Family Systems,[13] Relationship Centered Clinical Method,[14] and the Ecological Transactional Model,[15] and offered our residents ample opportunities for reflection and group support as they navigated the healer's path.

There was early resistance to this emphasis. Some residents and faculty members objected to a curriculum that placed so much emphasis on self-reflection and doctor–patient relationship skills, using language such as "too much fluff," or "not enough hardcore medicine." Within this conversation there was what we (the authors) saw as a false dichotomy between "biomedicine" and "the relationship stuff." In our thinking and our vision, they are inseparable. Yet, this split surfaced very early on and appeared in many of our early empowerment evaluations and in everyday conversations. Working with our faculty and residents in a relationship-centered way on this issue has been challenging, and ultimately, very fruitful.

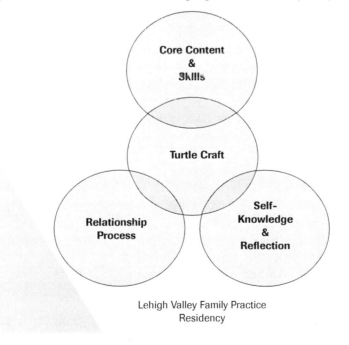

Lehigh Valley Family Practice
Residency

FIGURE 7.3 The "Turtlecraft" curriculum.

Some residents and faculty members objected to a curriculum that placed so much emphasis on self-reflection and doctor–patient relationship skills, using language such as "too much fluff," or "not enough hardcore medicine." Within this conversation there was what we (the authors) saw as a false dichotomy between "biomedicine" and "the relationship stuff." In our thinking and our vision, they are inseparable.

The residents' concerns about curricular balance first emerged in early focus groups, empowerment evaluations and exit interviews. The majority of people speaking about this issue seemed to take the position that the "psychosocial" parts of the curriculum were very strong, but there wasn't enough "pure bio-medicine." At the same time, a small but vocal minority of residents claimed that we shouldn't be spending much time at all trying to teach Relationship-centered Care because it is not teachable; it either comes naturally or it doesn't. This latter group also had tremendous difficulty with the extensive self-reflection built into our curriculum and with the use of the conceptual models of Relationship-centered Care, myth and the turtle symbol. But by the time of this writing, concerns about curricular balance and discussions of "fluff vs. real stuff" surface only occasionally and are no longer prevalent. It is interesting to reflect back on the evolution of this issue.

First, the split between "biomedicine" and "the soft stuff" is certainly present within larger medical culture. As junior members of a new department within the hospital, within a specialty that is often marginalized within medical culture for being not "scientific" enough, our early residents were vulnerable. They already faced the issue of having to prove themselves and their medical knowledge to their colleagues and attendings from other departments. This problem was particularly intense during our interns' rotations on other hospital services where they were clearly the "low person on the totem pole."

Our use of symbols, something that was clearly different and potentially "weird," may have further set us apart, perpetuating this dynamic of marginalization for some of our residents and the perception among other residency programs that family medicine was the "soft" stuff and the rest of medicine was the "real stuff." The work of faculty physicians Drs Armstrong and Stello in teaching relationship-based evidence-informed medicine was critical in reversing this problem. They demonstrated ways that evidence-based care works in harmony with and enhances a relationship-centered approach, successfully applying the work of Sackett *et al.*,[16] who view evidence-based medicine as integrating the best clinical evidence, the physician's clinical intuition about a patient, and the patient's values and preferences. This work demonstrates at a practical level that medical evidence and relationships can be integrated at the point of care. Our faculty are leaders in bringing this relationship-centered evidence at the point of care approach into the rest of LVHN.

Probably the most important strategy we used in helping with the split was to continue to listen to our residents; to provide a safe container in which these concerns could be voiced and heard. We regularly provided structure for them within the many forums discussed above (support groups, retreats, empowerment evaluations), to express concerns, and we attempted to find ways to meet their needs within the curriculum without compromising our own commitment to Relationship-centered Care. We continue to conduct annual year-end focus groups for each residency class with the help of an external facilitator to explore their experiences. This helps us understand the successes and gaps in our continuing quest to fulfill our vision.

Parallel culture change within the larger hospital network and support from network leaders were also critical. Many changes within the network signaled an admiration for and embracing of the principles of Relationship-centered Care. The more that the hospital began to get comfortable working side-by-side with family physicians and the more the larger network/hospital administration began adopting the principles of Relationship-centered Care, the less the residents have felt "weird" or "different" for emphasizing "that relationship stuff."

Other serendipitous events helped move the educational vision forward. In the summer of 2004, the chair of our Community and Health Studies Department at LVHN unexpectedly died at age 50. This caused great shock and grief in our system. Will was asked to fill in as interim chair of his department, essentially leaving us with a part-time chair for over a year. During this same summer, several core faculty members had major medical crises that were completely unanticipated.

One of the unexpected outcomes of this difficult summer occurred in the area of our resident–faculty relationships. Because we were severely short on family physician hospital attendings, we had to "borrow" the Internal Medicine faculty as attendings for our residents. Working with them increased our residents' appreciation for the culture of their own department with its emphasis on Relationship-centered Care. They began to complain that they wanted family medicine attendings who do things "the family medicine" way. At the same time, our residents and Internal Medicine faculty gained a better appreciation of each other. One of the residents trained during that time joined an Internal Medicine practice after graduating.

Interestingly, we saw this issue re-emerge very recently in our program. Once again, the value of deep listening in our relationships with residents was highlighted.

> I recently was preparing to relive the "biomedicine" vs. "the relationship stuff" as the residents were clamoring for more "didactic" time in the curriculum. I was reacting to these words and preparing for the old battle, but instead, I asked questions of the residents to help me better understand what they were really asking for. "Didactics" was a code word and we needed to decode it as we were not all

sharing a common code. This lead to a VERY rich conversation about how they learn, how they know they learn something, and what characteristics are important to them in their teachers. Their cry for didactics had very little to do with the mind–body dichotomy and everything about how they wanted more time to reflect, ask questions of themselves, colleagues, and faculty, and actively participate in answering these questions. I'm excited to help make those sorts of changes in the curriculum; and so are they. This dialogue contributed to the development of key portions of the P4 proposal.

Julie Dostal

RELATIONAL STRATEGIES

Creating a relationship-centered community of healing requires continual consideration of the relational consequences of every aspect of departmental structure and function. Three stories help to illustrate this approach: one relates to residents, one to faculty, and one to medical staff at our Family Health Center.

> Creating a relationship-centered community of healing requires continual consideration of the relational consequences of every aspect of departmental structure and function.

As a community of healing, we have placed a high priority on honoring the needs of our faculty, staff and residents for personal and professional balance. In 2002, we granted an applicant's request for a part-time residency slot that would allow her to complete the program in six years rather than three and to spend more time at home with her children. We subsequently received a steadily growing number of requests, not only for part-time positions but for job-sharing and other non-traditional training arrangements. Understandably, tension grew as scheduling became more complicated and the full-time residents became increasingly (and understandably) concerned that their call schedules would become overwhelming, and that they would be shouldering the brunt of these changes. Pam LeDeaux, the residency director, undertook the job of developing a policy for part-time and shared residency slots that was responsive to both the needs of prospective part-time residents as well as those of full-time residents.

She began by surveying faculty and residents as to their attitudes about part-time and shared residency training, finding that all faculty and most (75%) of the full-time residents agreed that part-time/shared positions do not compromise the educational integrity of the program. Full-time residents felt that the most difficult aspect of this situation occurs when a full-time resident changes to part-time. Part-time residents reflected on feeling some anger from their peers. Pam then convened a broadly representative work group to hear from faculty and residents, review the relevant literature, survey other residency programs and investigate administrative issues with an accountant and attorney and then recommend a policy. These discussions were sometimes challenging, but allowed for a diverse range of opinions to be heard.

The resulting policy recommendation was supportive of requests for part-time and shared training positions, particularly when they are planned well in advance, allowing for orderly scheduling. The policy also set conditions for mid-year requests to change from full time to part time, requiring the fulfillment of implicitly made commitments for full-time participation in call schedules, inpatient rotations, evening hours, and the class research project. The result has been much less tension around this issue, and has turned out to be a benefit in our recruiting.[17]

The second story is one where there has been success in helping a faculty member grow and maintain balance:

> When my first child was born in 2000, I realized over the course of the next year or two that, not only did I want to work part time, but also, I wanted to change the work I was doing. After years in residency education and becoming a mother in my late 40s, I no longer felt I had the energy and patience required to coordinate and teach the behavioral science curriculum. I struggled a great deal trying to figure out what to do next. I felt very supported in trying to figure out a way to adjust my job so that it fit with my new needs as a working mother and my new interests. Nevertheless, I finally decided to quit my job. The Department had already begun searching for my replacement, when I suddenly thought of another solution: to create a job share with a psychologist who had begun teaching in our department, which would allow him to assume more of a coordinator's role and for me to develop some other interests. My bosses immediately said "yes" to this idea, and have helped make it work.
>
> Over the next several years, as I developed a passion for teaching Mindfulness work, they continued to say "yes" to my many requests to adjust my job description to my new interests. It is always hard for me to ask directly for what I want, but I have learned to trust both that I will get, at least, positive consideration of my proposals, and that in the end the department benefits from these changes.
>
> There are other ways, too, in which this change has created challenges and opportunities to grow and stretch for me. Sticking around and watching someone else run what used to be "my curriculum," was not easy at first. Initially, I found myself feeling envious when I watched Jeff Sternlieb "getting credit" for running parts of the program that I had developed, even though I had chosen to give them up! I had several conversations with Jeff about what I

was experiencing. I remember one time we went to lunch and we talked in depth about it. His acknowledgment of my feelings, and of the fact that tremendous work had gone before him made all the difference for me in being able to let go. I am now genuinely, 100% happy when I see his success in putting his own mark on our program. And he and I have developed a very productive collaborative relationship, sometimes teaching together, and often consulting each other around professional or personal issues.

Joanne Cohen-Katz

Other faculty echo this theme: they have been able to have flexibility in their jobs and to identify and develop their professional passions.

In addition to saying "yes" to the things I am passionate about, this type of organization has forced me to think about myself and who I am in the world more than anywhere else I've been. If you're going to be effective in doing Relationship-centered Care, you have to know a lot about yourself. I've learned a lot about who I am as a leader, and I've had to think about how I put limits on myself. I've learned the most from failures by examining what went wrong. In one case, I failed to really take a stand on what I believe [by not questioning someone about] the way they were running something that didn't support our stated values.

What I most appreciate about the department is that, whatever negative stuff there is (which there is anywhere), I do believe that here people want me to succeed, and what I care about is part of the vision. And, at the core, we really like each other.

Abby Letcher, Family Medicine Physician Faculty

The third story has to do with the Family Health Center staff voicing their concerns about their personal safety. A few years ago, staff members were feeling threatened at times by a few of the patients who were extremely angry. There was some tension in the practice between the belief that Relationship-centered Care means being willing to acknowledge that patients are often frustrated and angry as a result of their illness, and the need to help the staff feel safe in their jobs. Through numerous meetings and conversations with members of various groups within the department, a violence policy was developed that includes a procedure whereby the medical director can ask a patient to leave the practice based on his/her behavior, and that also includes a "panic button" that staff can push immediately if they feel threatened. Dorene Svanda, our practice coordinator, feels that the development of this policy was important in helping staff members feel backed up and protected by the rest of the department.

Dorene also believes that the flexibility that she demonstrates is part of the success with her staff. She states: "*We are very flexible in helping them balance their personal and professional lives. When you give to them, they're willing to give back."*

OUTCOMES
Department and residency program

Our department has grown from 34 family physicians to 200, with a flourishing residency program, research initiatives, and many innovative patient-care and educational programs (some described under the faculty section). Our residency program, at the time of publication, has successfully graduated 11 classes of residents (6 per class), since we began training residents in 1998. In 2006, we had an extremely successful site visit from the Residency Review Committee, where we received full accreditation for five years with only two citations, far lower than the national average. In 2002, we received special recognition from the Fetzer Institute, which gave us an honorable mention in their annual Norman Cousins Award, which acknowledges a healthcare project that focuses significantly on relationships.

In 1997, our residency program's quest for innovative excellence took a giant leap forward, when we were designated a P4 site by the American Board of Family Medicine and the Association of Family Medicine Residency Directors. Their P4 program is administered by TransforMED, a practice redesign initiative of the American Academy of Family Physicians. We were one of fourteen family medicine programs chosen to participate. The purpose of P4 is to learn how to improve the graduate medical education of family physicians such that they are prepared to be outstanding personal physicians and to work in the new models of practice now emerging. The innovations tested by P4 residencies are expected to inspire substantial changes in the content, structure, and locations of training of family physicians and to guide future revisions in accreditation and certification requirements. For our department, we believe that all the groundwork we had laid in our first 13 years of existence prepared us well for this very exciting new era of innovation.

Residents

> The results showed evidence of relationship-centered behaviors and attitudes, even among those graduates who stated they had not been receptive to learning about Relationship-centered Care during residency. A rich tapestry of quotes showed Relationship-centered Care being practiced with patients, staff, other doctors, and the community.

Our residency graduates have done well. As mentioned above, in 2004 the second author and a research assistant conducted a study to see if our graduates actually practice Relationship-centered Care.[18] This study involved surveys of all graduates of our program and depth telephone interviews with 17 graduates who had been practicing at least two years post-residency. The results showed evidence of relationship-centered behaviors and attitudes, even among those graduates who stated they had not been receptive to learning about Relationship-centered Care during residency. A rich tapestry of quotes showed Relationship-centered Care being practiced with patients, staff, other doctors, and the community. Several examples follow:

> I think that I empower (him) to take some control over this (health issue), and he realizes this. That I'm willing to be a partner in these situations and offer all the advice and guidance I can and still allow him to make those choices and come to the conclusion himself.
>
> I'm always up front. I will tell them, if I don't know, I will tell you I don't know and I will find the answer for you or with you. I put a great emphasis on understanding the priorities of the patient. And my patients know that they can tell me all those other things that they're doing and I am not going to make them feel like they're stupid or they've made the wrong choice.

Physicians also provided rich examples of the ways in which patient care had changed them personally. For example:

> I think all of their stories kind of strengthens me as to who I am and I have a sense of gratitude. . . . In one sense I think it centers me. It kind of bolsters me. I like myself more and have much more self-confidence as a result of treating my patients. I think I've always been a pretty good listener, but maybe I have more empathy now.

Another promising indicator that our residents do indeed learn Relationship-centered Care has been the results of our work with the Patient Enablement Instrument (PEI), a tool that measures a patient's perception of their understanding and ability to manage their health after a doctor's visit. We have been using the PEI as a measure of our resident's relative Relationship-centered Care capability. We have been tracking this over the past three years and overall our residents have increased their PEI averages from 5.89 at the end of the first year to 7.39 at the end of their second year, and to 7.43 at the end of their residency. This suggests that our residents increase in their relationship centeredness. Although we do not yet have equivalent residency norms for comparison purposes, our residents are well above the norms for practicing primary care physicians established by the originators of the instrument.

In terms of our work on "healing the healer", one of our former residents says it beautifully in this quote from his exit interview. Dr Vladimir Iakomi, a Russian physician who trained in our program stated: "*I came to this program wounded and I was healed. I appreciate your support.*"

Faculty

One of the challenges often faced by academic medicine faculty is being able to present and publish their academic work, given the tremendous demands in their clinical and teaching roles. In our most recent annual report, we noted that our faculty increased their national and regional presentations from 14 to 36 and their refereed publications doubled from 4 to 8. In addition, our faculty has received many community service and teaching awards outside of our department.

Perhaps our area of greatest success with our faculty is in facilitating their pursuit of innovative work. The work of Lou Lukas is exemplary. Lou developed an interest during her residency in the question of why patients often have the experience of being over-medicalized and having their spiritual, social and psychological needs over-treated during end of life care. Working across silos, including Family Medicine leadership, critical care and oncology physicians, nursing and Care Management, as well as patients and their family members, she has collaboratively developed a hospital-wide, Pool Trust-funded initiative that is poised to dramatically impact the care of patients with advanced complex illness in both the outpatient and inpatient settings.

Abby Letcher's work has centered on combining clinical care and social change. She has developed a network of programs at an inner city youth development program center called The Caring Place. She describes her mission there as creating an atmosphere of Relationship-centered Care, where everyone feels welcome, and everyone, both patients and staff, have an opportunity to contribute and help get the work of improving health done. Programs at The Caring Place now include healthcare for children and families that is available at no cost to the uninsured, prenatal group visits, diabetes group visits conducted by a health promotora, a community interpreter training program and adolescent group visits. A local college uses this site as an important part of their service education model. This has expanded through regular conversations with all the stakeholders, identifying needs, wants, opportunities for shared gain, and recognition of barriers. It has created the opportunity for broader dialogue with other hospitals and community based agencies to consider more systems-based approaches to improved access to care. This site is the core practice for a Federally Qualified Health Center proposal. Abby feels one of her greatest outcomes to date is in being part of a group that has helped shift the conversation at the network level around how to provide care for the underserved in a way that respects people's dignity and builds relationships.

These are but a few of the many other examples of faculty who have blossomed and done extremely innovative work here. On the other hand, we have not always been so successful at cultivating our faculty. In one case, one of our most highly talented family physician faculty members bore the brunt of the work during the challenging summer, described above, when many of us were unavailable for medical or other reasons. His burnout also likely reflected our desire to take on too many innovative projects, and, perhaps the lack of balance that can occur when some people advocate for their own needs more directly than others. He did eventually leave our department to work in a non-academic setting. Our department experienced his departure as a major loss.

Staff

In terms of staff relationships, Dorene Svanda, our long-time clinical staff coordinator, believes that her staff has evolved over the years towards a very positive culture that promotes excellence among the staff members in providing Relationship-centered Care. Key ingredients of this success include regular forums for her team to voice concerns about the practice and to provide input into decisions about how to run the practice, as discussed above.

As a result, many staff people have developed areas of personal mastery and chosen to move into new positions of responsibility around our network. For example, Josefina Clark, one of our former staff members developed her interest and passion in the area of medical interpreting in our department and now holds a position as the coordinator of interpreter services in a new division of the hospital. Josefina is also the medical interpreter trainer for hospital employees.

Patient care

One of the indicators of excellence in patient care is length of stay in the inpatient, hospital setting. From the earliest years of our program, our length of stay has been consistently lower than the average in the hospital at large.

Another measure of quality of care is patient satisfaction. Our patient satisfaction scores (Press Ganey) for the Family Medicine network of practices are very high. Our most recent data shows that 11 out of 13 practices in our network were in the 90th percentile in terms of their patients' responses to the question "What is the likelihood of recommending this practice to others?"

Perhaps one of the greatest issues in quality patient care is increasing patients' capacity to access their care professionals in a timely manner. In 2003, our Family Health Center switched to a modified Open Access plan, which helped our average wait for a routine visit drop dramatically from 20 days to 3–4 days We have continued to explore with our staff and residents how to improve scheduling and Family Health Center operations. We currently have multiple cross-functional work groups addressing scheduling, efficiency, and quality-of-care improvement at the Family Health Center.

Health system

One of the most gratifying outcomes involves the many ways in which our relationship with the larger organization of LVHN has allowed the culture of Relationship-centered Care to spread outside of our department walls. For example, in 1999, faced with concerns about its referral base when a large competing hospital system began systematically purchasing practices, LVHN pursued an alternative strategy of creating mutually beneficial relationships with all of the primary-care practices. Seven years later, the success of this strategy is evident in our growth in market share.

After conducting site visits with us, and witnessing our commitment to Relationship-centered Care and to openness and transparency, the Pool Trust began promoting this in other areas of the hospital. With Pool's support, the Departments of Internal Medicine, Emergency Medicine, and OB-GYN have enhanced their teaching about Relationship-centered Care, self-reflection and interviewing skills.

In 2001, a challenging event actually served to further this process of the spreading of our culture. A fire occurred in our Family Health Center, forcing us to temporarily relocate our practice. Our practice manager called around to other clinics to see what space was available, so that our patient care could continue. Given her relationships with the managers of other clinics, fostered by a shared management structure, she was able to forge an agreement to use a section of unused space in the Internal Medicine clinic. We moved our entire operation there in one day. The temporary "joining" of the two clinics was both an outgrowth of our work and something which furthered this work. Having family physicians and internal medicine physicians working side by side created many positive changes. The IM clinic watched us work and commented on the more positive atmosphere they observed, including the positive relationships between staff and residents. As an outgrowth of this time together, the Medicine clinic integrated many of the processes of the Family Health Center into their own clinic, including modified open-access scheduling.

Similarly, our Future Search process, described above, has spread in our hospital. Many stakeholders outside of our department attended our Future Search. As a result, LVHN has now used Future Search in the development of palliative care services, future of nursing strategic planning, and a patient-centered experience initiative for the entire network. This hospital-wide spread of our culture has created a positive-feedback loop, where hospital and department gain mutual respect for each other and growing trust in the process of Relationship-centered Care.

CONCLUSIONS AND LESSONS LEARNED

As we reflect on our 13-year history as a department, we can clearly see a great deal of accomplishment, a great deal of messiness, and many lessons learned. In striving to implement Relationship-centered Administration, the organization needs to grow powerful roots in the culture of Relationship-centered Care, skills in relationship building both inside the immediate organization and with external allies and detractors, and nurture collaboration wherever possible, so that creative learning and growth is always occurring. All of this requires patience for a long time span and a larger organizational context that is supportive.

Roots are best defined as having clear values around what matters, values that are deeply embedded in the culture of the organization. We have found it enormously helpful to have culture-building strategies to grow and strengthen those roots. The intentional use of language, symbols and rituals in every aspect of the organization continually reinforce the cultural messages. Our posters of relationship-centered clinical tools hanging in the Family Health Center conference room, our videotape review forms using the vocabulary of these clinical tools, our resident, faculty and staff evaluation forms using the language of Turtle Craft: all of these remind us again and again of why we are here. So too, having whole-system events such as retreats and Years-in-Review creates a powerful message about what is valued. And using an organizational structure based on the stewardship model requires that we practice what we say we value: having work groups that are open in their membership and transparent in their work rather than managing from a top-down perspective. At times it does become necessary, as practitioners of Relationship-centered Administration, to hear about the ways in which strategies are not working for people or causing so much stress and resistance that they become ineffectual, and to then modify them accordingly. However, in modifying culture-building strategies it is critical not to lose the essence of what they are about.

> We have learned again and again that a critical set of skills is that involved in having difficult conversations. Relationship-centered Administration is all about conversations, and the difficult ones are the most essential. This includes having the courage to take risks to speak difficult truths. It requires deep listening . . .

We have learned again and again that a critical set of skills is that involved in having difficult conversations. Relationship-centered Administration is all about conversations and the difficult ones are the most essential. This includes having the courage to take risks to speak difficult truths. It requires deep listening, which involves toning down one's own inner reactivity so that non-judgmental listening and inquiry can occur.

> We have had many difficult conversations as we seek to understand what has heart and meaning for each of us as we go about fleshing out the reality of the innovations we have proposed, and we will have many more to come. When I listen for understanding rather than to find points to refute or disagree with, when I speak to further clarify my views rather than to convince others of my view's merits, the conversations are more productive and less difficult.
>
> Julie Dostal

When we succeed with this skill, great things happen, when we fail, people often are wounded or become disconnected from the community. We are by no means masters of these skills; we are always learning. As simple as they are, they are also enormously challenging and take great courage.

Another component that has fed our creativity and growth is our capacity to reach out and collaborate. Whenever we have been open to forging new connections and relationships, highly creative projects have been the result. Some examples of these, referred to above, are the Center for Mindfulness, a collaboration between our department and Psychiatry; and OACIS, a collaborative effort to improve the care of people with advanced complex illness that actually spawned a new division in the network's Home Healthcare department. Collaborations with Internal Medicine are focused on implementing innovations in Chronic Care using 'promotoras' and group visits. Collaborations with OB-GYN are working to improve low-risk maternity care and to improve the education of OB-GYN and Family Medicine residents in primary care of women and low-risk maternity care.

The most challenging lesson, however, is learning the "turtle wisdom" of patience. Growing roots, building conversational skills, and promoting collaboration require time to generate their creative magic. Relationship-centered Administration is inherently muddy and actually fosters challenging dynamic tensions. For example, we have learned that, in meeting any challenge, such as creating a new policy or a new curriculum, what being relationship-centered actually looks like often means systematically building in mechanisms for listening to a diverse range of opinions. If done well, this ensures that everyone experiences being heard, but it is time consuming and emotionally challenging to listen through the heated exchanges to get to common ground. Fortunately, the outcome is usually better when we take the time to patiently attend to diverse opinions.

> In meeting any challenge, such as creating a new policy or a new curriculum, what being relationship-centered actually looks like often means systematically building in mechanisms for listening to a diverse range of opinions. If done well, this ensures that everyone experiences being heard . . .

Being relationship-centered and creating a community of healing also involves balancing multiple needs and agendas. While this is true in any organization, in a relationship-centered one, it is impossible to get away with just giving a hierarchical ruling and ignoring the response. One person's desire to better meet his or her needs—for example, balancing personal and professional issues better by becoming part time—has ramifications for the entire system. In this example, the potential for the burden to shift to someone who has not explicitly asked for modification of their work status, especially in a system that has a great deal of creative energy and many new projects, is enormous, and can create great difficulty. If we are relationship-centered, we must attend to both sets of needs.

Another balancing act we continue to work with is balancing our tremendous creative energy and potential with the need to get things done at the practical level, to "make the trains run on time." There needs to be constant prioritization and reprioritization at the systems level to accommodate unexpected shifts in resources. Beware the dangers of overcommitment!

We have been delighted at the ways in which our culture has spread in our larger system. While this is an outcome we have long hoped for, the degree to which it has occurred has amazed us. We have come to deeply appreciate the importance of our home organization, LVHN, and the community in which we live and work. This local and organizational context has been critical for our success. The alignment of our longer-term goals of culture change towards relationship-centeredness and the financial strength of the network allowed our department to make mistakes and learn. LVHN was patient with us. We learned again and again the importance of building your nest in a good tree in a healthy ecosystem. In our attempts to be relationship-centered, we find ourselves constantly stretching to extend our trust: trust in ourselves, to know ourselves and to share with our community what we want and need to succeed and thrive; trust in each other, to listen and hear each other's stories, experiences, and dreams; and trust in the universe, that it will share what we need and will show us ways to move forward if we remain open hearted.

NOTES

1 Tresolini CP. The Pew–Fetzer Task Force. *Health Professions Education and Relationship-centered Care.* San Francisco, CA: Pew Health Professions Commission; 1994.

2 Lehigh Valley Hospital Department of Family Practice. *Initiatives in Family Practice: community, connections & collaboration.* Allentown, PA: Proposal to the Dorothy Rider Pool Healthcare Trust; 1996.

3 Miller WL, Crabtree BF, McDaniel R, *et al.* Understanding change in primary care practice using complexity theory. *J Fam Pract.* 1998; **46**(5): 369–76.

4 McDaniel SH, Campbell TL, Hepworth J, *et al. Family-oriented Primary Care.* 2nd ed. New York, NY: Springer; 2005.

5 Harrison GA, Morphy H, editors. *Human Adaptation.* Oxford, UK: Berg: Oxford International Publishers Ltd; 1998. Tattersall I. *Becoming Human: evolution and human uniqueness.* San Diego, CA: Harcourt Brace & Company; 1998. Barrett L, Dunbar R, Lycett J. *Human Evolutionary Psychology.* Princeton, NJ: Princeton University Press; 2002. Gunderson L, Holling CS, editors. *Panarchy: understanding transformation in human and natural systems.* Washington, DC: Island Press; 2002. Ludwig D, Walker B, Holling CS. Models and metaphors of sustainability, stability, and resilience. In: Gunderson LH, Pritchard L, editors. *Resilience and the Behavior of Large-Scale Systems.* Washington, DC: Island Press; 2002: pp. 21–48.

6 Berger PL, Luckmann T. *The Social Construction of Reality: a treatise in the sociology of knowledge.* Garden City, NY: Anchor; 1966. Shotter J. *Conversational Realities: constructing life through language.* London, UK: Sage Publications; 2000.

7 Senge P. *The Fifth Discipline: the art and practice of the learning organization.* New York, NY: Doubleday; 1990.

8 Block P. *Stewardship: choosing service over self interest.* San Francisco, CA: Berrett-Koehler; 1993.

9 Fetterman DM, Kaftarian S, Wandersman A, editors. *Empowerment Evaluation: knowledge and tools for self-assessment and accountability.* New York, NY: Guilford Press; 2005.

10 Cohen-Katz JL, Miller WL, Borkan JM. Building a culture of resident well-being: creating self-reflection, community, and positive identity in family practice residency education. *Fam Syst Health.* 2003; **21**(3): 293–304.

11 Weisbrod M, Janoff S. *Future Search: an action guide to finding common ground in organizations and communities.* San Francisco, CA: Berrett-Koehler; 2000.

12 Miller WL. The clinical hand: a curricular map for relationship-centered care. *Fam Med.* 2004; **36**(5): 330–5.

13 McDaniel SH, Campbell, TL, Hepworth J, *et al.,* op. cit.

14 Stewart M, Brown JB, Weston WW, *et al. Patient-Centered Medicine: transforming the clinical method.* Thousand Oaks, CA: Sage Publications; 1995.

15 Crabtree BF, Miller WL. *Doing Qualitative Research in Primary Care: multiple strategies.* 2nd ed. Thousand Oaks, CA: Sage Publications; 1999.

16 Sackett DL, Straus SE, Richardson WS, *et al. Evidence-Based Medicine: how to practice and teach evidence-based medicine.* 2nd ed. Edinburgh, UK: Churchill Livingston, 2000.

17 LeDeaux P. Non-Traditional Training: exploring part-time and shared residency positions [lecture/discussion]. STFM 38th Annual Spring Conference. New Orleans, LA; 2005.

18 Dostal J, Deitrick L. What does relationship-centered care look like in practice? [poster presentation]. NAPCRG. Quebec City; 2005.

Commentary: Family Medicine at Lehigh Valley Health Network

What would an organization be like if it was structured on the principles of Relationship-centered Care? Would such an organization be functional in the competitive world of healthcare practice? The story of the Lehigh Valley Health Network (LVHN) Department of Family Medicine answers both of these questions by describing such an organization and by showing that the answer to the practical "Will it work and be competitive?" question is a resounding yes. Like the previous case study of Clarian West (*see* Chapter 6), this case provides proof of the principle that an organization based on relational values can be a viable and contributing department in a large healthcare network, and remarkably successful, providing excellence in service, teaching and research.

The story of the Department of Family Medicine at LVHN is a story about organizational culture creation and change. It is the story of how a small group started a new family medicine department and residency program by intentionally developing a relationship-centered culture, and did so in the context of a traditional medical complex with traditional goals, expectations and values. In a sense, the new department of family medicine can be seen, in the terms of complexity theory, as a small perturbation with effects that are rippling out into the larger organization and into the community in which it is located.

A SYSTEMATIC EFFORT

This chapter provides a view of what a systematic effort to be relationship-centered could look like and offers much practical wisdom along the way. Over the years, Lehigh Valley developed and perfected a number of culture-building techniques that are relational in nature and also encourage the emergence of new forms. Some of these strategies are listed and examined in the section "Culture Building Strategies." They include the use of rituals and symbols, empowerment evaluation and whole-system events.

The role of ritual as a way of building group identity has been noted. Rituals clearly set the Department of Family Medicine apart from others, both in a stigmatizing and in an appreciative way, depending on who was involved and where the interaction was taking place. It is interesting, however, that as time passed, the stigmatizing began to disappear, and the appreciation was enhanced. This change in the perception of the rituals is an example of how the principles and practices developed in the family medicine department are insinuating themselves into the fabric of the wider organization.

The feedback provided by all members of the department through "empowerment evaluation" is also an important culture-building tool. It is a unique type of evaluation because rather than being primarily judgmental it provides an opportunity for everyone to have some input regarding the goals and direction of the organization as well as an opportunity to reflect on their own role and the extent to which they are accomplishing their vocational and organizational goals. Evaluation is no longer the dreaded confrontation between employee and supervisor, but becomes an opportunity for creativity and learning that can be of great value to the individual and the organization.

Two regularly scheduled system-wide events are described: the Year-in-Review and the Future Search meetings. Both flow from the methods of positive psychology and focus on empowerment, concentrating on individual and organizational strengths and accomplishments, deep collaboration, and a positive forward-looking emphasis.

THE STRUGGLE OVER STRUCTURE

The story of Lehigh Valley illustrates dramatically the messiness of developing an organizational structure based on relationship-centeredness as a fundamental value and principle. This messiness appears first in the evolution of an organizational structure. The leaders did not decide on one organizational form and stay with it, or even have a planned progression of ideas to try out. Instead, the writers note that they experimented with a number of structures before the current stewardship structure emerged, and they continue to consider their structure to be subject to experiment and change.

The original non-hierarchical structure did not have sufficient clarity of roles and lines of authority to efficiently accomplish the department objectives. However, they did want to listen carefully to the input of all department members and to honor and continue to encourage the creativity of the entire group. The stewardship contract eventually emerged as an organizing principle, in which each member of the department co-creates with management their roles and goals for the upcoming time period. They also convened conversations with members of the department around role clarity. This is very different from the usual hierarchical approach in which these roles would be dictated by management, assigned to individuals, and carried out machine like by the role occupants.

The stewardship contract is one more example of an emergent design in which everyone participates actively and creatively rather than passively receiving instructions and performing them. It would have been easy (and might have been tempting) to revert but they stayed with it, continuing to use their core practices of reflection and dialogue until they developed a better structure.

Several interesting lessons can be learned from the emergence of governance models. One is the notion that organizations have cycles. The type of governance important for one stage of organizational development may be different from that needed at another stage. People, too, have cycles. The type of structure that an individual finds most comfortable may change as a function of personal and vocational factors. And, in fact, some people may never be effective in the sometimes ambiguous environment created by a relational organization. These changing relationships, this "messiness," may always be part of changes in organizational culture. There are times when the fit is right and times when it's not. By recognizing and anticipating them it is possible to respond to them by relational means, such as deep listening.

AN ARCHETYPAL CONFLICT

Another issue that often appears in the context of relational culture change is specifically discussed in the section "Teaching Relationship-centered Care and searching for biomedicine." It is the conflict that often arises between process and content. At Lehigh Valley this conflict took the form of dissatisfaction on the part of some residents who felt that they were receiving too much input on relationships at the expense of training in biomedicine. The unstated assumption is that training in biomedicine is more important than developing a relational perspective. We use the term archetypal to describe this conflict because it arises frequently and across many settings when a process is introduced that is aimed at building relationships and group cohesiveness rather than directly aimed at solving problems, planning, improving professional competence in a specific skill or moving forward the stated goals of the organization. Process work, even when done with great rigor may be referred to derisively as "soft" or "just fluff." The rituals at Lehigh Valley such as the "Ceremony of Passage" became one flash point for this conflict. It is instructive that the leaders did not back away from the ritual, but used a relational approach to deal with it. They used listening, and surveys (which are a type of group listening), to determine how the rituals could be changed to accommodate the needs of most of the residents without compromising their intent to build a sense of identity and community.

OUTCOMES

Like the previous chapter on Clarian West, this story has an impressive list of outcomes. Where Clarian West achieved impressive quality, volume and financial outcomes, Lehigh Valley's achievements were in the areas of growth of the staff and faculty and innovation, the solid performance of residents and the emerging evidence that they carry relationship centeredness with them when they leave residency and the impressive accomplishments of the faculty and staff. Of course, patient satisfaction, measured at above average, is also of primary importance, as is the interesting observation, mentioned before, that the larger organization of which family medicine is a part is incorporating important aspects of the relationship-centered culture. Together, these two case studies demonstrate that a relationship-centered organization can yield highly successful outcomes over a wide range of measures.

FINAL NOTE

Chapter 5, on authentic presence, shows how self-knowledge and self-acceptance are important characteristics of the relationship-centered leader. That is clearly true in this story. It takes courage and maturity to hold steadfast in the presence of conflict and divergent opinions, and to work relationally in the context of a larger system that does not always hold relational values. Likewise, a willingness to listen to and learn from diverse perspectives is needed in order to hear divergent voices and to make appropriate accommodations when necessary. At Lehigh Valley, this was done by creating a supporting and nurturing environment (see Will Miller's comment) as well as one which is constantly challenging. It is this dynamic, of nurture and support as well as challenge and innovation, not unlike good coaching, which helped to guide Lehigh Valley to success.

CHAPTER 8

AMPATH: evolution of a weapon against HIV/AIDS

James L Greene

SYNOPSIS

Amkatwende—loosely translated—means, "Get up and go!" in Kiswahili and is the name of an agricultural cooperative for HIV-positive people. Perhaps this is a good glimpse at what the program described in this chapter embodies: it is the message for HIV-positive individuals who had little or no hope in years past; it is the message for numerous Kenyans—physicians and others—who want to "make a difference," as one of the founders often says; it is the message for westerners who come to serve and learn; since the devastation and displacement following the elections of December 2007, it is the message to staff and patients that AMPATH, our program, will survive: ***Get up and go!***

AMPATH (Academic Model for Prevention and Treatment of HIV/AIDS) was started as an on-going exploration, an evolving system, and an unfolding dream in the midst of the HIV/AIDS nightmare in Kenya, Africa. In November of 1988, four faculty members from the Indiana University School of Medicine (IUSM) had visited a number of third-world medical schools and recommended establishing a partnership with the yet-to-be begun Moi University Faculty of Health Sciences, in Eldoret. What began as a profound experience in International Medicine turned into a nightmare when AIDS arrived in Kenya. AMPATH was born in the midst of the pain of watching people die. It began as an effort to provide medicine to those who came to Moi clinics or showed up at the hospital with HIV-related life-threatening illness. Because AIDS is a multi-edged sword, however, the creative individuals who committed themselves to the struggle developed a system that became multi-edged as well. That system continues to evolve to this day.

The story of AMPATH is the story of an emergent, inventive, comprehensive system. AMPATH has grown from a vehicle for treating HIV/AIDS victims to a multi-faceted organization through which most of the spectrum of AIDS-associated needs can be addressed. As one facet of the program was instituted, that experience often led to the recognition of the need for another one. By December of 2007, those components included: care and treatment of HIV/AIDS patients; a program to curb mother-to-child HIV transmission; a far-reaching effort to eradicate tuberculosis; several farms on which People Living With HIV/AIDS (PLWHA) grow food for other patients and learn methods of sustainable farming; a food distribution program for patients "manned" by PLWHA; organized outreach and support services in each clinic area guided and staffed by PLWHA; crafts workshops and a restaurant in which PLWHA can begin to offer service to the larger community and support themselves; a program of support and aid for orphans and vulnerable children; a state-of-the-art electronic data gathering and management system; qualitative and quantitative research capabilities through a Research and Special Projects Department and a network of social scientists who are focusing on the work; and, most recently, a pilot effort in home-based counseling and testing organized and led by the program manager and the Community Mobilization Department.

> The story of AMPATH is the story of an emergent, inventive, comprehensive system. AMPATH has grown from a vehicle for treating HIV/AIDS victims to a multi-faceted organization through which most of the spectrum of AIDS-associated needs can be addressed.

AMPATH now serves western Kenya. Prior to the post-election violence and chaos of January 2008 (*see* Epilogue), the organization employed over 900 people and was treating over 60 000 patients. It was at work not only in the city of Eldoret, but also in 19 clinic locations throughout the area.[1] As the leaders of AMPATH are fond of saying, "We are reconstituting lives, not just immune systems."

Even beyond these admirable efforts, Joe Mamlin (co-founder and resident director) has written:

> When you think a moment, you realize the IU–Kenya Program at its core symbolizes what is so critically needed by Kenyan leadership. This is not a program dedicated to building medical schools or even stamping out a pandemic. At its heart, it is a program that screams, "Yes!" in a world too ready to say, "No!" This program puts love and compassion front and center. Those values build the rest . . .
>
> Joe Mamlin, co-founder AMPATH

In this chapter we describe highlights of the AMPATH story—charting the course of addressing immediate needs, seeking to understand additional needs and emerging problems in these new arenas, and then finding ways to tackle whatever comes next. It is a story of relationships, passion, commitment, and true emergence—no blueprint being available to this day, anywhere in the world. In fact, AMPATH is now being recognized as a highly successful program with calls to replicate it in other parts of Africa.

THE CREATION OF AMPATH

In 1989, a decade prior to the advent of AIDS in Kenya, four physician faculty members from Indiana's School of Medicine (Joe Mamlin, Charles Kelley, Dave Van Reiken and Bob Einterz) visited several institutions in various parts of the world in search of the most likely location for the beginning of a partnership in International Medicine. Their unanimous recommendation was to begin working immediately with the just-beginning Moi University Faculty of Health Sciences in Eldoret, Kenya. This partnership would, through 2009, be known as ASANTE (American sub-Saharan Africa Network for Training and Education in Medicine).[2] Beginning in 2010, the entire effort became "the AMPATH consortium."

> Our program in Kenya did not start with a goal of creating a robust and comprehensive HIV/AIDS program. When we began, HIV was not the scourge it is today so we did not create this program to attack that pandemic. Rather, our logic or goal was quite simple: to expose our students and residents to medicine in the developing world and thereby reinforce the altruistic spirit of medicine.
>
> Craig Brater, Dean, IUSM

In 1990 Bob Einterz (now Associate Dean for International Medicine, IUSM) and his family moved to Eldoret for a year, inaugurating a pattern that Indiana University (IU) has maintained ever since. From the outset, in light of his Peace Corps experience in Latin America, Bob felt strongly about the work being tied to the areas it served. Much of medical education in the States was still "orbiting around" the physician as s/he spent time on "the wards." Bob was determined that this effort should include but be broader than the hospital orientation. As he looks back, he remembers his concern:

> "Community based" was the buzzword, although very few understood what that meant. It—community-based—was almost all that mattered to me, and my efforts that first year, though wide-ranging and diverse, focused on championing community-based education and service.
>
> Bob Einterz, Associate Dean International Medicine, IUSM

The ultimate goal in those earliest years, says Bob, was "income generation, food, political action, organizing mothers, etc. . . . the stuff of health." He spent 1990–91 developing that focus and laboring to be certain that the community-based education and service emphasis for all medical students was solid.

Joe Mamlin and his wife, Sarah Ellen, were team leaders during the school year 1993–4. During that time, Mamlin's focus was the inpatient wards, wanting to build relationships and infrastructure. Each year the consortium trained American medical students and residents—who served in Eldoret for a specified length of time—and a few Kenyans who were sent to the States for brief periods of training and exposure to western-style practice.

The AIDS epidemic "hit" Kenya in full force during the 1990s and physicians stood by helplessly as countless patients died for lack of treatment. In late 2001 Mamlin, by then retired from IU and living full time in Kenya, was "on rounds" in the hospital in Eldoret and came upon a man being fed by an individual he recognized as a medical student. The patient was almost dead when Mamlin discovered him. At first he acknowledged simply that here was yet another HIV/AIDS victim. However, when he learned that the patient was a fifth-year medical student, Daniel Ochieng, he simply could not stand by and do nothing. He called back home to IUSM and said, in essence, "I want to treat ONE patient!"

After some debate among ASANTE personnel—about how their mission was education, not clinical care, and what good treating one person would do—they authorized treatment of this single individual. Mamlin and his colleagues were able quickly to raise the money to provide drugs for Daniel. They were determined that he would have the medicines needed to give him some chance at survival. Daniel's remembrance of that experience is poignant.

> It took them a lot of time to convince me that this medication was going to work well. I only had eyesight in one eye. I was really sick. I was getting worried that I might never continue with my education anymore. So I got depressed. After staying in the wards for some time with my mum taking care of me I managed to gain strength and once I was able to move around, I moved out of the wards and I was put in the private students' hostel. But the students did not want me there because they thought I might die in that hostel— so I was kicked out. So Mamlin then moved me to where he was staying.
>
> Daniel Ochieng (first AMPATH patient), AMPATH staff

Another staff member, Steve Lewis, who was instrumental in beginning the nutrition program, remembers meeting Daniel at this same time:

> Rounding with Joe Mamlin at Moi Teaching and Referral Hospital (MTRH)] I saw Daniel Ochieng, emaciated and deathly close to eternity. Professor [the term by which Mamlin is generally identified by those in Kenya] informed me that he had started Daniel on the life-saving ART (antiretroviral therapy) and expected a complete recovery. I shook my head in disbelief, said a prayer for

Daniel and left. Three months later Daniel was on the back of my motorcycle! The Lazarus effect.

Steve Lewis, Director, Amkatwende Agriculture Cooperatives

During this process, Mamlin began to function as more than a physician. His vision began to take shape: "We **must**, we **can** develop a system and build a team that will do more than simply keep those who come to us alive!" While he could not chart an exact path, he had a deep sense of commitment to move forward. He began, with the vigor and passion of an adventurer, to work within the channels set up by ASANTE. Here skills, sharply honed through systems development during his administrative career, came into play and here, as in all other dimensions of his work, Mamlin relied on and emphasized relationships. One colleague reflects, "Joe really thinks that those whom he trusts can do more than they are capable of—and they end up determined not to disappoint him!"

> "We **must**, we **can** develop a system and build a team that will do more than simply keep those who come to us alive!"

From a program of education and care giving, the confrontation with HIV/AIDS evolved.

When we created our Kenya program, one of our operating principles was that we were there as educators and as consultants. Our faculty, residents and students would participate in clinical care but we were not there to be medical missionaries. By that I mean we were not going to ship medications and equipment to Kenya Rather we could address health issues of Kenya. As HIV became overwhelming, we found ourselves in an untenable situation. On the one hand, the purpose of the program was to reinforce altruism. On the other hand, we were standing on the sidelines witnessing this carnage—the hidden curricular message was as far as one can get from altruism. Thus, we had to either engage or withdraw. We obviously chose the former course . . .

Craig Brater

Daniel Ochieng, when asked about the history of AMPATH, provided this poignant insight, relating it to his personal history:

If there was no Kenya project—[no] Moi and IU collaboration—probably I could not have met Mamlin in the first place. So you can see that it all boils down to that collaboration. That collaboration is like a mother to all the things that came up around it.

The emergent nature of problems and creative solutions
Providing medical care and support
The first task of patient care was to provide HIV-positive individuals with what drugs were available and hope that they could be saved. Almost immediately it was evident that medicine and medical care would not suffice; patients also needed support and encouragement from the program. Ochieng remembers his involvement as he moved from the role of "patient" to that of team member:

> We talked with Mamlin and at that time he was treating a pilot group of around 100 patients, some in MTRH and some in Mosoriot (an outlying clinic). He felt that we needed to find a way of providing some support to these patients. At that point he connected me with a colleague, a lady . . . who had been trained by the provincial AIDS control committee on support groups and on positive living— basically living positively—and we started thinking what we could do to help other people living with HIV and AIDS. We came up with the idea of starting a group. [We] put together the initial ideas and the initial paper, which helped us to get funding to start the group that we called the AIDS Interventions Movement.

It soon became apparent that physician attention, drugs and patient support groups were still not enough. AMPATH's growth demanded a restructuring of the PLWHA support/outreach strategy itself. Daniel remembers that effort:

> After some time, a program came in called the MTCT (Mother-to-Child Transmission) Plus program which was going to offer treatment to patients for life—mothers who are pregnant—with their husbands and families. They were really interested in keeping track of these patients, so that they don't lose [track of them], so that is the point that the idea of outreach also came into being. So we started filling in locator forms of the patients so that in case they defaulted from the clinic we could actually trace them and bring them back into the clinic. As AMPATH grew it became obvious that the two functions—outreach and support—were growing and could not be contained in one department. So we separated and support groups and outreach became separate entities.
>
> Daniel Ochieng

Creating systems for sustainable nutrition
In April of 2002, 34-year-old Salina Rotich, weighing only 73 pounds, was carried into the Mosoriot clinic, suffering from tuberculosis and pneumonia as a result of being HIV positive. Mamlin was the physician who saw her and immediately prescribed the appropriate antiviral medications. The following month when Ms Rotich returned, she was scarcely improved. In response to

Mamlin's probing about whether she was taking her medication, she insisted that she had missed no doses. He continued asking questions, including ones about her diet, and found that her husband had died of AIDS-related illness, that she was too weak to cultivate her small shamba (garden), and that she was eating almost nothing. The doctor gave her a few shillings for corn meal, milk and eggs. Mamlin and Kimaiyo (Dr Sylvestre Kimaiyo, Director, AMPATH) checked their patient population and found that at least one in five was getting inadequate nourishment. Salina Rotich was not unusual! They began to explore ways of providing food for the patients who needed it since that was a primary cause of lack of response to medication. At the time of Salina's six-month appointment, her body weight had doubled and she was caring for her five children and cultivating a couple of acres of maize. Food was the secret!

Implicit in the philosophy within which AMPATH has evolved is a commitment to involve PLWHA in every way possible—for at least two reasons: to provide a living wage for HIV/AIDS sufferers so that they can support themselves and their families and to give them the privilege of providing service to others. It was "natural," then, that concern for adequate food was followed almost immediately by the question, "How can we involve HIV-positive individuals in solving this problem?" The answer was relatively easy: teach them to grow and employ them to deliver fresh produce. Thus was born the idea of developing farms.

> Implicit in the philosophy within which AMPATH has evolved is a commitment to involve PLWHA (Patients Living with HIV/AIDS) in every way possible

Again and again, a new solution often unearthed new challenges leading to further solutions. A problem emerged with the food system, for example. It became apparent that patients often were not picking up their food, and for a variety of reasons: stigma, travel difficulties, conflicting priorities, the types of food provided, illness, etc. AMPATH leaders turned to the Research and Special Projects department of the system to investigate and develop recommendations to address the issue. Jim Greene (one of the authors of this chapter and a medical anthropologist who led many focus groups for AMPATH) said with amazement, "It is much like replacing a spoke in the wheel of a bicycle while you ride along."

> Again and again, a new solution often unearthed new challenges leading to further solutions . . . "It is much like replacing a spoke in the wheel of a bicycle while you ride along."

Preventing mother-to-child transmission

Another new challenge faced by AMPATH doctors as they began to treat HIV-positive patients was the critical need for some effective means to curb mother-to-child transmission of the virus. The physicians knew that without intervention, one in four pregnant women would infect their babies at birth. They were also quite aware that a large number of HIV-positive expectant mothers would not or could not come to a clinic or the hospital for testing, treatment or delivery.

The plan that AMPATH devised was again straightforward. Each mother who delivered at an AMPATH site was tested—unless she adamantly refused—and, if positive, given a single dose of nevirapine when her labor began. In conjunction with this, the new baby was also treated with the same medicine within 72 hours of birth. With this simple "double treatment," transmission dropped by more than 50%.

In keeping with the basic ASANTE philosophy that, whenever possible, Kenyans would lead any effort, Traditional Birth Assistants (TBAs) were chosen and trained to work in each location. Their job was to support and treat those mothers and their babies who would not or could not come to an AMPATH site.

Treating secondary illnesses

Another disease was always lurking in this country. Tuberculosis became a significant factor for those who were HIV positive. As one physician noted "HIV sets them up and TB kills them!" Jane Carter, a physician based at Brown University, developed a strategy by which TB could be confronted. Dr Carter is a creative behind-the-scenes strategist who spends every possible hour in the Kenyan countryside. She is exceptionally capable in developing deep relationships with Kenyan staff, Western colleagues and those who face tuberculosis, either personally or as members of the families of sufferers. The challenge was sometimes almost overwhelming, but Dr Carter reflected that she grew in many dimensions as she found ways of creating a system through which Kenyan personnel could test and treat those whose bodies were vulnerable to this killer.

Providing additional services

Those who deliver the PLWHA-grown food are HIV positive, as are employees who work with crafts, sew clothes and run a restaurant on the Moi campus. Benjamin Andama presently heads the Family Preservation Initiative (FPI) that encompasses farming and feeding of families. FPI's mission is to provide avenues for poor and vulnerable members of the community to achieve economic security. Andama is articulate in presenting in story form the personal challenge that he faced as he considered the new responsibility.

> When Professor Joe Mamlin approached me to take the lead on
> the FPI program I wasn't sure of what exactly I was going to do

because of fear. Those were the days when everyone around was scared of the pandemic. This happened when Joe came to visit me with his wife and we had dinner together. When we finished with the dinner, Joe broke the news on how he thinks I am fit for the job because I had been working with the community for a long time. It was easier to work with people when you didn't know their HIV/AIDS status than people you pretty well knew they have the virus. This was [scary] and my wife was worried. None of us knew a lot about the disease. My first case that "Prof" gave me was that of a high school student whose relatives had abandoned him because he was HIV positive. He dropped from school because he was very sick. He was a total orphan—both his parents had passed away—and he was left with relatives who were not ready to stay with him. They were terrified with his presence in the family; they went further and gave him a room including the utensils that he was to use. He was not to mix with the rest of the family members who feared contracting the disease. He was really discriminated upon by the relatives. Joe sent me to help. Surely it was one of the most difficult situations I had ever found myself in.

I visited the family with the clinical officer, Mr Keboi. I was shown by a finger [pointing to] where Steve [the patient] was sleeping. They were not ready to take us to the room. Steve was happy to hear that Joe had sent us to see him, because he had promised that we would visit him. We had talks with the family who were planning to take Steve away to his ancestral land, which was around 400 km away from Eldoret. They had given up on him to go and die, Remember this was very far away and Steve would not have been able to attend his clinic. This was Professor's great concern.

Our coming into the family changed a lot of things. With time, the family became very cooperative and friendly to us and to Steve. Although Steve passed away, this was a great moment in my life. I would say it was a training field for me to do what [I am] doing today. I realized the kind of discrimination that people who are HIV positive go through in the society. The program has become part and parcel of me and my family. My wife has given me a lot of support to realize much of the success story that we hear and see today. We keep by day hoping the cure for the disease will be found soon. My community suffers from double tragedy—that is poverty and the disease.

Benjamin Andama, Head, Family Preservation Initiative

Addressing the stigma of HIV/AIDS through community mobilization

Juddy Wachira, Co-Director Community Mobilization, spoke of another critical dimension of the work:

As AMPATH expanded, it was emerging that most of the clients enrolled in the program emanated from areas outside the program's catchment areas. Most clients accessed treatment when the disease had already advanced—hence limiting the treatment options. Furthermore, stigma and discrimination were evident in most of the communities. We realized the need to establish a department that would enhance HIV prevention, employ strategies to capture individuals who are infected as early as possible and link them to care and support services as well as prevent new infections. The Community Mobilization (CM) department was established in March 2006 with the aim of educating people about HIV/AIDS and encouraging them to get counseled and tested for HIV. The department also empowers individuals to make informed decisions in regard to HIV prevention, treatment and care. CM recognizes that collaborations are vital in the implementation of its programs. The program partners with stakeholders such as government agencies, NGOs, community-based organizations, faith-based organizations, self-help groups and the donor community. Linkages are established with local communities who work closely with AMPATH teams in all sites.

Juddy Wachira, Co-Director, Community Mobilization

She told of workshops for providers, training for faith-based groups and AMPATH's own research group, provision of education for community servants such as the police, school sensitization efforts and radio programs as illustrations of these collaborative efforts, and then reflected on CM's overall impact:

With time, Community Mobilization rolled out its activities to most sites—which meant enormous work for me as the manager. I had to learn how to multi-task and improve on my organizational skills. There were days when there was so much work that I thought I would go crazy. But what kept me going was the appreciation I got from the community at the end of a CM activity. The fact that you are making a difference in somebody's life by the information you pass, by them knowing their HIV status and for those who turn positive, AMPATH is there to offer hope by providing a free comprehensive HIV care and treatment package . . . that makes it all worthwhile. Sometimes I ask, "What if AMPATH had not initiated the CM department? How many lives would we have lost out of ignorance or lack of information?" And when a community member shakes your hand with a big smile and says, "Thank you for bringing these services to us" you are motivated to keep on.

Creating an informatics infrastructure

Bill Tierney, who succeeded Mamlin as Division Chief of General Internal Medicine at IU, told about the emergence of an Informatics program and the research dimension of AMPATH. His story is not unusual in terms of either leadership or expertise. He remembers, "I never anticipated being involved in international health, never, through the fifteenth year of being on the faculty. I couldn't justify getting involved in the Kenya program. I didn't think I had anything to offer."

While he was still Division Chief at IU, Mamlin passed a request for proposals to Bill, asking him to think through a program that would enhance the educational and treatment capabilities in Eldoret. As Tierney reports, the proposal was funded and he went to Kenya in late 1998 to make the proposed Internet access and computer network a reality. Joseph Rotich, who later became head of the School of Public Health, came to IU in 1999–2000 and returned with a completed informatics program for ASANTE. Like much of what has been tried in all aspects of the work, the program, as Bill says, "failed, was fixed . . . and has been in almost constant use ever since."

In early 2002, Tierney created an integrated informatics system for all of AMPATH.

> We knew we'd have to explore what we were doing in order to make data-based (quality-based) improvements and continually improve. Our mantra was "start small, make it better with information." You won't get better shooting baskets if you don't see if they go in. This was prospective Epidemiological and Health Services research.
>
> This is the most rewarding thing I've ever done in some ways. It is not very often that an informatics geek can save 10 000 lives. It means that AMPATH has gone from caring for 0 to over 60 000 patients. . . . I've always looked at . . . my role as researcher as an extension of my role as clinician. I see the research I do as clinical. More lives are saved in Kenya by creating records systems and enhancing care-delivery systems than by treating one patient at a time.
>
> Bill Tierney, Director, Research

Our mantra was "start small, make it better with information." You won't get better shooting baskets if you don't see if they go in.

At this point it is worth noting a fact—obvious to Kenyans who will identify the tribe to which each person "belongs" by his or her name—that may easily be overlooked by Western readers: AMPATH has consistently recruited individuals who appear best qualified for a particular responsibility—regardless of that person's ethnic background. As such, AMPATH has always been composed of people from many different tribes, all working together. This practice runs counter to the culture at large (where hiring by kinship or tribe is the norm) and AMPATH leaders often face counter pressure and resistance. But, it is this philosophy that, in large part, made possible what we consider to be *the* creative solution to an exceptionally difficult problem. Following the elections of December 2007, Kenya erupted in a firestorm of ethnic and tribal violence. During this period—described elsewhere in the chapter—members of the AMPATH "community" (and that is *not* too strong a term for the spirit of the organization) regularly risked themselves to serve and support each other and those outside the group regardless of their background and family ties. Following this time of upheaval, the fact that AMPATH was "up and running" quickly points similarly to the strength of a common commitment in a fractured world.

Leadership

Dr Sylvester Kimaiyo is, with Joe Mamlin, responsible for the major day-to-day work of AMPATH. He was attempting to care for a large number of HIV-positive patients, but medication was almost impossible to obtain because of the cost. He reported:

> In the year 1999, a month's supply of ARVs was almost $900 while the average monthly income in Kenya was less than $75. Thus a diagnosis of HIV was effectively a death sentence.

In 1995 Dr Kimaiyo had the chance to pursue a clinical fellowship in pharmacology in Indiana. During that time, he gained the clinical tools necessary for truly comprehensive HIV-patient care. He was positioned to become a leader, not a role he had seen himself in given his first loves of patient care and teaching. The real impetus for his interest in HIV/AIDS, as well as the call to service through leadership, was more personal.

> [Kimaiyo's] sister had always been an inspiration to him, as she represented Kenya in international running events as well as the national women's basketball team. However, in 1997, he received news from Nairobi that she had become severely ill. So, he immediately traveled to Nairobi and discovered his sister to be HIV positive. After bringing her back to Eldoret, he was able to obtain treatment for her cryptococcal meningitis. However, the family member who had been his inspiration ultimately succumbed to the lethal virus within one week, due to the lack of ARV accessibility. For Dr Kimaiyo, the consequences of limited ARV access and delivery mechanisms were painfully clear.
>
> While Dr Kimaiyo's growth as an HIV clinician has been facilitated by many outstanding individuals, his inner drive for

expanding AMPATH and his personal growth are clearly his own. He oftentimes reflects on his family, friends, and colleagues who unnecessarily suffered and ultimately perished at the hands of HIV without hope for sustaining a long, fulfilling life. Now, he is delighted to see HIV patients empowered and living a full life obtaining masters degrees or raising families. Too many fellow Kenyans have suffered, he says, and too many colleagues have helped him along the way for him to now become complacent. Dr Kimaiyo's life has been and will forever be affected by the victories and defeats in the battle against HIV.

Paul Park MD, student, Brown University

Caroline Opiyo, head of Human Resources for AMPATH, remembers her introduction to her leadership responsibility:

> My immediate mentors to this job were Prof Joe Mamlin and Dr Kimaiyo—and Joe's word to me always was, "Do what you can to make this thing work!" None of us really knew how to approach it, but by making constant mistakes and correcting ourselves along the way I managed to get four centers up and running within two months and currently the sites have been increased to 19 . . . This experience has really developed me and made me believe that with commitment and hard work everything is possible. This success in fact earned me a promotion to Associate Program Manager in charge of operations.

None of us really knew how to approach it, but by making constant mistakes and correcting ourselves along the way I managed to get four centers up and running within two months and currently the sites have been increased to 19.

Opiyo also describes another important feature of AMPATH's leadership philosophy, which leads to a complex interweaving of the new approaches introduced by AMPATH within a traditional Kenyan framework.

> AMPATH's style of leadership is embedded in the culture of Kenya. AMPATH tries to use the Ministry of Health system to identify leaders. Some AMPATH clinics are . . . headed by Ministry of Health Employees (Clinical Officers). All AMPATH employees in each facility report to the Medical Superintendent in charge of the Hospital or the Clinical Officers in charge of the health centers. Therefore, all positions fit within the existing systems of

Kenya—from high administrative levels (i.e. Program Manager) to the lowest levels.

Caroline Opiyo, Head, Human Resources, AMPATH

In 2006, Tony Suchman and Penny Williamson, external consultants to the IUSM with expertise in relationship-centered healthcare, were invited to develop leadership training for AMPATH leaders. Here are Penny's reflections on their first three visits.

Our first visit to Eldoret in February 2006, at Bill Tierney's invitation, was exploratory—to meet many of the AMPATH leadership, build relationships, begin to learn about the complex cultures of Kenya, and to see whether our style of leadership development might be useful in this very different context. We were excited, curious and open to learning all that we could. We also held the possibility that our experience might not fit in Kenya. Much to our delight and surprise we found that our ways of approaching leadership training (e.g. as an emergent process based on shared stories, enhanced relationships, and useful skills of interaction) seemed to resonate with and be of immediate interest to our new colleagues. We found a group of young professionals who had been thrown into complex leadership positions with no training other than their original preparation for the roles of doctor, nurse, social worker, or counselor, and informal mentoring by their American colleagues. They were hungry for anything we could teach them, and eager to begin. For them, this was not simply a job, but a chance to save their communities from the scourge of HIV/AIDS—to make a difference. By the end of that brief but intense week, we were as eager to be of help as they were to have it. We, too, wanted to make a difference.

With Joe Mamlin, Sylvester Kimaiyo and Bill Tierney's guidance, we planned a multi-stage program. A return trip in September 2006 focused on intensive training for the four senior leaders of AMPATH (Sylvester Kimaiyo MD, Abraham Siika MD, Winstone Nyandiko MD and Caroline Opiyo, who was named as leader-facilitator in training to carry on the work after us). In addition to focused work with this group, we carried out a 2½ day off-site workshop for the 30 leaders of AMPATH, those with oversight for the different functions—Pharmacy, Outreach, Counseling, Nutrition, etc.—that comprise AMPATH in Eldoret and each of the rural clinics. In the daytime we focused on the sophisticated yet basic skills of advanced communication, feedback, delegation and accountability. In the evenings, two Kenyan associates who had helped manage all the details of the workshops led interactive games that added delight and levity to the work and helped build community.

The success of that first workshop led to a third visit in February 2007. At that time we held two consecutive retreats for the clinic officers, nurse managers and physician directors of the 19 clinics. In her role as trainer-in-training, Caroline Opiyo participated in the first of these retreats and helped to lead the second one. During our visit we also met with the senior leaders and program managers, with whom we had previously worked, to explore the impact of our earlier sessions. The senior leaders told us that they had successfully incorporated lessons of delegation and communication into their ongoing practices. This was very gratifying. But we also learned that ongoing practice among others had not taken place. They were too busy and the ideas too unfamiliar to incorporate newly learned practices on their own initiative. Tony and I had also hoped to conduct regular coaching sessions by phone with the senior leaders and this proved not to be possible due to their busy and unpredictable schedules. We did have regular phone meetings with Caroline, and in this way, at least, kept up our links of communication. But some in the larger group expressed disappointment and skepticism about the value of these widely spaced, single trainings. Although disappointing to us as well, this rang true to our experience. Single training events, no matter how informative, cannot create sustainable change without practice, reinforcement and ongoing learning. We hoped to return to Eldoret in a renewed learning mode, to explore with our Kenyan colleagues other approaches to sustainability that would have a better chance of success.

Penny Williamson, External Consultant

Juddy Wachira talked briefly about the leadership development provided by AMPATH.

Initially, it was difficult to delegate and not worry whether things were being done right. I had to learn how to communicate, give feedback and appreciate the uniqueness of each one of the staff members. I am grateful that AMPATH took all its managers for a leadership workshop because it equipped me with necessary leadership skills. I came to realize that management is not all about being bossy and giving orders. It is about creating a conducive working environment where team spirit and commitment to the end result is the driving force. In addition, concern about each others' well-being is also important in building a good working relationship. I have learned to take one step at a time, learn from my mistakes and build on my strengths. Cry if I have to but never ever give up. I now believe in team spirit and that success comes from consulting, involving and appreciating all parties concerned.

As is the case with all AMPATH work, leaders learn from those who deal with AIDS personally on a day-to-day basis. Wachira almost laughs at herself as she recalls one such insight-providing experience:

> One day, a gentleman came to the office and introduced himself as a client who has been involved in sensitizing the community about HIV as well as referring patients to AMPATH for treatment. He went on and on about the way he would be a useful tool in CM if given an opportunity to work within the department. . . . This guy (Michael Rono) never gave up. . . . He shared his life experience and pointed out that he was alive because of AMPATH. He was willing to go to all lengths to help his community even if it meant working with no pay. I was touched. I had never met a guy so courageous and determined. Mr Rono is currently our MTRH community liaison and I owe a great bit of our success to his dedication and passion to mobilizing the community for HIV testing. His testimonies proved to be effective in encouraging individuals to get tested because he represents a symbol of hope. We now have clients share their life experiences.
>
> Juddy Wachira

Abraham Siika, MD, tells this story about his professional growth and the impact of leadership training:

> As Prof Mamlin once told me, "It is better to be at the bottom rung of a long ladder than at the top rung of a short one." This is best exemplified by AMPATH, which grew from just a desire in one man to treat a medical student (what I would consider the bottom rung) and thus show the world that HIV can be treated in Africans, to treatment and care for thousands of patients. The ladder continues to grow longer with each patient added into treatment and care—not only at AMPATH but also in all of sub-Saharan Africa. I have also learned that dreaming isn't such a bad thing, as long as you only dream at night and work all day to fulfill those dreams. Identification of targets, methodical planning and patience will more often than not lead to success. In a leadership workshop for AMPATH leaders in 2006, I learned that it is easier to achieve your objectives through proper delegation and supervision. Indeed, life has become so much better since delegating to and empowering the people I work with. This has left me with enough

time to concentrate on doing what I do best—treating patients and teaching students.

Abraham Siika, Senior Leader, AMPATH

After his near miraculous rehabilitation and joining the AMPATH staff, Daniel Ochieng has continued to grow as a leader and to make a significant contribution to care for PLWHA:

I went and did a course with Kenya Institute of Professional Counseling in Medical and Psychological Counseling and managed to graduate with a higher diploma. And I have, of course, managed to initiate the first HIV/AIDS support group in the region and also I initiated outreach services within AMPATH and am currently heading the outreach services. I can also say that as of now I have also managed to get a readmission into the university and I am pursuing a bachelors degree in psychology. (Note: because of his HIV-positive status, Daniel was dismissed from Medical School and not permitted to re-enter).

Daniel Ochieng

OUTCOMES

One summary report in the fall of 2007 was succinct:

With over 60,000 current patients and new enrollment exceeding 1000 patients per month, AMPATH serves as the Ministry of Health's designated HIV training center for western Kenya, a leading HIV research institution in sub-Saharan Africa, and the largest HIV care program in East Africa. AMPATH is currently the fastest-growing HIV care system in Africa, and operates over 19 sites in North Rift Valley, Western, and Nyanza Provinces in Kenya.

Paul Park reported from "the top."

While Dr Kimaiyo will adamantly claim that he still cannot pinpoint a specific event that led to his position as Director of AMPATH, his weekly meetings provided a specific, comprehensive plan. The first meetings had less than five attendees, but after just five years, the number has increased to over one hundred. Likewise, AMPATH has grown from 3 staff to 1,200 staff and from 40 patients to over 60,000 patients. To this day, Dr Kimaiyo still chairs monthly meetings with the sole agenda of directing the future of AMPATH.

Paul Park

A late January 08 report to IU leadership from Eldoret included a picture of Kimaiyo again gathering staff in the AMPATH conference room after the post-election violence. Some individuals had not yet been able to return, but "the team" was meeting once again to plan and work. Their spirit and determination prevailed even in the midst of the crisis.

Steve Lewis reported prior to the riots in January 2008, saying:

> Today we receive in excess of 130 metric tons of maize, beans, corn soy product and vegetable oil on a monthly basis. The Japanese embassy (one of the biggest supporters for relief food in Africa) provided AMPATH with a grant to build a WFP food store worth over $90,000. Our farms are currently producing up to 4 metric tones per week of fresh culturally acceptable nutritious food.
>
> Steve Lewis

FPI's urban-based intervention, the Imani workshop, is a sustainable social enterprise run and managed by AMPATH patients. The Imani workshop is a fair trade certified craft workshop which provides full and part time employment opportunities for AMPATH patients and paid internships for 150 patients per year to develop business skills and access capital and financing for client-run micro enterprises. The Imani workshop produces and markets jewelry, textiles, handmade paper products, and ceramics.

The Amkatwende Agriculture Co-operatives (AAC) is AMPATH's primary rural based intervention. AAC provides access to high value commodities markets, co-operative administrative support, agricultural extension support, and operations management and services for small-scale farmers living with HIV. Amkatwende, which loosely translated, means '"get up and go" in Kiswahili, is a comprehensive agricultural cooperative for small-scale farmers living HIV/AIDS.

In addition, FPI offers a business consultancy and micro-finance service for both rural and urban-based patients. They provide financial management advice, business development services, and micro-finance for entrepreneurial clients enrolled in AMPATH.

One of the latest FPI projects is a poultry project that will provide eggs to the AMPATH project. "Now we are producing our own feeds," boasts Benjamin Andama, head of FPI, "and we are hoping very soon to supply eggs to the commercial shops in town and western Kenya. " The clients, of course, can access our feeds for their broilers and layers.

No one is certain what to expect in AMPATH's future. The story we have outlined here makes us feel, however, that when this winter of upheaval, terror and chaos begins to show evidence of spring in the form of some normalcy, AMPATH will, like the perennial plants of Indiana, also begin anew to serve, bringing hope again to those who need it most. Everlyne, an Imani worker, wrote to friends during the riots:

> We use our lives to give hope and encouragement to others, say-
> ing that we, being HIV positive, were once considered death
> walking with no hope and now we have hope! We are living and
> going about our lives positively. In the same way, those feeling
> devastated and hopeless should not lose hope. The future can still
> be bright!
>
> Everlyne, Imani Worker

We use our lives to give hope and encouragement to others, saying that we, being HIV positive, were once considered death walking with no hope and now we have hope!

EPILOGUE: AMPATH CONTINUES GROWTH IN THE FACE OF CHALLENGES

At least four system-changing events have occurred since these words were written. They are: a) the post-election turmoil and terror, b) the beginning of Home-based Counseling and Testing (HCT), c) the evolution of AMPATH towards holistic primary care, a transition that is just now beginning, and d) the drying up of funding for continued expansion and service.

The death, riots and turmoil that followed the national election in December of 2007 brought about, perhaps, the most significant challenge that AMPATH has faced. As the program was beginning to serve about 100 000 people and function in more than a dozen locations, it faced *actual* disbandment because of the trauma throughout the country. Juddy Wachira, who was originally charged with co-developing the Community Mobilization Department speaks, demonstrating some of the resilience and focus that has emerged among staff members:

> I was part of the post-election crisis committee that looked into pro-
> viding access to care and treatment for affected patients and staff.
> We formed a medical team and went to the camp. At first I could
> not go to the Internally Displaced Persons camps for a long time, I
> just couldn't! We began to find AMPATH patients there and organ-
> ized a team and did counseling and testing for HIV in the camps,
> though we had to ensure the safety of our staff who came from
> various ethnic groups. AMPATH also organized for psychosocial
> therapy for its entire staff. This really helped me forgive and work
> comfortably with colleagues from the other ethnic groups without
> fear. I also benefit from the financial support given to the affected
> staff which went to pay the hospital bill and funeral arrangements

for my cousin [who, like Juddy, was Kikuyu and had been killed during the violence]. God rest his soul in eternal peace!

Juddy Wachira

Home-based counseling and testing is a second major shift in the work of AMPATH. Although they were treating thousands of HIV-positive patients, AMPATH leadership realized that only about 15% of the residents of western Kenya knew their HIV status. *Voluntary* counseling and testing had been conducted by government employees in VCT centers for years—but, in 2008, few were actually taking advantage of this. Uganda had previously tried a program of home-based counseling and testing (HCT) and partially succeeded in the effort. Mamlin and Kimaiyo—learning from the work done by colleagues in that country—decided to attempt a similar program in AMPATH sites throughout western Kenya. Funding was identified and obtained, communities were targeted, information about pitfalls and stigma, dreams and fears was collected and studied, teams were put in place—and the hard work of house-to-house visitation was begun. The community of Mosoriot was small enough and homogeneous enough so that it became the prototype effort. Learning from and changing as a result of that experience, AMPATH moved on to the Turbo area and then to Webuye, each larger and more complex than its predecessor.

About this time—and partially because of what clinicians learned through HCT—it became clear that AMPATH should evolve towards provision of primary care in a broader sense; the people needed, wanted and deserved more holistic care than "just" HIV/AIDS identification and treatment. (There is even, among some of the leaders, discussion of changing the name from **A**cademic **M**odel for **P**revention **a**nd **T**reatment of **H**IV/AIDS to **A**cademic **M**odel for **P**rovision and **A**ccess **to** **H**ealthcare.)

The stigma that still surrounds AIDS and the identification of AMPATH facilities and vehicles *exclusively* with that disease have meant that treatment of individuals identified as HIV positive has sometimes been difficult; the opportunistic diseases that kill those whose immune systems have been compromised by the disease point towards the necessity of broadening the AMPATH mission. As one of the leaders verbalized it, "HIV knocks folk out—and malaria kills them!" (This comment echoed for tuberculosis as well.) In addition, as the region evolves and as patients become more "consumer-oriented," demanding broader care, attention to hypertension and diabetes, as examples, come into focus. This is a next step for the system's growth.

As one might guess, with the emergence of these additional challenges at the same time that funding is questionable, AMPATH leadership has postponed formal leadership training for the time being. Individuals are still receiving scholarships and attending institutions of higher education in several countries; regular study of critical and interesting issues is being conducted by a growing cadre of researchers in Kenya and the States; creative work is continuing at every level in the system. However, for the moment, there is no organized formal training program in leadership development.

Diminished funding is painful, angering and to be expected in the world economy of 2010. Funding for identification and treatment of HIV/AIDS seems to be drying up just when AMPATH has learned, as an organization and as a community of caring individuals, how to do the job that has become their passion and mission. Those who lead AMPATH are driven by personal experience, compassion for suffering people in all walks of life and hope for the future of Kenya. They have developed relationships of caring and service among themselves and with those for whom they offer that hope. The task of tomorrow is to guide this system towards a future that is sustainable. As Joe Mamlin wrote to his home church during the post-election days in 2008:

> When you think a moment, you realize the IU–Kenya Program at its core symbolizes what is so critically needed by Kenyan leadership. This is not a program dedicated to building medical schools or even stamping out a pandemic. At its heart, it is a program that screams, 'Yes!' in a world too ready to say 'No!' This program puts love and compassion front and center. Those values build the rest . . .
>
> Joe Mamlin

At its heart, it is a program that screams, "Yes!" in a world too ready to say "No!"

NOTES

1 By 2010 AMPATH had evolved into a primary care system responsible for some two million individuals in Western Kenya. The system involves about 2000 employees and operates in twenty-three full-time clinics and an additional thirty satellite locations.

2 The partnership would include at various times as many as fifteen institutions. The consortium presently includes Indiana University, Purdue University, Brown University, the University of Toronto, the University of Utah, Duke University, Providence Portland Medical College, Lehigh Valley Hospital and Health Network and George Washington University School of Public Health and Health Services.

Commentary: AMPATH

The AMPATH Chapter tells the riveting story of the development of a program to serve patients in western Kenya with HIV/AIDS. It is a story of "reconstituting the lives, not just the immune systems" of patients living with HIV/AIDS (PLWHA). More than that, it is a story of creating and sustaining hope in the face of despair and against daunting odds of combating a devastating pandemic. Just as important it describes an effort to build a trustworthy community of competent, compassionate service in the midst of a country struggling with corruption and self-serving bureaucracies.

The story of AMPATH is unique on several fronts: its scale is global; the nature of the programs is emergent; and the vision it serves is evolving to this day. It began with the intention of procuring medicines to treat patients with HIV/AIDS and grew by necessity to include myriad additional aspects of patients' health and well-being. Today it is changing into a comprehensive primary care program with an emphasis on testing people for HIV/AIDS as well as treating those positive for the illness.

Like the stories of IUSM and Clarian West (Chapters 13 and 6) this is a good illustration of emergent design; however in those other two chapters there was a clear and guiding vision from the outset. In this story the vision itself emerged.

CREATING KEY DISTURBANCES IN PATTERNS OF SOCIAL ORGANIZATION

This chapter includes several examples of intentional efforts to disturb strong ongoing social patterns. One is the current practice in Kenya, based on a culturally ingrained tradition, of hiring staff based on kinship ties. By basing hiring practices of its ever-enlarging staff on meritocracy instead, the leaders of AMPATH created a disturbance in a pattern of social organization that had profound effects on the program. Instead of selecting only members of one's own tribe, every branch of AMPATH was staffed by people from many different tribes, based solely on their qualifications. This allowed relationships to be built on trust and anchored in respect as well as accountability. It opened the way for real conversations and effective teamwork. It meant, for example, that after the post-election violence in 2008, the program was able to reconstitute immediately, as team members' loyalty to each other and to the program triumphed over allegiance to their individual tribes. AMPATH has created a trustworthy model of leadership that one hopes will spread to other parts of the country.

Another social pattern being disturbed involves the status of patients living with HIV/AIDS. They have been a stigmatized, helpless group—so much so that people would not even get testing. By following the principle of empowering PLWHA wherever possible, AMPATH began the process of transforming a vulnerable, weak group into a source of strength and hope for others. PLWHA routinely contributed to programs and offered innovations as well as being recipients of care. As one HIV-positive patient recounts, "We use our lives to give hope and encouragement to others . . . once considered death walking with no hope . . . now we have hope. We are living and going about our lives positively." Another PLWHA gentleman insisted that he could serve AMPATH as it had saved his life; he is now a community liaison whose "testimonies [are] effective in encouraging individuals to get tested because he represents a symbol of hope."

Two stories illustrate the profound effect on others of a return to health from the near death of untreated AIDS: the story of Daniel Ochieng (the medical student who became the first AMPATH patient and is now a healthy staff member) and Selma Rotich (the patient brought to the clinic at 73 lbs and near death). Both suffered the stigma of the disease. As people saw their miraculous rehabilitation they realized HIV was not a certain death sentence but a condition that could be treated. PLWHA could still lead a normal healthy life. They called this "the Lazarus Effect." Stories such as these and the examples above are gradually changing the stigma of HIV/AIDS in Kenya.

BUILDING RELATIONSHIPS OF TRUST AND FREEDOM TO CREATE

A hallmark of the AMPATH culture is that individuals are encouraged to try new things and to learn from their mistakes. People are not afraid; rather they understand that there is no blueprint and that their creativity is essential to moving forward. Thus creativity is fostered and the results are often astounding. Abundant stories point to Joe Mamlin, co-founder of the AMPATH program, as a model for this philosophy; as one person wrote, "He really thinks [we] can do more than we are capable of . . . and [we] end up determined not to disappoint him."

Capacity is built at every level: from leaders who grow into their positions through experience and courage, to patients who learn to farm or to create and sell crafts as means of feeding and providing for their families. It is inspiring to read accounts of people accepting leadership responsibilities and rising to meet them through trial, error, fixing and moving on. Unlike the usual administrative stance (the machine metaphor), mistakes are accepted as learning opportunities rather than as occasions for punishment. Caroline Opiyo, the head of Human Resources for AMPATH, recalls, "None of us really knew how to approach it [building new rural clinics], but by making constant mistakes and correcting ourselves along the way I managed to get four centers up and running within two months." Experiences like this allowed staff to grow in confidence as well as competence, learning-in-action and inventing new ways to meet new challenges.

AUTHENTIC PRESENCE OF LEADERSHIP

Undergirding this remarkable story is the equally extraordinary authentic presence of the leaders and members of the AMPATH community. Their stories show a deep commitment to values. For all involved this is so much more than a job. People are working to save their very communities; most have lost relatives and friends to the scourge of AIDS. Additional losses accrued during the post-election violence of 2008 where people were killed because of their tribal affiliation.

To keep steady and hopeful in the face of these relentless challenges takes self-differentiation and attunement, as described in Chapter 5. In one poignant example, Juddy Wachira, an AMPATH staff member, told of overcoming her reticence and joining a multi-ethnic team to treat affected staff and patients in the camp for displaced persons following the post-election violence. (During the turbulence, her cousin had been killed and the situation was not yet safe.) She was able to rise to the occasion "with comfort and without fear" due to the therapy sessions that AMPATH provided the entire staff. In this example, Juddy maintained focus on the work and on the principles involved in doing each part fairly and well, even as trust was being rebuilt among the care team. Clearly, the trustworthiness of the AMPATH community is vital to success; the work is too emotionally and physically demanding to be in it alone.

KEEPING AN EYE ON WHAT IS POSSIBLE

The spirit evoked by members of the AMPATH community along with myriad and impressive accomplishments, building one on the next, are heartening and inspirational. This story is proof of concept that small disturbances can result in near miracles, and even change the course of history. The heart of an appreciative approach (as described in Chapter 3) is to look for the positive core in the most daunting of circumstances in service of creating a better world. The AMPATH story is a profound example of such an approach made manifest. As Joe Mamlin so beautifully writes: "It is a program that screams, 'Yes!' in a world too ready to say, 'No!' This program puts love and compassion front and center. Those values build the rest . . ."

CHAPTER 9

A community of influence: clinician researchers join to make a difference to people affected by consequences of cancer treatment

Alison Donaldson with reflections by Jane Maher and Patricia Shaw

Editors' Note: We thought that a brief comment might be helpful *before* this case study. The story that follows takes place at an entirely different level than the previous stories. We will not see the emergence of a new clinical program or department, but rather the formation of a team (a "community of influence") that the conveners hope will go on to do transformative work in the future. Recall in Chapter 2, our description of how an organization is created:

> An organization is a conversation before it is anything else: it begins with people talking together about something they would like to do that is beyond their capacity to do as individuals. At some point, their shared idea gains sufficient coherence—there is sufficient similarity in what each of the individuals is understanding—that they can begin to coordinate their actions effectively. That's when the organization begins to function.

It is exactly this process—a shared idea gaining sufficient coherence—that we are privileged to observe in this case study. What emerges here are a shared identity and common purpose that are vital prerequisites if this group (this new organization) is to function. Notice how this happens and how the conveners manage a skillful balance between providing facilitative structure while also leaving plenty of space for serendipity and emergence and for the participants to be co-creators of their enterprise.

SYNOPSIS: A COMMUNITY OF INFLUENCE

This story is about a group of 12 clinician researchers, formed to improve the patient experience by influencing research, education, services, practice and policy in an increasingly topical field: adverse consequences of cancer treatment. The story, which includes three episodes from the group's early life, gives a flavour of its face-to-face meetings, the benefits (and drawbacks) of informal email exchanges, and the part played by narrative writing in tracking and making visible what the group achieves. Although this particular community of influence is still young, a number of themes and outcomes are beginning to emerge: in the first few months, members have pooled resources, identified numerous issues worth pursuing jointly, and made some first collaborative moves.

WHAT LED UP TO THE CURRENT STORY?

The group of professionals whose story is told here is made up of clinician researchers with nursing or allied health professional backgrounds. We have come to think of these people as "hybrid creatures," because of their multiple identities. These place them well to influence research, education and policy as well as services and practices on the ground.

But to explain how this group came into being, we first have to talk briefly about doctors. The roots of the story go back at least two decades, to debates in the UK around cancer and palliative care in the 1980s, when many still viewed cancer as the preserve of specialists administering radiotherapy, chemotherapy, surgery and other treatments in hospital. Others, however, were starting to argue that General Practitioners (GPs) could make a valuable contribution to caring for cancer patients "in the community", i.e. outside hospital.

One particular organization that recognized the role of GPs in supportive care was Macmillan Cancer Support—a major charity and household name in the UK. Known especially for its "Macmillan nurses," the organization provides practical support for people living with cancer. In the early 1990s, Macmillan started to invest in its relationship with selected GPs by paying them for "protected time" (typically one day a week), which they could use to educate and influence their peers. There is now a community of some 300 "Macmillan GPs," influencing practice and policy both locally and nationally. The collective voice of Macmillan GPs has been influential on many levels. For example, it helped to establish new processes in primary care (in order to improve the quality of care given to dying cancer patients) and to persuade the UK government to include supportive care among the services for which it rewards GPs. Apart from these highly visible achievements, myriad initiatives have emerged on the ground and been shared whenever the GPs meet.

After a decade of working with the GP community, the team at Macmillan decided in 2004 to form a slightly different kind of group. This time, the intention was to encourage collaboration between researchers and "service developers," clinicians who have a track record not just in caring for patients but also in improving healthcare more widely. Its core members were clinically active academics, mostly doctors, with a track record in researching end-of-life care. The group, which came to be known as the "Macmillan Palliative and Cancer Care research collaborative" (MacPaCC for short), represented six UK universities. By 2009, its members had produced more than 60 peer-reviewed publications (often as principal authors), and it had succeeded in both advancing knowledge and achieving recognition in the field of end-of-life care.

Meanwhile, the number of people surviving cancer in the UK had been steadily growing and a whole new set of issues was beginning to emerge around adverse consequences of cancer treatment.

Consequences of cancer treatment: time to act

In 2008, a National Cancer Survivorship Initiative (NCSI) was launched as a partnership between Macmillan Cancer Support and the UK's Department of Health,[1] with a major stream of work focused on the adverse consequences of cancer treatment. Planned activities included: articulating a vision for cancer

TABLE 9.1 Members of Consequences of Cancer Treatment Collaborative Group (CCaT)

Clinician researchers:	
Jo Armes	Research Fellow, King's College London
Natalie Doyle	Nurse Consultant, Royal Marsden NHS Foundation Trust
Mary Wells	Senior Lecturer in Cancer Nursing, University of Dundee
Karen Robb	Consultant Physiotherapist, Barts Hospital, & King's College London
Diana Greenfield	Nurse Consultant, Sheffield Teaching Hospitals
Claire Taylor	Lecturer in Gastrointestinal Nursing, St Marks Hospital, Harrow
Isabella White	Remedi / Macmillan Clinical Research Fellow in Cancer Rehabilitation, King's College London
Karen Roberts	Nurse Consultant/Visiting Fellow, Northumbria University
Sara Faithfull	Professor of Cancer Nursing Practice, University of Surrey
Deborah Fenlon	Senior Research Fellow, Macmillan Research Unit, University of Southampton
Gillian Knowles	Nurse Consultant, Edinburgh Cancer Centre
Theresa Wiseman	Joint appointment: Senior Lecturer, Guy's and St Thomas' NHS Foundation Trust, and King's College London
Supporting team:	
Jane Maher	Chief Medical Officer, Macmillan Cancer Support
Janice Koistinen	Macmillan Projects Support Manager
Alison Donaldson	Writer / consultant
Patricia Shaw	Consultant / facilitator
Chris Steele	Project manager

survivors, developing a model of care, testing the model in the specific area of "pelvic cancer," reviewing data collection, producing guidelines, and pursuing research and development.

The team at Macmillan responsible for the consequences of treatment work stream (which included Jane Maher, Macmillan's Chief Medical Officer) spotted an opportunity to take the learning from the academic GP group mentioned earlier and to create a second clinician–researcher group. The story of this group, which has since adopted the name "Consequences of Cancer Treatment collaborative group" (CCaT for short), is told in the rest of this chapter (*see* Table 9.1 for a list of members).

How many people suffer negative consequences of cancer treatment?

Among people living with a diagnosis of cancer today, about a quarter are also living with consequences of treatment. This means about half a million people in the UK are suffering reduced quality of life. Many visit doctors or have tests for symptoms they do not understand, costing the UK's National Health Service tens of millions a year. The risks differ according to type of cancer, form of treatment and the individual's constitution, but evidence (some of which was published by members of the group described in this chapter) shows that different problems appear at different stages:

- nearly all patients will have moderate or severe treatment-related effects, either physical or psychological, during the first few months after treatment,
- the proportion falls to around a quarter of patients after six months,
- for others, e.g. those with pelvic malignancies, troublesome bowel, urinary or sexual problems may not develop until months or years later,
- in 5–10% of all people who have had cancer treatment, these problems will become complex or life-threatening over a 10-year period,
- for still others, consequences may result in chronic illnesses decades after treatment, e.g. heart disease, second malignancy or osteoporosis after breast or prostate treatment.[2]

During 2009, Jane Maher and her colleagues invested considerable time seeking support in order to be able to fund the new group. The initiative sparked strong interest and by the time of the first community meeting (in November 2009), there was sufficient funding (more than £½ million) to create and sustain a new group of research-active senior health professionals, with the intention of improving the experience of people living with the consequences of treatment.

Jane Maher writes:

> We needed buy-in from a whole range of stakeholders—the

Department of Health, Macmillan senior management, and the Macmillan regional teams (all of whom provide funding and support for this work). In particular, we wanted the Macmillan regions to recognize the value of having clinician researchers. So we invested a lot of effort early on in engaging our regional colleagues in the work. For example, we invited them to suggest people who might be interested in joining a new community focused on consequences of treatment, and we made sure we had people from the regions on the selection panel. In seeking financial support, there was no fixed amount on offer. Rather, as the year went by and people saw the quality of the group, offers of funding grew.

There was a striking experience quite early on in the process, in which we used pictures to describe the "communities of influence" work to senior managers and Department of Health officials. A series of images—sculptures set in rural landscapes—enabled people to "get it," to grasp the concepts that had been difficult to explain just in words, such as "hybrid creatures" (referring to the kind of clinician researchers whom we hoped to attract to the new group) and "working across boundaries" (*see* Figure 9.1).

The power of the pictures first became clear after some teleconferences with Macmillan regional heads of service, the National Cancer Director Mike Richards, and Department of Health representatives. After these calls, we followed up by sending round the slides containing the photos, and it was then that people really started to show an interest in what we were doing. We had tried meetings, words and papers. Pictures influenced people in a different way.

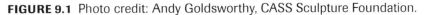

FIGURE 9.1 Photo credit: Andy Goldsworthy, CASS Sculpture Foundation.

Helpful concepts emerge

As we (the authors of this chapter) continued to refine the way we were talking about our experience of cultivating influential communities of health professionals, we found ourselves coining the phrase "communities of influence." We had long been conscious of Etienne Wenger's notion of "communities of practice." Wenger first became associated with this term in the 1990s in the context of learning theory, positing that learning is a fundamentally social phenomenon.[3] We all belong to and participate in informal communities of practice, he argued, in which we refine our practice, negotiate meaning and develop a sense of identity. The groups Macmillan had been cultivating seemed to fit this notion of a "community of practice" quite well. However, it struck us that the term didn't quite capture the essence of the groups we were studying, whose main *raison d'être* was to *have an influence on practice and policy*. In general, people join them and stick with them mainly because they want to make a difference to the patient's experience, hence our term "community of influence."

It may be helpful to add a few words here about the terms "community" and "network." In everyday language, network sounds perhaps looser than community. For our purposes, however, the difference is unimportant. What matters, whether one is talking about communities or networks, is *relationships and conversations*. Relationships make a community, but they also emerge and grow from community conversations.

With time, we have become increasingly convinced that cultivating communities of influence offers a fresh approach to service quality improvement, organizational change and policy development. This may be welcomed by those who are frustrated by top-down bureaucratic control, especially in the public sector.[4]

> We have become increasingly convinced that cultivating communities of influence offers a fresh approach to service quality improvement, organizational change and policy development. This may be welcomed by those who are frustrated by top-down bureaucratic control

During the months running up to the creation of the Consequences of Cancer Treatment group, other concepts emerged in our conversations, including "hybrid creatures" and "no man's land," which helped us to explain that clinician researchers have the potential to cross boundaries, influence a range of colleagues and make a difference to patient care.

Jane Maher writes:

> I began to realize that between the clinical world and academic research there was this zone, a "no man's land" that was full of "corpses," including broken down research projects, and researchers ready to give up their search for funding. This was true for

both GP and nurse researchers, but the nurses faced additional difficulties. There was a common view among clinicians that "we don't need nurses with PhDs." So my wish was to create bridges across no man's land, to help people develop from "alien visitors" into recognizably different but valued colleagues.

Patricia Shaw adds:

> In organizations, people can only recognize activity that they can draw one another's attention to in their speaking together and so sustain its life. So as we began to talk about hybrid creatures (we even had an image of a man/beast sculpture—a minotaur), people started to recognize themselves and be recognized. They also started noticing how hybrid creatures work and thus eventually bring new terrains of professional activity into active recognition. We speak of this as "populating no man's land." We are helping people take more seriously activity which is neither within one professional discipline nor in another, and so does not "count"; it is literally not measured or officially reported as a substantive contribution. This imaginative language provides a way of speaking on the way to the eventual emergence of new practices and roles which will have new names. Listening for and using imaginative language which resonates with what is happening allows otherwise "invisible" activity to be "caught" in conversations and slowly become more formally named and organized.

GETTING STARTED
Recruiting a team of hybrid creatures

As soon as funding was in place (in September 2009), Jane Maher and Macmillan colleagues invited suitable candidates to bid for membership of the new hybrid group. They all had a track record in the field, e.g. they were already involved in developing services, educating clinicians or doing research into consequences of treatment.[5]

The selection panel chose 12 individuals from across the UK, with either nursing or physiotherapy backgrounds.[6] Some were based in academic institutions (e.g. King's College London, University of Surrey, University of Southampton, Northumbria University, University of Dundee), others in hospitals or cancer centers (e.g. the Royal Marsden NHS Foundation Trust, St Marks Hospital, Sheffield Teaching Hospitals, Edinburgh Cancer Centre).

Early exchanges with the 12 chosen to make up the new group confirmed the challenges faced by hybrid creatures. They may get caught in academia, unable to get back into clinical work to implement their findings, or they may get trapped in clinical or management roles, unable to get the funding they need to do research.

Assembling a supporting team

From experience we knew that certain kinds of support are vital if communities of influence are to enjoy fruitful collaboration. The supporting team set up therefore included:

➤ an experienced manager to negotiate and manage funding arrangements (Chris Steele),

➤ a project support manager to organize document sharing and other important administrative tasks (Janice Koistinen),

➤ a writer/facilitator to track the evolution and achievements of the group (Alison Donaldson), and

➤ a facilitator to make the meetings and conversations among group members as productive as possible (Patricia Shaw).

As a team, we spoke and corresponded regularly, meeting to prepare community meetings and later to reflect on them after the event, as well as participating in ad hoc teleconferences as need arose. We also encouraged progress and connections among group members between community meetings.

STORIES ALONG THE WAY

The early stages of any new community are significant—they set the tone and start to form a "direction of travel" for the group. To shed light on how a community of influence develops, therefore, we have chosen three stories from this particular group's early life:

➤ an early "conversational" email exchange among members,

➤ the first meeting of the group, and

➤ the first episode of narrative writing.

In the accounts below, we deliberately include more detail than is normally found in a managerial report. In our experience, it is often seemingly small moves that create a collaborative atmosphere, shift thinking, and move people to act. The stories are written in the present tense to make them more immediate.

Story 1: An email exchange among members

in which members of the group start to become visible to each other, preparing the ground for a productive first meeting.

Often in organizations, when a new group is about to meet for the first time, the kind of paperwork circulated includes agendas, objectives and the like. Rather than follow these managerial habits, as we anticipate this group's first meeting we want to prepare the ground, so that when they finally meet they can quickly get down to real and fruitful exchanges. We therefore jointly formulate an email to all 12 members, which goes out in early November 2009 from Jane Maher as convener. The style is deliberately informal, inviting people to join a "conversation." It begins like this:

Now that you and others have agreed to become part of a community focused on consequences of cancer treatment, I wanted to start reflecting together in the run up to our first meeting. By sharing some early thoughts and starting to make connections with each other, we will be better prepared to make the most of our time together. So I hope you will read this and send any responses by using "reply to all" so that we can start a conversation which we will continue when we meet.

> An initial email reiterates the issue that brings this particular group together (to help people suffering consequences of treatment). Then it tells the story of how the idea of creating a new community emerged from a conversation . . .

The email goes on to reiterate the issue that brings this particular group together (to help people suffering consequences of treatment). Then it tells the story of how the idea of creating a new community emerged from a conversation a year ago with three members of the future group about the particular challenges faced by "hybrid creatures."

Patricia Shaw adds:

> Following on from my last comment, we encouraged Jane to acknowledge the early beginnings of the forming of the community, the real story so far, including risking allowing the uneven processes of involvement to be revealed. Yes, some people may seem more central, others more peripheral, some feel well established, others feel like new joiners, some feel confident of welcome and regard, others wonder if they need to prove themselves. . . . The official version begins supposedly with a fair and rational process of selection in which everyone starts at ground zero, but instead we actively acknowledge the history, the different experiences of inclusion and simultaneous worries about exclusion. We want to work with this explicitly all along the way so that the difficult processes of power and influence, leading, following, risk taking will be available for reflection and learning amongst us all.

> We actively acknowledge the history, the different experiences of inclusion and simultaneous worries about exclusion. We want to work with this explicitly all along the way so that the difficult processes of power and influence, leading, following, risk taking will be available for reflection and learning amongst us all.

Next, Jane's email introduces each member of the new community, with a few words about their background and field of research. To give a flavour, here are just two of these introductions:

> Sara first encapsulated the concept of the "hybrid creature" for me: she has experience of education, research and clinical work. As well having written a definitive book on long-term problems after radiation therapy and served as president of the European Oncology Nursing Society, she is also a professor with experience in establishing commissionable education for nurses; and she has a Dimbleby-funded project whose aim is to improve rehabilitation of prostate cancer patients, especially in relation to urinary symptoms. Despite all this, she has had difficulty returning to a clinical role, so she is looking for help in buying some of her research time to enable her to work clinically in a Primary Care Trust, giving her a chance to implement her research. She has a particular interest in how to develop and implement commissionable services.
>
> Mary has a long interest in the consequences of cancer treatment and is a particular expert in head and neck cancer. She also epito-mizes the challenges of being a clinician researcher. She has written guidelines on the effects of radiotherapy on the skin and, like many of you, knows the challenges of implementing evidence-based guidelines. She has also tested an assessment tool that identifies patients' priorities, so that services can be designed around them. Yet, like Sara, having got into research, she has found it difficult to find a foothold in clinical work again. She knows that to really make a difference you need "to get out there in the field and warm people up" before you attempt to implement research or new ideas.

After introducing all members of the group, including the supporting team, the email concludes:

> I know this email is longer than most! I hope if you have read to this point it means you will reflect on your experiences so far in the very early stages of this project and write in response in any way that will start to flesh out who we all are, the connections you are beginning to see between us and to say more about what you hope we can achieve by coming together rather than each ploughing a lone furrow.

It ends by again urging people to use "reply to all" so that everyone will see any written responses, since experience suggests that otherwise people often reply just to the sender. Over the next few days, we wait with curiosity to see how people respond. After a week has gone by, only one person writes back—to ask if she has missed something: has an agenda for the first community meeting been circulated? Then, one evening, about a fortnight after the original email, I send a short note to the group, starting like this:

> I am very much looking forward to seeing you all on November 30. I haven't noticed any other responses to Jane's email of November 2, so I am curious to know if you all read it! I gather a lot of you know each other already, so perhaps there are lots of bilateral conversations and exchanges happening anyway.

The very next day, there is a burst of responses from group members, starting with the following:

> I think your assessment of the potential explanation for the lack of response to Jane's introductory email is astute and certainly not because we haven't read the email, rest assured. Most of us do already know each other if not closely, then by reputation, and there have indeed been a number of parallel conversations about this initiative when we have met in other contexts.
>
> Clinical Research Fellow, based at a UK university

Another member makes a suggestion:

> Since Jane's email, I have been thinking about the short summaries she provided of each of us (this can't have been easy, and it is interesting to reflect on how someone else perceives you!). I wondered whether it would be useful if we all attempted to do our own (very short) summaries too—not to give everyone loads of work to do but just perhaps to jot down a few key issues related to the consequences of treatment that we feel most passionately about, ideas we are bringing to the table (even if very early or obvious ideas) and maybe a summary of one or two pieces of work or a couple of publications that we care most about and that have some relevance to the work of the community.
>
> Senior Lecturer in Cancer Nursing, based at a UK university

Over the next few days, a steady flow of emails appears, responding to this invitation. Below is one example, which further illustrates some of the difficulties faced by clinician researchers.

> I have been a nurse working with cancer patients (mostly breast cancer) for over 20 years. . . . Seeing how women suffer menopausal problems without the prospect of being able to relieve them through HRT launched me into my PhD. I am also a "hybrid

creature" having spent three years as a full-time lecturer and now working as a full-time researcher. However, funding streams mean that I have to be contained within a discrete "box" and so I now have little direct clinical contact with patients. It frustrates me that medics have specific posts that allow and even expect them to work both clinically and in research, yet in nursing you can only do one or the other. I am also very concerned about the divide that we are forced into, because of funding streams that keep "practice development" and "research" as separate entities. My clinical colleagues may want to develop a new service and ask my advice on getting some research evidence out of the change in practice. However, they can't wait until we have put together a proposal, got it funded and gone through ethics [equivalent of the US institutional review board]. Unless we do that we can't get our work published in high-quality journals and no one will fund us. If we in this group can find ways round this then we will have the potential to make a huge difference. It has always been my passion to get nursing underpinned by research evidence and I know the AHPs feel the same way.

Macmillan Senior Research Fellow, based at a UK university

By introducing themselves, often in quite a personal way, members are becoming more visible to one another. The benefit, we hope, is that, when they meet for the first time face-to-face at the end of the month, they will already be aware of many common interests and experiences.

There is a small catch to the story, however. After a subsequent exchange of emails, some of which include attached documents, someone sounds a protest:

> Dear all, I am finding the scale of email and messages coming from the group difficult to keep up with especially as I have a full-time job where I am not sitting at my desk most days but also have European responsibilities. We keep being asked to respond but in reality I am reacting rather than developing considered pieces of work. Could we at the meeting next week take stock, talk about this approach, and have a more considered communication strategy and action plan. I would find this very helpful. Despite feeling a little overloaded I am looking forward to seeing everyone next week. Best wishes . . .

This seems an important moment. Somebody has been honest enough to express their frustration. It provokes two kinds of response: 1) some group members write to echo the concern about the volume of email, and 2) the supporting team offers to investigate creating a web space to accommodate some of the communications and documents circulating between meetings. At time of writing, an online "learn zone" has been created, though people are making relatively little use of it, and email traffic continues to flow.

This whole episode highlights the constant challenge faced by groups who want to stay in touch but all have busy lives. The technologies now available for this can be helpful. Email has the advantage that it is generally easy to access—most people know how to use it, and no web link or special password is needed. A web space, if people get used to it, can offer a tidy way of collecting shared documents, even if few individuals actually post comments in the discussion areas. But these electronic forms of communication can also start to feel like a burden. The pragmatic approach emerging for this group is to: 1) continue using email for quick exchanges, and 2) use the web space to store documents and useful information about the group, such as contact details, profiles, lists of publications, and so on.

Story 2: Gathering for the first time

> in which an "iterative conversation" enables members to become more and more fluent in expressing their interests and hopes for the group.

Shortly after the first email exchange mentioned above, the first community meeting takes place. Nine out of the 12 group members (three are unable to make this first meeting) travel to a venue on the University of Warwick's campus outside Coventry to gather as a group for the first time.

The supporting team, which is also present, has given considerable thought to this first community gathering. We see it as much as an opportunity for the group to bond as a chance for its members to explore the topics they would like to take on together in coming months. We know from past experience that seemingly small things can do much to develop relationships, e.g. the opportunity to arrive the evening before the community meeting, and time within the agenda to share experiences and tell stories.

FIGURE 9.2

> We see the first gathering as much as an opportunity for the group to bond as a chance for its members to explore the topics they would like to take on together in coming months. We know from past experience that seemingly small things can do much to develop relationships.

Our suggested agenda for this meeting also leaves plenty of room for improvisation, as we want the flexibility to "work emergently." We break the day loosely into 90-minute intervals, with topics phrased as simple but important questions, such as: "Who knows whom, what are the opportunities and challenges in forming this community, and what is our experience of influencing in a complex world?" Improvising is not just a question of making it up as we go along. Rather, we take seriously what is arising in the group so that, for example, when people become excited about a particular issue, they can explore it together in depth without somebody cutting in to say "and now we are going to move on to the next item on the agenda." This can test the patience of those who feel more comfortable with a firmer "structure" or who are anxious to achieve clear and quick results. However, in our experience, this way of working does lead to many of the "results" desired, such as coherence, learning, trust and desire to act. This is where it starts to be paradoxical: we develop an imaginative sense of what kind of outcome is required, yet at the same time we work with the energy in the room, staying alert to what is emerging.

> It starts to be paradoxical: we develop an imaginative sense of what kind of outcome is required, yet at the same time we work with the energy in the room, staying alert to what is emerging.

On the day, we begin at about six o'clock in the evening. As the sponsor for this work, Jane Maher starts by clearly stating her goals for the group in its first year: 1) to make it more visible; 2) to start thinking about a program of work that, by the end of the year, could become a platform to attract further funding in this field. She particularly emphasizes an insight from working with MacPaCC (the other hybrid group mentioned earlier): the importance of sharing resources—papers, reference lists, proposals, tools, etc.—from the beginning. To this end, we hang large sheets of paper on the walls and during the next day and a half an impressive list grows, making visible the extensive pool of resources available to the group. These include good research papers that could be revived to influence practice or policy, literature reviews on various aspects of cancer survivorship, promising grant applications that were turned down but could be resurrected, and knowledge and skills that could be used to create new services for patients.

Jane Maher comments:

> There may be a tension between getting papers written versus spreading the message. Once a researcher has a good paper, rather than rushing on to the next, it may be worth putting effort into "giving it a social life." That way, good research is less likely to "get lost in translation."

In the meeting, the natural thing to do next is for people to explore who already knows whom and what common interests exist. It becomes strikingly clear that most know more than half the other members already. They have met through a range of circumstances—working on projects, studying or training together, supervising another member's PhD, working on papers or books together, being in the same post-doctoral forum, taking part in key committees and collaborative bodies (including the National Cancer Survivorship Initiative), or just sharing special interests.

People are invited next to talk about what kinds of topics they want to pursue as members of this group. Again, we hang large sheets of paper on the walls so that, if they wish, they can put up their topics for us all to see, though we do not expect these formulations to be the final word.

Over the next 24 hours, we intend to give people a number of chances to articulate and re-articulate their interests and aspirations. In practice, the process began two months ago with the bid presentations. However, today people are not simply repeating what they have already said. As they address their peers in the new group, they may express themselves differently compared to what they said in their bids. Over the next 24 hours, they will have several chances to practice describing what they care about and want to take on together in coming months. We think this is useful, since one of the key skills for people who want to influence is the ability to speak engagingly about issues that matter to them.

Thus, next morning, after an opening discussion of the challenges faced by "hybrid creatures," people are invited to return once more to exploring their common interests. This time, anyone who wants to can stand up, walk to a spot in the room and declare a topic they care about and would like to take on as a member of this group. Next, we urge anyone else who feels a connection to that topic or who wants to offer another one, to stand up and add their voice. More than once, Patricia invites people to give examples of relevant experiences. After three individuals are already standing, she explains why this matters:

> What we're looking for is exactly what three of you have already done: you put the high-level topic very articulately and at the same time you give a clear picture—which is often omitted—of the concrete experience that this relates to. If we can get that mixture over time that's the best kind of material to do stuff with.
>
> Patricia Shaw

Below are two examples of how people describe a personal experience before going on to suggest what needs to change:

> I had a patient in the supportive care needs survey who filled out the questionnaire, then wrote to me and then rang me to talk about her supportive care needs that she felt hadn't been met. She had been going round the houses [futile or inefficient action] speaking to different people who she perceived to not be helping her. She was obviously in a black hole and the clinicians around her seemed unaware or unwilling to help her.
>
> Research Fellow, based in a UK university

The insight that this group member draws from this experience is that nurses, at the end of treatment, should be able to conduct a systematic assessment of patients' supportive care needs. And nurses should also be skilled up to provide patients who are suffering fatigue with active lifestyle management (not just supplying patients with information). Another member of the group tells another story:

> In our original study we skilled up a nurse and she blooming well got run over! And then we were really stuck. She had a broken leg doing consultations because we had nobody else with the skill sets. And really what we know is you have to skill up a team and everybody has to take responsibility for changing the system. It taught me a lot about how to look at designing systems.
>
> Professor of Cancer Nursing Practice

FIGURE 9.3

The individual uses this example to stress the importance of working out how to maintain supportive care skills. It's not just skilling up one individual (which is what tends to happen), she says, but skilling up a team, making sure that everybody takes responsibility—or as she puts it, "designing systems for sustainability."

Eventually, every member of the group is standing, having indicated what matters to them and whose interests feel close to their own. As people literally stand up for their interests in this way, a kind of "map of connections" emerges in the room over the next 45 minutes.

From here, people are invited to move into clearer groupings of threes and fours, and to continue exploring an issue that connects them, this time using large sheets of paper. After about 20 minutes, three distinctive areas of interest emerge:

➤ shifting the context from illness to wellness after treatment,
➤ developing assessment skills for follow-up care among Clinical Nurse Specialists,
➤ making interventions sustainable/understanding barriers and systems.
Patricia Shaw adds:

> This process of taking up positions in relation to each other in the room was another step in creating a working community. It is not easy for people to show the affiliations, disquiets, differences they may be experiencing amongst themselves. As facilitator I was trying to find ways to begin this process: questions such as "shall I start?", "shall I go next?", and "shall I wait for x or y to declare themselves first" all acquire a sudden life and urgency and everyone learns a little more about themselves, each other and the relationships which are forming. It was noticeable how people tended to cluster close together, a bit reluctant to open up spaces between them. One person who found herself "in the middle" rapidly moved back out from this "exposed" position.

This process of taking up positions in relation to each other in the room was another step in creating a working community. It is not easy for people to show the affiliations, disquiets, differences they may be experiencing amongst themselves. As facilitator I was trying to find ways to begin this process: questions such as "shall I start?", "shall I go next?", and "shall I wait for x or y to declare themselves first" all acquire a sudden life and urgency and everyone learns a little more about themselves, each other and the relationships which are forming.

Later, we go through yet another iteration of the same process (of members exploring what they want to do together—what a joint program of work might look like). So far during this meeting, people have been addressing each other—the members of the new group. Now, Jane Maher spontaneously and unexpectedly urges everybody to try speaking to a different audience—a future potential funder. She invites them to talk about a project or idea they would like to bring to the group, addressing their words this time to an imaginary "Mr Moneybags":

> Let's pretend we're making a story up about a program of work that we're doing. I am Mr Moneybags or Mr Very Important Person and everybody has been invited to describe the work that they're doing and how it fits together into a kind of program—or not.
>
> Jane Maher

Again, people are "iterating," not just repeating themselves. With each round of conversation, the emphasis shifts as they further develop the way they are talking about what the group might do in coming months. They are constantly finding new ways of expressing what matters to them, and through this process we start to get a glimpse of the ingredients that might go into a program of work as the year progresses.

Story 3: Making the invisible visible

> in which a narrative account gives shape to the group's first steps together.

In our experience, written narrative accounts help to track a community's evolution and influence over time. This can enable interested parties to understand the work of the group and, perhaps most importantly, it can help to satisfy funders/sponsors that money is being well spent. It can also stimulate people to reflect on and learn from what has happened. And finally, it provides a shared story of the group that can be re-consulted and re-used as much or as little as people want.

> Written narrative accounts help to track a community's evolution and influence over time.

As narrative writer, I (Alison Donaldson) take an active part in the meetings and email exchanges, recording people's words and stories by taking notes and/or audio-recording. In other words, I do not just observe silently.

In this case, my official involvement begins when I am invited to sit in on the day of bid presentations in September 2009, where candidates talk about why they want to join the new group and what they would contribute.

I listen, noting phrases that particularly strike or move me. Later, when we are formulating the introductory email to the group (*see* Story 1), I use a few of the striking phrases to add colour to Jane's descriptions of individual group members. For example, one said "At the moment the whole nursing agenda is around chemotherapy . . . I want people to know what is available so they don't get on their knees before they get support." I find these spoken words honest and moving, refreshingly free of medical jargon. I imagine that somebody might use less-engaging language if they were asked to write down their own thoughts.

My first real challenge as writer, however, comes when I sit down to capture the first community meeting in writing. At the meeting itself, after several hours of listening, everything seemed frustratingly complicated and amorphous to me. And now, four weeks later (Christmas holidays have intervened), the memory has faded. I start by re-reading my handwritten notes from the meeting, immersing myself in the detail. This makes it possible for me to sketch out a contents page and, as I do so, a story starts to take shape. Next, as I begin describing in detail what happened, I feel a need to re-listen to parts of the meeting, which I audio-recorded. I transcribe some passages in full and my draft grows into a lengthy collection of raw material. When Patricia and I meet up a few days later, we take time to go through the material, reflecting on how we might use it, e.g. to stimulate further conversations at a future community meeting. For example, the discussion about the nature of influence (fully transcribed) may provide a useful starting point for further exploration of this topic at a future date.

We also explore the form of the narrative writing in some detail. For example, does it work best to leave people's comments (e.g. on the challenges they face) in chronological order (as spoken), or is it better to reorganize them under theme headings? The latter version is more common in business writing—the headings do part of the work for the reader. The "unstructured" version leaves readers to notice what themes and connections emerge in their minds as they read. I notice that my initial tendency is to create headings, because I imagine the reader getting impatient reading a lengthy, unedited transcript. However, on this occasion I choose to maintain the chronological order, without introducing any subheadings, because our intention with the narrative account is to stimulate group members into reflecting on experience. By playing their own comments back to them, without imposing my own structure, I hope to give them a chance to judge the meaning for themselves. At the end of the chronological account, I simply offer one possible way of summarizing people's comments (*see* box).

Challenges faced by "hybrid creatures"
A number of possible themes seem to emerge, e.g.
- managing time and coping with the reality of the NHS
- getting connected/being known
- finding good mentors/senior allies
- developing/maintaining relationships with clinicians
- finding appropriate research methodologies
- getting what you want can be scary.
(From the first draft narrative account about the group)

Next, I send the draft narrative account to the supporting team, which is meeting in a few days to reflect on what has been happening and to plan the next community meeting. In my covering email, I insert a "health warning" by explaining that the account should be viewed as "raw material" that can later be reworked and adapted for other purposes.

Despite my warning, I discover (when the supporting team meets) that my revised, still lengthy draft has left at least one individual bewildered. My "health warning" about the unfinished nature of the writing has not been taken up quite in the way I expected. This experience reminds me that no amount of precise instructions to readers can determine how they will respond—nothing can shortcut the important process of learning from others' responses to a draft. I go home and revise the account again, this time including some orienting material near the beginning, e.g. a proposed "direction of travel" for the group in its first year—which has emerged from today's conversation among the supporting team, who think it will reassure group members.

The draft that eventually goes to the whole group has come a long way. It still has no executive summary—a conscious choice, as we want to use the writing to stimulate further thinking, and the time for executive summaries and peer-reviewed articles will come later. There is, however, a new Foreword to guide readers—my second attempt at a health warning!

> Much of what you see in this paper is "raw material." It aims to make visible some of the early events and conversations in the life of the new community of influence. It is not designed as a summary nor is it meant for publication in its current form.
>
> There are different ways of reading documents. When reading this one, I would like to invite you as group members to notice what strikes you, what seems important to you, what you find yourself reflecting on, what you want to take up in future conversations.

Finally, the draft now also has an Afterword containing some provocative questions, which have arisen during a spontaneous phone call between me and Jane Maher.

For example:

> If one way of making yourself more visible is to "be useful" to others,
> is there a risk of becoming taken for granted? Could you become a
> useful colleague rather than "top-table material" [a leader]?

The draft narrative account now goes to the whole group with a covering email,
including the following words:

> Dear all,
>
>   I am attaching a draft narrative account of the group's early life
> ("episode one"). I'd like to give you some context and suggestions
> for how to read it.
>   First, it is quite long (28 pages plus appendices), as I wanted to
> get down the story of the group's formation and include enough
> detail and verbatim material to help you recall the first meeting
> and what emerged from it. For those unable to be there, it should
> give you a flavour of the conversations.
>   Patricia and I have given it a lot of thought and we came to the
> conclusion that you would all be very good judges of what is sig-
> nificant in the account, which bits interest you, what themes and
> insights arise as you read, and what you would like to take up in our
> live discussions in February. So, it is not meant to be a streamlined
> account or executive summary of "objectives" and "outcomes."
>   We see the writing process as iterative. So the account will
> evolve and change as time goes by and I get a chance to weave
> in your responses. The writing is meant as much to stimulate
> sensemaking as to establish a visible record of the group's life and
> achievements . . .
>
> Best wishes,
Alison

The only response to this email is one of those automated "Out of Office" replies!
Meanwhile, having sent off the draft narrative, I now have time to start writing
the present chapter, a task made much easier by having the "raw material" at my
finger tips. (We are light-heartedly referring to this raw material as a "kitchen
sink document" as it contains "everything but the kitchen sink.") I am therefore
quickly in a position to send round a first draft of the present chapter. This time
we do receive some interesting email responses. First, the mention of giving
documents a "social life" seems to have stimulated some members into thinking
about where the group might publish to make it more visible; and second, one
particular individual sends me the following comment on the chapter: "For me,
it definitely captured the flavour and unfolding of the community so far and it
also drew me back in to feeling part of a group."

Next, I also send the draft chapter to two guests whom we have invited to join the second community meeting. When the day of the meeting arrives, one of these guests confesses that, as described in the chapter, the group seemed rather "intimidating." A week later, Jane Maher and I bump into this individual again and she remarks that the group she met seemed much less "intimidating" than the one in the chapter. They seemed uncertain, she adds, about what they wanted to focus on. This encounter serves as a helpful reminder that there is never just one narrative about any group or event.

Reflecting back on the whole process of drafting the first narrative account, including people's comments along the way, I am reminded how writing enables us to "give form" to conversations and processes that may otherwise feel amorphous or ephemeral. It may be harder for critics to say it was all "just talk" when they see a crafted, detailed written account. Yet a narrative account is always just one possible story about what has happened. As the writer, I hope that the group described in it will recognize something of itself and that the account will help to make it more visible, as well as stimulating thinking about its future direction.

For those interested, below are some of the writing methods that have emerged for us over the years when working with communities of influence:

➤ creating both an evolving group story and some individual written portraits of selected community members; this provides two complementary ways of making the life of the group more visible

➤ trying to reflect complex causality in the writing; this involves: avoiding oversimplified "a led to b" accounts, always striving to describe what happened, rather than giving an idealized picture, and including different perspectives where appropriate

➤ keeping an eye and an ear open for "serious anecdotes," specific experiences, and stories, as these stimulate a particular quality of reflection; real examples are also helpful in "evaluating" the work of a community

➤ writing "iteratively," using successive drafts to stimulate further reflection and sensemaking, so that the account that emerges is to some degree inter-subjective, even though my voice as author may prevail

➤ looking for ways of giving the writing a "social life"—using it to stimulate further reflection and action, making sure it does not disappear into a "black hole" like so many reports.

Some of these insights have been enriched by studying relevant literature, e.g. in fields such as historiography, ethnography, storytelling in organizations, complexity and emergence.

Jane Maher adds:

> I am confident that this community is beginning to become more visible and influential. I am also keen for the group to make some short video clips. For example, a researcher might show some

statistics, describe a problem and give a patient example. I have seen the effect this can have on the people whom we need to influence—a short video often allows people to "get it" instantly, where words and writing have failed. Nevertheless, writing plays an important part because it provides a way of securing what is otherwise ephemeral.

OUTCOMES SO FAR

At time of writing, the community has met just twice, so it is rather early to give a definitive list of "outcomes." Nevertheless, we feel confident from our experience of working with other communities of influence that this one will make a difference. Indeed, by forming a group that meets and communicates regularly, much has already been achieved—as one group member put it, "nobody has ever asked us to get together before." And we know from our experience with the Macmillan GP community that a collective voice tends to be more influential than just one practitioner pressing for improvements in her local area. In the case of the group described in this chapter, some early progress is evident, as we shall see next.

A pool of knowledge and resources

As mentioned earlier, at the group's first meeting people were encouraged to make a start with identifying resources they could share with one another. After the first meeting, the list already included:

➤ 6 literature reviews on various aspects of cancer survivorship (e.g. interventions related to fatigue, self-management in prostate cancer, female sexual problems)
➤ 8 research papers that could be revived to influence practice (e.g. on quality of life in patients with skin reactions to radiation, quality-of-life priorities in patients with bowel cancer)

FIGURE 9.4

➤ 9 grant applications that could be resurrected (e.g. randomized controlled trials on nurse-led service delivery, and on different exercise regimes for postoperative breast cancer patients)

➤ 21 examples of knowledge or skills (e.g. related to risk stratification, exercise for cancer patients, rehabilitation services, psychosexual therapy, and cognitive behavioral therapy). These could be the seeds of new services for patients.

Preliminary statement of the group's goals

In the first narrative paper we decided to include a section near the front called "proposed direction of travel for the group," as we felt that a preliminary statement of the group's purpose, even if it would be modified over time, might ease people's anxiety at this early, uncertain stage. Table 9.2 shows the text as it appeared.

TABLE 9.2 Proposed "direction of travel" for the group

Main intentions:

• Develop the capacity of its members to influence research, service development and education

• Help ensure that the shared vision (see box below) of the Department of Health and Macmillan Cancer Support is taken forward

• Demonstrate the benefits of working as a "community of influence."

Aspirations for the first year:

• Make the group more visible and influential, in order to make the issue more visible (how to care for those living with consequences of cancer treatment), e.g.

    — Identify, tell, retell stories/experiences that move and influence;

    — Become expert at presenting your "gems" (e.g. projects, products, stories) to influence practice and policy;

    — Publish (e.g. good papers that proved hard to publish in the past);

    — Demonstrate changes in practice, including examples of collaboration across primary and secondary care;

    — Use video clips to convey a patient problem, evidence for it, research under way, how that research should be translated/implemented, and the challenges involved in doing so.

• Identify skills and services that you can market or get commissioned

• Secure funding for and start relevant projects

• Spread knowledge/skills

• Show evidence of collaboration

• Secure promotion/new roles where appropriate

• Achieve new qualifications where appropriate.

A vision for cancer survivors

Our vision is that consequences of cancer treatment are acknowledged and therefore described, measured, coded, enumerated and reported routinely by the NHS. Preventable consequences are avoided through universal access to the safest and most effective treatments for cancer. Where adverse consequences cannot be prevented, effective and accessible services are available for all patients in order to reduce functional impairment and to alleviate distress, whether physical or psychological. The nature and content of the services provided is matched to need using stratified assessment tools. There is a continuing research and development program to improve our understanding of the consequences of cancer and its treatment, and this research program is seamlessly integrated into mainstream research into the treatment of cancer.

From the National Cancer Survivorship Initiative Vision
published jointly by the UK Department of Health and
Macmillan Cancer Support in January 2010

Opportunities emerging from conversations

Email exchanges among members between the first and second meeting highlighted a range of opportunities that could be followed up. A few examples give a flavour:

➤ *Rehabilitation pathways.* The UK's National Cancer Action Team launched these pathways in January 2010, and one group member prompted a discussion about them, suggesting that the group pursue this further

➤ *Health and well-being clinics.* Stimulated by this email exchange on rehabilitation, one member mentioned that she and her colleagues were bidding to provide a Macmillan-funded health and well-being clinic. This prompted another member to say that she and her colleagues had just secured funding to run such a clinic for gynecological patients. These two emails sparked a debate about the merits of different forms of follow-up, e.g. hospital-based, community-based, and telephone.

➤ *Sexual problems.* Two members shared views with the group on managing patients' sexual problems after treatment, sparking useful debate about the pros and cons of guidelines, and about the ability of clinicians to talk to male and female patients.

➤ *Hybrid careers.* Two members reported increased interest from their universities in sustaining the "hybrid creature." This may help towards one of the goals suggested to the group: that at least half the group secures both nurse consultant and senior lecturer posts within three years.

Meanwhile, informal phone calls brought to light further stories of collaboration and influencing activity. For example, after the second community meeting, two members worked together to revamp a proposal for a trial of telephone follow-up for women finishing treatment for ovarian cancer. One, a professor of cancer nursing, had failed with this so many times that she had become disheartened. The other, a nurse consultant who was able to contribute a clinical perspective, responded with enthusiasm. A subsequent teleconference between their two teams enabled them to use unpublished research to strengthen the bid document. They also modified the language to emphasize the practical relevance of the trial in terms of "service development." Meanwhile, the nurse consultant got the professor invited to speak at a key meeting in Glasgow. This was at the other end of the country, so it took some encouragement for her to go, but afterwards she was delighted she had gone, as several people came to speak to her after her talk. As a result, she was able to include three extra collaborators in the new bid, which also came to involve six centers instead of three. Both women were optimistic about its prospects.

Moving towards a collective sense of purpose

At the second community meeting, in February 2010, there was a distinct shift towards the group finding its own words to articulate its purpose. From our experience with such groups, we know that they tend to develop new ways of speaking that become useful for the purpose of influencing. This "common language" cannot be created by individuals on their own. Only a community can develop a language.

Despite the pleasure of seeing each other again, people also expressed a degree of frustration at this second meeting. One put it like this:

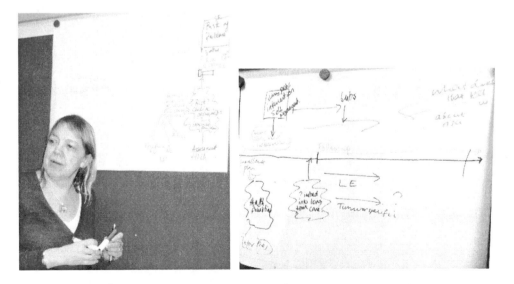

FIGURES 9.5 AND 9.6

I feel we are stepping into the Tardis [the "time and relative dimensions
in space machine" from the TV series, Dr Who]. We are trying to get
a feel for where we are going. We could do almost anything.
Professor of Cancer Nursing, group member

Some way into the conversation, however, something of a breakthrough
occurred. The group agreed to sketch out a map of the cancer patient's journey,
from diagnosis right through to possible consequences of treatment several
years down the line, using large sheets of paper fixed on the wall.

The drawing (*see* photos on p. 170) helped us all get a much clearer sense of
where the work of individual group members was located in relation to different stages in the patient's experience. In particular, it became apparent that the
group's research interests were clustered around the time of treatment, with few
of them looking at the period some years later when negative consequences of
that treatment may first come to light for patients.

In a post-meeting email exchange, several members pointed to this sketch as
having been helpful. For example, one wrote:

I am most excited about how from the process map we were able
to see where best to place ourselves and how there is a huge gap in
the market that is just waiting to be filled by us . . .
Nurse Consultant

Towards the end of the meeting, after people had done further sketches and
explored ways of articulating a collective purpose, four members agreed to draft
a one-page "introduction" to the group. A couple of weeks later, they circulated
their first attempt. There is not enough space to include the whole text here, but
to give a flavor, below is the first paragraph, summarizing the purpose of the
group in members' own words:

To improve the experience, outcomes and care of people who are living with
the consequences of cancer treatment, by:
1   conducting meaningful and rigorous research
2   developing sustainable services/systems of care
3   raising awareness and delivering education
4   influencing policy and strategy
5   changing the culture of care.

At the second meeting, the group also began to explore what it might call itself.
A few weeks later, a vote among members pointed to "Consequences of Cancer
Treatment Collaborative group" as the preferred name, with the short form
"CCaT" (we suggested using the short form with care, given the sea of acronyms
health professionals often find themselves swimming in.) It is worth noting that
settling on a name only became possible after people had met twice and had an
opportunity to explore aims and activities in their own words.

EPILOGUE: GETTING READY FOR FURTHER COLLABORATION

As this account draws to a close, the third community gathering is approaching, and a number of between-meeting activities have come to our attention.

For example, towards the end of the second gathering, members agreed to pair up and write short profiles of one another in the coming weeks. We urged them to "talk up" the skills, knowledge and achievements of the other person, since this is something that many find hard to do when writing about themselves. Many chose to pair up with somebody they didn't yet know well. Thus, as well as generating profiles, this exercise is creating new pairings within the group that may facilitate future collaboration and influence.

Another example is the phone conversations we (Alison and Patricia) have had with each member to gauge their feelings about the group and their wishes and concerns about the future. (We sometimes refer to these informal connections and calls between meetings as "weaving"—it is a vital part of cultivating communities of practice.) This group has seemed unusually cohesive from the start, yet we have learned from these informal conversations that the usual hard-to-talk-about feelings are present, at least for some. For example, one person gently raised the question "who owns the work?"—she wondered if this might be a worry for those pursuing academic careers. Her own view, however, was "as long as it gets to a patient, it doesn't matter who owns it." Another expressed her concerns about how we were going to use the recordings of the meetings and the narrative accounts. She had missed the first community gathering, where we had spoken about these methods, so the phone call provided an opportunity to explain our way of working to her more fully.

The calls have also drawn our attention to influencing activities going on between meetings. For example, one member related how she had offered to speak about her research to a group linked to UK charity *Beating Bowel Cancer*, stressing that she might not have made this offer if she hadn't been part of the consequences of treatment group.

Finally, we were able to use the calls to encourage and accelerate collaborative activities. For example, there had been some email exchanges about whether the group might approach the editor of a relevant new publication, the Journal of Cancer Survivorship, but this suggestion seemed at risk of remaining "just a good idea," so in one of our informal calls we encouraged a member of the group to take the lead on it. She swiftly took up this suggestion, and in no time a teleconference was set up for members interested in getting the group a place on the editorial board. As a result, instead of one individual singly approaching the editor, five members of the group agreed to offer their services collectively to the journal, and the email sent to the editor received a positive response.

In this chapter, we have told the story—just one possible account—of the early months of a new community of influence. With other groups, it might be more customary to wait until two or three years have passed and then write a report of their work, with conclusions and recommendations. We hope, nevertheless, that this story proves useful to anyone who is wondering how they might create and sustain a similar group with a view to influencing an important issue, whether in the health sector or elsewhere. It is during the early stages of such a community's life that there is the greatest opportunity to build trust, develop a collective sense of purpose and identity, and demonstrate some early achievements.

NOTES

1 *See* www.ncsi.org.uk (accessed November 11, 2010): The NCSI aims to "improve the ongoing services and support for those living with, and beyond, cancer—currently two million across the UK. This number is likely to grow by over 3% per annum, reflecting the increasing incidence of cancer and better survival rates. The aim of the NCSI is, by 2012, to have taken the necessary steps to ensure that survivors get the care and support they need to lead as healthy and active a life as possible, for as long as possible. The initiative is a partnership between the Department of Health and Macmillan Cancer Support and is co-chaired by the National Cancer Director, Professor Mike Richards, and the Chief Executive of Macmillan, Ciaran Devane.

2 Based on: Armes J, Crowe, M, Colbourne L, *et al.* Patients' supportive care needs beyond the end of cancer treatment: a prospective, longitudinal survey. *J Clin Oncol.* 2009; **27**: 6172–9.

3 Wenger E. *Communities of Practice: learning, meaning and identity.* Cambridge: Cambridge University Press; 1998.

4 A book on this subject, entitled *Communities of Influence*, by Alison Donaldson, Elizabeth Lank and Jane Maher, is shortly due for publication by Radcliffe Publishing.

5 For example, a seminal article previously published by a member of CCaT was: Armes J, Crowe, M, Colbourne L, *et al.*, op. cit.

6 The selection panel included Jane Maher, Stephen Hindle (Macmillan Survivorship Program Manager), Chris Steele (Workstream Support—Late Consequences of Treatment), Donal Gallaher (Macmillan Development Manager) and Jacqui Graves (Macmillan Clinical Program Manager).

Commentary:
Macmillan Cancer Trust

The story of the Macmillan Consequences of Cancer Treatment Collaborative Group shows the "micro moments" of a team forming and, through conversation, developing a collective identity and common purpose. While our other case studies don't describe the communication processes in this depth of detail, we can be certain that such dynamics (inclusion/exclusion, emerging and evolving understandings of purpose and direction, etc.) were taking place in every moment of every story; it's happening all the time in human interaction. We just don't usually notice it. We tend to get so absorbed in the content of the work that we don't attend to the process. Yet we can see in this story how exquisite mindfulness of the conversational process and very small interventions can make a big difference.

For example, the conveners explicitly attended to diversity and responsiveness in order to foster creativity and innovation. As they assembled the group, they were thoughtful about the diverse perspectives that would be needed to seed the emergence of novel patterns (creativity). And they actively encouraged the group members to bring that diversity forward (i.e. to be authentically present). For example, at the very outset (in Story 1) they invited members to share self-introductions. Later, in Story 2, we see them invite people to spontaneously propose discussion topics, rather than specifying the topics themselves. Not only does this invite expression of diversity, but it also is a gesture of partnership, sharing control of the discussion agenda with the entire group—a clear example of a relationship-centered meeting practice (*see* Appendix 2).

To enhance responsiveness, the conveners share observations back to the group about its process and offer empathic reflections about discomfort that the group members might be experiencing (Story 2). They also use sequential rounds of narrative writing to foster reflection on both the themes and the process of the group's conversation (Story 3). Curiously, this chapter itself was a part of that process! This technique of narrative writing is an interesting variation on the method of "reflective time outs" described in Appendix 2.

The conveners used various methods to provoke small disturbances in how people were thinking (patterns of meaning) that subsequently grew into transformational changes. For instance, they offered a variety of images as visual metaphors for the group members and their work. One of these pictures, of a minotaur, helped introduce and reinforce the theme of "hybrid creature." The clinician researchers recognized themselves in this image, and gained a new way to make new sense of their previously enigmatic and under-appreciated position. It offered them a valuable new identity as boundary spanners, laying out an effective new direction that they were uniquely qualified to undertake. Hence we see a small disturbance in a conversation—a new phrase—amplify and spread, resulting in a transformative new way of thinking about roles.

There was more going on here than people just meeting each other. Most of these people already knew each other, but they were not taking any sort of action. Over the course of the story, we see the group develop a sense of coherence—shared purpose, an understanding of how to work together, even a shared vocabulary—that allowed them to truly become a community of influence. And by the end of the chapter, after three months of elapsed time, they began to take effective action. The conveners skillfully stewarded the entire process by fostering dialogue, and being attentive and responsive to what was emerging. And so we have witnessed the ephemeral change in the organizational conversation that is the heart and precursor of every kind of organizational change.

CHAPTER 10

Using the Positive Deviance approach to reduce hospital-acquired infections at the Veterans Administration Healthcare System in Pittsburgh[1]

Arvind Singhal and Karen Greiner[2]

SYNOPSIS

On the evening of May 16, 2006, Tanis Smith walked into the recreational room of the HJ Heinz III long-term care facility of VAPHS (Veterans Administration Pittsburgh Healthcare System[3]), mingling easily with the 34 male veterans who had gathered for the scheduled Bingo game. As she deftly handed out the Bingo cards, Tanis understood, from her previous 23-years of work experience in nursing homes, how much these recovering war-scarred patients looked forward to getting together in such recreational evenings.

As the churning Bingo balls rhythmically spun up to the surface, Tanis scooped them up, announced the number, and lighted the called digit on the electronic screen behind her. As the evening unfolded, we could hear Tanis' melodious number-calling, followed by several loud exclamations of "Bingo!"

After the game was over, Tanis' booming voice came over the microphone: "Prior to you getting your snack, I will come to you and squirt some foam on your hands. It is foam, not shaving cream. It is foam, not whipping cream. Rub your hands with the foam or the little critters in your hands, which you cannot even see, will nibble at you."

Then with a flourish, Tanis walked down the aisle, squirting antibacterial foam into the patients' open palms, repeating, "Get your zap and get your snack." Almost all the present veterans accepted Tanis' squirt, rubbing their palms together to do away with any lurking critters (germs, in common parlance).

Tanis Smith's easy going, friendly, and rapport-building approach with the veterans, and her playful routine to zap their hands with alcohol foam, signified an important process unfolding at the VA healthcare facility in Pittsburgh (VAPHS) to combat and neutralize "critters." And hospital staff members like Tanis Smith, as well as her cohort of Bingo patients, represent soldiers in this battle.

What follows is the story of VAPHS' quest to combat methicillin-resistant *Staphylococcus aureus* (MRSA), a dangerous and devious bacterial infection. Interestingly, the story is not one of commanding doctors and powerful medicines but one of conversations, dialogue, self-discovery and, above all, coordination and collaboration among individuals who ordinarily would not have talked, and among silo-like hospital units whose unstated mission is to preserve their boundaries, identities, and expertise. A true cultural transformation occurred at the VAPHS, supported by a leadership that placed faith in its people, and the hundreds of small solutions they implemented to combat MRSA.

> A true cultural transformation occurred at the VAPHS, supported by a leadership that placed faith in its people, and the hundreds of small solutions they implemented to combat MRSA.

MRSA: A DANGEROUS BACTERIUM AND A COMPLEX PROBLEM

"Just how dangerous are these MRSA bacteria?" we queried our escort Dr Jon Lloyd,[4] a retired general and vascular surgeon, and from mid-2004 to 2007, Coordinator, MRSA Prevention for VAPHS and Southwestern Pennsylvania.[5] Besides its Highland Drive campus, the VAPHS has two other major facilities in Pittsburgh—University Drive, an acute-care facility with 146 beds, which carries out both cardiac surgery and transplants, and the Heinz long-term care facility with 256 operational beds.[6]

To answer our question, Jon launched into a riveting story about MRSA Coordinator Heidi Walker's[7] self-conceived macaroni MRSA routine at the VAPHS' Heinz healthcare facility. Heidi purchased a large bag of uncooked macaroni and had the neighbor kids count the number of individual pieces it contained. Estimating that 21 bags would contain about 100 000 pieces, she purchased that many bags and loaded them on to a gurney along with a hand foam dispenser, gloves, gowns, and nasal swabs. Gathering a curious audience of patients, nurses, doctors, and other staff persons, Heidi would first provide basic information about MRSA and other hospital-acquired infections (HAIs), and then crack open a bag, scoop up a handful of macaroni, and drop the uncooked pieces into an empty plastic bowl one-by-one. While so doing, she told the group that each piece represented a human life lost as a result of HAIs. As the pieces clattered in to the bowl, Heidi would point to the 21 macaroni bags on the gurney, emphasizing that they contained a total of 100 000 pieces—the total number of lives lost each year to HAIs in US hospitals.

"What impact did Heidi's demonstration have on the participants?" we asked.

"It had a strong emotional effect," noted Jon. Heidi took an abstract, invisible issue and made it both concrete and observable by humanizing the needless deaths.

Over a six-year period in the United States, from 1999 through 2005, estimated MRSA-related hospitalizations more than doubled, from 127 036 to 278 203.[8] Jon explained that in contrast to the US certain northern European countries— notably Netherlands, Norway, and Denmark—have tamed MRSA. For instance, he said, "in Denmark, MRSA infections peaked in the mid-1960s—accounting for about 35 percent of infections, and have dropped precipitously to account for only 1–2 percent of *Staph aureus* infections over the past three decades. This means that a Danish patient with a *Staph aureus* infection can be treated with an old-fashioned beta-lactam antibiotic with faster response, higher cure rate, and quicker hospital discharge at lower overall cost to society."

Over three decades ago, when MRSA was recognized as a problem in these northern European countries, they embarked on a search and destroy mission. The government mandated complete surveillance, meaning that every patient was swabbed for MRSA both at the time of hospital admission and discharge. Those who had MRSA were isolated, decolonized, and treated. The MRSA loads in the environment decreased to very low manageable levels.

"Why is active MRSA surveillance not mandated in the US?" we asked.

The response was complex: If active MRSA surveillance is mandated, hospital costs will spike up dramatically, at least in the short run. More swabbing for MRSA means more lab work, more identified cases of MRSA, more isolation rooms, more supplies (e.g. disposable gowns, gloves, and the like), and heavy investments in information systems that can track patients' MRSA status from admission to discharge. In the day of highly managed healthcare and spiraling medical costs, MRSA is low on the radar of most hospitals. It is simply considered as a cost of providing healthcare. At best, routine swabbing for MRSA is reserved for patients in ICUs and surgical units, where the risk of infection runs high.

In the day of highly managed healthcare and spiraling medical costs, MRSA is low on the radar of most hospitals. It is simply considered as a cost of providing healthcare.

In essence, MRSA represents a formidable foe that has, over time, gained a stronghold in US hospitals. In Jon's words, "We are wading upstream in an ever-widening and deepening MRSA river." The VAPHS is trying to turn the tide of this rising water.

Understated in the US media and public policy discourses, hospital-acquired infections kill as many Americans each year as do AIDS, breast cancer, and auto accidents combined.[9] However, as noted previously, most Americans are likely to be clueless about MRSA.

At 95 percent of US hospitals, when patients are admitted they are not swabbed for MRSA. Some 75 percent of people who are colonized (who carry MRSA) do not know it. Of those colonized, approximately 30 percent will develop a serious MRSA infection. The most vulnerable include those who are older, immunosuppressed, chronically ill, and/or undergoing a surgical procedure.

Unlike the HIV virus, which cannot survive outside the human body for more than a few minutes, MRSA is a "very hearty organism," notes Dr Robert (Bob) Muder, the hospital epidemiologist at the VAPHS. MRSA can survive for up to six weeks on environmental surfaces. Further, MRSA transfers very easily by physical contact with a colonized person's skin, bedding, or personal effects. A simple skin break—even through a needle prick—can cause an MRSA infection among the colonized, leading to life-threatening complications and even death.

Further, to decolonize an MRSA carrier is a rather cumbersome process. A colonized person needs to apply an antimicrobial nasal ointment twice daily under medical supervision and take chlorhexidine showers for five consecutive days. Such decolonization is especially critical for patients who are about to have surgery.

The most common treatment for an MRSA infection is an antibiotic called vancomycin, usually given to a patient through a central intravenous line over a three to four week time period. During this time the patient needs to be quarantined—put in an isolation room. Attending hospital staff need to don new pairs of gloves and gowns each time they enter the patient's room. Also, very strict hand-washing is essential.

MRSA takes not just a "heavy physical toll" on its patients, it also takes "a psychological and economic toll of both the patient and their family members," Dr Muder emphasized. "Nobody wants longer hospital stays; neither the patients, nor the family members, nor the nurses, doctors, or healthcare administrators." An MRSA infection can cost a hospital tens of thousands of dollars (averaging $35 000) in patient care costs.

"Why is MRSA such a big problem in the United States?" we ask Dr John Jernigan,[10] an infectious disease specialist at the US government's Centers for Disease Control (CDC) with expertise in the epidemiology of HAIs, including MRSA. Based at the nation's premier public health agency, and recognized widely for his work on HAIs and pathogen-based bio-terrorism, Jernigan is one of CDC's most strident advocates for MRSA prevention and control.

John considered our question and then answered that the roots of the MRSA problem in the US were technical, social, and cultural.

Doctors tend to over-prescribe antibiotics—even when they are not required: for instance, in combating viral infections. Further, patients often do not finish their course of prescribed antibiotics, increasing resistant bacterial strains.

In addition, hand hygiene is poorly observed in most hospitals. As per CDC guidelines, doctors, nurses, and other staff should wash their hands both before and after attending to a patient, preferably in view of the patients. However, most of them only wash their hands after attending to a patient. The hierarchical culture within US hospitals also makes it difficult for patients and less-credentialed staff members to remind doctors and surgeons to follow hand hygiene precautions.

> The hierarchical culture within US hospitals also makes it difficult for patients and less-credentialed staff members to remind doctors and surgeons to follow hand hygiene precautions.

COLLECTIVE MINDFULNESS: CHANGE FROM WITHIN[11]

"So what can one do to control and eliminate MRSA?"

Jon Lloyd replies, "The environment does not clean itself. MRSA will not tackle itself. But it is not hopeless. The power to change lies with the people."

As we reflect on Jon's words, it dawns on us that at Heinz, VA's long-term healthcare facility in Pittsburgh, Tanis Smith is playing precisely such a role to control MRSA. By zapping patients with alcohol-based foam after the game, Tanis' actions reduce the risk of MRSA transmission. Also Nurse Heidi Walker's 100 000 macaroni-piece demonstration—which spurred numerous conversations at the VAPHS—represents another spirited example of a Heinz staff member taking a self-motivated action to prevent and control MRSA. As we spent more time at VAPHS facilities spread across four field visits in 2006, we met with what seemed like an army of soldiers fighting MRSA in the trenches.

What explains this collective mindedness for an MRSA-free environment at VAPHS? How did the VAPHS get involved in preventing MRSA from the inside-out?

Toyota production system

The VAPHS got involved in MRSA prevention and control serendipitously. In 2001, Dr Jernigan began to collaborate with the Pittsburgh Regional Health Initiative (PRHI) on "zero goals," an initiative to reduce hospital-acquired infections and medication errors to zero.[12] Jernigan recalled, "The CDC wanted to pilot an MRSA prevention and control initiative with internal funds from our Antibiotic Resistance Working Group and PRHI, given its regional focus, was a logical partner. However, to meet our fiscal requirements and funding cycle deadlines, we needed an expeditious mechanism to channel funds to PRHI. The Veterans Administration, as a fellow federal agency located in Pittsburgh, seemed like a viable go-between organization." Peter Perreiah, formerly Production System Manager at Alcoa, served as team leader of the MRSA prevention initiative at the VAPHS from 2001 to 2004.

Perreiah, trained in the principles of the Toyota Production System (TPS),[13] put into place similar industrial processes at the VAPHS to reduce errors that jeopardized patient safety. Nurse Practitioner Ellesha McCray joined the TPS team for one-on-one mentoring with Perreiah.

Consistent with the TPS method, McCray and Perreiah gathered baseline data by keenly observing staff–patient encounters in 4 West. They noted, rather quickly, that the general perception among the staff was that "MRSA infections were primarily because of overuse of antibiotics, and not because of what *they* did or did not do." A lot could be done to raise the efficacy of MRSA "countermeasures"—that is, basic prevention precautions such as gowning, gloving, hand-washing, and use of hand disinfectant. Rather than focusing on forcing *individual* compliance, McCray and Perreiah were more eager to unearth *systemic* issues. If nurses weren't wearing gowns or gloves, or were not using the disinfecting alcohol rub, they wanted to know *why*.

One systemic problem they discovered involved management of supplies. The nurses could don gowns or gloves only if they were easily accessible, available on a rack, and the stock was replenished before it ran out. This was not happening, perhaps because accountability was diffused: for instance, it was unclear who was responsible for replenishing gloves.

Ellesha told us, "Our challenge was to develop processes and systems to make it easy for them to adhere to isolation procedures. . . . TPS is about standardization . . . about *Kaizen* [Japanese for "continuous improvement"],which are often small but important changes, like the perceptual shift from hand *washing* to hand *hygiene*. Standardization also meant improving systems to ensure that staff had what they needed to ensure patient safety." (*see* Figure 10.1)

FIGURE 10.1 Needs list.

By mid-2005, internal discussions were raging on VAPHS' executive floor about how to expand the MRSA prevention and control program beyond the two units on University Drive. While some systemic streamlining aspects of TPS (e.g. the organized supply room and equipment room) were implemented hospital-wide by directive from the upper administration, the MRSA "countermeasures" to improve quality of patient outcomes (e.g. through gloving, gowning, hand hygiene, and the like) did not naturally spread to other units. Should the VAPHS management continue with the implementation of TPS to reduce MRSA infection rates unit-by-unit?

VAPHS' Chief of Staff Dr Jain explained, "We made a strategic decision to move away from TPS in order to scale up the fight against MRSA. TPS was not failing, quite the contrary, but it had shortcomings on two important fronts. First, it required additional resources—and we were not in a position to hire another 10 to 12 Peter Perreiahs and Ellesha McCrays for our other units. It was slow and expensive. Second, based on my regular participation in unit briefings, I got the sense that the program had the appearance of being run by the team leaders."

Jon Lloyd added, "TPS has several drawbacks." For instance, it is highly regimented, expert-driven, and teacher-centric. It requires accredited teachers and other dedicated staff, making it extremely resource intensive. These attributes also make it very difficult and expensive for TPS to be replicated and scaled up.[14] Of the 13 units at VAPHS, TPS' impact on MRSA control was mainly felt on the 4 West Surgical Unit at University Drive and to a lesser degree in the SICU. "In light of our TPS experience, I was looking . . . rather searching . . . for other approaches to combat MRSA—approaches that were more people-driven, sustainable, and not as resource intensive." Such approaches do not come easily.

Positive Deviance: communicatively tapping the wisdom that already exists

Just like the first (TPS) stage of MRSA prevention and control at VAPHS, the second stage also began serendipitously. In November, 2004, when Jon Lloyd was browsing the website of the Plexus Institute, he found a link to an electronic copy of an article published in Fast Company magazine.[15] The article—about combating malnutrition in Vietnam—caught his eye.

"The only reason I read the article was because its setting was Vietnam," noted Jon. "In 1970–71, during the Vietnam war I served as a surgeon in the 3rd Field Army Hospital in Saigon. During this time, I fell in love with Vietnam and its people . . . including their hopes, aspirations, and dreams."

"What did this article do for you? How did it speak to combating MRSA?" we asked.

"The article was like a ball of hot fire on my computer screen," Jon noted with enthusiasm. "It was the first time I heard about the Positive Deviance (PD) approach to change. PD advocates local solutions—solutions that are owned by the people, not imposed by experts. Unlike the TPS approach to MRSA which was all about eliminating errors and defects, PD focused on amplifying what was going right."

PD advocates local solutions—solutions that are owned by the people, not imposed by experts. Unlike the TPS approach to MRSA which was all about eliminating errors and defects, PD focused on amplifying what was going right.

Jon was intrigued by the PD mindset and by the facilitative approach advocated by the late Jerry Sternin, a former Peace Corps Director in several countries and founder of the Positive Deviance initiative at Tufts University, and his wife and collaborator, Monique, who oversaw the PD initiative in Vietnam. He shared the article with Dr Jain who was intrigued and supportive.

Positive Deviance (PD) is an approach to social and organizational change that enables communities to discover the wisdom they already have, and then to act on it.[16] PD initially gained recognition in the work of Tufts nutrition professor Marian Zeitlen in the 1980s when she began focusing on why some children in poor communities were better nourished than others.[17] Zeitlin's work used an assets-based approach, identifying what's going right in a community in order to amplify that, as opposed to what's going wrong in a community and fixing it. The community itself must discover the solutions (including the resources) that it already possesses, and find a way to amplify them through peer-based social proof.

The Sternins built on Zeitlin's ideas to organize various PD-centered social-change interventions around the world. They institutionalized PD as a social-change approach by demonstrating how it could be operationalized on a wider scale.

In 1991, the Sternins faced what seemed like an insurmountable challenge in Vietnam. As Director of Save the Children in Vietnam, Jerry was asked by government officials to create an effective, large-scale program to combat child malnutrition and to show results within six months. More than 65 percent of all children living in the Vietnamese villages were malnourished at the time. The Vietnamese government realized that the results achieved by traditional supplemental feeding programs were rarely maintained after the programs ended. The Sternins had to come up with an approach that enabled the community to take control of their nutritional status. And quickly!

Building on Zeitlin's ideas of PD, the Sternins sought poor families that had managed to avoid malnutrition without access to any special resources. These families were the positive deviants. They were "positive" because they were getting good results, and "deviants" because they engaged in behaviors that most others did not. Coached by the Sternins in a process of inquiry, the communities discovered that mothers in the PD families collected tiny shrimps and crabs from paddy fields, and added those plus sweet potato greens to their children's meals. These foods were accessible to everyone, but the community believed they were inappropriate for young children.[18] Also, these PD mothers were feeding their children three to four times a day, rather than the customary twice a day. PD mothers were also more likely to actively feed their children by hand, in contrast to other mothers who just placed the rice bowl in front of their children.

The Sternins helped the community design a program for itself whereby community members could emulate the positive deviants in their midst. Mothers whose children were malnourished were asked to forage for shrimps, crabs, and sweet potato greens, and in the company of other mothers learned to cook new recipes that their children ate right there. Within weeks, mothers could see their children becoming healthier. After the pilot study, which lasted two years, malnutrition had decreased by an amazing 85 percent in the communities where the PD approach was implemented. Over the next several years, the PD intervention became a nationwide program in Vietnam, helping over 2.2 million people, including over 500 000 children improve their nutritional status.[19]

Positive Deviance challenges the traditional role of outside expertise, focusing instead on building the internal capacity to solve the problem. Social and organizational change experts typically take upon themselves the role of discerning the deficits in a community, prioritizing the problems, and implementing solutions. All this work is done from the outside and presumes that communities can't do this for themselves. In the PD approach, the role of experts is to lift up the community's capacity: to find positive deviants, the people in the community who have already identified new solutions, and to coach and mentor internal change agents in disseminating these innovations by presenting social proof to their peers.[20] The consultant works behind the scenes to facilitate a process for identifying and amplifying local wisdom, with the expectation that local solutions (and their benefits) will be more sustainable than solutions introduced from outside.

> Positive Deviance challenges the traditional role of outside expertise, focusing instead on building the internal capacity to solve the problem.

Another hallmark of the PD approach is its emphasis on hands-on learning and actionable behaviors. As Sternin emphasized, "It is easier to act your way into a new way of thinking than to think your way into a new way of acting."[21] So the PD approach turns the well-known KAP (knowledge, attitude, practice) framework on its head. Rather than increasing knowledge to change attitudes which then changes practice, PD focuses on changing practice directly with the idea that new knowledge results from the direct integration of (and subsequent reflection on) concrete action steps.

Evaluations of PD initiatives show that it works because the community owns the problem, as well as its solutions.[22] PD is *not* about experts or top management securing *buy-in* from the various stakeholders or about securing compliance by way of directives, tacit authority, or punitive action. The power of PD is foundationally anchored on people *owning* the change enterprise. Far too many change initiatives fail as they depend upon buying into an expert vision, usually imported from outside (*see* section on Self-Determination Theory in Chapter 3).

That is what grabbed VAPHS' Jon Lloyd as he read the PD article in *Fast Company*. In PD, people are not told what to do—even if that seems to be efficient and the "right" thing to do. Instead, they're supported in figuring things out for themselves. It dawned on him that this might be the problem with the Toyota Production System (TPS) approach that the VAPHS had implemented. It was focused on "telling" people (through designated "teachers") the "right" way to eliminate bottlenecks and errors. While the MRSA reduction outcomes were dramatic for one surgical unit, TPS had required a substantial infusion of human and material capital from the outside. Further, attempts to transplant the lessons learned to other units, even in the same facility, met with tacit resistance and yielded disappointing results.

Jon was intrigued that the Sternins had effectively used the PD approach to address such diverse and intractable problems as preventing childhood anemia, eliminating female genital cutting in Egypt, curbing the trafficking of women in Indonesia, increasing school retention rates in Argentina, reintegrating returned girl-child-soldiers in Northern Uganda, and increasing rates of condom use among commercial sex workers in Viet Nam and Burma.[23] Why not try the Positive Deviance approach for MRSA prevention and control at the Veterans Administration Healthcare System in Pittsburgh?

POSITIVE DEVIANCE COMES TO VAPHS

In March 2005, Jerry Sternin conducted two workshops on the PD process in Pittsburgh. Some 50 representatives from 10 Pittsburgh-area hospitals— all interested in MRSA prevention and control—were invited to attend. The VAPHS' two major facilities (the University Drive acute-care hospital and the Heinz long-term care facility) were well represented. The workshop outlined the "4 Ds" of Positive Deviance.[24]

1 *Define* the problem.
2 *Determine* if there are any individuals/entities already exhibiting the desired behavior/status. (Identify the "Positive Deviants.")
3 *Discover* the uncommon, but demonstrably successful practices/strategies enabling the PDs to find a better solution or outperform their "neighbors" with access to the same resources.
4 *Design* an intervention enabling others in the "community" to begin to practice the PD strategies. (Note: Focus is on *providing opportunities for practice* rather than just sharing information.)

The Sternins stressed that PD is, in some ways, "a leap of faith": one needs to trust that the solution can and will be found *within* rather than having to be imported from without. Once discussion got started and workshop participants began identifying successful behaviors and practices already underway in the hospital, things began to roll. Unlike "best practices" and "benchmarking," which rely on an external source to "identify and introduce a superior template,"[25] the Positive Deviance approach relies entirely on existing talent and solutions. Although many at VAPHS were skeptical that an approach that was effective to combat childhood malnutrition in Vietnam would hold relevance for MRSA control in a US healthcare system, others, including Jon Lloyd, were excited by the notion of amplifying "what works" instead of fixing "what does not work." As Jon noted, "The US healthcare industry has been too focused, for too long, on fixing errors. Too preoccupied with making right what is wrong. Nurses and hospital staff have been bombarded with a litany of top-down expert-driven directives to fix a broken system. In this context, PD's focus on 'what works' was greeted with open arms." Referring to Tanis Smith's foamy zap before the snack in Heinz's Bingo room, Jon emphasized, "The expertise to tackle MRSA was right under our noses. There are hundreds of experts here; the key was recognizing and harnessing their presence."

Inviting participation

In July 2005, Jerry and Monique returned to Pittsburgh to do a follow-up PD workshop and consultation with the staff at VAPHS. After issuing a broad invitation to participate, the Sternins knew that the next step in planning the workshop was out of their hands: participants would have to "self-select"—those with time and energy to dedicate to the fight against MRSA would show their commitment simply by showing up. The invitation yielded a core group of PD champions including two recently-appointed full-time MRSA prevention coordinators—Cheryl Creen at the Heinz facility and Candace Cunningham at University Drive. Cheryl and Candace had both "self-selected" by applying for the open positions. With support from top management, notably VAPHS CEO, Mike Moreland, and Chief of Staff, Rajiv Jain, these internal champions led the PD process from the front.

> Participants would have to "self-select"—those with time and energy to dedicate to the fight against MRSA would show their commitment simply by showing up.

Dozens of "Discovery and Action Dialogs" involving hospital staff from all walks—nurses, doctors, custodians, van drivers, and lab technicians—were conducted over several weeks to solicit all kinds of ideas for preventing and controlling MRSA and to invite further involvement in pilot-testing solutions. Patients, a previously untapped resource, also began participating in earnest.

At first glance, it may seem that a "field of dreams" model was in operation—that if the MRSA cause was broadcast loudly and widely enough, interested individuals would simply emerge, i.e. "they would come." But the logistical reality of working in a hospital dictated that more than a good cause was needed in order for people to "self select" and rally to the cause: leadership was also required. Supervisors had to agree to release staff members from their regular duties to attend meetings, and also to create the space and time for those staff members to report back what they learned.

Some of these meetings went on for hours, sometimes past midnight. They yielded several walls of sticky yellow Post-it Notes capturing diverse, internally generated ideas on controlling MRSA. Out of these dialogues emerged several patient-generated solutions, including recommendations about placing foam dispensers in the recreation room, in the cafeteria, and in the library—locations where a lot of people touch the same bingo cards, the same serving spoon, or the same newspaper, making the risk of MRSA transmission very high.

Many participants, who ordinarily would never be consulted, and whose voices were routinely overlooked, rejected, or silenced came to Jon, Cheryl, and Candace, noting that, "For the first time, we felt that someone cared about our ideas."

Joyce Ewing, a Nurse Manager of the Surgical Intensive Care Unit at the VAPHS explained that it was management's responsibility to create an atmosphere where staff would feel comfortable sharing their ideas and concerns. "The evolution of the PD program has been phenomenal in helping to support a model of what, in nursing, we call 'shared governance.' The clinical practice issues are back in the hands of the frontline workers—where they belong. The traditional management paradigm of 'You need to do this or that' or force-feeding top-down solutions has been replaced with all staff taking responsibility for MRSA prevention and control. And because the staff *own* the solutions they propose, they comply with them." People don't turn their backs on what they've created themselves.

"How does the staff come up with new solutions?" we asked.

"When staff members see that a patient on their unit has converted from MRSA negative to MRSA positive, they put on their Sherlock Holmes hat to deduce how that transmission might have happened. Then they develop an intervention to address the problem" (*see* Fig 10.2).

Joyce Ewing emphasized that while staff ownership of MRSA problems and solutions has been key, the support of the administration at the VHA has also been crucial. "Take Dr Muder, for example. He really comes to bat for nursing. He and Dr Rajiv Jain are open to suggestions and willing to listen. In Pittsburgh, a historically union town, this type of relationship between 'management and labor' is unique."

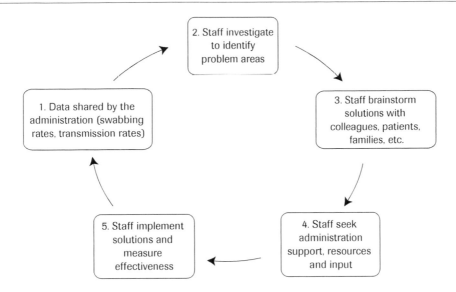

FIGURE 10.2 Data driven problem-solving model.

Expanding the solution space

During our visits to Pittsburgh in 2006, we were introduced to many worthy people—doctors, nurses, patients, housekeeping staff, van drivers, and the like—who had come up with many worthy ideas to prevent, control, and eliminate MRSA.

An aura of pride and accomplishment was palpable in the nursing stations we visited during the weekly Wednesday morning MRSA stock-taking rounds. In at least two units, prominently displayed multi-color charts announced no new MRSA infections during the past few weeks. In one unit, there was one MRSA infection recorded in the past week. The display of this data served as a reminder to staff members that an infection had occurred, and that it was necessary to determine the cause and get back in the "MRSA free" zone. From what we were observing and hearing in our discussions with staff members, it appeared that several hundred brains at VAPHS, previously busy with other routine tasks, were now actively working to expand the solution space to combat MRSA.

> From what we were observing and hearing in our discussions with staff members, it appeared that several hundred brains at VAPHS, previously busy with other routine tasks, were now actively working to expand the solution space to combat MRSA.

Let's engage with some of these people, ideas, and actions for they signify the expanded solution space for MRSA prevention, control, and elimination at the VAPHS.

In fall, 2005, when Cathy Hill,[26] LPN at Heinz's long-term care unit, first heard that the hospital staff were being encouraged to provide suggestions about how to combat MRSA, she was initially hesitant. Usually such directives were imposed from the top, with little or no input from floor nurses. Further, 12 years of nursing experience had taught Cathy that MRSA was a formidable, invisible enemy, lurking on curtains, light switches, bed linen, gowns, counter tops, handrails, and, on the patients' skin and clothing.

"So, Cathy, what did you do to tackle such a sneaky, invisible enemy?" we asked.

Beaming, Cathy responded, "I'm a visual person. I started to think how invisible germs could be made more visible." Someone, somewhere (she doesn't remember who or when), told Cathy about a product that made hand-to-hand transmission visible, perfect for simulating how germs are transmitted. After searching on the Internet, Cathy found Glo Germ, an invisible substance—available as liquid, gel, or powder—that glows when exposed to ultraviolet light.

The Glo Germ arrived at Heinz just in time for Cathy and her accomplices to set the stage for a stealth demonstration. The setting was perfect: In March, 2006, VAPHS had organized a day of MRSA stock-taking and results demonstration, and Cathy smeared Glo Germ powder on the pens that folks used to sign in. Around the corner, out of sight, was an ultraviolet light apparatus, awaiting the unsuspecting participants. As the day wore on, several scores of people were ushered to this apparatus.

Cathy recounts, "People were shocked to see how the Glo Germ had unsuspectingly spread." Under the UV light, the Glo Germ powder glowed on their hands and heads, shirts and skirts, glasses and watches, and on plates and cups. MRSA, hitherto an abstract, invisible idea for most folks at Heinz, was becoming concrete and visible.

One of the most visible signs of the VAPHS' efforts to combat MRSA is the army of alcohol hand-rub dispensers lining its hallways; they are to be found everywhere—in the recreation rooms, dining rooms, ceramic rooms, and even the library. In the Dementia Unit, where such dispensers are a hazard, nurses

FIGURES 10.3A AND 10.3B Precaution signs.

may be seen with hand rub "holsters" on their belts or hand rub "necklaces"— miniature dispensers strung on a yarn and worn around the neck. While hand-rub dispensers, stationary or ambulatory, are highly visible, there are hundreds of MRSA "countermeasures," which according to Dr Jon Lloyd are "hidden from plain view." These anti-MRSA efforts result from empowered staff members and patients, not from an administrative directive from the executive floor or from a CDC guideline.

Kathleen Risa's anti-MRSA trick is "the knuckle." As a long-time nurse and the newly appointed MRSA prevention coordinator for the VA-led national initiative, Kathleen is constantly thinking of how to subvert the transmission of these pathogens. So, as we rode the elevator up, Kathleen pushed the button with a knuckle, not a fingertip (which is likely a more potent vector of MRSA transfer). As we did the math for the MRSA transmission potential of a panel of buttons on one elevator car—used by hundreds of people round-the-clock, we concluded that knuckling a panel might be one way to thwart, or slow down, the transmission cycle. Most interestingly, when we mentioned Kathleen's knuckle-trick to others at VAPHS, numerous other home-grown anti-pathogen strategies surfaced: For instance, the "inside jacket gloving" technique in which the inside of a jacket is used to (un)lock doors of toilet stalls; the "foot flushing" maneuver in which the foot is used to operate toilet flush levers; and the "elbow side-arm swivel" to shut off the water faucet.

Glenn Buzzelli, one of the RNs in the Surgical Intensive Care Units (SICU) spoke about the several newly-initiated anti-MRSA measures in his unit. When his narrative on the "disposable" EKG lead wires drew a blank expression from us, he guessed, rightly, that we were not medical professionals. He continued, "You wouldn't *believe* all the stuff that can get on these EKG lines."

We asked, "So how do you clean them?"

"We don't," he said. "One of the other RNs, Dave Tzakas, hunted like crazy . . . and finally found [an EKG line] that was cheap enough to make it disposable. . . . So now we just throw the dirty ones away."

Another visible indication that the fight against MRSA at the VAPHS is in full swing could at first glance go unnoticed. Passing a meeting room at the Heinz long-term care facility, one might catch a glimpse of Peter Knickerbocker, a pre-med student at the University of Pittsburgh and a hospital volunteer, sitting and dialoguing with a group of patients. This gathering is one of the weekly meetings that Peter organizes to discuss strategies to promote hand hygiene and to listen to patients' ideas about their own involvement in combating MRSA. A typical meeting yielded the following recommendations from patients: 1) Ask MRSA patients to share their stories with other patients in future meetings. 2) Issue a hand sanitizer to each patient upon admission along with written instructions on its use. 3) Ask patients to share what they've learned about hand hygiene with other patients when they play bingo, gather in the smoking areas, and watch football games together. For the VAPHS staff, such respectful, dialogic feedback sessions with patients have proven to be a valuable way to increase knowledge flows, and increase ownership of both problems and their solutions by all stakeholders.

Rock to water logic

Edward De Bono, in his 1993 book *Water Logic* describes two different types of thinking: Rock logic is rock-like—hard and unyielding; something that sits on a surface and does not budge. Water logic, on the other hand, is water-like—soft and fluid; it spreads out and explores when flowing on a surface.

While rock logic leads to questions that focus on "what is" (e.g. that's the way it is, or that's the way it is not), water logic leads to questions that focus on "to" (e.g. What does this flow to? What does this lead to? What does this add up to?) Bono argues that while both ways of thinking are functional and useful, they yield very different outcomes.

Hospitals are bastions of rock logic. Operating in a highly controlled regulatory environment, strict guidelines govern the practice of medicine. Processes are prioritized and protocol reigns supreme. Uncertainty and ambiguity are unwelcome and need to be vanquished. The metaphor of a "well-oiled machine" is valorized; each part should know what "is" and "should be." Clearly this rock logic serves a very useful purpose in the implementation of technical processes. However, it can be limiting (*see* Organizations as Machines in Chapter 2).

Jennifer Scott, a nurse in Heinz's 2 South Unit, described to us a series of recent events on her floor that illustrate some shifts in thinking from rock to water logic. Jennifer credits the PD-inspired processes at Heinz for such a cultural shift.

A patient on Jennifer's floor was sinking rapidly and a "code red" alert went out on the hospital intercom. "The patient had 'alphabet soup'—all the germs one could possibly get. And I remember, outside the patient's room someone was playing the role of a sentry, dispensing gowns and gloves at the door. You couldn't get in unless you were properly gowned and gloved. There were people dashing in—doctors, nurses, nursing assistants, respiratory therapists, and others—from other floors. One of the doctors, Dr Hubicz, had 10 extra pairs of gloves in her pocket that she handed out to people as they came in."

While the patient's room was a beehive of activity, Jennifer remembers thinking, "What about the crash cart [the portable cart used to wheel in all the emergency supplies and resuscitation equipment]? How is it cleaned? What happens to a monitor that has to be placed on an infected patient's bed, just so that the cord could be plugged into the nearest electric outlet? Or for that matter, what happens to the electric cord itself?"

Jennifer's acute awareness of how people and equipment move in an emergency led to her to pose questions inspired by water logic. Her thoughts focused not only on "what is", e.g. code red, but also on the "to", e.g. where the crash cart, and its equipment and supplies, go to *during* and *after* the cart's use.

Jennifer's new way of thinking, which she calls her "MRSA radar," travels with her. "I went to this conference with my colleague, and there was this vendor, selling ceiling-mounted lifts," Jennifer recounts. "There was a crowd around him, and he was going on and on about how this new lifting machine, with canvas straps, could be mounted on the ceiling of every patient's room. He said, 'Now every patient could have their own ceiling lift—and it would last for 50 years!'"

The first thought that hit Jennifer was, "Okay, but how do you *clean* it? If we can't clean it, we have no use for it." She went on to describe the vexing hygiene challenges they face. "One issue is that we have designated MRSA isolation rooms, but then we have *portable* equipment. So it's not enough to have staff put on gowns and gloves when entering a MRSA isolation room. They have to remember to take them off every time they exit and dispose them safely. They also have to make sure that the *equipment* doesn't go from room to room without being cleaned."

"Ah, that explains the disposable stethoscopes and blood pressure cuffs in isolation rooms," we stated.

"Yes, that's part of it," Jennifer concurred, "but most of the equipment is not disposable."

"So how do nurses feel about going into these isolation rooms, given the complicated hygiene routine? Do they dread it?"

"When everyone's MRSA radar is on, you get used to it," Jennifer replied.

Another person engaging in water logic on Heinz's 2 South is Unit Clerk Karen Stofan. When we met her in 2006 (she passed away in 2007), Karen was concerned that once patients get stuck with a MRSA diagnosis, it stays with them throughout their hospital stay. Her goal was to not just be on top of who is *MRSA-positive*, but to know when they've become *MRSA-free*.

"That's the biggest switch for me from what we used to do," Karen said. "Now we're getting people cleared from the MRSA list." She described how this is done. "I check the list and see who tested positive but hadn't been cultured for months. We swab them again and if the results are negative, we re-swab to be sure. Another negative culture and they are cleared from the list."

Jennifer added: "It used to be that once you went MRSA, you were MRSA forever. Just recently we cleared five people off the list!"

Another newly introduced feedback and feed-forward loop at VAPHS' Heinz facility was sharing the MRSA list across the hospital units. This purposive sharing is especially important at Heinz facility as the patients here stay for longer periods and receive care in multiple units located on different floors. Sharing the MRSA list allows everyone from physical therapists to Bingo facilitators to know who the MRSA-positive patients are so adequate precautions can be taken in a respectful manner without stigmatizing. In her book *Communicating in the Clinic*, Laura Ellingson emphasizes that information sharing in typical health-care establishments mostly happens between "dyads and triads of [existing] team members."[27] However, the VAPHS seems to be establishing some new benchmarks in information-sharing, given ideas on MRSA prevention are shared beyond traditional teams: nurses now share "what works" across units;

and housekeepers share MRSA prevention tips with physical and occupational therapists.

> Nurses now share "what works" across units; and housekeepers share MRSA prevention tips with physical and occupational therapists.

As we were leaving Unit 2 South, we saw Jennifer heading back to the crash cart. "I'm thinking that sooner or later this screen is going to go if we keep cleaning it," she said, pointing to the EKG monitor sitting on the top shelf of the mobile cart. After a pause, she continued. "What if we wrapped the screen in plastic *separately*? Then if we used the EKG monitor we could just change the plastic instead of cleaning the screen and everything else on the cart . . ."

At Heinz, new ideas, like water, continue to flow.

A key component to keeping the "flow" of good ideas coming is management support. Jennifer's eagerness to improve the process of cleaning the EKG monitor is fueled by her knowledge that if she comes up with a good idea, it will find a receptive audience in someone like Cheryl Creen.

Enabling innovation and ownership

One of the first things you see when you enter Cheryl Creen's office is a typewritten sheet of paper on the bulletin board: "The question isn't who is going to let me, it's who is going to stop me." As MRSA coordinator at Heinz, one of Cheryl's major duties is to follow up on ideas and suggestions offered by staff.[28]

British sociologist Anthony Giddens warned against the tendency to identify structure solely as constraint. Structure, he points out, can also be enabling. Within the enormous structure that is the Veterans Administration and its necessary framework of guidelines, rules and regulations, Cheryl creates structures that enable her staff to think creatively.

FIGURE 10.4 Jennifer Scott and crash cart.

Prior to her selection as MRSA coordinator at Heinz, Cheryl Creen was a much-loved Unit Manager for 2 South. She constantly gets emails from the nurses there. "They'll write, 'Has anyone considered this or that?' They're not afraid to share their ideas," Cheryl noted with pride.

Cheryl credits the close-knit relationships in her previous unit as the reason why "people speak up and are not always on their guard." Unit cohesion is what made a member of the housekeeping staff feel comfortable enough to teach "a thing or two" about hygiene to the rest of the unit. One day, she recalled, some staff members were talking about cleaning the room of a patient with the C-Diff (*Clostridium difficile*) bug, "and Eddie, from housekeeping stepped forward and said 'alcohol won't work on spores of C-Diff. We have to use Clorox.'"

One of the resident doctors exclaimed, "Why didn't anyone tell us this before?"

One of the reasons that the doctor hadn't been told before was the lack of opportunities for doctors to interact with housekeepers, or for other such cross-functional conversations. So Cheryl created them. "We held a lot of floor-wide social events," she recalled. "And I made sure *everyone* was invited—doctors, nurses, patients, and even staff from the environmental (housekeeping) unit."

Such events promote non-hierarchical, stress-free informal interaction between individuals with diverse functions, creating what Cheryl described as a "culture of cohesiveness." These events build a *relational infrastructure* that facilitates information sharing and the dissemination of innovations. The relational infrastructure is built slowly, as staff members get to know one another not just as colleagues but as people. By attending one of Cheryl's floor-wide events, the hospital resident mentioned above could now learn not only about the need to fight C-Diff with Clorox but also that Eddie Yates is a Veteran himself and that he has a BA in economics. Knowing Eddie as a person makes it easier to approach him later with questions, comments and requests for suggestions.

Cheryl's social events brought together people with diverse perspectives adding new ideas into the mix of what Anthony Suchman has called the "organizational conversation" (*see* Chapter 2)[29]. Another effort to bring different perspectives together was the weekly briefing on MRSA transmission and infection rates attended by unit staff and management. As noted by Suchman, the outcomes of such conversations couldn't be predicted or controlled, but they offered an ideal opportunity for new ideas to emerge and spread.[30] Take the example of "the list."

Jon Lloyd recounts the story: "Fred Chen from physical therapy began attending the [MRSA] briefings." He started getting to know several people on the unit. One day, he asked one of the LPNs if he could have a copy of the list of MRSA-positive patients. As a result of that question, wheels started turning. Other people began asking for the list, which prompted more people to begin thinking about how MRSA could be transmitted in their areas, which prompted the development of new precautions.

Nursing Program Leader Ginny Rudy observed, "Once staff members come up with their own interventions, they *own* the solutions." Management plays a supporting role, attending the briefings on each unit, listening, providing resources and removing barriers—but it does not direct or control the process. Staff members have *ownership* of the solutions, ensuring that the solutions will be implemented more readily.

Henri Lipmanowicz, a former executive with Merck Pharmaceuticals, articulated the important difference between ownership and the concept of "buy in," which is frequently used to describe organizational change processes. These terms, he stresses, are not interchangeable. Ownership of an idea, he writes, "means that you have participated in its development, that it is your choice freely made. . . . Buy in is the opposite—someone else or some group of people has done the development, the thinking . . . and now they have to convince you to come along and implement their idea."[31] Lipmanowicz argues that it is essential for leaders to recognize the difference between these two terms because only ownership can lead to true enthusiasm and true commitment. He writes: "If leaders involved UPFRONT all the people that will be involved later on in the implementation there would be no need for buy-in . . ."[32]

> Ownership of an idea, he writes, "means that you have participated in its development, that it is your choice freely made. . . . Buy in is the opposite—someone else or some group of people has done the development, the thinking . . . and now they have to convince you to come along and implement their idea."

Dr Bob Muder echoed the importance of supporting staff-led innovation. "We now rely very little on punitive measures. Healthcare workers are professionals—they want to do the right thing. If you give them support and the resources they need, they're going to do what's necessary [for patient safety]."

Cheryl Squier, an infection control nurse with 27-years experience at the VA described the VAPHS's successful fight against MRSA as being due not only to the trusting and patient attitude management demonstrates towards staff but also to the pride staff feel in fixing problems on their own. "What amazes me the most," she confided, "is that things happen without me even knowing about it. Staff come up with very localized solutions—they find a way to make things work for their area—and the changes that come from MRSA prevention impact the practices for preventing other infections."

Sometimes change comes about only because the guy who cleans the rooms feels comfortable enough to explain to the [Chief Medical Officer] what he thinks needs to be done.

Just as solutions can emerge in dialogue, so too can new problems. The day we spoke with Cheryl Creen in her office, she was working to track down the fire hazard regulation that barred foam containers from being installed in the hallway. "We'll do what we can," Cheryl said enthusiastically.

> Sometimes change comes about only because the guy who cleans the rooms feels comfortable enough to explain to the [Chief Medical Officer] what he thinks needs to be done.

Reports from the "red zone"

VAPHS patients who are infected with MRSA at the acute-care University Drive facility are kept in isolation rooms. The floor around their bed is painted with a large red rectangle. Hospital staff know if they enter the "red zone" they need to don fresh gowns and gloves and remember to remove them when exiting. At the Heinz long-term care facility, patients are often ambulatory and also stay for longer periods and therefore cannot be completely isolated. Nonetheless, special precautions are required with MRSA patients there, too.

The way most hospital staff exit and enter rooms is not lost on the patients. "They'll wash their hands *on the way out*," noted Darryl, a veteran who had been diagnosed with MRSA, "but only a few wash them *on the way in*." Darryl does agree that, in the past year or so, the staff is doing a lot better with hand washing on their way in.

"When a doctor, or a nurse, enters my room," continued Darryl, "and doesn't wash their hands, I deliberately do not make eye contact with them. Instead I just look at the sink." As Darryl talked, he mimicked the obvious sideways glances he would make. "If they do not understand, I'll just look back at the doctor, and then back at the sink, until they wash their hands."

Darryl, on his own, has cracked the communication code to neutralize power and hierarchy at VAPHS. It is hard for patients, lying on beds and hooked to tubes and monitors, to verbally tell their attending doctor to wash their hands. Such a good-faith request may be construed as being rude, and patients fear reprisals. So patients usually silence themselves. Darryl has learned to use silence with some simple non-verbals to politely convey his main point.

The trick, Darryl will tell you, is to smile when looking at the sink. A smirk could backfire. If one did not wish to look at the sink, one could just look up at the newly-plastered poster on the front wall.

"Patients are not the problem. We could be part of the solution," noted Darryl. "If one guy is contaminated, he can contaminate others." Darryl rues not having informed a fellow veteran about the dangers of MRSA in a timely manner. The veteran ended up infected. "If I could have gotten to him two days earlier . . ." Darryl lamented, his thoughts trailing off.

"What has the patient group been up to?" we asked.

For one, the patients decided to create their *own* anti-MRSA brochure.

The hospital-produced brochure is entitled "Resistant Bacteria: Methicillin

Resistant *Staphylococcus Aureus* and Vancomycin Resistant Enterococcus." The patient-produced brochure has a different title: "Keeping America's Veterans Healthy—A guide to MRSA—A simple way to shorten your stay." Both brochures have a section on risk. Interestingly, where the hospital-produced brochure notes that healthy people are at very little risk of *getting* an infection with resistant bacteria. the patient-produced brochure stresses that everyone who enters a hospital is at risk of *becoming a carrier.* Both risk statements are true but they frame the situation differently. The patient-produced brochure exhorts veterans to become active in MRSA prevention. Lines on the last page of the brochure read: "Join in the effort to prevent its spread to other veterans. Ask a nurse how you can help." Inviting patients to expand the "solution space" has provoked new, insightful perspectives on MRSA prevention and control.

The patient-produced brochure is more credible with other patients because the messages come from fellow veterans. Trusting a fellow soldier, and covering each others' flank, is key to survival in a battlefield, and veterans at the VAPHS are expanding the application of these principles in another form of combat—with a lurking, invisible, and dangerous enemy.

> The patient-produced brochure is more credible with other patients because the messages come from fellow veterans. Trusting a fellow soldier, and covering each others' flank, is key to survival in a battlefield, and veterans at the VAPHS are expanding the application of these principles in another form of combat—with a lurking, invisible, and dangerous enemy.

Gathering a group of patients and asking for their insights is "resource neutral" since it involves tapping into *existing* resources rather than requiring that additional resources be brought in from outside. Of course, the patient-produced brochure couldn't have happened without the support of hospital leadership. Asking hospital volunteers like Peter Knickerbocker to organize and record these meetings was an efficient, low-cost way for management to support the MRSA prevention effort while supporting the veterans' desires to be part of the effort to solve problems that affect them directly. At the VAPHS, veterans aren't restricted to the "sick role,"[33] nor even to the role of decision makers in their *own* care: mechanisms have been created for patients to also have a role in the safety of other patients.

Hanging the results for all to see
Through Glo Germ demonstrations, foam zaps after Bingo, macaroni routines, and "discovery and action dialogues," a collective mindfulness about combating and eliminating MRSA is shaping up, especially at VAPHS' Heinz facility. Cheryl Creen and Jon Lloyd, Heinz's MRSA commanders, have worked hard to create feedback loops, so that experiences of one Unit can be shared with other units,

victories can be celebrated, and disappointments can be met with resolve.

An important feedback loop consists of rainbow charts which are prominently displayed at all nursing stations at Heinz reporting on new MRSA infections and transmissions during the past week. The pride of the unit staff is evident at the weekly briefings when they can report no new MRSA infections.

During our four visits to VAPHS, we attended several weekly MRSA briefings. Usually Jon Lloyd and MRSA coordinators Cheryl Creen (at Heinz) and Candace Cunningham (at University Drive) meet with the unit staff to discuss progress, identify bottlenecks, and address concerns. What was palpable in the units we visited was the individual commitment to patient safety displayed by the staff—from doctors, to nurses, to housekeepers, to van drivers. It became apparent in these 15-minute briefings that the responsibility and accountability for a new MRSA infection lies with the entire group. No one person can be held responsible and no unit member should be excluded when discussing patient safety.

In our July 2006 visit, the weekly briefing on Heinz's 2 South Unit was lead by housekeeping staff member Edward Yates. Twenty-two staff members were in attendance, including three patients. Ed happily reported that 2 South had zero MRSA infections, zero colonizations, and had achieved 100 percent nasal swabbing rates.

Dr Muder explained that even though the briefings are now led by "front-line" staff like Ed Yates, the presence of senior management is nonetheless crucial. If problems arise, for example, staff can request what they need directly to management rather than having their requests languish in traditional bureaucratic channels. Furthermore, Muder explained, "It is important that staff get feedback when things are going well so they can see the impact of what they're doing *right.*"

And yet, Muder stressed, fighting MRSA is not just about feeling good. "It's about patient safety—and when you see the data that demonstrates that you're

FIGURE 10.5 Eddie Yates.

doing something right—that infection rates are down—*that* makes people feel good. They can see the link between their actions and the results." As illustrated in the "Data-driven problem-solving model," once front-line staff see that what they are doing is working, and that their actions have the support of hospital management, they are free to try new things, some of which will succeed and some of which will fail. The key is that ideas—good, bad *and* ugly—continue to flow.

> It's about patient safety—and when you see the data that demonstrates that you're doing something right—that infection rates are down—*that* makes people feel good. They can see the link between their actions and the results.

DECLINING MRSA RATES AT VAPHS

What evidence exists for declining MRSA rates at the VAPHS? How much of this decline may be attributed to the system-wide adoption of Positive Deviance? MRSA surveillance data at VAPHS show the following trends:
➤ Incidence of MRSA from clinical cultures dropped house wide at VAPHS' University Drive facility by 20 percent (64% to 44%) from January 2002 (when TPS was launched on 4 West) to October 2006 (*see* Figure 10.6).
➤ About half of this 20 percent decrease can be attributed to the dramatic reductions in MRSA incidence on 4 West and SICU (these two units contributed a significant number of MRSA infections to the house-wide total). The other half of the decrease has occurred since July 2005 when PD was introduced.
➤ Hospital-acquired Surgical Site MRSA infection rates declined by 50 percent at VAPHS from July 2005 (when PD practices were implemented) to October 2006.

The following qualitative outcomes have also been achieved:
➤ The MRSA data and accompanying feedback and feed-forward loops are shared across hospital units, enabling the staff to learn when an MRSA transmission has occurred and to take adequate precautions.
➤ Weekly unit briefings with MRSA coordinators provide an opportunity for the staff to monitor and investigate new MRSA transmissions and to take individual and collective responsibility for preventing recurrence.
➤ The ongoing discovery and action dialogues result in a constant flow of new ideas to tackle MRSA.

Reflecting on the VAPHS' Heinz facility, Dr Jon Lloyd observed, "A true cultural transformation has occurred from within—with support from the leadership that demonstrated faith in its people—which manifests itself in a growing sense of ownership among staff and patients of the MRSA problem and their creation

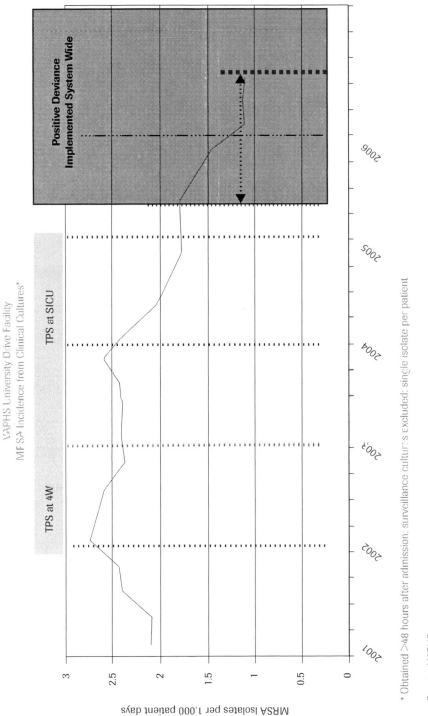

* Obtained >48 hours after admission; surveillance cultures excluded; single isolate per patient

Source: VAPHS

FIGURE 10.6 Trend in MRSA rates.

and implementation of hundreds of small solutions." Both Jon and Cheryl Creen emphasized the importance of celebrating stories of staff members' contributions, however small.

A RIPPLE CREATING A TIDAL WAVE

The VAPHS' quest to prevent, control, and eradicate MRSA, supported by early indicators of its effectiveness, has not gone unnoticed at the CDC, at the Veterans Affairs Department in Washington, DC, at the Agency for Healthcare Research and Quality, and with private granting agencies such as the Robert Wood Johnson Foundation.

On August 17–18, 2006, the VA administration held a kick-off event in Pittsburgh to launch its national initiative to combat MRSA entitled "Getting to Zero," with VAPHS as the lead implementing agency (under the leadership of Dr Rajiv Jain). Representatives of the 17 VA hospitals participating in Phase 1 descended on Pittsburgh for this event. The remaining 150 or so VA hospitals across the country will be covered by the national initiative in phase two.

"So what are the remaining challenges?" we asked.

Candace Cunningham, the MRSA prevention coordinator at the VAPHS acute-care facility, said a major challenge was what she called the "not supported by the literature" issue. Hearing Candace's comments, Dr John Jernigan from CDC agreed. "Everyone wants to see a randomized controlled trial before they'll believe something is effective." He then noted that the British Medical Journal has questioned the exclusive dominance of evidenced-base medicine by publishing an article highlighting the lack of randomized controlled trials to support the effectiveness of parachutes in "preventing major trauma related to gravitational challenge."[34] The article concluded with a call to the medical community to "accept that, under exceptional circumstances, common sense might be applied when considering the potential risks and benefits of interventions."[35] And just as one does not need a randomized controlled trial to know that parachute use is a good idea when jumping out of a plane, one might also defer to common sense when assessing the value of increased communication and staff ownership.

Jon Lloyd agreed with the need for a "common sense" approach to MRSA prevention. "You have to respect the process . . . opening the floodgates of communication between staff may not be clinically proven to help prevent MRSA, but it certainly can't be hurting!" Jon then noted that the ideas of such luminary figures as Ignaz Semmelweis[36] and Oliver Wendell Holmes[37] were also met with skepticism in their day.

"MRSA is a great unifier. Every patient and every healthcare worker is potentially affected. . . . Once you start tackling MRSA head on, it's like the genie is out of the bottle—you can't put the genie back in."

Dr Bob Muder added that other hospitals have an 'enlightened self interest' in joining the battle against MRSA. "Many people seem to have an 'aha moment' when they see the preliminary data on how many infections we've prevented—how many *deaths* we've prevented—at the VAPHS. When people see the data, they become partisans—and once data at other hospitals starts becoming available there will be nowhere to hide—facility managers will start being held accountable. There's no reason other hospitals with the same resources can't do what we've done here. Even from a fiscal, legal or public relations perspective, it's a win–win situation."

IN CLOSING

VAPHS' quest to vanquish a dangerous and devious enemy necessarily requires waging a battle on many fronts. Faith in the local grounded intelligence is essential to navigate the difficult and often unknown terrain. By identifying "home-grown" solutions, making them visible and sharing them widely, the VAPHS was able to expand the solution space and get a cross-section of hospital staff members involved in the fight against MRSA. The struggle continues, but the burden is now carried across more shoulders.

Twenty-five hundred years after his death, the Chinese philosopher, Lao-Tzu, founder of Taoism, makes an appearance. Presiding over an audience of MRSA warriors who seek his advice, he says:

"Go to the people. Live with them. Learn from them. Love them.

"Start with what they know. Build with what they have. But with the best leaders, when the work is done, the task accomplished, the people will say, 'We have done this ourselves.'"[38]

NOTES

1 This narrative documentation effort is supported by the Positive Deviance Initiative at Tufts University, as well as VAPHS. The Plexus Institute, as its President Curt Lindberg does best, helped bring us all together. A special thanks to Dr Jon Lloyd, Dr Rajiv Jain, Mr Michael Moreland, Jerry and Monique Sternin, Curt Lindberg, and Henri Lipmanowicz for their support. Thanks also to all the MRSA warriors at VAPHS, who honored us by shared their experiences and insights. Portions of this chapter draw on an unpublished report, Singhal and Greiner (2007), available at the Plexus Institute website: www.plexusinstitute.org/ideas/show_elibrary.cfm?id=664 (accessed November 11, 2010).

2 Arvind Singhal is the Samuel Shirley and Edna Holt Marston Endowed Professor, and Director, Social Justice Initiative, Department of Communication, The University of Texas, El Paso. Karen Greiner is a Post Doctoral Scholar at the University of South Florida in Tampa Florida. She served as Peace Corps volunteer in Cameroon and was a 2008–09 Fulbright Fellow in Bogotá, Colombia. Both authors are interested in the diffusion of social innovations as well as complexity science-inspired approaches to organizing for social change.

3 VAPHS is part of the US Department of Veteran Affairs (VA), a government agency that regulates and administers all matters pertaining to war veterans,

notably providing them with quality medical care. Some 25 percent of the US population is eligible for VA benefits as veterans, family members, or survivors. The VA's 2005 fiscal year spending was $71.2 billion, including $31.5 billion for healthcare, $37.1 billion for benefits, and $148 million for the national cemetery system. Source: http://www1.va.gov/opa/feature/history/history10.asp (accessed November 11, 2010).

4 Lloyd was previously Chair of the Department of Surgery at Shadyside Hospital and Medical Director of the Pittsburgh Regional Healthcare Initiative. From the first day we met him in Pittsburgh in May, 2006, Jon Lloyd served as our escort, teacher, and connector to VAPHS' staff, patients, and facilities. Throughout the writing of this story, he sent us both pithy and detailed email messages sharing the MRSA struggles and triumphs at the VAPHS, and keeping us in the loop through phone calls. He opened many "doors" for us, and provided insightful "windows" to the nuances, subtleties, paradoxes, and contradictions we observed at the VAPHS.

5 This position is supported by an inter-agency agreement between the Centers for Disease Control and Prevention and VAPHS.

6 As noted previously, the 4 West Surgical Unit on VAPHS' University Drive facility had, since 2001, implemented the Toyota Production System method to reduce MRSA infections; however, this best practice yielded disappointing outcomes when replication was attempted on other units.

7 Heidi Walker was appointed MRSA coordinator for the VA's Heinz facility in August 2005 and worked there until December 2005.

8 Klein E, Smith DL, Laxminarayan R. Hospitalizations and deaths caused by methicillin-resistant *Staphylococcus aureus*, United States, 1999–2005. *Emerg Infect Dis*. 2007; **13**(12): 1840–6.

9 Saco R. *Good Companies: organizations discovering the good in themselves by using positive deviance as a change management strategy*. [Dissertation] Paris, France: HEC Paris/Oxford Executive Education; 2005.

10 Jernigan is Chief, Interventions & Evaluation Section Division of Healthcare Quality Promotion, CDC.

11 This section draws upon Papa MJ, Singhal A, Papa WH. *Organizing for Social Change: a dialectic journey of theory and praxis*. Thousand Oaks, CA: Sage; 2006.

12 PRHI and the CDC worked with the University Pittsburgh Medical Center (UPMC) on reducing catheter-related bloodstream infections, which according to Dr Carlene Muto, medical director of infection control at UPMC, was very expensive to treat and had high mortality. The thirty-two hospitals in 10 southwestern Pennsylvania counties that participated in the intervention averaged a 68% decline in infection rates during April 2001–March 2005.

13 TPS was developed by the Japanese auto giant Toyota. Other industrial quality initiatives include Lean and Six Sigma.

14 Saco R, op. cit.

15 Dorsey D. Positive deviant. *Fast Company*. 2000; **41**: 284–92.

16 *See* Chapter 3. See also Sternin J, Choo R. The power of positive deviance. *Harv Bus Rev*. 2000; **2–3**: 14–15. Singhal A, Buscell P, Lindberg C. *Inviting Everyone: healing healthcare through positive deviance*. Bordentown, NJ: PlexusPress; 2010.

17 Zeitlin M, Ghassemi H, Mansour M. *Positive Deviance in Child Nutrition*. New York: UN University Press; 1990.

18 Sternin J, Choo R, op.cit.

19 Sternin J, Choo R, op.cit. Sternin M, Sternin J, Marsh D. Scaling up poverty alleviation and nutrition program in Vietnam. In: Marchione T, editor. *Scaling Up, Scaling Down: capacities for overcoming malnutrition in developing countries*. Amsterdam: Gordon and Breach Publishers; **1999**: pp. 97–117.

20 Pascale RT, Millemann M. Gioja L. *Surfing the Edge of Chaos: the laws of nature and the new laws of business*. New York: Crown Publishing Group; 2000.

21 *See* Sternin, quoted in Sparks D. From hunger aid to school reform: positive deviance approach seeks solutions that already exist. *J Staff Dev*. 2004; **25**: 46–51.

22 *See* Buscell P. The power of positive deviance. *Emerging*. 2004. Aug–Oct: 8–15. Dorsey D, op. cit. Sternin J. Practice positive deviance for extraordinary social and organizational change. In: Ulrich D, Goldsmith M, Carter L, *et al.* editors. *The Change Champion's Fieldguide: strategies and tools for leading change in your organization*. New York: Best Practice Publications; 2003. pp. 20–37.

23 To learn more about these PD experiences, *see* www.positivedeviance.org/resources/wisdomseries.html (accessed November 11, 2010). *Positive Deviance Wisdom Series* 1 through 4, published by Boston, Tufts University: Positive Deviance Initiative; 2009. #1. Singhal A, Sternin J, Dura L. *Combating Malnutrition in the Land of a Thousand Rice Fields: positive deviance grows roots in Vietnam*; #2. Dura L, Singhal A. *Will Ramon Finish Sixth Grade? positive deviance for student retention in rural Argentina*; #3. Singhal A, Buscell P, McCandless K. *Saving Lives by Changing Relationships: positive deviance for MRSA prevention and control in a US hospital*; #4. Singhal A, Dura L. *Sunflowers Reaching for the Sun: positive deviance for child protection in Uganda*.

24 This section is adapted from material distributed at an October, 2005 workshop offered by Jerry and Monique Sternin entitled "Social Change from the Inside Out: Addressing Intractable Social Problems through Positive Deviance."

25 Pascale RT, Sternin J. Your company's secret change agents. *Harv Bus Rev*. 2005; **83**(5): 72–81.

26 In June, 2007 Cathy participated in a session on Innovation in Infection

Control at the annual conference of the Association for Professionals in Infection Control and Epidemiology (APIC). The title of her presentation was "Use of gown counts to assess and improve compliance with contact isolation." Commenting on Cathy's initiative, Ira Richardson, Associate Director for Patient Care Services at the VAPHS, said: "Cathy is taking her work to the next level. Usually, at APIC conferences, one sees RNs present, but rarely LPNs like Cathy. It is impressive to see how much Cathy has grown, professionally."

27 Ellingson L. *Communicating in the Clinic: negotiating frontstage and backstage teamwork.* Cresskill, NJ: Hampton Press; 2005. p. 143.

28 Nonetheless, Cheryl works within the constraints of the VA system. She acknowledges that keeping abreast of government regulations is challenging. But, she adds, that it's important that the staff know the regulations. This may mean having to explain "why a seemingly good idea can't be implemented—at least, in the short term."

29 Broekstra G. An organization is a conversation. In: Grand D, Keenoy T, Swick C, editors. *Discourse and Organization.* London: Sage; 1998.

30 *See* Suchman AL. A new theoretical foundation for relationship-centered care: complex responsive processes of relating. *J Gen Intern Med.* 2006; **21** Suppl. 1): S40–4.

31 Lipmanowicz H. *Buy-in versus ownership,* unpublished document shared with the authors via personal communication.

32 Lipmanowicz H, op. cit. p. 2.

33 Parsons T. *The Social System.* Glencoe, IL: Free Press; 1951. p. 437.

34 Smith GC, Pell JP. Parachute use to prevent death and major trauma related to gravitational challenge: systematic review of randomised controlled trials. *BMJ.* 2003; **327**: 1459–61.

35 Smith GC, Pell JP, op. cit. p. 1460.

36 Semmelweis introduced the practice of hand washing with chloride of lime to block transmission of the disease.

37 Holmes authored the essay *Contagiousness of Puerperal Fever* in 1843 which concluded that Puerperal Fever was transmitted by healthcare practitioners.

38 *See* http://thinkexist.com/quotes/lao_tzu (accessed November 11, 2010).

Commentary: Veterans Administration Pittsburgh Healthcare System

As we read in this case study, methicillin-resistant *Staph aureus* (MRSA) infections claim 100 000 lives every year. The fact that the bacterium is tenacious and difficult to treat is only half the story. The other half, which is arguably more critical, involves self-propagating patterns of thinking and acting among healthcare professionals: initially the inappropriate prescribing of antibiotics that fostered the emergence of drug-resistant bacteria, compounded by persistent inattention to the everyday behaviors that spread bacteria from one person to another *in healthcare facilities*. But there may be an even deeper level.

For many decades, there has been a general belief that a certain low postoperative infection rate is normal, even inevitable, and is therefore acceptable. Efforts at prevention were focused entirely upon the more heroic realm of invasive procedures with clinicians trying to be meticulous in their practice of sterile technique. But humdrum activities like touching patients, hand washing, passing food trays, and using the same stethoscope on one patient after another were of little interest, and the associated infection control practices were inconvenient. Infection control personnel were often dismissed if not derided for even raising these topics. This pattern of meaning—that hospital-acquired infections are a normal part of doing business—may be the single biggest factor that has enabled the MRSA epidemic to continue. And so 100 000 more people die each year.

The MRSA team at the Veterans Administration Pittsburgh Healthcare System was artful, persistent and effective in trying to change these toxic patterns. The story of its work exemplifies every one of the major principles in this book.

First, complexity: at the heart of the initiative was a process of fostering mindfulness of the patterns people were creating in each moment and attempting to alter the problematic ones. Using bags of macaroni to make the number 100 000 visible—and then translating that into lost lives—disrupted the pattern of complacency and acceptance. The use of Glo-Germ helped with this, too, vividly demonstrating how everyone was part of the network of hand-to-hand transmission. The project depended upon emergent design: following the direction of the group as more and more people got involved and contributed their ideas.

At many points in the story, we see small accidental disturbances cascading to become transformational patterns. The first person to be in charge of the MRSA prevention initiative happened to be familiar with the Toyota Production System; using those methods he demonstrated that lowering the infection rate is indeed possible. Then, one of the MRSA Prevention Coordinators happened upon an article about Positive Deviance, which he read only because it described a project in Vietnam where he had served decades earlier. That chance encounter altered the direction of the entire project. A physical therapist asked to receive the list of MRSA-positive patients, prompting others to do likewise, thus engaging lots of people who never thought about MRSA before to start noticing and modifying potential paths of transmission in their work processes.

Second, this story is positive psychology *par excellence*. As we saw in Chapter 3, Positive Deviance presumes and calls forth the capacity of a community to solve its own problems; the Pittsburgh VA was no exception. Experts did not provide answers; their role was to coach internal leaders about processes of engagement, discovery, communication and rapid implementation. By having both the solutions and the leadership come from inside the community, PD supported the autonomy of the VAPHS staff and highlighted their competence. Instances of MRSA transmission were used as occasions for learning and further innovation rather than for blaming and shaming, keeping people constructively engaged and fostering their creative thinking.

Third, the story demonstrates relationship-centered process. In Discovery and Action Dialogs, floor-wide social events and weekly MRSA briefings, people were invited to join as partners, across all occupational and professional roles, across all levels of hierarchy, staff and patients alike. Everyone's perspective was valued. There was a deeply felt understanding that everyone together was much more powerful than anyone alone; indeed, it would take everyone to solve this problem. Positional leaders fought down their urge to give directives, recognizing that a shared sense of ownership and decision-making would ultimately lead to greater effectiveness and efficiency.

This case study illustrates an important dimension of change management that may seem paradoxical—the intentional use of organizational structures to foster emergence. Recalling from Chapter 2 that diversity and responsiveness are the key factors that foster the emergence of new patterns (innovation and adaptability) we can appreciate the value of the relational infrastructure that the Pittsburgh VA staff created. They designed forums that regularly brought together in conversation patients, housekeepers, physicians, nurses, van drivers and everyone else, calling forth the full diversity of the organization—the difference that seeds new patterns. The forums were structured to help people listen to each other, celebrate each others' ideas, and build relationships and trust; all this enhanced responsiveness, allowing new patterns to evolve and spread.

The project leaders could not command people to innovate, but neither were they passive. They could and did create a fertile environment that unleashed creativity. They developed open, enabling structures that supported emergence, dissemination, and widening engagement. Their strategy of "supported emergence" succeeded: data presented in the chapter show a 20% decrease in positive MRSA surveillance cultures at the acute-care hospital and a 50% reduction in surgical site MRSA infections. By 2009, the entire VA system in Pittsburgh had achieved a 60% reduction in all MRSA infections.[1]

One last point for us to consider: this case study provides our first look at the Toyota Production System, more widely known now as Lean Production. While TPS was very successful in reducing MRSA infection in the intensive care unit, the project leaders found it to be too expert-driven and too costly. Later in the book (Chapter 13) we'll have a chance to explore a different and more relationship-centered implementation of TPS, so you might want to suspend judgment on this methodology for the moment. For now, let's celebrate the VAPHS staff and their outstanding and inspiring application of Positive Deviance.

NOTE

1 Singhal A, Greiner K. Small solutions and big rewards: MRSA prevention at the Pittsburgh Veterans Hospitals. In: Singhal A, Buscell P, Lindberg C, editors. *Inviting Everyone: healing healthcare with positive deviance.* Bordentown, NJ: Plexus Press; 2010. p. 75.

CHAPTER 11

Designing buildings for student-centered learning: the Science Centre at University College Dublin

*Michael Monaghan, Joe Carthy, Kathy O'Boyle,
Emma Sokell, William Wilson and Gopal Naidoo*

SYNOPSIS

This chapter describes the conversational processes which comprised the early design stages for a new science teaching facility at Ireland's largest university. In a proposal to the national funding authority, the university promised a transformation of the undergraduate experience of studying science, which would follow the provision of funding for new buildings. When the funding was awarded, the authors participated in a series of design workshops in a variety of different roles. It might be expected that a common understanding of learning processes would inform the design of such teaching facilities. The reality described here is that there were many different understandings of what constituted effective teaching and learning strategies. During the wide range of different conversations which took place, the faculty moved quite a distance from a conventional lecture/laboratory approach to teaching and began to embrace contemporary approaches which enable the social aspects of learning. Some of these understandings were aided by participation in conversations about building design which were not unlike the kind of classroom conversations we are now trying to encourage with our students. Towards the end of the process it began to look like the transformation in the undergraduate experience, which the university administration had promised in the initial proposal, might become real. At the time of writing, the new facility is in the final stages of design.

THE ORGANISATION AND THE IMPETUS FOR CHANGE

University College Dublin has its origins in the Catholic University established by John Henry Newman in 1854 and is now the largest university in Ireland. It has 23 000 students of which 25 percent are engaged in research. Its mission is to "advance knowledge, pursue truth and foster learning, in an atmosphere of discovery, creativity, innovation and excellence, drawing out the best in each individual, and contributing to the social, cultural and economic life of Ireland in the wider world". In 2009 it became one of the top 100 universities in the Times Higher Education Supplement World Rankings. Prior to 2004, it had conducted its business in conventional ways, but with the appointment of a new President, the declaration of an ambitious agenda (being in the top 30 universities in Europe) was soon followed by a radical restructuring of the university and an equally radical overhaul of the undergraduate curriculum. An especially ambitious program, which was explicitly linked to national objectives for the development of a "Smart Economy", was put in place for the sciences.

The university remained in the city center until the 1960s but gradually began to migrate to a 320-acre campus on the south side of the city which now houses its academic facilities, research institutes, libraries and archival collections, enterprise facilities, student villages and sports facilities. The Science Centre was the first complex to be completed on the new campus in 1963. Forty years later, in common with many scientific buildings of that era, it had become tired and unsuitable for contemporary research and teaching needs; generating the funds for a major investment in new science infrastructure quickly became a high priority for the new administration.

The buildings in which science is done in UCD range from extremely modern (a minority) to dowdy, old-fashioned and dysfunctional buildings dating back to the 1960s. These buildings are not only ill-suited to the needs of the existing population of scientists; they are also a significant impediment to the recruitment of the world-class scientists from the international academic marketplace.

This narrative will primarily describe the experience of trying to implement the university's vision of transforming the undergraduate experience in Science. The existing position and the ambition were set out as follows in a 2007 proposal to the Higher Education Authority:

The Old Model

The traditional degree program:

- is accessed almost exclusively by school leavers, and frequently without real commitment or sense of the career possibilities in science;
- features a fixed curriculum with little choice or flexibility; traditional, large-group teaching approaches; minimal adoption of educational and e-learning technology; and minimal exposure to research and discovery;
- fails to keep pace with new interdisciplinary areas of study underpinning key areas of innovation and with new technological advancements;
- offers little opportunity to broaden education beyond the core subject area of the degree, leaving students ill-prepared for the challenges of change encountered in a rapidly evolving society;

- uses laboratory facilities designed for science in the 1960s;
- approaches learning as a solitary activity, with little development of teamwork, project management and problem-focused skills.

The New Model

An open and flexible set of learning opportunities prepares graduates for work and lifelong learning in the knowledge economy, where:

- the recent advances in technology are fully exploited so that many traditional classes are enhanced;
- students are admitted to an attractive environment that matches the expectations and potential of modern science;
- an environment where small-group problem-based interactive learning is the norm rather than the exception;
- students are able to move where necessary between institutions and between sectors (universities, institutes of technology, further education) as required to pursue their specific learning pathway;
- degree programs are flexible and responsive, allowing subjects (including non-science subjects) and disciplines to be combined to prepare students to work in new and emerging areas at the forefront of knowledge and innovation;
- research and entrepreneurship are mainstreamed into the science curriculum;
- students have access to innovative courses that will specifically prepare them for a working life in a vibrant knowledge economy, including skills in business, management, economics, technology, ethics and civic/social responsibility;
- learning approaches recognize that the primary purpose of university education is to develop skills for lifelong learning at advanced levels;
- the fundamental scientific disciplines such as Math, Biology, Chemistry and Physics support the applied disciplines such as Food Science, Agriculture, Engineering and Biomedicine.

This narrative will include a number of voices describing their own experience and the kinds of conversation (some of which were quite unusual) which took place over a period of months, as we moved towards signing off on the design of new teaching facilities for our students in science.

GETTING STARTED: THE PROJECT DIRECTOR'S NARRATIVE

(The role of Project Director is to work with the senior administration and the science community on doubling the size and transforming the quality of the Science Centre at UCD, a project which will cost in excess of €300 million.

The funding will come from a variety of sources including the State, borrowings and philanthropy. The functions undertaken by the Project Director are various and include interacting with a design team on the master plan and on the design of specific buildings, assisting with a donor campaign, commissioning cost-benefit analyses over a 25-year period, keeping the UCD community informed on what is happening, persuading colleagues to migrate to highly unsuitable places while refurbishments take place, chairing a committee on allocation of space and dealing with occasional conflict. It is an intermediary role assisting with the implementation of the university's vision of being in the Top Thirty.)

In August 2008, we commenced work on a master-plan for the new science center with a design team which was led by Wilson Architects. I had worked with Bill Wilson before on a pilot project redesigning part of the Chemistry building and I had come to greatly admire his style. He has spent his entire career working with academic scientists, has a great knowledge of science facilities and their design and has exceptional skills in eliciting what he needs to know from every group that he works with. As part of the master-planning process, we had a number of workshop sessions over a period of months trying to decide what we needed in terms of classrooms, laboratories and other facilities for teaching the large numbers of first-year students and the smaller numbers of science-degree students who go on to specialize in fields like Synthetic Chemistry, Physics, Computer Science, and Neuroscience.

The architect's experience

> We are often asked by University administrators to assess science and engineering facilities and recommend changes to improve them. As a rule, the initial request is triggered by poor facilities—too tired, too small—and actually driven by a deeper need, the inability to recruit and retain students and faculty. Generally, the solution to aging facilities is not to replace as is, but to rethink and re-create the science and engineering community in alignment with, and as an articulation of, the University's mission. In other words, what starts as a leaky roof (at Chapel Hill) or a lack of a certain kind of lab space (at Harvard) becomes, through a process of interdisciplinary discussions, a deliberate plan to change the culture of an institution in a way that empowers and defines the academic community.
>
> At University College Dublin, the change in culture is made more dramatic by the way the existing complex sits frozen in time. Built in the early sixties, the Science Centre is the literal core of the campus, surrounded by newer, more handsome buildings and landscapes. When walking through the campus, one passes by modern buildings, sophisticated sculpture, and arrives at four

glass and aluminum warehouse buildings. It is impossible to walk through the complex. One can enter, but most students walk around, bypassing the complex.

Walking into Michael Monaghan's office in the summer of 2007, I had the usual checklist of concerns:

- The central question about process: What is the dynamic of schools and faculty within each school?
- How are decisions made? What combination of hard and soft data points are sought by upper management?
- What is the culture, the identity of the community?
- What is their vision?

The only way to help would be to understand their faculty: their decision making, their culture, and their mission. And what kind of help could an American architect be in Ireland?

Michael's office is sparsely furnished, and it is two-thirds table and chairs with a small office around the corner, sending out the message that it is a place where people meet, talk, and make decisions collectively. With a furrowed brow, he had one question about the risks ahead: "I don't think the faculty is ready for this." I asked him why, and he said that they would revert to their old ways. I understand that "they" meant senior faculty, often defending the turf of their academic units, and the way things are done.

Changing organizational culture is like baking bread. There is an aroma when the bread is ready. One sign of faculty being "ready" is when they start making references to the importance of other departments, or placing a higher value on future faculty than on existing ones. How long would this take, I wondered? Two or three workshops? How would the lines be drawn—and they would—with the one camp trying to prevent the inevitable change asked for by other, more interdisciplinary, voices?

I left Michael's office knowing that when the project went ahead, there was a guardian angel in place. He did not have, or want, a title, but he was ready for the responsibility, and occupied an office in the exact center of the three-story complex at the middle level where connecting bridges intersected.

> Changing organizational culture is like baking bread. There is an aroma when the bread is ready. One sign of faculty being "ready" is when they start making references to the importance of other departments, or placing a higher value on future faculty than on existing ones . . .

In the summer of 2008, the project was released and we had two important first steps—to organize the process and to inventory the buildings. Our approach to the process required learning the Irish nomenclature for academic life—departments are schools, chairs are heads of schools, deans are called heads of colleges, and science academic coordinators are in fact called deans. At the start, our approach did not vary from other planning projects.

- Set up a small working team with Michael on the academic side, and Tadgh Corcoran, and occasionally his boss Aiden Grannell, on the facilities side. This way both sides agree on shared priorities.
- Organize representatives in each school (department) to report back to their faculty.
- Organize stakeholder groups for special interest topics such as vivarium, materials handling, engineering, and computing.
- Ask for periodic audiences with the upper-level group, which at UCD is called the Senior Management Team or SMT, and includes the President, the Chief Financial Officer, and the Director of Research.

We proposed six workshops—one a month, to allow time for information to sink in, and for "corridor conversations" to occur.

The physical inventory began on a quiet Sunday in August of 2009. We had a guide with a master key that worked on every door. We have learned to read organizational culture from the usage of buildings, and the tour spoke volumes.

The first clue was the well preserved, original condition of the building. It was not a beauty, but it had original woodwork, signage, light fixtures—all untouched. Was this due to austerity, like many public institutions? There is worry to build it, but not to renovate or refurbish it.

On the exterior, the building is unloved. In Ireland, this is a message. The exterior of loved buildings have geraniums, palm trees, and gravel paths with inviting benches. The UCD exterior is surprisingly abandoned as a campus space, and instead of quadrangles, the spaces in between the buildings are service yards, metal buildings (for chemicals, it turned out), loading docks, and dense plantings with no paths. This explains why, in the center of campus, students passing east–west would go around the science center.

Just as the exterior was underused, behind the locked doors we found evidence of an academic community bustling with life. Tea areas were gathered in unlikely places—the plumbing room, a chemistry instrument room, and in rooms next to teaching labs.

Hand-painted murals, classrooms with very tight seating, and in one case we found a housekeeping closet wall papered with colorful postcards sent by appreciative graduate students from faraway places. Still we did not come across rooms filled with students at computers, or classrooms with new technologies. While the schools had their turf, there was little space for students themselves, or for technology. And the biggest target for conversation became the large teaching labs.

Biology's large Intro lab has small varnished wooden stools to allow students to sit close together for popular labs. Geology uses rows of long narrow counters, also varnished wood, while around the room are rock specimens. The Chemistry teaching lab spaces are also large rooms with tall, operable windows for fresh air, a concept originally from anatomy teaching labs of the turn of the century, and now a popular way to save energy.

The age of the facility meant that a full renovation was inevitable. A full renovation would occur in phases, and over a period of time, but new systems (electrical, plumbing, teldata), carpet, lighting, and paint were unavoidable.

We began our first workshops by asking simple questions, verifying space and headcount, gaining an understanding of each academic unit, and letting them see our reports and maps, so we had a sense that we were going to work together, even though none of us knew the outcome. We asked them to interact with us and each other, and let them know they would be party to the outcome.

At our second workshop, we went beyond inventories and asked about vision (what were their strengths and weaknesses?) and about benchmarking (who did they compete with for students?).

One discussion brought out important themes already at UCD, and new frontiers they wanted to expand, particularly in computation, disease, environmental health and nano-science (nano-biology and nano-physics). Selecting these themes was a milestone, because they served as umbrellas that covered all the stakeholders. Discussions allowed differences to be aired. Were large 400-seat classrooms an ideal teaching setting? Some said yes, some said no. And discussions recognized the financial limitations on capital and operating costs. Yes, any work would be in phases. Yes, the renovations would mean interim hardship. And yes, small-format teaching was affordable if teaching assistants were trained to handle sections, two per room for a 24-seat lab.

Bill Wilson, Architect

I started the project by inviting a couple of the directors of teaching and learning and the dean of science to a discussion about how we should proceed; my suggestion was that we invite anyone they thought might be helpful rather than confining it to those who held relevant titles. We had a reasonably good turnout at the first meeting, which took place in a new-style teaching room in the School of Nursing. The meeting opened with a chemist saying, "I'd hate to teach in here, it's horrible." Bill was pleased with this as an opening gambit and we had a spirited debate about the design of that room and about what might happen in it. Ironically the room was designed along the lines of a parliamentary debating chamber and it seemed to be working very well! Very soon the conversation moved to availability of large numbers of additional staff "if we're to move to small-group teaching." This issue arose in 2008 just at the time the university, the country and the developed world moved into financial crisis; hiring additional staff for teaching seemed like a very unlikely outcome. I was also fairly sure that I was being tested as someone with a reputation as a zealot for small-group teaching.

It was starkly obvious that there was not going to be a dramatic increase in the number of teaching staff, yet we had promised our funders "an environment where small-group problem-based interactive learning is the norm rather than the exception." I was also beginning to realize (again!) that the approach of developing a strategy (new teaching/learning practices underpinned by what I regarded as well-established principles of learning) in advance of deciding on the infrastructure was an unlikely sequence of events. I was also, again, overestimating the level of interest in and understanding of the learning process on the part of my academic colleagues. Their primary concerns centered on their own performance in the lecture theater and maximizing efficiency in order to increase the time available for research. Raising topics like employers' interest in generic skills such as team-working, finding and analyzing information, writing skills, etc. caused mystification if not irritation. The students were here to become scientists and they would do so by the tried and tested methods of the lecture followed by the 2–3 hour practical class (which sometimes has a 45-minute introduction with PowerPoint!). I started to feel a bit pessimistic that we might finish up spending millions on more of the same facilities which just looked nicer . . . and change nothing.

When I was pressed about a potential increase in staff, there was only one answer: it wasn't going to happen. UCD was likely to stay at a staff/student ratio of 20/1 as compared with our UK counterparts where the ratio is 10/1. I suggested that a total move to problem-based learning was neither appropriate nor possible and that since we were obviously in the mass education business, we should work towards some kind of blended approach. Then someone said what we really need is a 600-seater lecture theater; this would give huge efficiencies and get the mass knowledge transfer part of the process done much more quickly. My heart sank even further. I thought about a conversation I had with the President a year earlier in which I expressed my view that there had been a profound change in the value system of the university since the emphasis on research had increased; teaching was now regarded as "academic housework" for which there were few rewards in the promotions system. His response had been, "We've got to do both."

A critical moment occurred when Bill suggested that if UCD wanted to be a Top 30 European University, perhaps some of the faculty should visit Top 30 institutions and see what was going on there. I endorsed this suggestion and kept repeating it to anyone in the corridors who would listen over the following weeks. So Physics went to Manchester and Leicester, Computer Science went to Purdue and Chemistry went to Bristol and a couple of places in Canada. The narratives started to change.

> A critical moment occurred when Bill suggested that if UCD wanted to be a Top 30 European University, perhaps some of the faculty should visit Top 30 institutions and see what was going on there.

PHYSICS

The head of Physics and a colleague came to the second master-planning workshop with a presentation on how their approach to teaching first-year Physics could change radically if they had a different classroom layout. The conversations with colleagues in other places had revolved around the fact that the great majority of their first-year students would never think about Physics again; was it time to question the conventional approach of treating them as if they were going to become career physicists? They had seen that first-year Physics could be taught as a series of problem sets which uses Physics concepts to develop other generic skills which the students could apply later in medicine, engineering, agriculture as well as in the sciences. Physics students in second year could be treated as embryonic physicists and might learn in a different way. They had floor plans on how all this could be done. I was so taken with this presentation that I asked the Physicists to repeat it to the wider teaching and learning group later in the day.

Emma's story

Physics is a laboratory-based subject and a significant amount of the undergraduate experience centers on practical work. Physics at UCD is no different and close to 1000 students pass through our first-year laboratories each year, most en route to non-physics degrees. The School has long recognized that students do not always gain as much as they might from their time in the first-year laboratory but, for a variety of reasons, things today are in the main little different than they were decades ago.

Recently the School radically changed its approach to physics for 1st-year medical students; the traditional lab was replaced by inquiry-based learning focused on medically relevant problems. Examples include the calculation of the forces involved in the development of lower back pain and the fluid dynamics of intravenous infusions.

Mindful of this recent innovation and at the suggestion of Michael, the Head of School and I, as Head of Teaching and Learning, visited three Physics departments in England, learning different things from each department. One, Leicester, has pioneered problem-based learning in physics and we came back with ideas about flexible classroom space for our first-year laboratories, which would facilitate inquiry-based, group learning. We envisaged sets of equipment that would allow different cohorts of students to explore physics through inquiry that was appropriate to them and within a context that made physics relevant to them. We also imagined furniture that would allow traditional experiments and inquiry-based group work.

From my point of view there was not so much a "Eureka" moment as a motivation to crystallize thinking of how we might do things in the future. There was the chance of a real opportunity for change, with institutional support. The idea of the visits suggested that the consultation process was genuine. After all, Michael could not forecast what we would pick up from departments that we had chosen to visit. It also eased some of my own frustration associated with the apparent "ad hoc" nature of the planning process. If the master plan was being shaped rather than rubber-stamped then a certain amount of confusion was inevitable. My own experience of the planning process in many ways paralleled that of students accustomed to traditional lectures encountering problem-based learning for the first time.

Emma Sokell, Physicist

Architect's story

The Physics teaching labs spread over three floors with rooms filled with experiment set-ups ready to go, laid out like an obstacle course as students move from lower to upper levels. The whole department occupied one end of north block, and the administrative head was gracious and strategically located at the bridge level.

The Physics faculty—Lorraine Hanlon and Emma Sokell—were obviously caring and thoughtful in their approach. How would they react to change, I wondered? I had heard they visited some newer teaching labs in England and when I saw their slide show, it was a knock-out. They showed examples of recent renovations where labs were designed as flowing spaces, suites along an open circulation spine instead of rooms along a closed corridor. Could their walls be removed? At the end of the day I checked and they could be. Could they have a loft-like space? The structure was elegant, and had lots of glass so it could be an easy refit.

Lorraine asked the most dangerous question of all: "Why are we doing this [teaching Physics]? We should be showing all levels how to use physics, not training PhD physicists." I laughed inside. Did she know that I had to take Physics for Architecture?

Lorraine and Emma had a new vision of three different programs for three different clients: Physics for non-majors, Physics for engineers, and Physics for scientists. A PhD physicist will probably go elsewhere. This humility and clarity of purpose came as a result of their trip, which gave them an objective view of their mission, their program and their space. If we had done an analysis of their options—an inventory, alternative layouts, and the usual approach, it would have taken longer to get to the same place. A visit is worth a thousand pictures.

The Physics story has two levers on the process at UCD: one, they were the first group to announce a new approach—and they articulated a new curriculum; two, their request had the potential of being a less-expensive "dry" renovation. Organizations can do a lot with simple refurbishments, sending out messages with projects that can be done in a semester or over the summer. If they reflect the mission of the institution, small renovations are powerful transmitters internally and catalyze larger changes.

Bill Wilson, Architect

COMPUTER SCIENCE

Computer Science had seen a system at Purdue in which a teaching lab was laid out as a series of round tables as opposed to linear benches. Teaching assistants (TAs) roved from one table to another as students worked on problems in computer science. A seminar by a visiting Australian scientist described how a similar banqueting hall arrangement had been used to teach biology.

Joe's story: intelligent design or serendipity?

Computer Science and Informatics (CSI) took a decision to "go laptop" in 2008, i.e. we required our students to supply their own laptop and the school would no longer maintain labs of desktop PCs. This meant that our three computer labs (64-seater, 2 × 40-seaters) would be refurbished to remove fixed benching and replace them by rectangular tables so that they could be used as teaching rooms as well as labs. We were fortunate to win a university grant to cover the cost of the refurbishment. Having 25-years' experience of teaching

CS, I knew exactly what the labs would look like and the university took our specification and ordered the supplies.

At the same time, the university was designing a new science facility and lots of meetings with architects were being held to look at the design of science facilities. I attended these and heard ideas about design facilitating teaching but they did not strike home to me. This was partly because CSI was in the happy position not to require labs in the new facility and so we would only be looking to use "standard" classrooms.

Then at one meeting Prof Mick McManus, a visiting academic from Australia gave a charismatic presentation which covered classroom/lab design. The highlight for me was a four-minute video from the University of Minnesota on an active learning space for a Biology class.[1]

The classroom was designed using large round tables in a "banqueting style." It was a "eureka" moment—I immediately saw that we could do this with our large 64-seater lab. I invited Mick to come and see our lab and he agreed that it would be ideal for such a design. Michael was also very supportive and Bill came to see it and we had drawings done up. Our IT Manager, Gerry, also bought into the concept and took responsibility for delivering it. The new design comprised eight large round tables with nine student places, with a wall mounted LCD screen for each table as well as power for the laptops. This meant we could accommodate 72 students in a lab where previously we could handle 64 and still have lots of circulation space.

But what about the cost? The tables and chairs were already on order and could not be cancelled. Gerry suggested that we take the opportunity to refurbish our two classrooms with these supplies, as they were in need of upgrading—a no brainer so we did that. We still had to find a substantial sum to cover the new supplies. Fortunately, the school had a reserve account for emergencies and while this was not such an occasion we felt that the new lab was worth depleting this account.

The outcome: We now have a world class teaching facility that is getting rave reviews from teaching staff across the university as well as from students (undergrads, graduates, professionals on CPD courses). It also has a wow factor that really impresses high school students who come on visits to see what it would be like to study CS at UCD. I use the lab for teaching a module that I have previously taught in a lecture theater with some difficulty. It is a fantastic experience for me and, I hope, students. Students now "flow" into groups and work together—this took valuable time to organise in the lecture theater. I can check easily on each group and interact with them—the design facilitates the teaching.

As a CS academic I would have never expected to learn about CS lab design from looking at non-CS labs. I now realize the importance of design for teaching but only came to that realization from seeing it in practice—in my case by video. I think an actual site visit is the ideal way to learn these lessons and I know colleagues from other disciplines have benefited from such trips. My strong recommendation to anyone looking at refurbishment/new builds is to talk to people like Bill who can propose creative solutions and suggest appropriate places to visit.

This was an occasion where the right circumstances came together—world class experts were in UCD discussing design; we had a change leader (Michael) leading the process; we in CSI had money to carry out the project; we had an IT manager who bought-in to the idea and led the delivery; we were willing to learn even though we thought we knew all that was needed for CS lab design!

Joe Carthy, Computer Scientist

Architect's narrative

This was the quickest turnaround on campus. Joe Carthy, head of Computer Science, showed that he cared personally about details, even though his department (called a school) was not based in the Science Centre but was overflowing into the North Building from its home directly across the main east–west campus path. Computer Science Departments on most campuses are open to new approaches, and they embrace new technologies and ideas like self-directed learning and peer tutors.

In December, Joe, energetic and a good listener, took us over to the department home with a mission in mind: he showed us a large carpeted room with parallel countertops dead-ending into one wall. Computers lined the rows of counters. We love flow and the ability of students to gather around and look at a screen together. We could instantly see that just pulling the computers away from the wall was going to help. Joe had a plan of round tables similar to the active learning lab set up for MIT and Minnesota. We did a simple layout over the holidays and a year later, in February 2010, the Biology group has been able to experiment successfully with the room and now we are planning four more.

I feel personally involved, as other clients make similar requests: can we have an open room with computers on round tables and instructors so they can work in teams solving relevant problems? In March I sat in the room watching students and instructors.

The mood was upbeat; the instructor in the middle was informal and humorous, giving an aura that this was going to be a good session.

Bill Wilson Architect

As Project Director, I was recently invited to participate in one of Joe's classes on project management. We asked a group of 72 students to devise a scheme for managing the construction of the new Law School at the university with a minimalist formal introduction. The students got down to work immediately in a very focused and business-like way. A colleague and I went to visit each group over the next half-hour and provided some occasional orientation, encouragement and no specific information. At the reporting stage, when we aggregated the findings of each of the seven groups, we had 90 percent of the high-level components for the management of a construction project. When Joe came in at the end, his parting words to the students were to be sure to record their reflections on this in their diary. The levels of engagement and interaction that we achieved in this room ensured that the social aspects of the learning process were given real opportunity for expression. Compared with the lecture we had planned (and then abandoned when we saw the geography of the room), I feel certain the students gained a great deal more from this experience.

CHEMISTRY

Chemistry had taught first-year practical classes in groups of 90–100 in a large and intimidating laboratory. These labs are very dated and among the most ill-suited for purpose of all of the university's stock. There is a large amount of first-year service teaching and this is typically done in big groups with the help of teaching assistants. Prior to the design process, the chemistry faculty believed that what was required was updated but similar facilities with a greater emphasis on safety; the size and layout of the laboratories would likely remain very similar. This view was challenged by the design team quite early in the process and examples of more contemporary teaching lab layouts were presented for discussion. Key differences were the size of the labs (24 students as opposed to current group size of up to 72) and a layout that would enable a higher quality of contact between the students and the teaching assistants. Chemistry faculty also went on visits to the UK and Canada to review contemporary teaching methods there. As the design workshops proceeded, enthusiasm for the layouts proposed by Bill's team grew among the small group of chemists attending the workshops and we proceeded to more detailed design. However at a school meeting where the plans were presented to the wider faculty group, considerable disquiet was expressed about the designs; they flew in the face of conventional university (not just UCD) thinking about how Chemistry is taught and were attacked by a number of very vocal people. Student safety was the overt reason given for the objections, but some chemists later conceded that this was a frequently used ploy to fend off unwelcome proposals.

A much larger group attended the penultimate design workshop and it became a very difficult discussion. One of the attendees later told me that he was so concerned that he wished he'd had my mobile phone number to summon me to the event. I joined the conversation after attending another design session with a different group and I found a room which seemed filled with conflict; some chemistry colleagues were suggesting that we needed to go right back to the beginning and start again while others expressed vehement objections to the new layouts; those who had attended the workshops were doing their best to defend the proposals. At this point we were well into the design process and had spent a very large amount of money; going back to the beginning was simply not an option. I was also determined that the progress we had made with the small group of enthusiasts in the earlier session was not to be lost.

I listened to the increasingly fraught debate for a while and, with considerable anxiety, eventually decided on a confrontational and fairly hostile intervention in which I described my own experience of being a lost, 17-year-old first-year chemistry student in a huge teaching lab with what seemed like hundreds of strangers. I had a cookbook lab manual and there were small groups of older-looking people (the TAs) who might have been there to help, but I wasn't about to interrupt their conversation to ask. I was attempting to describe in the most graphic terms I could, what was the very opposite of what we were trying to achieve. I declared that the new layouts would help enormously with generating a higher-quality learning experience for our first-year students and that we owed this to them. I later discovered that there were several people in the room who related very much to my contribution, but there were some things that the chemists simply couldn't say to one another in a public arena.

There was another meeting of the chemists a few days later and agreement was reached that we would develop more conventional labs for the senior students, but that we would also continue with the design of the 24-person student-centered labs for the first years. The design of these is now complete and similar laboratories are being designed for students in Biology, Biochemistry and Pharmacology.

Architect's narrative

Evaluating chemistry teaching labs in older buildings means looking at the worst conditions in any teaching complex—small rooms full of bottles with strong, noxious odors, shelves of glassware and porcelain mortars and pestles, old fume hood cabinets that surely do not work, and large open rooms with years of accumulated stains on the original linoleum floors and stone counters. The only modern upgrade in an old chemistry teaching lab like UCD is likely to be some new analytical instruments on the counter of an adjacent room. The UCD chemistry labs were large rooms with wooden casework, unchanged since the early 1960s.

How will this conversation go, I wondered, when we had our first meeting in September at workshop 3? The Department Chair had no clear vision but was of an open mind and by our October workshop we had a list of labs and prep spaces, but no one showed up for the meeting. No alarms rang.

At our next session in November, we met with the Stockroom Manager and got a ground-level understanding of how the Chemistry group actually works: yes, they stored bulk solvents in a temporary rental shed outside. He explained the flow of chemicals out of the building and he was as delighted to have a person who knew how the building worked as he was to see that someone else cared about his space and safety problems. By workshop 5, in December, we had a review of the three kinds of teaching labs used by Chemistry—the Intro Suite, the P-Chem Suite, and the Synthetic Suite. By workshop 6, in January, we had agreement from the chair, Earle Waghorne, and Michael Monaghan, and a new direction.

A month later, we found ourselves facing a room of doubters. Workshop 7 in February 2009 was supposed to be a sign-off session for the C-shaped design. We thought we would be covering familiar territory with pleased users. Instead, we had a new cadre of seasoned instructors and they were not happy. We retreated to a previously proposed position of "looking at options" and left for a month. We used the computer to render 3D views and returned in March at workshop 8 to a room with more new people from Chemistry.

The concept of change was trickling through the chemists and it was an important part of the process to challenge it. Some were complaining; some were advocating. It was a heavy moment for the chemists as they publicly agreed with each other not that the new proposal was patently better, but that it was a different approach, one worth trying. The room quietly listened to a chemical biologist express her concern about being able to supervise a large number of students working in smaller rooms. In response, they agreed to have a suite of rooms along a circulation spine. This created "flow" and was an improvement in our minds.

We got sign-off in April at workshop 9, which took more meetings than usual in what was not a linear process—but that is the nature of designing chemistry teaching labs—probably the most challenging because of the overlay of multiple requirements: chemicals, fumes, and equipment with a large number of students of varying backgrounds.

Consensus in a Chemistry Department comes from within and it comes from reaching an understanding with several constituencies, the faculty who teach, the staff and the instructors who orchestrate the process as their prime day-in and day-out activity, and also with some third-parties in the administration who care about the students, the value of the program and the image of the program on the campus.

For the faculty consensus, there was no single person to decide, though any single faculty was willing to decide and each had a unique opinion so the best approach was to have them react to our sketch concepts and hear each other's views in a symposium style. The winner was nominated, in effect, by this group process. The presence of younger faculty in the debate—the chemical biologist in this case—added a critical dimension, openness to new ideas. The most friction occurred with the instructors with a split over the question of the old way versus the new way. The arguments on both sides were heard by the faculty and this was important. The third party in this case was Michael Monaghan and he weighed in only after all parties had spoken and he spoke not as a chemist, but from the higher ground of moving all disciplines to a new place.s

Bill Wilson Architect

For the faculty consensus, there was no single person to decide, though any single faculty was willing to decide and each had a unique opinion so the best approach was to have them react to our sketch concepts and hear each other's views in a symposium style. The winner was nominated, in effect, by this group process. The presence of younger faculty in the debate—the chemical biologist in this case added a critical dimension, openness to new ideas.

As these experiences unfolded I couldn't resist the temptation to draw attention to the potential that was now opening up for a different learning experience for our students and that all of the approaches we were hearing about moved us towards a much more interactive experience, where students would have opportunities to learn through dialogue and argument, to discover through real experience, to review their findings with peers and much of it would be done with a light hand of facilitation. Here were all those generic skills I had been preaching about to no avail at an earlier stage and the students would be picking them up while learning some Physics, Chemistry and Computer Science. We have now moved on to detailed design for the rooms in which these activities will take place and there is some measure of excitement about the possibilities.

THE CLASSROOM CONVERSATION

In the middle of 2009 we heard that the state was prepared to invest €65 million in our proposal to transform teaching and learning in the sciences at UCD. We had not yet started to talk seriously about the kinds of classrooms we needed. I was keen for us to have as creative a conversation as we possibly could around the type of classrooms we might design and decided to use four techniques from a suite of "Liberating Structures."[2] These are designed explicitly to increase the chances of novelty emerging from a fast-moving and intense set of encounters. I chose to use the "celebrity interview", "conversation café", "creative destruction" and "minimum specifications" and these are described below. We had two architects present and the challenge that I set for the group was to generate some preliminary instructions for the design team on the new classroom facilities we required.

Celebrity interviews: One of the architects rather bravely agreed to act in the role of chat show host and we had a number of guests for him to interview, including a recent winner of a national teaching award, the president of the students' union, some recent graduates and Kathy O'Boyle who had recently attended a meeting in the USA on the design of teaching facilities. The "host" adapted to the role very quickly and succeeded in raising many of the difficult issues around the quality of the learning experience. It was extremely interesting to hear the students' views on the value of the different attempts to provide them with education.

Conversation café: There are some specific rules here which we didn't quite manage to keep. The group was subdivided into smaller groups with a host in each group whose job it was to ensure that each person spoke for a minute about what they had just heard in the interviews. When the entire subgroup had spoken there was a second round of uninterrupted one-minute contributions and after that there was a fifteen-minute discussion. I asked that someone make a note of anything interesting that happened.

Creative destruction: The groups were mixed up again and I asked them to spend ten minutes compiling lists of the worst possible things we could do in the project; i.e. design features that would militate *against* the learning opportunities for our students. They seemed to enjoy this. After we collated the list of "don'ts" I asked how many of these we were doing already. There was a chorus of "all of them!"

Minimum specifications: We again moved the groups around and I asked them to compile a list of things we really ought to do now. Again there was a lively discussion at the end of which the flip-chart made its first appearance. I compiled a list of the dos and don'ts which have now gone on to inform the next stages of the design process.

Gopal's story: chat show host

> Being asked to be a "chat show host" was certainly the strangest request I have received from any client in my short career as an architect. Michael's explanation of the process that was to be

facilitated and his very brief introduction to the techniques to be used did nothing to build my confidence or assist in my rationalization of how the ultimate goal was to be achieved with the process.

With my background I would have been familiar with various types of collaborative problem-solving techniques, all of which would broadly take the form of a facilitator helping the participants to "information dump" issues, neatly group them into boxes (or sub-boxes and so-on . . .) and then prioritise them. A process not without its inherent flaws . . . those who shouted loudest (had the most confidence in a group situation) got heard and would advance their requirements high up the priority list with the result that we would usually end up with a de facto decision for the group.

The "chat show" interviews gave a number of people the opportunity to address outline issues relevant to the subject, in this case "Learning/Teaching Environments" and the current thinking about same. It allowed "specialists" in the field to address the group in an interactive environment but in a one-on-one situation. The outline ideas were thus on the table. This served as a genesis of ideas and considerations for the audience during the "conversation café" and the "creative destruction" sessions that followed. These sessions gave every person in the group equal opportunity to reflect on the discussions and add their issues/considerations to the discussion.

What was interesting about the outcomes to the latter part of the "creative destruction" session and more so in the "minimum specifications" part of the process was the amount of consensus that was being built around topics. With traditional collaborative problem-solving techniques, the object is to create a neat set of "pigeon holes"—a process in which consensus is built on the back of inevitable compromise on the part of the participants. The technique employed at our workshop provided an alternative and undoubtedly more robust form of consensus building by reflection and discussion by all of the participants. It didn't mean everyone was in agreement but we got more agreement in a shorter period of time as compared with the traditional technique.

> With traditional collaborative problem-solving techniques, the object is to create a neat set of "pigeon holes"—a process in which consensus is built on the back of inevitable compromise on the part of the participants. The technique employed at our workshop provided an alternative and undoubtedly more robust form of consensus building by reflection and discussion by all of the participants. It didn't mean everyone was in agreement but we got more agreement in a shorter period of time as compared with the traditional technique.

On further reflection on the techniques used, I would say that the interviews need to be quick, fast paced and should not allow any prolonged oratory from the speaker . . . they should be as engaging as possible for the audience. The interview panel should be from opposing sides of the spectrum to spark debate on the floor during the "Conversation Sessions." All of it should run to pre-arranged time constraints (but not rigidly so) . . . I feel this was the key to the process—short enough to keep the participants interested, but long enough to address the issues. I felt that the added bit of time pressure helped everyone to at best galvanize to a position, at worst to speak up about their considerations.

As to the ultimate outcome of the process, we got a set of dos and don'ts without a preset agenda or set of imposed objectives, but by means of an organic set of considerations and ideas that became apparent during the process and which, by agreement of all the participants on the basic principles, has led to a tangible set of requirements that will inform the design brief for the project.

Gopal Naidoo, Architect

Kathy's story: celebrity interviewee

In the 12 months leading up to November 2009 the faculty had had several lengthy meetings with the architects about the new science center. During this time we were encouraged to think about what new facilities we thought we needed but also, and more fundamentally, to think about how we wanted to teach going forward. Despite this encouragement, however, many of us were limited by our own experiences and were reluctant to commit to changing our teaching styles. A key turning point for me occurred when I had the opportunity to attend a design workshop in the USA on undergraduate science learning spaces. In particular, listening to a compelling account of how student-centered active learning classrooms encourage teamwork, problem solving and creativity amongst students persuaded me that this was a different, but probably better, way to teach. For the first time, it sounded not only desirable but also do-able. I was aware that we had a newly commissioned active learning classroom on campus so I reorganized one of my courses and ran a couple of short problem-based sessions in this facility. The class enthusiastically embraced the challenge posed by, what was for them, a new approach to learning. As well as discussing the problem, sharing ideas and working and re-working solutions, they had opportunities to present their work to the rest of the class. Above all, the students talked science to each other. Even in the small number of sessions available to the class it was possible to delve deeper into the topic than would have been possible using a more traditional, lecture-intensive teaching style.

I have been completely converted to this style of teaching and now have plans to introduce elements of it into most of the courses that I teach. Having gone to the USA to learn about the design of better undergraduate learning spaces I have ended up changing my whole approach to teaching and learning.

Kathy O'Boyle, Pharmacologist

CONCLUSIONS AND LESSONS LEARNED

The project remains a work in progress, but the design workshops are about to resume for a three-month period when we will finalize the layouts of the laboratories and classrooms. The conversation has moved on in significant ways and we are now talking frequently about the learning experience of our students rather than our own experience of teaching. This is the most striking change and it is interesting to think about the high-level objectives outlined in our proposal documents to the funding authorities, the starting point of our initial discussion (the 600-seater auditorium) and the fact that we are now talking explicitly about how we change the learning experience of our students. It is also interesting to think about the reality that, in my experience, it is always difficult to generate conversation around these topics in the abstract, but the prospect of new facilities was a key factor in changing the conversation. The high-level aspiration, developed at the senior administration level in the organization was not sufficient on its own to change the discussion.

My role as project director has multiple facets to it. I report on progress directly to the senior management team of the university every few weeks. Their interest is in knowing that the university's vision, as set out above, is being achieved. When I leave the administration building, my role is one of trying to work with my colleagues in the sciences to reach the goal of "transforming the undergraduate experience." My approach to doing this is based on a strongly held view that academics believe passionately in the importance of dialogue and feel an intense need to creatively sustain the academy as a living tradition; they must feel able to fashion their own position within the arguments which have to do with constituting and re-constituting that tradition.[3] By way of trying to achieve this I was deliberately trying to create what Stacey describes as more fluid, spontaneous types of conversation, with a view to creating conditions where some novelty might emerge.[4]

My role and status give me some power; a significant part of that power is in determining the kind of conversation that takes place. Stacey, drawing on the work of Foulkes, the founder of group analysis, states that: "Given the power relation of the leader to others, he or she is in a particularly well-placed position to create opportunities for conversation that may foster greater spontaneity.

Such spontaneity is likely to be fostered through the manner in which a leader handles a situation, encouraging others to create and shape the situation rather than simply giving instructions.[5]"

The other significant way in which my approach to "leading" or "managing" these conversations has changed in recent years relates to the question of conflict. In previous roles I used spend very large amounts of time traveling the corridors in advance of meetings to try to ensure there was a reasonable chance of consensus at the actual event; essentially I was managing conflict out of the discussions. As I joined the difficult Chemistry meeting in the middle of a heated debate, it seemed to me that there was a real possibility of the chemists regressing to the design of another large "teaching barn" rather than the family-sized units we had been discussing in more recent times. I felt compelled to take a deliberately conflictual position and described with some passion my own wretched experience as a 17-year-old first-year student of first-year chemistry. I urged them to consider the advantages that would accrue from the new layouts and how they could significantly enhance the experience of our students and probably increase the pass rate at the end of the year. This had the potential for throwing a can of petrol onto a roaring fire, but I felt absolutely bound to support those who had been advocating change in the face of more recent arrivals to the conversation who held more conventional views of the learning experience. I learned later that several of the chemists were quietly agreeing with me.

The classroom design session was the most experimental of the techniques I used in my attempts to generate different kinds of conversation and indicates the frustration I feel with what frequently passes for dialogue in organizational life; typically we are exposed to a PowerPoint lecture or talk to introduce the topic and then invited to discuss or participate in the version of life the presenter has put before us. This is now so embedded in the university teaching ideology as to be almost unquestioned, yet it flies in the face of contemporary views on how the learning process takes place. My objective was to expose the participants in the discussion to an unconventional experience that enabled a physical demonstration of how learning, which is characterised by activity, social exchange and real engagement, can greatly supplement individual learning. This is based on the belief that meaning frequently emerges from the exchange of conversational gestures and that learning that takes place in this kind of environment is much deeper than passively sitting listening to an "expert" presenting the material. I wanted frequent movement, different conversations and chose to introduce the "experts" in an interview format. It helped greatly that Gopal took to the role like a natural as "chat show host." We generated outputs together in two hours which provided the starting point for the next conversation. We are now planning a suite of four rooms which will be set out like the new computer science room with capacity of 100 students each and which are designed for science students to work in conversational groups in which they can discuss anything from the principles of evolution to the resolution of difficult problems in mathematics.

We now seem a long way from the aspiration of having a 600-seat auditorium.

It is very clear that the university has made definite moves towards being more forceful in its approach to planning and implementing its strategies since 2004. The development of Science at the university has been explicitly linked to national strategies to develop a "smart economy" and funding proposals to government have made explicit promises in relation to the quality of the research and teaching which will take place if investments are made. We have now been awarded a substantial amount of funding for the development of the undergraduate teaching program and it has been my job to try to ensure that we design and deliver transformative facilities. Of course, this has not been a linear process and there have been many unexpected turns in the road. While it is not so difficult to *write* about transforming the undergraduate experience, making these things happen is a rather different thing. My despondence at the opening discussions we had was based on a fear that the gap between the high-level aspiration of the university and what those delivering the teaching perceived as the real world was too great to be bridged. The suggestion that colleagues visit what they perceived to be their peers to discuss how learning processes could be improved was pivotal. Inviting those who were already trying innovative approaches to participate fully in the discussion was important, as was being aware of the role and potential value of diversity and conflict. Clearly, planning was very important for this project, starting from the point at which the initial idea was conceived, through writing persuasive proposals for the funding agency and finally developing the drawings which would be used by the contractor to construct the building. What this narrative attempts is to describe how solutions were reached, sometimes by rather unexpected means, and some significant points in the journey. The role of free-flowing conversation was deliberately developed, sometimes by slightly artificial means but this also took place against the backdrop of deadlines that needed to be met and the clearly expressed strategies of senior management in the university. It was never the case that we could just do anything we liked.

There is considerable debate in university circles about the competing values of managerial versus the traditional collegial approach to decision making. Managerial approaches are frequently denigrated by those holding conventional views, but when pressed they often concede that traditional approaches were often characterized by late and inappropriate decision making. In this project there was no doubt that senior management in the university held substantially more power than their predecessors, but it was equally clear that they alone could not sustain the vision through to completion of the project. The approach being taken is to try to maximize the extent of involvement of colleagues in the process of decision making, while making it clear that decisions will and must be taken in a timely manner to ensure completion of the project. The narrative makes clear that it is possible to include academics in the discussions, arguments, conflict even, which help us as academics, in Shotter's phrase, to position ourselves within the arguments which have to do with constituting and re-constituting the university tradition.[6] There will always be tensions in the university around the competing values of managerialism and collegiality; I would argue that, in this project, those tensions have generated good interim outcomes which should be sustained throughout the design process and deliver the quality learning outcomes that we have promised for our students.

The most surprising element for me as project director was the impact on colleagues of visiting other places and their having the chance to discuss plans with their peers in the scientific disciplines. These discussions obviously had considerable depth and got down to the detail of what constitutes a good learning experience of students. Despite the fact that conventional wisdom would hold that physical planning should be part of the implementation of an established teaching and learning philosophy, this project indicates how the emergence of an embedded teaching philosophy went hand in hand with the planning of the infrastructure. Ideas brought back from other places often are fruit that quickly wither on the vine; in this case their incorporation into the master-planning process very soon after they were brought home gave them a lifespan which might not have been expected. As one of the stories above indicates, one was fully implemented within a few months of its conception.

> Despite the fact that conventional wisdom would hold that physical planning should be part of the implementation of an established teaching and learning philosophy, this project indicates how the emergence of an embedded teaching philosophy went hand in hand with the planning of the infrastructure. Ideas brought back from other places often are fruit that quickly wither on the vine; in this case their incorporation into the master-planning process very soon after they were brought home gave them a lifespan which might not have been expected.

Anxiety, anger, shame, exhilaration, frustration were emotions which became manifest at various stages during the project. Some colleagues experienced anxiety at conventional ways of teaching being challenged, others were frustrated by the demands on their time of a more student-centered approach in a research university and some of the chemists were angered by the dramatic changes proposed to the layout of teaching labs. When things seemed to be going the wrong way in the Chemistry argument, my intervention could be described as a deliberate attempt at shaming my colleagues but, in fact, the actual response to this intervention was quite mild and we reached a solution which seemed to meet the needs of all parties. The pleasant emotions were exhilaration at the great ideas coming from colleagues on new ways of thinking about how we do things and the frequency with which we found ourselves talking about the learning experiences of our students, as compared with earlier conversations which were more about ways we could help the teachers "perform" better or more efficiently. It really does feel like we are on our way to designing facilities which will enrich the experience of our students in significant ways.

NOTES

1 www.classroom.umn.edu/Interactive_Classroom225p.mov (accessed November 11, 2010).

2 Lipmanowicz H, McCandless K. Liberating structures: innovating by including and unleashing everyone. *Performance.* 2010: **24**: 6–19.

3 Shotter J. *Conversational Realities: constructing life through language.* London: Sage; 1993. p. 183.

4 Stacey R. *Strategic Management and Organisational Dynamics: the challenge of complexity*, 5th ed. London: FT Prentice Hall; 2007. p. 286.

5 Stacey R, op. cit.

6 Shotter J, op. cit.

Commentary: The Science Centre at University College Dublin

This chapter makes real the metaphor "an organization is a conversation." It tells the story of how the design of a new science facility at the University College of Dublin was informed through dialogue, and illustrates how even the tangible aspects of an organization (its buildings) emerge through conversation (*see* Chapter 2). Creating two key disturbances changed patterns of relating and meaning and led to more comprehensive, innovative and inclusive dialogues and a robust consensus about the way forward. The smaller scale of this project, being closer to the ground compared with other case studies in this book, reveals to the reader the rich details of the moment-to-moment conversational process. It is at this level of detail that change happens.

WHEN STUCK, CREATE A DISTURBANCE TO CHANGE PATTERNS OF MEANING

An enlightened leader (Michael Monaghan) and an innovative architect (Bill Wilson) attempted to engage the science faculty in dialogue about how the design of a new facility could align with optimal student-learning environments. At first these ideas fell on deaf ears. The existing patterns of thinking were very strong and faculty members were resistant (perhaps afraid) of leaving familiar ground. They seemed fixated on updating familiar environments to maximize their teaching efficiency using traditional methods. The idea of change in the abstract perhaps raised anxieties of incompetence. Then came a pivotal intervention: Since the goal was for UCD to rank among the Top 30 European Universities, Bill suggested that faculty visit peers at other high-ranking sites to see how they did things. Motivated by the goal of becoming a top site, faculty were willing to take up Bill's suggestion.

The site visits shook up conventional ways of thinking ("disturbed patterns of meaning," in the language of complexity) and opened people to new world views. Something about going to other places and seeing new ideas in action made these ideas more accessible than when they simply heard about them in the abstract. In one instance, seeing a four-minute videotape of an interactive learning environment led to a "Eureka moment" for a member of the Computer Science Faculty, who commented, "I now realize the importance of design for teaching but only came to that realization from seeing it in practice—by video." The inclusion of the video-link is an innovation of this chapter that will allow readers to experience this for themselves.

The site visits also served to assure the faculty that their views were truly welcomed and would help shape the outcome. After all, the project leader couldn't know what they would find in these visits. This was clearly an open invitation to gather the best wisdom from all sources. Although there was a defined timeline for the project, faculty input was needed and welcomed to help shape the outcome. There was no master plan; no hidden agenda.

In being sent on this discovery expedition, faculty who were given the autonomy to learn for themselves and in their own way, came to see that they could develop competence in innovative methods of teaching, and felt they would be respected for their opinions. These are the hallmarks of Self-Determination Theory (Chapter 3) and, as predicted by that theory, led to changes in attitudes and conversations.

It was not only seeing other venues, but also conversations with peers in other places that opened minds to new approaches. When members of the Physics faculty returned from conversations with colleagues at other sites fired up about a new way of thinking and teaching their first-year students, they were invited to present their insights to their UCD colleagues. This project has much in common with a Positive Deviance project (Chapter 3). It engaged a community in finding its own solutions and in using the positive innovations within that group to inspire change in others.

DETERMINING STRUCTURES FOR DESIRED CONVERSATIONS

To further harvest faculty wisdom from the site visits for designing the next generation of classrooms, Michael used a series of unique conversational formats that were engaging, interactive and fast paced. He invited all stakeholders to be present for this gathering, including top teachers, students, recent graduates, and faculty. These modalities gave everyone a voice (rather than the most vociferous persons having the most influence), allowed mixing of ideas, and plentiful opportunities for serendipity, innovative thinking, and finally, a deep consensus based on robust dialogue. (Again, in the language of complexity, they fostered diversity and responsiveness creating the conditions under which transformative new patterns could emerge.) The experience also provided a lived example of engaged interactive learning, the very innovations that faculty were being asked to adopt in their teaching of students.

FACILITATING AND SPEAKING ONES TRUTH

As Project Director, Michael was more than a facilitator of process. He also spoke his truth at a critical juncture—sharing his own wrenching experience as a chemistry student at 17 to confront the intellectual argument for a large impersonal teaching auditorium with the hard reality of his experience as a young learner. His personal authenticity in that moment engaged others and invited people into a deeper and more balanced dialogue.

By his own lights, his major contribution was the belief in the faculty: "their passion for dialogue and . . . need to creatively sustain the academy as a living tradition." His choice of methods and structures was in service of creating conditions for greater spontaneity and novelty, inclusive dialogue and robust respectful consensus. His stance was both bounded and open—maximizing the involvement of colleagues in the decision-making process, while making it clear that decisions would be taken in a timely manner to ensure completion of the project.

WITNESSING A SHIFT IN PARADIGM

Through the course of this process, the dominant pattern of conversation shifted from what constitutes an effective environment for teachers to what constitutes a good learning environment for students. The faculty came to recognize the profound impact of physical space on learning experience which led to engaged and creative ideas for the design of the new facilities.

In sum, this chapter dramatically illustrates how small changes in interpersonal interactions seed new patterns of thinking. Being mindful of the very structure of how people are talking together is critical to the outcome.

CHAPTER 12

The Harvard Vanguard Kenmore Practice experience: a focus on human development and relationship building

Zeev Neuwirth

SYNOPSIS

This narrative describes the beginning stages of the transformation of an Internal Medicine department within Harvard Vanguard Medical Associates (Harvard Vanguard). This initial effort laid the foundation for the subsequent beginning of a transformational journey for the larger organization, a 600-physician multi-specialty group practice.

In 2005, many of the Internal Medicine clinicians and staff at the Kenmore center, one of the urban practice locations of Harvard Vanguard, were discontented and felt disenfranchised. Not surprisingly, patient-satisfaction survey scores reflected dissatisfaction as well. The patient-satisfaction scores of the Kenmore Internal Medicine practice were among the lowest in the organization. Customer service was less than desired and it was difficult for patients to get the kind of personal attention they wanted from the staff. On the larger scene, Harvard Vanguard was recovering from a difficult financial situation resulting from its separation from Harvard Pilgrim Healthcare and was struggling to establish itself as a financially strong and independent, physician-led group practice.

To address this situation, we used a combination of team-building activities, community-organizing principles and Relationship-centered Care practices, all of which culminated in the adoption of organizational-change principles and process-improvement techniques from Toyota Production Systems ("Lean") within the department. The staff describe this experience as emotionally and professionally fulfilling and transformational on multiple levels—from professional satisfaction to improved relationships with each another and, most importantly, to the provision of care that is patient centered.

In the years that have followed our initial efforts, Internal Medicine teams at Kenmore have kept the momentum going with continuous improvements in healthcare delivery and service to patients, as well as positive changes for clinicians and staff. The early pilots at Kenmore became a model for several other practice sites that began to adopt similar principles and approaches. Now, four years later, key aspects of Harvard Vanguard's organization-wide strategic plan and deployment methods are based on the same principles of respect, culture change, and process improvement that were defined and initiated at the Kenmore practice.

THE ORGANIZATION

The Kenmore practice is one of 17 locations through which Harvard Vanguard, a non-profit, multi-specialty group practice, provides coordinated primary and specialty care to more than 460 000 adult and pediatric patients in Greater Boston. Harvard Vanguard's 4000 employees include more than 600 physicians and 1000 other healthcare professionals. During 2005 and 2006, the time period described in this narrative, the Kenmore Internal Medicine Department had 23 000 patients served by 19 primary care physicians and 6 advanced practice clinicians (nurse practitioners and physician assistants), as well as 24 medical assistants and medical secretaries.

The Kenmore practice dates back to the origins of Harvard Vanguard. In the late 1960s, a group of physicians, healthcare administrators and academic leaders led by Robert H Ebert, MD, then dean of Harvard Medical School, created the Harvard Community Health Plan (HCHP). When it opened its doors on October 1, 1969 in Boston, HCHP became the first managed-care organization (also called a health-maintenance organization, or HMO) sponsored by a medical school. The Kenmore practice became the first HCHP clinical group.

The model created by HCHP represented a revolution in the delivery of healthcare in Boston, replacing fee-for-service care with a prepaid group practice that provided high-quality ambulatory healthcare within the community, serving the sick while also providing preventive care to the well. Comprehensive care services were available under one roof, delivered by a multi-disciplinary practice staffed by salaried physicians working with clinical teams. Affiliation with Harvard Medical School provided training for future physicians, and the program cared for patients from all sectors of society, including low-income, underserved populations.

The history of Harvard Vanguard is the history of a social dream: a vision for healthcare delivery that inspired all who were involved during the early years and one that continues to attract clinicians and staff with a desire to improve our healthcare delivery system. It was this vision that drew me to the practice in the summer of 2005 and convinced me to accept the position of Chief of Internal Medicine at the Kenmore practice. The inspirational power of the organization's original mission brought into particularly sharp relief the difficulties within Kenmore Internal Medicine at the time that I joined the organization.

IMPETUS FOR CHANGE: SETTING THE STAGE

By the late 1980s, with more than 200 000 patients and several additional practice locations, HCHP had formed one of the most successful quality-of-care management programs in the nation. In 1993, HCHP became one of the first HMOs in the nation to be fully accredited by the National Committee for Quality Assurance. This cemented HCHP's position as a leader in clinical quality improvement, a trajectory that formed the philosophical base and gave momentum to the changes within the Kenmore Internal Medicine Department to be described in this narrative.

At the time of my arrival in 2005, Harvard Vanguard was still recovering from a series of significant and disruptive organizational changes. In 1995, HCHP had merged with Pilgrim Healthcare, an insurance company and HMO whose physicians were members of an Independent Practice Association, a network of independent-physician practices that contracted with Pilgrim to form Harvard Pilgrim Healthcare. By 1998, this larger combined entity was experiencing severe financial troubles. The healthcare delivery side of Harvard Pilgrim, known as the Health Centers Division decided to separate from the insurer to form a completely independent, not-for-profit, physician-led group practice named Harvard Vanguard Medical Associates.

The start was rocky. Beginning in 2000, Harvard Vanguard had three CEOs in two years. During this same period, Harvard Pilgrim, the group's primary payer, was on the verge of financial collapse. The focus for Harvard Vanguard at that time was clearly economic survival.

The organization-wide turmoil was being played out within the microcosm of the Kenmore Internal Medicine (IM) Department, which was also struggling with its relationship to senior management. This narrative begins with the department's frustration and anger over the central administration's decision to reduce RN staffing at Kenmore IM, and with another top-down decision—to roll out a Patient Centered Care (PCC) initiative, which had been developed at another Harvard Vanguard practice site with external consultants and as a result of a collaborative research survey. As one person within the Kenmore IM department stated:

> The IM Department is a superb clinical team taking care of the practice's most difficult and needy patients—and we, far more than the off-site senior administrators, are able to make the right decisions about how to manage our practice. In other words, stop meddling and let us keep doing what we have been doing, and doing well, for more than twenty years.

WALKING INTO IT

Just a month prior to my joining the practice, the PCC "deployment team" arrived at Kenmore. Their plan to roll out a centralized, standardized practice model could not have come at a more difficult time. The Kenmore administrative team and I supported this new model of care, but the larger context and the way in which it was being deployed, especially following the elimination of several RN positions, created a problem.

The PCC model was built upon two basic premises. The first was that patients could be grouped into "categories of need": those who required basic preventive and wellness care, those who required more intensive preventive care, those requiring chronic disease management (often complex and multidisciplinary), and those who required intensive home-bound and institutional-assisted care. This approach would allow the practice to create protocols of care that would provide more appropriate medical attention focused on what patients in each group required. The second premise was that patients wanted to have their primary relationship with their physician, who would be supported by a multi-disciplinary, integrated and coordinated team. These two premises, the resulting standardized clinical team roles and responsibilities, and the clinical protocols of care represented a huge departure from the way in which medicine had been delivered at Harvard Vanguard. As one example of this change, nurse practi-tioners and physicians assistants who for years had been regularly assuming the front-line role in patient care and in the patient-clinician relationship would now be serving a more supportive and secondary role.

All of us on the Kenmore management team felt that the new practice model was quite positive and forward thinking. What concerned us was the *way* it had been developed and the *way* it was being deployed. Clinicians and staff were being asked to be collaborative and relationally oriented with one another and with their patients, yet the internal deployment effort was not collaborative and relational. The model had been largely developed at the central office with only a handful of people involved. It had been piloted at only one practice site without much input from the clinicians and staff from the other sites.

Most importantly, the focus of the initiative had been on the technical aspects of the team in this new model of care. Little attention had been paid to the socio-cultural aspects of change. The intention of this initiative was to be patient (people) centered, but the people part—the cultural, leadership, and change issues—were missing from the model. As we were observing the situa-tion and struggling to balance the deployment of the new care model with the needs of the practice, the Kenmore management team began to realize that if we wanted to create teams that could provide "patient-centered" care, we would also have to create a department that cared for its clinicians and staff in the same way. We would need to create a department in which respect, trust, open dialogue and communication, and collaborative problem solving were the norm, i.e. a "relationship-centered" culture. On the surface, the problem was to get the department to adopt a patient-centered model. On a deeper level, the challenge was to develop and foster the kind of collaborative culture and supportive team dynamics that would be the essential components of any patient-centered model. The challenge of making those changes in this department was overwhelming.

The Kenmore management team began to realize that if we wanted to create teams that could provide "patient-centered" care, we would also have to create a department that cared for its clinicians and staff. We would need to create a department in which respect, trust, open dialogue and communication, and collaborative problem solving were the norm . . .

As soon as I arrived at Kenmore in June of 2005, a steady stream of unhappy nurses, doctors, medical assistants, physician assistants, medical secretaries, technicians and other staff began arriving at my door. There were tears, anger and bilious resentment that, as one staff member told me, "had been building up for years." I was shocked at the lack of respect and trust among the staff. People clearly felt disenfranchised and unheard. A number of people said, "This used to be a great organization. Now it is over." One physician told me that he and his colleagues had, for the past few decades, adopted a "seek cover" approach. Whenever a new initiative appeared, they would simply seek refuge in their offices and exam rooms, and eventually the initiative would lose steam.

Another physician informed me that his medical assistant was "an idiot." When I interviewed his medical assistant, I discovered that she had a Masters in communication and wrote fluently in five languages. Most upsetting to her was that the physician with whom she worked was unaware of her capabilities. This was not an isolated case. A number of doctors were disparaging of the staff in their conversations with patients and often worked *around* their staff instead of with them. The staff knew this and often responded by making only a minimal effort to assist the physicians. It was a negatively reinforcing cycle of disrespect and distrust. It was clear that no clinical improvements or initiatives would be possible without first addressing the underlying relationships and the difficult emotional dynamics within the department.

As medical chief my first critically important step was to develop a strategic partnership with the Kenmore site administrator, Michael Knosp. Michael is a highly skilled and intuitive healthcare administrator who had been with the practice for years. Within a few weeks, I came to respect his values and principles and to trust his administrative acumen, experience and wisdom. We met every week in a collegial mutual mentorship. My goal was to learn from him, to confirm my perceptions and ideas, and to plan together. We also began to work with the management team at Kenmore Internal Medicine. On our team were:

➤ Dr David Meenan, a bright, intuitive, and gifted healthcare administrator and experienced physician leader who served as associate chief of the Kenmore practice and also ran the urgent-care department for the entire organization;

➤ Noelle Lawler, the other associate chief of the department and an exceptional physician assistant who is passionate about patient care and also highly creative and forward thinking about new modes of healthcare delivery;

➤ Joanne Svenson, our nurse leader whose enthusiasm, openness and positive attitude were critical to our team;

➤ Jennifer Whitworth and Dagmar Eglitis, the Internal Medicine supervisors who had been through tough times but were also amazingly responsive and willing to try new things;

➤ Sue Cantor, the department administrative support person, a warm person with a huge heart. If you needed to know something or to get something done, Sue was the person to turn to.

FIRST STEP: LISTENING AND OBSERVING

Our Kenmore management team believed that in order to change the socio-cultural dynamics within the department we needed to engage the staff both individually and collectively, with a view to honoring each person's emotional and professional perspective. In order to create a plan of action, we needed information from a fresh and unbiased source. So, as someone new to the practice, I began conducting individual interviews with each and every member of the staff, filling my notebook with detailed pictures of the complex dynamics that had developed and trying to piece the entire picture together.

During my first 2–3 months at Kenmore, I met with every person in the department for a one-on-one interview. Although I had a few questions outlined, I spent the majority of these one-hour sessions just listening. I invited staff members to speak honestly and then listened closely to them, promising that I would maintain confidentiality. Some interviews required a follow-up to complete the picture or to allow the individuals to get comfortable speaking with me. As I told each of them, my goal was to create a respectful working environment within the department that afforded each clinician, staff member, and patient the dignity he or she deserved. I also made it a point to walk the hallways during my administrative time to see how things were actually working. I spent time sitting in the staff break room, eating lunch with folks and mostly just being friendly. These informal and impromptu dialogues were invaluable to getting past the barriers to open, meaningful and trusting dialogue.

The leadership team and I reviewed the notes I had taken during these interviews to look for patterns and the underlying structural issues. As the newcomer to the practice, I was able to bring a fresh perspective and listen with an open mind. The rest of the management team was able to provide their firsthand experience and hard-earned intimate knowledge of the people and the situation. More than just data gathering and analysis, the dozens of one-on-one interviews and the management-team debriefs were the beginnings of a practice-wide dialogue within the Kenmore IM practice.

One clear picture that emerged from these interviews was that the different professional groups within the practice were not communicating well with one another. The nurses were at odds with the medical assistants. The medical assistants were in contention with the physicians and also with the medical secretaries. The physician assistants had disagreements with the nurses and nurse practitioners. So, to address this communication problem, we developed an initial plan.

REBUILDING MUTUAL RESPECT

Believing that mutual respect requires knowledge of the other person's perspective, we set up a series of staff get-togethers. Initially, we began meeting with the professional groups separately to discuss their frustrations and difficulties. We met with the nurses, the medical assistants, the medical secretaries, the physician assistants, and the physicians. Then, once the groups had a chance to vent and be heard separately, we began pairing these groups. For example, we scheduled a number of one-hour lunch time dialogues between the nurses and the medical assistants over pizza and soda. The facilitation process was simple. Each person had a chance to speak without interruption and to voice their experience. We simply went around the table until everyone had spoken. We did not initially include cross-talk or dialogue, instead emphasizing the importance of simply giving people the opportunity to speak and to be heard. As time went on, the process became more of a dialogue. Before, the various staff groupings often had been criticizing each other for not performing adequately. This began to change as each group heard the circumstances and pressures under which the others were operating.

> Believing that mutual respect requires knowledge of the other person's perspective, we set up a series of staff get-togethers. . . . The facilitation process was simple. Each person had a chance to speak without interruption and to voice their experience.

At first, it was obvious that people were angry and resentful. However, attitudes began to change within minutes as people listened to one another, and as they heard the frustrations and challenges that others faced. People were genuinely surprised at what they were hearing from, and learning about, one another. We continued to hold these cross-group dialogues until we realized that the groups were beginning to hold them on their own in both formal and informal settings.

The second group meeting we constructed was within each individual professional or staff grouping. These sessions initially began as a way for people to air their concerns, but over time they became more like opportunities for community organizing. Two groups on which we focused were the medical assistants and the medical secretaries. What became surprisingly clear was the ability and power of the medical secretaries and medical assistants to influence the day-to-day delivery of healthcare. Whereas the clinicians were largely focused on the technical aspects of medical care and on their individual relationships with patients, the assistants and secretaries were focused on the system as a whole. They were the process and flow-oriented personnel.

We shared this perspective with the medical assistants and secretaries and began building their understanding of how much positive influence they could have in healthcare. Together we began to develop ideas and plans for how they could organize themselves and the department in order to deliver better care. We appealed to their values, principles and sense of dignity, reminding them that our shared goal was to provide the kind of service to our patients that we would want for our own families and ourselves. It was a powerful message and it motivated all of us.

EMPOWERMENT AND SELF-DETERMINATION

As we improved relationships and trust among staff members in the IM practice, we also had to address the difficult relationship between the Kenmore IM Department and the central administration. As front-line middle managers, we were faced with a dilemma. The central administration had planned a fairly rapid roll out of the PCC initiative at Kenmore. The Kenmore management team, however, had determined that a purely top-down initiative was not going to work. We thought instead to improve patient care through a more "grass-roots" approach, which would draw upon the knowledge and experience of staff at the front lines of care. Now that the staff members were talking to each other, they would be better able to collaborate to provide Relationship-centered Care to patients.

This dilemma required two simultaneous negotiations. First, we needed to persuade senior management that we could achieve the PCC objectives using this more bottom-up approach to change. Second, we needed to sell the idea of creating some of our own patient care improvements to all levels of staff within our department. Fortunately, the senior administration supported our request and agreed that we could launch our own clinical care improvement program in conjunction with PCC. This gave a tremendous boost to the IM staff in terms of being heard and in achieving the balance of self-determination and empowerment they were seeking.

TEAM BUILDING
Team building in the Kenmore IM management team

A foundational aspect of our early work was team building. We began with the management team. Initially, we held off-site sessions introducing the principles of Relationship-centered Care, the importance of allowing people to speak openly and honestly, the fundamental necessity of listening to people and being present in the moment. We practiced these skills by role playing. I also introduced the concept of the management team as a "learning organization": learning from our shared experiences through dialogue and reflection, learning from the people we worked with through listening and inquiry, and learning from people outside our organization and even outside of healthcare. I began to bring articles and case studies for people to read prior to the management team meetings—sort of a book club. I also brought in speakers from outside of the organization to provide us with fresh ideas and the experience of other provider groups. Within a few short months our management team was turning into a vibrant "learning and doing" club. Our weekly management meetings became inquiries and explorations into improving the practice and patient care rather than administrative fire-fighting. These management team meetings, coupled with the weekly mentoring meetings I had with Michael Knosp, created a powerful coalition for change.

Team building in the Kenmore IM clinical teams

After our initial large group "round table" lunch-time dialogues with the clinical staff, we initiated a team-building program. I constructed a series of three 2 hour seminars for the clinical teams. These sessions were held during the lunch hour to have a minimal impact on patient-care time. A typical clinical team in our practice consisted of a physician, an advanced practice clinician, a nurse, a medical assistant and a medical secretary. The first session was an introduction that was similar to what we had done with the management team, focusing on the importance of respectful listening, inquiry, dignity, meaning and purpose. We spent some time discussing how to adopt a "learner" rather than "judger" mindset when listening to colleagues. Another concept, learned through the practice of improvisational performance techniques, was learning how to say, "yes and" instead of "no, but."

The second session was a deeper dive into listening in which the group learned concepts and techniques of inquiry. In one exercise the group members asked each other questions about their work day, including what they did, how they did it, what their challenges were, and how they measured success. It was startling to the clinical team members just how little they understood each others' perspectives and roles. I also shared with the group a powerful listening technique learned from a mentor, Robert Fritz. This technique involves "picturing" what the other person is saying. We began by having the team members simply picture colleagues' descriptions of rooms in their houses. The picturing requires intense listening as the listeners try to visualize what is being told to them. It is the most challenging and rewarding form of "active listening" that I've ever encountered, and it had a real impact on the clinical teams. These exercises afforded the team members the opportunity to hear one another in new and deeper ways and simultaneously to develop their listening skills. As one medical assistant recently recalled:

> I still, several years later, remember visualizing the teddy bear on top of the bureau of my physician's son. I began to see her as a person I could talk to and ask questions of rather than someone intimidating.

One of the most memorable bits of feedback I received came a week or so after this session from a quiet and rather non-participatory physician who had been in the practice for years. He told me how he had gone home and taught his children how to listen using the techniques he had learned in that session.

In the third session we conducted an Appreciative Inquiry exercise within the clinical teams. In it, the team members shared stories of past successes and from these stories derived themes that would frame a vision for their future. It was an intense, bonding, vision-setting group activity that changed the way that people on the team interacted with one another.

A COMMUNITY OF CARING

Our underlying hypothesis during this time was that changes in the interpersonal and working relationships among staff created by these large-group dialogues and smaller team-building sessions would result in changes in the ways in which staff related to patients, thereby developing the department into a "community of caring." There was clearly a community-organizing aspect embedded in our approach. People were engaged because they were co-authoring a new chapter in the Kenmore story that was about mutual respect, dignity and being empowered and self-determined. They were engaged because they were listening to one another and constructing shared meaning and purpose together. As our assistant chief put it,

> The true meaning of the roles of all members of the team became illuminated during this period, as if flickers of light were beginning to shine. The question became, "is the right person doing the right job in caring for the patient?" If not, what can we do to help all staff feel empowered to be part of the team so that we can make the patient experience and patient care better?
>
> Noelle Lawler

Our underlying hypothesis during this time was that changes in the interpersonal and working relationships among staff created by these large-group dialogues and smaller team-building sessions would result in changes in the ways in which staff related to patients, thereby developing the department into a "community of caring."

Over the course of a few months, the staff went through a remarkable transition—from invisibility to recognition, from helplessness to empowerment, from feeling self-limited and constrained to being creative and collaborative, from simply doing their jobs to looking for ways to support one another and improve patient care. There was a sense of hope and purpose. Once staff began treating each other with respect and dignity, they also began treating patients in the same way. Even now, after four years, some of the language that managers and staff use in the practice is the language we created together during those few months.

The following quotes, taken from interviews held four years later, provide some insight into the changes the clinical teams went through and the impact they were beginning to have on patient care at that time.

From medical assistants:

> Before the team building, I felt like a lemming, just doing what the doctor said, sometimes the doctor didn't even know my name. The team-building exercises were the first times I had ever had a conversation with a clinician; I felt like we got to know each other as people; like I had a voice, could ask for clarification, be less intimidated. I have a brain, and I can use it.

> Now, I feel like I could go up to anyone on the team—including doctors and nurses, and say, "What can I do to help you here? Can you explain to me a bit more why we are doing this?" It is fun to be part of a group that wants to improve patient care, no matter what your title, and not just move patients in and out of exam rooms.

> Before the team building we were scared of the doctors. Now, we joke with each other, know what to expect, and respect each other. Before, all I did was take vital signs, and I was afraid to interact with the patient—I didn't want to ask the wrong questions. Now, I have more responsibilities: I check their medications, discuss allergies, ask about smoking, arrange lab work, reinforce the importance of getting labs done and follow up appointments like eye exams, and answer questions that patients might not feel comfortable asking doctors.

From a physician assistant:

> The doctor was no longer the judger leader; he was the learner leader, and he brought that mentality to us. This was liberating to feel that we had voices, that it was safe to have a voice, and safe to be able to talk honestly to each other and listen with respect.

From a physician:

> When a patient comes in with a complaint, certain things will be done (e.g. urine test), and the results handed to me before I even go into the room, or an EKG for chest pain will be in the works often before I see the patient. This is because the MAs now know the patients well enough to detect when something is wrong. The MA now feels [to me] like an extension of my practice.

DISCOVERING "LEAN": A RELATIONSHIP-CENTERED APPROACH TO CONTINUOUS ORGANIZATIONAL IMPROVEMENT

As we began to improve our working relationships, another problem surfaced which challenged our hypothesis about the importance of relationships among staff and forced us to augment our approach. The clinical teams were clearly engaged with one another and more engaged with their patients. They had even begun to adopt some of the roles and responsibilities of PCC in which team members played a supportive role to the physicians. However, it became painfully apparent that their daily workflows and work processes were burdensome instead of supportive and, that as a result, the system was not working well. The doctors, not only in Kenmore IM but throughout the Harvard Vanguard practice, were complaining about "job do-ability." Even though these were outstanding physicians with sophisticated electronic medical record systems, they were constantly falling behind schedule during the day and completing their charting at nights and on weekends. Some physicians had unfinished charts from visits that were held weeks ago. As Noelle Lawler observed:

> We were feeling good about each other, and staff relationships had dramatically improved. However, we did not feel that we had the tools to improve the work were doing to care for our patients.

So our Kenmore management team did what it had now been trained to do. We looked into the problem and together we sought a solution. Instead of blaming the doctors or the staff, we tried to understand the situation and create a better one. Early on in this exploration, we happened upon a couple of articles about a "Lean" process-improvement methodology. This was an approach to organizational management developed by Toyota, the car manufacturer, and tested over many decades. It had been highly successful in the car industry and had been adopted subsequently by other industries, including healthcare. The Lean approach was based on very similar principles to the ones we had been trying to manifest in the practice. It was a people-focused approach as much as a technical one. The fundamental tenets of Lean that really attracted us were, "Go see for yourself, ask non-blaming questions focused on the processes within the system rather than on individuals, and show respect." "Respect" in the Lean methodology meant challenging people to think about continuously improving what they were doing and excelling in their performance, supporting them in understanding the situation, and mentoring them in creating and piloting solutions. The basic rules of Lean as applied to healthcare are: 1) Create value for your patients, 2) Respect your clinicians and staff, and 3) Cut out the waste in the system. It was a perfect fit for us—a principle-based, relationship-centered approach that was integrated with a process improvement method.

> Our Kenmore management team did what it had now been trained to do. We looked into the problem and together we sought a solution. Instead of blaming the doctors or the staff, we tried to understand the situation and create a better one.

In addition to the readings that we did together on Lean, we also invited people to come and speak to us. Luckily, the small group of academics who had initially piloted the Lean methodology in healthcare were at the Harvard Business School, only a couple of miles away from our practice. We created a series of lectures and seminars to further delve into this new methodology. These training and early mentoring sessions included not only our Kenmore management team, but also some of our nurses and medical assistants.

It all felt quite timely and serendipitous. It reminded me of the phrase, "when the student is ready, the teacher will appear." The Lean approach and methodologies felt like a natural extension of what we were already doing. The approach engages every individual's unique perspective, knowledge, wisdom and creativity in a disciplined and supported approach to problem solving, innovating and implementing, with a focus on transforming the value created for the customer, in this case our patients.

Although Lean is often described as a process-improvement and efficiency-enhancing methodology, we viewed it as an extension of our relationship-centered activities; as much a cultural intervention as anything else. We also knew that if any process changes were to be incorporated into the practice, the physicians and staff would have to be integral to making it happen. From our perspective, interpreting Lean purely at the level of process improvement techniques was misguided. Lean is a principle-based approach to organizing the workplace. At its core, Lean is about people—it is a philosophy about how people should interact with one another in the pursuit of creating value for themselves, for their customers, and for their communities.

> Lean is a principle-based approach to organizing the workplace. At its core, Lean is about people—it is a philosophy about how people should interact with one another in the pursuit of creating value for themselves, for their customers, and for their communities.

At Toyota, front-line employees are allowed and expected to contribute their ideas, creativity, innovations, questions, and concerns on a daily basis; and to take these ideas and translate them into action. The job of their managers is to support them in these endeavors, and to create accountability and alignment for outstanding performance and continuous improvement in the delivery of value to customers.

A RELATIONSHIP-CENTERED PROCESS-IMPROVEMENT (LEAN) PILOT

After the preparatory readings and trainings, we piloted Lean to see if it would work in our setting. We thought it seemed prudent to begin solving the most painful and immediate problems of the practice—and particularly of the physicians. The approach was to start small and start where the pain is. For years the physicians had been telling us that they were drowning in a sea of overwork. Some administrators and clinical leaders wrote it off as "belly aching." Others blamed individual physicians for simply "falling behind" or "not keeping up" with their work. But we (the Kenmore management team) focused our efforts on understanding the system.

We asked two primary-care physicians and their teams to participate in a pilot to test out the application and utility of the Lean approach in our clinical setting. These two wonderful physicians, Drs Shanthy Sridhar and Sheila Tapp, were courageous in opening up their practices to us. This was especially true since they allowed us to study their workflows and processes and to observe their clinical visits. They had seen the benefits of improved team functioning from the team-building activities we had been through together, and they were hoping that the focus on workflow operations would add even more benefit.

We decided to address the issue of workflow in the primary care practice with a focus on making the job of primary care more do-able for the physicians and freeing up the physicians to spend quality time with their patients. The purpose of the pilot was to understand the current state of the team workflow, including why the physicians were overwhelmed and falling behind during their day and to measure the results following an intervention. Interestingly, the concept of job do-ability for primary care has since been verified and even reported in the *New England Journal of Medicine*. Tom Bodenheimer has estimated that it would require nearly 18 hours a day for primary care physicians to completely fulfill their duties.[1]

Our pilot was a Lean "A4" problem-solving approach, the steps of which are:

Step 1: Make direct observations at the place that the work is happening or the value is being created and measure your observations so that you have a quantitative and qualitative understanding of the current situation.

Step 2: Conduct a root-cause analysis of the current problems by simply asking, "why?" repeatedly (the so-called "5 why" exercise).

Step 3: Develop "countermeasures" to the root causes.

Step 4: Pilot the countermeasures as experiments and measure the new state to see if, and by how much, an improvement has been made.

We trained the members of the two clinical teams in this process and then organized the observations.

Step 1: Observation and data analysis

We spent six hours observing each physician and their teams using a simple time–motion observation sheet to record and measure our observations. As observers, we were dismayed by what we saw. The physicians seemed to be running behind schedule from the moment they began seeing their patients. It was frustrating even to us as observers because it seemed like the system was working against the doctor. The processes in place were interfering with the doctor–patient relationship instead of supporting it. As we analyzed the data, two major items were even more upsetting than our qualitative impressions.

First, the physicians were spending about two-thirds of their time in the exam rooms working on the electronic medical record system and less than 10% of their time talking directly with or listening to their patients. Even when you combined the physical exam time with the dialogue time, the combination was still less than 40% of the total time in the exam room. When we expanded this observational data to include the entire physician workday, the actual face-to-face clinical time was less than 25%!

Second, we noted that it took about 10 minutes to prepare a patient for the physician after the patient was checked into the system. So, even if a patient arrived on time, the doctor was already 10 minutes behind by the time the patient was prepped. All it took was one patient coming in on time to set the doctor behind for the rest of the day! If the patient came a few minutes late, the physician was even further behind.

These results were quite helpful. We presented the findings to the two doctors and their teams.

Said one physician:

> It surprised me to realize how much time I was spending on reviewing the chart during the visit. I was actually spending less personal time talking to the patient than I had thought. The data made me realize— God, how far away had I gotten from what I had always wanted to do as a doctor, and thought I was doing. I made a decision that I was not going to short change my patients anymore in this way.

The other physician remarked, with obvious relief:

> When I looked at the time–motion study results, I realized that the problem was the process rather than something I was doing wrong. I literally ran down the hall saying, "it's not me!"

Step 2: Root-cause analysis

The observation data made explicit and transparent what the physicians had been saying all along. It also provided them and us with the ability to make a change and measure whether the change improved the problem. The problem was that physicians were spending too much time doing preparation work, performing visit follow-up work and engaging in other visit-based work that their medical assistants could do.

Step 3: Countermeasures

Based on the root-cause assessment, the two clinical teams constructed a number of countermeasures. One team came up with a dozen changes, the other, nearly two dozen. The fundamental changes involved shifting to the medical assistant and other support members of the team much of the preparation, post-visit work, data entry and data retrieval that the physician had been doing during the visit; having much of the preparation work completed prior to the visit; and having much of the post-visit work done after the visit. Some specific examples of these changes included having the medical assistants conduct medication reconciliations, schedule screening tests, look up lab data and test results, and schedule follow-up appointments.

These changes allowed the physician and patient to maximize the limited time they had together during the visit; they had more time to focus on what was important. From the Lean perspective, it allowed the physician to do more "value-added" work, that is, work that contributed directly to creating value for the patient.

Step 4: Deploying the countermeasures and measuring the results

Once the team had determined the countermeasures, they began to deploy them and test them out. Remarkably, the entire time for this A4 process, from the initial training of the team to the follow-up measurement, was only six weeks. Even more remarkable were the positive results. In less than two months' time the team had nearly inverted our initial findings in the exam room observation. The physicians were now spending about two-thirds of their time in dialogue with the patient and only about 13% of their time doing data entry and data retrieval on the electronic medical record. From the Lean perspective, the value-added time for the physicians had increased considerably. And these two physicians were now running on time considerably more often than they had prior to the intervention.

The Lean effort had not only changed the efficiency of the team and the value to the patient of the clinical visit, it had also transformed how the team was working together with positive ramifications for its members. Medical assistants felt empowered to take on more responsibility, to make suggestions for workflow improvements, and to engage in relationships with patients. Most importantly, they felt like valued members of the care team. Patients began to look forward to contact with their MAs, seeing them as an additional valued caregiving resource.

> The Lean effort had not only changed the efficiency of the team and the value to the patient of the clinical visit, it had also transformed how the team was working together.

Below are several representative comments from staff and physicians.
From a physician:

> It was a little daunting at first to agree to have my practice observed. But I then learned that it was a way to improve. It gave me the chance to stop, think and communicate with the team, which is not usually built in to the work of the day. I was also excited to realize that I could have input into the way the work was done. You validated me and it felt good.

From a medical assistant:

> When this reassignment of responsibilities and tasks was put into place, the results were dramatic. Before, all we did was check vital signs. I had been afraid to make conversation with patients in case what I said was the wrong thing. I was also afraid of being rejected by the patient. Now I check medications, ask about allergies, ask about smoking, check on diabetes management, reinforce the importance of lab work, print up recent lab results for the doctor, help patients with their referral appointments, and answer questions patients may not be comfortable asking the doctor.

From a physician:

> My medical assistant is now an extension of my practice, my right-hand person. Now, before I even see the patient, the MA may have already done a pregnancy test and handed these and other lab results to me before I walk into the exam room. Now that the MAs know the patients well, they may spot problems in advance, warning me, for example of a certain kind of rash or telling me that someone looks paler or more frail than usual. Their observations are usually correct.

From a physician assistant:

> My experience in the exam room has been transformed. . . . Now that the exam room is less cluttered with micro activities, I can spend more time with the patient doing the job I have been trained to do—discussing, for example, chronic disease management. The extra time and more meaningful dialogue I am now able to have with the patients means they understand their disease better. Being free to focus on the patient as a person provides a more robust patient experience.

Although we do not have patient comments to share, the anecdotal feedback from these physicians' patients was enthusiastic and positive. Patient-satisfaction survey scores also improved, with a near 10% increase for one physician in her patient-satisfaction scores within one year's time—a truly unprecedented improvement.

OUTCOMES, SPREAD AND SUSTAINMENT
Widening engagement at Kenmore

The news of our Lean pilot studies spread throughout the Kenmore Internal Medicine practice. Other clinicians and their teams began to adopt some of the approaches. The initial spread came through the medical assistants (MAs) who had participated in the Lean pilot studies. They began to meet with the other MAs during their lunch hours to share their enthusiasm, results from the pilot, and the standard protocols that they had developed and were deploying. It was a great example of spontaneous organic spread, and a reflection of the impact of the team building and community organizing we had done over the past few months with the medical assistants in the Kenmore IM practice.

The other clinicians who had participated in the Lean pilot (the physicians, nurses and physicians assistants) also started meeting with their colleagues in the practice to share their enthusiasm and results. Within a few months, we launched a second Lean pilot that was much larger than the first and included many more physicians and staff. Then we launched a third Lean pilot that extended beyond the Internal Medicine Department into the Gastroenterology Department, focused on how the two departments worked together on internal referrals and cross booking. These events began to break down the barriers between the departments and led to a larger sense of teamwork within the practice. It served to spread the Lean principles and concepts to other departments in the larger practice.

It was clear to us that the combination of team building, community organizing and process improvement was having a positive impact on our clinicians and staff. Over the course of 15 months, we saw nearly a 10% improvement in the physician-assessment survey scores that team members were filling out about their physician team leaders. The greatest improvement was in the area of the physicians' communication and relationship with the patient. This particular improvement was particularly notable because we had not instituted any patient communication skills training programs or customer-service initiatives. This was all due to "spillover" from the internal team building and relationship-centered work with the clinicians and staff. Yet the impact on increased patient-satisfaction scores was dramatic. Patient care was becoming much more respectful, streamlined and efficient, and this was clearly reflected in the Kenmore IM department patient-satisfaction survey scores. Within a little over one year, the Kenmore practice went from among the lowest scoring sites to one of the top scoring Internal Medicine departments at Harvard Vanguard.

Patient care was becoming much more respectful, streamlined and efficient, and this was clearly reflected in the Kenmore IM department patient-satisfaction survey scores. Within a little over one year, the Kenmore practice went from among the lowest scoring sites to one of the top scoring Internal Medicine departments at Harvard Vanguard.

We conducted a series of follow-up interviews four years after the initial Kenmore experience and found that the principles, relational behaviors and operational continuous improvement efforts that we put into place remain very much alive. Every person we interviewed describes that time as a significant and positive period of growth—personally, professionally and communally. It is clear from the present activities at Kenmore that the changes we instituted have spread. Productive ways of communicating are now habitual among staff members, who still frequently respond to each other in meetings with "yes and" comments, rather than "no but"—the language skills from improvisational performance that we had introduced in the initial relationship-building effort.

The site administrator and senior IM staff have a consistent focus on team practice of healthcare in several ways that grew out of the experience, as evidenced by a recent comment from the site administrator:

> Our approach was to think differently about how we wanted to do our work that did not sacrifice the positive aspects of the original patient-centered care initiative but rather emerged from within the practice itself. We wanted to own the process, to make it part of our culture; and some of the Lean principles were helpful ways to do this, specifically, respect for all staff and engaging people in decisions about their own work.
>
> Michael Knosp

Expanding to the larger organization

Using a similar "grassroots" approach, we began to pilot this relationship-centered Lean approach in a number of other Harvard Vanguard sites. Our Chelmsford practice conducted a larger, site-wide initiative which created important advances in our care model. Our Burlington practice also initiated a Lean pilot and created hundreds of small improvements in patient-care processes.

In 2009, the Harvard Vanguard senior management team adopted the integration of a Lean approach as one of its key strategic imperatives. Lean was viewed as a way to empower the sites, departments and clinical teams while simultaneously improving quality, efficiency and the patient-care experience. Over the past year and a half, we have attempted to use a participatory approach in implementing

Lean into the organization to make patient-centered, Relationship-centered Care the standard in our practice sites and departments.

Harvard Vanguard is now utilizing a relationship-centered Lean approach as the organizational operational platform—not just in process improvement but also to transform our thinking about quality improvement, financial and data analysis, and day-to-day management at the front line. The approach is becoming integrated across clinical departments and functional service areas including finance, human resources, and quality and safety. We currently have eight large-scale organization-wide Lean projects underway as well as numerous smaller initiatives.

Although this effort has shifted from a single department to a central organizational approach, the "pull" from the sites and departments continues to fuel the effort. The demand from the practice for this new approach, even at this early stage in our journey, now exceeds our ability to facilitate and support the widespread change. As a result, we are beginning to transition from a purely centralized approach to a centralized approach for system-wide processes combined with a coordinated but distributed effort for local initiatives. One example of this distributed effort comes from the Kenmore practice with the recent creation of a daily nurse-run hypertension clinic. A nurse leader, along with the two current Internal Medicine chiefs at Kenmore, and with the support and backing of the medical and surgical specialty chiefs, used a Lean problem-solving effort to construct this much needed clinical ambulatory center. It was a wonderful story of spontaneous front-line initiative and leadership, and an example of how far the Kenmore practice and Harvard Vanguard have come over the past four years.

The Harvard Vanguard Leadership Academy

One critical ingredient in our transformation and a huge accelerant of change has been the 2008 launch of a Harvard Vanguard Leadership Academy. Created as a team effort with Tanya Chermak, a Senior Project Manager, the Academy is a nine-month program with over 70 hours of group-based seminar time. In developing the curriculum, we listened to the needs of clinician leaders and managers across the organization and built upon some of the learnings from the Kenmore experience. The program focuses on enhancing skills in four areas: leadership, management, financial stewardship, and clinical operations such as quality, safety and process improvement. To date, we have trained over 150 clinical leaders and managers from across the organization. Reviews have been very positive; we now have lengthy waiting lists for participation.

Two attributes of the Leadership Academy appear to be particularly powerful in making it a change catalyst for our organization. The first is its social and communal aspect. Every month nearly 80 people get together for six hours to learn together, and to share their stories of challenges and successes, fostering an enhanced sense of community. We have heard numerous anecdotes about relationships formed in the Academy that have allowed leaders distributed throughout our multi-site practice to support one another and to create innovations together.

The second source of effectiveness for the Academy is one of the requirements for participation, namely, that the participants commit to transforming themselves from "thought leaders" to "action leaders." From the very first session, the participants are reminded that leadership is about action. The leadership values and principles matter only to the extent that they drive tangible action and behavior that create positive change in patient care and in the workplace. The curriculum we have constructed requires active participation in creating change at the front line of care—not necessarily completing a project, but at least beginning the journey of becoming a change agent in healthcare delivery.

CONCLUSIONS AND LESSONS LEARNED

We believe that the requirements for a high-quality relationship-centered patient care system include: 1) creating a safe and respectful work environment in which each clinician and staff person is treated with dignity; 2) engaging clinicians and staff in the process of assessment, improvement and innovation and making this an integral part of each person's scope of responsibilities; and 3) creating a systematic approach to continuous improvement that incorporates both the cultural and technical aspects into the daily work practices of the group. Particularly important are a continued focus on understanding the current reality and generating solutions, and the promotion of social learning and human development.

People often assume that the introduction of Lean training or the deployment of some other approach to process improvement within an organization is synonymous with continuous improvement. Quite the contrary: these training and quality/process-improvement programs are just "technical fixes." They do not by themselves create a culture of continuous improvement or Relationship-centered Care. They can even quash engaged and responsive learning.

The culture that complements the technical components and brings them to life depends upon the following principles: 1) including daily dialogue as a core business practice; 2) recognizing that the people who are closest to patients and who actually do the work have the best knowledge about the care processes and the patients; 3) supporting and facilitating the front-line people in assessing their performance and improving upon it; 4) understanding that the wisdom of the team is often superior to the wisdom of any one individual; 5) transparency; 6) aspirational thinking rather than constraint-based thinking; 7) using rapid prototyping and rapid piloting (fail fast to succeed) rather than prolonged planning; 8) transitioning the role of manager into one of organizer and coach; 9) focusing on process-oriented as well as results-oriented metrics; 10) focusing on understanding and critiquing processes rather than on blaming individuals; 11) including all staff members as creative thinkers to be challenged to grow and develop through continuous improvement and innovation efforts;

and 12) understanding that everyone has two jobs—doing their current job and improving the value proposition of their current job.

One noteworthy aspect of our journey at Harvard Vanguard over the past four years is that we've begun to create a community of action-oriented learner-leaders who are creating nodes of positive change that are spreading and connecting rapidly throughout the organization. This phenomenon is not simply an attribute of a process-improvement deployment but rather a consequence of a more broadly conceived change. We are creating a community of leaders distributed across every level of the organization and in every professional category—leaders who can organize and support their colleagues in improving the processes of healthcare delivery and making continuous improvement a way of life. This leadership community has the commitment and capacity to make much needed and difficult changes. It is a community of innovators, initiators, and sustainers. It is my firm belief that this sort of internal leadership community is the most practical nexus and even a requirement for any aligned and accountable care organization.

Another unique aspect of our journey is that we have wed the development of our internal working environment and of our clinicians and staff to the development of a better-value proposition for patients. This is an approach that respects the integrity of parallel process: to create an environment of active engagement for our patients, we must treat our staff in the same way. It is a balanced, holistic approach that treats people—patients *and* staff—with dignity and respect. And most importantly, it is an approach that recognizes that it takes people's motivation, enthusiasm and energy to create sustainable positive change. This approach values and harnesses the power of the creative human spirit and the strength and resilience of community.

In our organization, everyone is struggling to learn and adapt these new philosophies and tools, from the CEO and senior management team to the clinical leadership and middle management to the front-line clinicians and staff. As we move throughout the practice, we share stories of how the senior management team is succeeding and fumbling with this new approach. A critical aspect of success is that not being perfect is becoming acceptable. Everyone adopting these new tools and new behaviors must be willing to become a learner. That means not being a "knower" but a "doer", and at times this learning involves failing.

From my perspective, the socio-cultural formula we've begun to craft within Harvard Vanguard is a powerful, adaptable and sustainable force for positive change in healthcare delivery. Given the current turbulent times that face our healthcare system, it seems to me to be a timely imperative. "Leadership," according to Marshall Ganz, the noted community activist and Kennedy School of Government Professor, "is about accepting Change, Paradox, Chaos and Complexity. [It is] accepting responsibility for enabling others to achieve purposeful action in times of uncertainty." The recent inflection in our organization, which can, in large part, be traced back to the Kenmore experience in 2005–06, is exactly that, a relationship-centered approach to enabling others to achieve purposeful and meaningful action that continuously enhances the value of the care delivery environment for clinicians and staff, and of the healthcare delivery system's value for all of us.

NOTE

1 Bodenheimer T. Primary care: will it survive? *N Engl J Med.* 2006; **355**(9): 861–4.

Commentary: Harvard Vanguard Kenmore Practice

This chapter contrasts the introduction of organizational change using a traditional top-down strategy with a more relationship-centered approach. As the story begins, the Kenmore practice of Harvard Vanguard Medical Associates is reeling from significant changes in the parent organization and reacting poorly to the imposition from above of a new team-based "patient-centered care" model. The staff is being asked to be more relational with patients as well as with one another, but the organization, in its deployment of this new care model, is not using a relationship-centered approach itself. The front-line reaction to this imposed change has been swift and negative—resistance and distrust—despite the fact that the local managers and many staff agree that the new care concept is sound.

A short time later, we see this same front-line organization becoming a model of efficiency and cohesiveness for the entire system and its patient-satisfaction scores improving dramatically And we see that these gains are still intact four years later. How has this happened? This is the story of the Kenmore practice.

The turnabout was comprised of two phases: an intensive effort focused on listening and relationship building followed by the introduction, in a deeply relational way, of a quality-improvement process borrowed from manufacturing and gaining acceptance in healthcare—Toyota Production System or Lean.

RELATIONSHIP BUILDING

When Dr Zeev Neuwirth arrived at Kenmore as Chief of Internal Medicine, he found a culture of deep division, distrust and resentment. In that kind of interpersonal environment, it would have been impossible to implement the new model of patient-centered care, regardless of how good a model it was. In keeping with the aphorism, "whatever hinders the work *is* the work," Zeev and his management immediately set about the work of organizational healing and relational repair. People needed the opportunity to hear and be heard by each other; to learn about each other's perspectives, roles and needs; and to trust that they could depend on each other.

The story of the relationship-building phase offers a wealth of practical methods, the effectiveness of which can be accounted for by the various theories we've been considering throughout this book.

➤ Weekly mentoring meetings with the site administrator—note that the mentoring went both ways (enhancing interpersonal connection, building competence, supporting autonomy).

➤ Offsite sessions with the management team to teach the principles of Relationship-centered Care, practice interpersonal skills and introduce the concept of a learning organization (enhancing connection and competence, introducing new patterns of meaning).

➤ Individual interviews with all staff and listening to build trust (enhancing connection, reflective listening, valuing difference and diversity).

➤ Walking the hallways observing and interacting and sitting in the staff break room in order to have informal conversations and, again, to listen (enhancing connection, creating opportunities for serendipity and relationship building, changing the culture by "being the change."

➤ Facilitated meetings between professional groups allowing people to speak openly and honestly about their experience of the workplace (fostering new patterns of relating and new patterns of professional identity, i.e. how people see each other; eliciting expressions of difference; reducing fear; building communication competence; enhancing connection).

➤ Meetings for intact clinical teams to build communication skills and reflect on their successes (building competence, enhancing responsiveness, Appreciative Inquiry).

➤ Negotiations with the parent organization to diminish top-down control and support the autonomy of the local staff as they implemented the patient-centered care program (supporting autonomy, changing patterns of relating).

The combined effect of all these techniques was a marked improvement in trust and morale. People saw each other in new, more positive ways and had a much stronger sense of common purpose.

With good relationships and a learning orientation as a foundation for organizational change, the Kenmore practice was then ready for the second phase: redesigning work processes to improve the efficiency, effectiveness and customer experience of healthcare delivery. For this, they turned to Lean.

RELATIONSHIP CENTERED LEAN

Like the relational methodologies featured in other case studies, such as Positive Deviance (Chapter 10) and Appreciative Inquiry (Chapter 13), Lean presumes and engages the capacity, creativity and resourcefulness of the entire staff. It empowers staff at all levels to make decisions and suggestions and rewards them for doing so. This is in marked contrast to the widely used, machine-inspired systems that were in place at Kenmore at the beginning of this story where management makes the decisions and the staff are expected to compliantly carry them out.

Even Lean could be just another tool imposed from above on an unwilling staff, but here it was much more. It was applied in a way that exemplified the principles of Self-Determination Theory, thus favoring its adoption: it was highly relational, it enhanced the autonomy of the practice staff, and it developed competence. Lean occasioned conversation between co-workers, bringing forth diversity and fostering responsiveness, thus creating conditions conducive to innovation—the emergence of new patterns. It also fostered objective reflection, gathering data to challenge beliefs, thus disrupting static and inhibitory patterns of thinking.

For all these reasons, the Lean program was enormously successful, enhancing the performance and productivity of the practice while simultaneously furthering the development of its relational culture. And these effects were not confined to the Kenmore Practice; they produced ripples of change in the larger organization.

We've now seen two examples of Toyota Production System in our case studies—one here in the Harvard Vanguard story and the other in the story about reducing hospital-acquired infections in the Veterans Administration Pittsburgh Health System (*see* Chapter 10). In the latter, Lean produced a substantial decrease in infection rates, but at a high cost and in an expert-driven fashion, prompting the leaders in that project to move on to a more grassroots-oriented approach, Positive Deviance. But here in the Harvard Vanguard story we see a different version of Lean, one that is, in fact, oriented around grassroots wisdom and that, rather than being expert-driven, teaches Lean methodologies to staff members who successfully continue the work on their own.

Lean is a "socio-technical" methodology. It rests on two foundations: first, rigorous observation and analysis of work processes with regard to the value they produce for the customer, and second, respecting and engaging workers, who are closest to and therefore most knowledgeable about both production processes and customers. It would be hardly surprising if, under the sway of the machine metaphor and an inclination towards control, some managers or Lean practitioners were attracted towards the technical component and lost sight of the social. But they depart from the original intent of Lean and fail to realize its full potential. The phrase "relationship-centered Lean" appears in the Harvard Vanguard chapter. It's a useful reassertion of the social component and reminds us that Lean has been relationship-centered from its inception.

The Harvard Vanguard story offers great inspiration and hope. It show us that it is possible in a short period of time to transform a negative work environment characterized by mistrust and animosity into a high performing, relationship-centered learning organization. Mindful relationship building and Lean instigated a cascade of positive behavior and events. As these positive changes took hold they were noticed and eventually incorporated into the larger organizational context, a small change in one part of a system spreading to have a dramatic impact on the whole. The potential was there all along; the key to unleashing it was Relationship-centered Administration.

CHAPTER 13

Transforming the professional culture of a medical school from the inside out

Penelope R Williamson, DeWitt C Baldwin Jr, Ann H Cottingham,
Richard Frankel, Thomas S Inui, Debra K Litzelman,
David L Mossbarger and Anthony L Suchman

SYNOPSIS

Since 2003, Indiana University School of Medicine (IUSM) has undertaken an unique and courageous experiment—the Relationship-centered Care Initiative (RCCI)[1], a four-year effort to initiate self-sustaining culture change throughout the entire medical school. The intent was to foster widespread reflection on, and mindfulness of, the values being conveyed in everyday personal interactions and organizational behavior. The goal was to cultivate a social and professional learning environment (the informal curriculum) that consistently reinforced and exemplified the values and principles of the competency-based formal curriculum in the domains of professionalism, communication, ethics and self-awareness.

> The intent was to foster widespread reflection on, and mindfulness of, the values being conveyed in everyday personal interactions and organizational behavior.

The RCCI leadership group adopted a strategy of emergent design, describing the change process with the metaphor of a pebble dropped in a pond causing ripples. The first step was a set of 80 appreciative interviews conducted by the Discovery Team, a group of 12 students, faculty and staff volunteers, to elicit stories of IUSM's culture at its best. These stories were analyzed and the themes presented back to the community in a number of venues. As a positive and hopeful image of IUSM began to emerge, more volunteers stepped forward (at the start of year four, over 170) offering to bring the RCCI to their departments, committees, offices or projects. Discovery Team members reached out to involve more students, residents and alumni, each subgroup now active in spreading the culture change.

Many volunteers requested opportunities to learn more about being effective internal change agents. To that end, the Discovery Team met monthly for peer coaching and instruction on organizational change in support of the many projects they have initiated. Two other programs were offered: the Courage to Lead program, a year-long seasonal retreat series on strengthening leadership capacity from the inside out; and the Internal Change Agent program, a five-session skill-development program for internal change agents.

This initiative has done more than begin a process of change in the culture of a large medical school. It has affected all of us who have participated in it. From the beginning we believed that change occurs one person at a time, and from the inside out: from inside the personnel and culture of the organization and from inside the identities and values of each person in the organization. As Gandhi so eloquently said, each person must "be the change" he wishes to see in the world. This chapter interweaves the chronicle of the RCCI with the personal stories of some of the main players: members of the leadership group, IUSM deans, faculty, staff, residents and students. This story offers rich examples of emergent design, Appreciative Inquiry, and applications of formation approaches and principles. It also shows that large scale change is possible.

> From the beginning we believed that change occurs one person at a time, and from the inside out: from inside the personnel and culture of the organization and from inside the identities and values of each person in the organization.

The biggest 'psychosocial' problem facing us may be the need for our own personal transformation—to understand and promote change within ourselves.[2]

THE ORGANIZATION

Indiana University School of Medicine (IUSM) is the second-largest allopathic medical school in the United States, with over 1100 students, 1200 faculty, 1000 residents and thousands of administrative staff and health personnel. Students in the first two years study basic sciences at one of nine campuses around the state. All students come to the Indianapolis campus for their clinical rotations in their third and fourth years. IUSM is the only medical school in Indiana. Many of the faculty received their training there and then stayed on, creating a network of long-term connections. In the mid-western culture of Indiana, civility is the norm. A new member of the faculty commented when he arrived in 2002 that the culture seemed "congenial but impersonal." Everyone focused on the agenda; there wasn't extra attention given to relationships or relationship-building.

THE IMPETUS FOR CHANGE

In 1999 IUSM introduced a new competency-based curriculum, the culmination of a 10-year effort. Included among its nine core competencies were professionalism, ethics and moral reasoning, self-awareness and communication. However, as was generally true in medical education, the social and professional behavior that students observed and experienced in their day-to-day encounters did not consistently reflect the values of the core competencies. In other words, the informal curriculum did not always support or match the formal curriculum.

An additional impetus came from results of the annual Graduation Questionnaire administered by the Association of American Medical Colleges to every graduating medical student at all accredited medical schools in the US. It achieves extraordinarily high response rates by virtue of the broad interest of medical administrators and educators in the results. These responses are analyzed nationally, as well as individually for each school, allowing educators to compare the responses of their own students with national norms. For many years, IUSM students rated their overall satisfaction with their medical education well below the national average.

> IU School of Medicine was faced with a student body that felt it had been ignored and was disrespected. Faculty members were feeling the pressures of outside forces such as tight grant funds and decreased reimbursement for clinical care. Leaders were challenged to instill a spirit of optimism and mutual respect among learners, faculty, and staff. We recognized we needed a change in culture that combined increases in accountability with more collegial interactions among everyone in the institution. More accountability implied more pressure while at the same time striving for interactions that were less pressured and stressed. The easiest way out would have been to throw up our hands in surrender saying that we were no different than any other academic medical center and it is impossible to change culture in such a large organization that has people continually fluxing in and out.
>
> Instead we decided that we needed to do as an organization what we admonish individual faculty members to do; namely, role model. Said in another way, what institutional role would we be modeling if we decided to stay the course? We started with an exercise to seek broad input in articulating our values. We then knew we had to live them. Many things were done including strengthening

our process that allowed students to safely bring issues forward, and committing to taking action when our values are transgressed. We stressed service learning; we created more opportunities for teaching people how to teach; we developed programs for leadership development and on and on.

Craig Brater, Dean, IUSM

Craig Brater did more than espouse role modeling, he walked the talk.

Clearly the most memorable time was the Saturday morning when [Dr Brater] approached a division chief who had been absent for months while undergoing treatment for his newly diagnosed cancer and warmly hugged him with tears in his eyes. This rare showing of humanism was life affirming and modeled the depth and power of relationships. I knew at that moment that if we could all be more like this more often, that our department, our school, our culture would be transformed. I knew it could be a different place, but it would take a different way of being, personally as well as collectively. In 2000, this Chair with the capacity to publicly hug his critically ill division chief became Dean . . . setting the stage for other courageous change agents to step forward living out a new way of being together.

Deb Litzelman,
Associate Dean for Medical Education and Curricular Affairs

It was into this fertile combination of a broad-based curricular change and supportive leadership that Tom Inui and Rich Frankel, senior leaders with expertise in professionalism and medical school culture, were recruited to IUSM. Both had been members of the Pew–Fetzer Task Force on Health Professions Education that first introduced the term "Relationship-centered Care." Tom had a long-standing interest in improving the environment in which students formed their professional values and identities. He could envision a relationship-centered medical school and was eager to pursue a large-scale organizational development project to realize that vision. Rich was a renowned scholar in the field of healthcare relationships and communications. They brought with them a three-year grant from the Fetzer Institute to conduct a demonstration project in organizational culture change—the Relationship-centered Care Initiative (RCCI). While the work was to take place at IUSM, the grant was intended to have much wider impact:

Movement in the direction of Relationship-centered Care in the life world of academic medicine would be galvanized if even one medical school/academic medical center could seriously undertake this kind of change process (organizational formation), document its journey, share perspectives with peer schools, and measure the impact of what it has done on the members of the academic community . . .

Thomas Inui in the RCCI grant proposal

GETTING STARTED
The Formation Team

To steward the RCCI, Tom and Rich assembled a six-member leadership team which we immediately named the "Formation Team" (FT). Formation, a term popularized by Parker Palmer, refers to the personal development that is necessary in preparing for a professional role.[3] Individual formation work involves intensive personal reflection to gain self-knowledge, to clarify one's values and to develop an authentic personal ethos of service. The RCCI was an experiment to conduct formation work at the level of an entire institution.

Tom and Rich were the first two members. Tom was the project director; Rich led the research arm of the RCCI (a parallel project that convened a national network of healthcare communications researchers) and had responsibility for faculty development activities and the teaching of professionalism at IUSM. Having just arrived at IUSM themselves, Tom and Rich sought a partner who was deeply immersed in the IUSM culture and committed to its enhancement. They chose Deb Litzelman, the Associate Dean for Medical Education and Curricular Affairs, who had helped to lead the design and implementation of the competency-based curriculum. They also engaged a program coordinator, Dave Mossbarger, to track finances and manage the project and two outside consultants experienced in culture change and personal formation work, Penny Williamson and Tony Suchman.

Each of us brought unique perspectives and gifts to the work, but there was also something more: this project had enormous personal significance for us. Most of us had worked for many years to improve communication and relationship processes in healthcare. Our work up to this point had consisted of teaching relationships skills to individuals, preparing faculty members to do this kind of teaching, working with single departments or pursuing culture change at small community hospitals. In the RCCI, we were attempting to take this work to a wider scale than ever before. It felt to us like our professional careers had led up to and uniquely prepared us for this extraordinary opportunity. We were both excited and intimidated by the scope of what we were undertaking, and we realized at the outset that we would need a very different approach to organizational change than anything we had ever tried or experienced before.

> It began on the airplane as I was en route to the first meeting of the Formation Team. Over the months since Tom's invitation to help with this project, my initial elation—a long-held dream come true, bringing relationship-centered process

to an entire medical school—was being increasingly accompanied by a sense of anxiety and even intimidation. "How, exactly, are we supposed to do this? Do we have any idea of what we're doing here?"

Sitting on the plane and re-reading the grant proposal, it occurred to me that "not knowing" was precisely what we had to do. If my Masters Degree program had taught me anything, it was the unpredictability of organizational change. Group process cannot be designed and controlled. I realized that if we expected that we could plan and implement a three-year change program, complete with interim targets and measures and run charts, we would be off track from the outset. We couldn't process people through workshops, officially stamp them "relationship-centered" and expect them to act differently ever after, nor could we prescribe specific actions or behaviors to literally thousands of people. Such an approach could never work; it could only lead to frustration which would then make us anxious as we faced our fear of failure, which would then make us clutch at control ever more desperately and this whole historic opportunity would slip away.

The prospect of warning my colleagues of this danger also worried me. This was such a large grant and a very visible project; how could they possibly accept the idea of not planning? And what did I have to offer as an alternative? A new complexity theory, that I could barely articulate, about self-organizing patterns? Reassurance that small disturbances sometimes spread and grow unpredictably? A glorified rendition of "we'll make it up as we go along?" Some strategy! Yet even as I questioned whether I could persuade my colleagues to adopt this approach, I felt in my very bones that it was the only way the project could possibly succeed. I spent the rest of the flight mapping out a logical and orderly line of argument and designing a visual aid to make the new complexity-based theory comprehensible.

The Formation Team gathered for its first meeting in the spacious refurbished attic of Tom's center-city house. I felt like I was going to burst; it felt urgently important to share these ideas. We introduced ourselves to each other and reflected on how we came to be part of this project and what it meant to us. As we finished and started to plan the agenda for the day, my heart started pounding. "Look, I've been thinking about this project all the way out here," I burst in. "I need to tell you about a new perspective that I think will be perfect for the project." So with my heart still thumping and feeling a bit breathless, I proceeded to tell my colleagues about Complex Responsive Process.[4] It wasn't very clear but it was good enough. They understood the approach and were excited about it, maybe even relieved that they didn't have to know how to do this either.

Tony Suchman,
external consultant

> "How, exactly, are we supposed to do this? Do we have any idea of what we're doing here?" Sitting on the plane and re-reading the grant proposal, it occurred to me that "not knowing" was precisely what we had to do.

And so we came to better understand our role as stewards of the RCCI—not to plan and implement, but to notice patterns of relating at IUSM, instigate what we hoped would be constructive disturbances in those patterns, observe the results and discern the next steps. And we hoped to engage a growing number of people in this same process. We called this strategy "emergent design."

> ... our RCCI external consultants shared with the group their vision of organizational culture as conversations, and organizational change as key events that alter the nature of those conversations in a rippling way, like dropping a pebble in a pond. The vision focused on the ways people understand and relate to one another. Rather than trying to engineer a massive change by mandate, we were going to attend to and alter relationships from a more grassroots level. Theoretically the process sounded great. Practically, I was not sure exactly what "dropping the pebble" meant in terms of specific action at IUSM.

Ann Cottingham,
Director of Special Programs for Medical Education and
Curricular Affairs

We also recognized early on that we needed to conduct the project in a relationship-centered fashion—to foster culture change in a way that modeled the new culture. Mindful of this, we organized our Formation Team meetings to have ample time to reflect on how we were working together. Meeting twice each month (a four-hour meeting during the external consultants' monthly visits to Indianapolis and a two-hour conference call in between visits), we tracked the various threads of the project, followed up on new leads, and identified potential cross-links between various people or projects. We explored and challenged our assumptions in a trustworthy setting. And we supported each other during difficult times. We began each FT meeting with two practices that quickly became traditions throughout the RCCI: the reading of a poem to set the tone and an in-depth check-in: sharing personal and professional news or reflections to help us become fully present to each other.

One day, our check-in was particularly poignant. Something chal-lenging was occurring for each of us—overwork, strain in the family, illness, excessive fatigue, desire for a change in work role. We took all the time we needed, each person sharing and receiving the group's warm and compassionate attention. We didn't try to fix or advise each other. We simply listened, knowing that this shar-ing would help us be mindful and supportive of each other as we continued our work. When we turned to the main agenda, we were perceptibly lighter of heart and moved through it in a noticeably thoughtful and efficient manner.

Remarkably, that was one of our most creative meetings. Tony and I shared our excitement at the growing number of new people being drawn to the work of the RCCI. Rich likened the RCCI to the Lewis and Clark expedition (just then celebrating the 150th anni-versary), and Tom Inui, in the moment, created a vignette based on the Lewis and Clark journals, which he titled "drawn to the light." We were heady with joy and enthusiasm.

Penny Williamson, external consultant

At FT meetings, we also made time to reflect on our experience of working together and on the culture we were creating within our own group.

I sometimes worried that I wasn't good enough to be part of this highly creative, relational, articulate "dream team." Was I contrib-uting often enough? Were my contributions smart enough? At one meeting, I found the courage to ask for feedback in the spirit of wishing to contribute my very best to this work and to this group. I had observed that others' comments often received verbal affirmation whereas my words did not seem to evoke a response. I wondered whether I was being clear. My colleagues listened to me with respect, empathy and seriousness. A member of the group commented that he might have been taking for granted that I would know I was affirmed without the need for verbal response. After this meeting, I noticed a shift in the behavior of the group (more verbal acknowledgment of my comments) and I felt a welcome internal shift as well—more comfortable that my contributions were valued. Voicing this most vulnerable of concerns helped remove a barrier so I could give my best to the group. What made it possible was the trust we had established and the norm of speaking about our own relationships as an integral part of the work.

Penny Williamson

What made it possible [to voice this vulnerable concern] was the trust we had established and the norm of speaking about our own relationships as an integral part of the work.

The Discovery Team

Once we realized we couldn't plan the whole project in advance, the question then became, "if we can only plan one step at a time, what should the very first step be?" We decided to begin with a project to discover the best of IUSM's culture by means of appreciative interviews with students, residents, faculty and staff. We planned a three-month process for designing, conducting and analyzing the interviews that would culminate in an Open Forum to present the stories and themes of exemplary culture back to the community. To carry out this work, we convened a "Discovery Team" comprised of 12 faculty, staff and students who were known to be invested in the well-being of the medical school.

> When I was asked to participate in the Discovery Team with a goal to improve the IUSM informal curriculum, I was excited. My work at IUSM involves issues of ethics and professionalism and my background is in theological and philosophical ethics. Improving the way IUSM models excellent medical practice was very appealing. And I was curious to discover how this complicated and huge task was to be accomplished.
>
> The consultants invited us to participate in planning, conducting and coding appreciative interviews with individuals in a wide variety of roles across the IUSM campus. Interviewees were asked to recall high-point experiences at IUSM, times when their work felt most meaningful, collaborative and effective. The interviews were long for many of our busy colleagues. They required about an hour. Yet of the six I conducted, most went over the time allotted. Everyone I met was able to identify good experiences, and gained excitement and energy as they remembered and related them to me. It was a rewarding and energizing event for all involved. We seemed to be off to a great start. What would be next?
>
> Ann Cottingham

The Discovery Team interviewed a total of 80 people and performed a content analysis of the interviews. Their analysis revealed four themes about the positive core of IUSM at its best:
➤ believing in the capacity of people to learn and grow: trusting them to take on a higher level of responsibility;
➤ connectedness: between students and teachers, patients and clinicians, members of interdisciplinary healthcare teams; research collaborators,

bench scientists and clinicians, and members of different departments and institutions;

➤ passion: for all aspects of the work—patient care, learning, teaching, trying new ideas and methods, creating new knowledge; and

➤ the wonderment of medicine: the continuing discovery of and appreciation for the profound nature of our work.

The DT members found the process re-energizing. The optimism of the stories and themes was contagious. But would the Open Forum succeed in engaging others?

> Everything went wonderfully and before we knew it, the time for the Open Forum was upon us. We wondered nervously if this plan would work—if the first step would indeed give rise to a second.
>
> We had invited all the interviewees, the deans and other leaders and interested individuals. We had no idea how many people to expect. It was a rather small turnout, around 20 people. But the stories and themes were enthusiastically received. One person said, "I never realized how good we are. When I see what we're capable of, I can no longer be silent when I see someone throw something in the operating room, or humiliate a student. We're too good for that." The dean was also there and he said, "We're working on a lot of things in the school right now, including a major effort to expand our research activities. But of all of them, I believe this is the one we'll look back on as our most important accomplishment." Many of the people hearing the presentation then volunteered to join the Discovery Team to help us think about where the project could go next.
>
> Tony Suchman

> "When I see what we're capable of, I can no longer be silent when I see someone throw something in the operating room, or humiliate a student. We're too good for that."
>
> "I believe we'll look back on the RCCI as our most important accomplishment."

STORIES ALONG THE WAY
Emergent strategies

True to the spirit of emergent design, the Formation Team continued to meet to discern next steps for the RCCI. Four general strategies emerged, none of which was part of an *a priori* plan:

> disseminating relational practices and the discipline of reflecting on the relational implications of personal and organizational behavior;

> focusing on key areas of leverage regarding culture formation: how people are brought into the organization, how performance is assessed and rewarded, and how cultural breaches are addressed;

> identifying and engaging sub-communities within IUSM that had not yet been involved in the RCCI; and

> seeking out individuals who were already involved in activities that contribute to a relational culture, but had been working in isolation. By making them aware of one another they could become a community of change, strengthening their collective skills, confidence and momentum.

These strategies are reflected in the priorities and activities of the first three years. In Year One, following the Discovery Interviews and Open Forum described above, the Discovery Team redefined itself as a community of internal change agents. We sought to enlarge this cadre and enhance their change agentry skills by means of monthly peer-coaching meetings. We began to introduce the RCCI's goals and practices to the committees at IUSM that deal with cultural breaches: the Professional Standards, Academic Standards and Teacher-Learner Advocacy Committees. We invited these committees to reflect on the degree to which their practices and procedures manifested core professional values of respect and partnership. For instance, the Academic Standards Committee reconsidered its long-established practice of informing faculty about poor student-course evaluations by means of a form letter (called the "ding" letter). They realized at once that this process was not sufficiently relational, and could unintentionally be contributing to the perception of IUSM as an impersonal and uncaring organization. They immediately ceased sending "ding" letters and redesigned the process. We met with other standing committees at IUSM as well, introducing them to various practices to "humanize" their meetings, e.g. checking-in, noticing successes, and appreciative debriefings (*see* Appendix 2 for a more detailed description of these practices).

The external consultants also made "getting to know you visits" to an expanding network of department chairs, program directors, nurse researchers, administrators, staff, students, residents, other school leaders and other potential change agents to let them know about the RCCI, to invite their participation and support, and to learn from them about others who were involved in related work. Many of them came to Discovery Team meetings to learn more about the project and its methods and to meet kindred spirits.

In Year Two, noting that there had been much more participation by faculty members than by students and residents and that the eight regional education centers had not yet become involved (all our work to that point had been at the Indianapolis campus), we formed the Student Engagement and Resident Engagement Teams to plan outreach activities and we decided that Penny or Tony would personally visit each of the other eight campuses around the state.

We also arranged to have teleconferencing equipment at each of our Discovery Team and Student Engagement Team meetings to facilitate participation by people on the other IUSM campuses. Several center faculty members began to participate regularly.

We also continued our monthly meetings of the Discovery Team and intensified our teaching of change agentry (described in more detail below). And finally, based on our conversations with department leaders, it seemed that two departments were interested in undertaking intra-departmental culture-change initiatives. We conceived of these as "Vanguard Departments," establishing an example for other departments to follow. As it turned out, these attempts proved unsuccessful (*see* the Barriers and Challenges section below).

In Year Three we focused on sustainability and dissemination. We added four members to the Formation Team to help steward the culture-change movement. The external consultants' roles began to change from the principal implementers to coaches in anticipation of the end of their monthly consulting visits. We gave more attention to external dissemination, sponsoring a National Immersion Conference (described below) and preparing publications and presentations for a national audience. We also sought several grants to extend the work to more groups both within and outside IUSM. We obtained funding to allow the external consultants to make five bi-monthly visits in Year Four to help conduct an Internal Change Agent Program (described in more detail below), helping more people prepare to carry on the work of culture change.

With this overview of the emergent strategies of the RCCI, we can now trace several spreading and intersecting ripples of change within specific subgroups subsequent to the Discovery Interviews.

Internal change agents

Following the Open Forum, its work as an interviewing team completed, the Discovery Team decided to continue to meet, taking on a new purpose: to be a learning community for internal change agents. It grew steadily as more people volunteered to help; anyone who was interested was welcome. People got involved after hearing about the RCCI at the Open Forum, from having participated in Discovery Interviews, through the external consultants' outreach visits, through personal contact with other RCCI participants, or through other serendipitous circumstances.

> About six months into the project, while at a social function, an acquaintance asked me what I did for a living. As I explained the RCCI, she exuberantly suggested that I talk with her former sorority sister who was treated horribly by medical personnel at a local hospital on the night that her husband was fatally injured in a car accident. She explained that the woman was no longer bitter but rather sought to improve things for others as she tried to educate medical personnel about compassion for the dying and their

families. That's how I was introduced to Chris Mulry, who became a consistent and significant addition to the Discovery Team and the project as a whole.

David Mossbarger,
RCCI Project Manager

I was out west sitting in a ski lodge at 10 000 feet when I discovered the RCCI at my own institution. I was having a conversation with a longtime leading medical educator from the AMA who began to tell me a story about Tom Inui's activities at IUSM. That meeting led to a lunch with Tom when I returned to IU and I embraced the concept immediately. Actually, the changes that the RCCI were espousing simply fit in with my way of thinking about what medicine is, and how it should be taught. It was from personal interactions that I was drawn into the program and it is through these interactions that the program will continue and build.

Jeff Rothenberg,
OB-GYN Faculty

Discovery Team members included administrative leaders, physicians, nurses, junior and senior faculty, department chairs, residents, students, patient advocates and staff.

This initiative emphasizes how interconnected we all are, irrespective of discipline, position, or level of training. Indeed, one of the interesting aspects is how many non-physicians have been brought into the process. This has not only enhanced the program, but made people realize that medical centers are not just for physicians and patients—without the ancillary staff we would readily fail and lose one of our most important assets—the people who make up our academic family.

Jeff Rothenberg

Ten to twenty-five people showed up at the monthly Discovery Team meetings. Chairs were arranged in a circle. Titles and roles were left at the door: everyone had an equal voice.

When I came to my first Discovery Team meeting, I expected to sit in the back. But I discovered that there are no corners in the Discovery Team, and no back rows, either.

Michelle P Elieff,
then a 4th year pathology resident

> When I came to my first Discovery Team meeting, I expected to sit in the back. But I discovered that there are no corners in the Discovery Team, and no back rows, either.

Tony and Penny facilitated these two-hour gatherings in what soon became a customary format:

➤ check-in: giving participants a chance to reflect on how they are at the moment or what might be occurring outside of the meeting that might be diverting their attention;
➤ appreciative reflections: sharing stories about either relational moments or new relational patterns of behaving that participants initiated or observed since the last meeting;
➤ peer coaching: participants seeking ideas and/or support regarding specific challenging situations or projects;
➤ peer teaching: Discovery Team members teaching each other methods, skills, or relevant theories related to organizational change; and
➤ appreciative debriefing: inviting each participant to name a moment during the meeting that s/he found particularly useful or engaging.

As Discovery Team members became familiar with these meeting formats, they brought them to many other groups, both educational and administrative, such as the Curriculum Steering Committee, the Competency Directors Committee, Medical Education and Curricular Affairs Staff meetings, a variety of teaching rounds, a community group for troubled youths and another community group for sex offenders.

Courage to Lead program
The Discovery Team soon identified a deeper learning agenda:

> At one meeting the consultants asked us what we felt we would need to move forward. At some point the responsibility for continuing the RCCI would rest in part with this team. I quickly suggested that I would need a better understanding of the RCCI process and some tools for furthering it in order to know how to take this initiative forward. Shortly thereafter the Discovery Team and others from IUSM were invited to participate in a retreat series, led by Penny and Tony, called the Courage to Lead.
>
> Ann Cottingham

The Courage to Lead program was a year-long series of four seasonal retreats based on an approach to personal and professional development pioneered by Parker Palmer called leader formation. This work was "rooted in the belief that effective leadership flows from the identity and integrity of the individual."[5] These retreats provided the time and support to reflect on the connection between participants' inner lives and the relationship-centered values and practices they hoped to foster across the medical school. In large-group, small group and solitary activities, we explored the "heart of the leader" through personal stories, reflections on work experiences, and insights from poets, storytellers and diverse wisdom traditions. The participants discerned principles and practices that underlie Courage work, and explored how to use them in furthering relationship-centered work at IUSM.

> This [Courage to Lead] experience was pivotal for me. It gave me a much deeper understanding of the theory behind the strategy that the consultants had been using—"be the change you want to see in the world"—and some good tools for helping to improve interpersonal relations in my spheres of interaction. During the retreats we learned how to ask open and honest questions, focus on our listening skills, use a poem to stimulate discussion, and foremost to consciously focus on, and value, how we are relating to others and how they are responding in all our interactions. It was tremendous to finally find a direction!
>
> It also became clear to me that this seemingly bold idea of changing the direction of the IUSM curriculum by improving relationships at the grassroots level would work. It was not hard to see the link between frustrating or demoralizing experiences that students sometimes reported, or difficulties I encountered in working to move the curriculum forward, and stress, professional fear, and distrust—feelings and perceptions that could be dramatically alleviated through improved relationships and communication.
>
> Ann Cottingham

> It became clear to me that this seemingly bold idea of changing the direction of the IUSM curriculum by improving relationships at the grassroots level would work.

A behavioral scientist faculty member who participated in the first Courage to Lead program describes its impact on her:

> CTL led to my own re-connection with my goals. When I entered the area of teaching, I wanted to create life preservers for patients and their families by changing the system of education for doctors. Somehow, I got caught up in the "shoulds" of an academic career

in medicine—I should want to do research, I should want to get a job requiring shoulder pads, I should want to get promoted. I rediscovered my truth in the retreats: I really come alive when I am teaching students or residents at the bedside of a patient, in the waiting room with a nervous family member, or in the office working with a patient in crisis. The best part is helping the trainee see, in that very moment, that the patient's greatest needs are for connection, truth, trust, and caring, not medicine. No one can make another person hear, but helping someone have the courage to listen is the most important part of teaching.

Throughout the retreats, the silence, the asking myself hard questions, and being asked hard, unanswered questions by others, felt very different than any other group-training experiences I have had, professionally or personally. The ground rules of being non-invasive and non-judgmental were foundational. No one was more an expert on my needs than me. This is not a common experience in the workplace, where often everyone else has an opinion that's presented as more important than one's own!

> Kathy Zoppi, then Competency Director, Communication
> and Family Medicine Faculty; currently, Director of
> Behavioral Sciences, Community Health Network
> Family Medicine Residency.

We conducted the Courage to Lead retreat series for three consecutive years, each time inviting 20 members of the Discovery Team or other IUSM leaders to participate. Over the three years, leadership of the retreats transitioned from the external facilitators (Penny Williamson and Tony Suchman) to IUSM faculty (Deb Litzelman and Rich Frankel), who had by then completed facilitator training with Parker Palmer and colleagues at The Center for Courage and Renewal.

Internal Change Agent program

As the three-year grant period came to a close, we recognized that the sustainability of culture change in a large, complex organization like IUSM would require a broader-based understanding of organizational change on the part of its leaders. Therefore, six members of the expanded Formation Team (including the external consultants) created and taught the Internal Change Agent program, a five-session, 20-hour program offering an in-depth curriculum on organizational change theories and facilitation skills. This program offered more rigorous instruction in change agentry than that provided at Discovery Team meetings, and was presented to a cohort of 28 faculty and administrative leaders.

Students

Early in the RCCI, we heard about a group of student change agents who had initiated the creation of a school-wide honor code in response to an episode of cheating. Their initiative was strongly supported by the student body, the Dean and the faculty. We invited the leaders of this project to join the RCCI; they turned out to be active members and were instrumental in engaging other students.

The creation of a student story book

Early in the first year of the RCCI, a fourth-year student volunteered to join the Discovery Team after participating in the Discovery Interviews. She had related a powerful story about finding a mentor who "embodied what she expected us to do."

> Telling my story [to the Discovery Team interviewer] propelled me into motion. I wanted other student voices to be heard. I wanted more students to be involved in RCCI—after all it was conceived for our benefit! I had an idea and acted on it. I decided to take an elective month in my last year to pursue this goal. Several other students and faculty joined me to create a team and we set out to collect student stories of student culture at its best from all nine campuses of IUSM. We collected nearly 100 stories. What we acquired was breathtaking. The stories themselves were amazing and the process was even more exceptional. Each center was eager and willing to have us visit them. During our visits to each center we were struck by the number of positive stories students told about each other as well as their school/center. The students, too, were impressed with the qualities and values that they heard in their own stories. You could feel the positive energy and uplifted attitudes in the room after one of our sessions. That was the beauty. We saw what students and our classes could become.
>
> We compiled exceptional student stories into a booklet, "Taking Root and Growing: Becoming a Physician at Indiana University School of Medicine." (We even found a student artist to design the cover of the book.) We distributed it to . . . incoming students at their White Coat Ceremony. By sharing the positive stories of so many students from all over the state, I dreamed that students would be proud of our medical school before even starting. But the real goal would be to nurture new students' positive attitudes throughout their experience at IUSM. The interactions with our team and the experience with other students give me hope and optimism that IUSM can be a place where people appreciate and care for each other in every interaction.
>
> Vani Sabesan, then a 4th year medical student

> The interactions with our team and the experience with other students give me hope and optimism that IUSM can be a place where people appreciate and care for each other in every interaction.

The book was not something we would ever have planned. It emerged from one student's initiative, and has proven to be a popular and enduring tradition. In each of four subsequent years other students have taken the lead in creating new booklets for the incoming class that are compilations of student and faculty art, poetry and narratives.

Medical student admissions

Another major unplanned change that emerged during the first year of the project—a transformation in the medical student admissions process—resulted from a spontaneous dinner invitation.

> After a particularly engaging and enjoyable meeting with one of the deans, Lyn Means, we suggested that we go out together for dinner. (We ended up having dinner with many people over the course of the project—it both reflected and contributed to the building of relationships—and friendships.) Lyn ended up inviting us to her home, and over the course of the dinner conversation she wondered aloud about the effect of the student selection process on the culture of the school. "Instead of choosing students with the highest academic credentials and then having to do remedial education in relationship skills, what if we assessed their relational capacity as part of the admission interview and made that one of our criteria for acceptance?" She took this idea back to the Admissions Committee, which then redesigned the entire admissions process, even going as far as engaging a group of "simulated applicants" to help committee members improve their interviewing skills.
>
> Tony Suchman

Six classes of students have now been selected according to the new process that involves eliciting actual stories, exploring hypothetical situations and observing behavior. The change in process was demonstrated early on when a candidate with outstanding academic credentials, who would certainly have been offered admission under the old process, was asked, "What would you do if you saw another student cheating?" She responded dismissively, "It's not *my* business." The committee decided not to accept her based on the mismatch between her values and the community of scholarship and practice envisioned by the committee.

Student Engagement Team

In year two of the grant period, hoping to get more students involved in the RCCI, The external consultants convened and facilitated bi-monthly Student Engagement Team meetings that included students, faculty and staff. These meetings offered students an ongoing opportunity to share examples of relationship-centered practices they had tried or observed and to receive peer and senior coaching about how to introduce positive change in their daily activities. At the students' request, the Dean established a permanent student body leadership position—the "Student Professionalism Liaison"—to focus efforts to promote mindfulness of relationship in all campus activities. In addition to sitting on the Student Council, the liaisons became ex officio members of the Formation Team during their terms. Students, with support from staff and faculty, also initiated the publication of "Incident Reports," vignettes describing either problematic or exemplary communication with accompanying discussions about relational strategies and dynamics.

Residents

We found it especially challenging to meaningfully engage residents in the RCCI and assumed that their busy schedules were the biggest obstacle. One resident affirmed that it was difficult for her to attract her peers, and she believed that it was disillusion and guilt as much as lack of time that kept residents from opening to this appreciative approach to self and others—the disillusion of having been changed in untoward ways by their training, and the guilt of subsequently behaving towards students in ways of which they were not proud.

> During my first two years at the Bloomington Medical Sciences Program, a community-based branch of IUSM, I had the opportunity to work with professionals who were dedicated to community service. They encouraged students to do likewise. Our advisor exemplified the best of the doctor–patient–community relationship. In an environment of mutual respect, he and the other doctors taught us to see the individual in the context of a social, family and personal setting.
>
> Moving to Indianapolis as a third-year medical student, I recognized a huge cultural difference between the community hospital and the academic medical center. Students were told to be compassionate in an environment that denied them simple respect and compassion. Healthcare professionals ridiculed patients and their families, not to mention staff, students, and colleagues. I didn't want any part of it, but sometimes I saw myself sink into playing the game. Disgusted, I almost quit medical school near the end of my 3rd year. Instead, I, like many of my IUSM Class of 1999 colleagues, transformed my med student idealism into bitter resident cynicism.
>
> But nothing constructive comes from cynicism. I wanted to see

if there was anything I could do to heal, so I joined the RCCI. I tried to enlist some of my fellow residents, but many were distrustful. They had already been badly "burned" and assumed this was just more hypocritical lip service. Also, it was difficult for some of us—myself included—to see the project so willingly embraced by idealistic students.

I didn't know what to think of these foreign concepts. At first I was utterly terrified by the authenticity of it all, thinking that anything that real just had to be fake. It took me a long time to allow myself to trust and experiment with such genuineness. . . . Eventually, I grew to understand and appreciate it as a foundation for awakening people to the possibilities that exist within the community.

This work is much more complex than I originally thought. We fall victim to so many pervasive mindsets that we don't even think about. Cynicism like mine is just one example. So is the "this is acceptable because this is the way we always did it" mentality, which stifles innovation and perpetuates negative behaviors. It takes effort to wake up and change stereotyped behaviors. . . . Only when we are aware of what we are doing and why, can we truly relate to people—ourselves and others. It's uncomfortable at first. And it requires considerable effort to forgive ourselves and our role models our imperfections and strive to be cooperatively better. Just knowing there's an effort on the part of some people at IUSM is comforting.

Michelle P Elieff

> At first I was utterly terrified by the authenticity of it all, thinking that anything that real just had to be fake.

Michelle often described herself as a cynic. Yet in the company of her Discovery Team colleagues, she found the inner capacity to turn from cynic to advocate and to become a significant force for change as we moved forward. She observed:

I've learned a lot . . . from working with quite a few people I had never met like Drs Meg Gaffney, Janet Hortin, Ed Hollenberg and others. . . . Having the opportunity to see them in action at Discovery Team meetings was inspiring. . . . Seeing once again that physicians could be positive role models changed me. It helped me rediscover the positive side of myself that drew me to medicine in the first place. . . . I wonder if these experiences had occurred earlier in my training whether my medical career might have taken a different direction. I know I would have been of better service to the community.

Michelle P Elieff

In the second year of the project, the external consultants formed a Resident Engagement Team in parallel with the Student Engagement Team, to find ways to engage more residents. After some efforts that didn't "take" (e.g. meetings with residency program administrators and noon conferences with residents that used storytelling to discover the principles of Relationship-centered Care), the idea emerged to connect the RCCI with something that already mattered to residents and residency program leaders—the ACGME competencies.[6] Several team members came up with the idea of conducting a workshop for residency directors and faculty from across disciplines on teaching professionalism using the appreciative and relationship-centered approach that was the signature of the RCCI. This workshop would also help us pursue an additional project goal—to empower Discovery Team members to be effective internal agents of change. The planning and facilitation of this workshop was carried out by five IUSM behavioral science faculty members with only light coaching and collaboration from the external consultants. As indicated by the formal evaluation and our own observations, the workshop was a great success. (A detailed personal account of this workshop appears below in the Outcomes subsection on Personal Change.)

This retreat gave rise to many ideas about how IUSM's graduate medical education infrastructure could become a means for disseminating culture change within and through residency programs. Unfortunately, this initial momentum stalled in the face of the retirement of the Associate Dean for Graduate Medical Education and a prolonged search for a successor. But the fire may now be rekindled as the new Associate Dean begins to incorporate appreciative storytelling into meetings of the residency program directors, a marked departure from that group's traditional behavior patterns.

Senior leadership

Three months into the project, around the time of the first Open Forum, the external consultants paid a courtesy call to the Dean and the Executive Associate Deans (EADs) to tell them about the RCCI and to share stories and themes from the Discovery Interviews. During that meeting, this senior leadership group for IUSM recognized their major effect on the culture of the school. They invited the external consultants to meet with them monthly to help them reflect on how they were conducting their work and how the challenging issues before them could be informed and addressed by a relationship-centered approach.

Partly as a result of these conversations, the Dean included rigorous data on the work environment in performance reviews for department chairs.

He initiated and personally conducted these reviews in a relationship-centered manner. Also, the deans undertook a school-wide initiative to introduce mission-based management (known at IUSM as Data-driven Decision-making or 3-D) with the expressed intention of fostering partnership, engagement, and trust. It was a remarkable and unprecedented milestone when the Dean presented to the 3-D Steering Committee (which included most of the department chairs) a complete accounting of where all funds in the medical school come from and where they go, including the allocations to each department. He thereby transformed a traditional pattern of secrecy, self-interest and competitiveness (back-room deals between the dean and department chairs) into one of shared information, collaboration and collective thinking. Each of the department chairs saw their allocations in the context of the whole institution and conversations became more participatory and open.

More recently, the Dean and the EADs dealt in a trustworthy and collaborative manner with a budget crisis generated by a major decrease in appropriations from the state government. One of the EADs describes her experience:

> Approximately, one year ago, largely due to a decrease in State appropriations, the IUSM faced the biggest budget crisis in our history. We discovered that we were about to experience a shortfall of more than $6 million. The EADs held numerous emergency meetings to decide how to handle this.
>
> Early in the discussions, a unanimous decision was made to protect the School's departments from the impact of the shortfall and to place the majority of the burden from the budget deficit on the various Dean's offices. That was the easy part . . . then, the hard work began.
>
> Each one of the EADs had a mission area to protect: the EAD for Education had to protect the educational mission, the EAD for Clinical Affairs had to protect the clinical mission, the EAD for Strategic Planning, Analysis and Operations had to protect the administrative infrastructure and the EAD for Research had to protect the research mission.
>
> Each of us was passionate about our respective areas and lobbied for the cuts to be made "elsewhere." I argued that Research was core to our existence and that it was also our future. Short-sighted reductions in the research infrastructure would severely restrict IUSM's future potential to become one of America's great medical schools. There were many tense moments . . . and for me, some tears as well. There were days and weeks when it seemed that we were facing insurmountable obstacles, disputes and roadblocks that could not be overcome.
>
> In the end, I believe that we, as a team, made some of the best decisions that could have been made under such difficult

circumstances. How did we negotiate these impasses? The RCCI played an inimitable role. To me, Relationship-centered Care is a compilation of ideas that emphasize the importance of relationships in moving initiatives forward. While not an exact science, I have learned a great deal from the RCCI. I believe that successful relationships are vital to an institution's advancement and have discerned five key elements that allow relationships to thrive. I believe these elements enabled us to reach a solution to IUSM's budget crisis.

- *Common purpose:* The Dean and the four EADs shared a sense of common purpose. We were all rowing in the same direction for this common purpose . . . to make the IUSM the best medical school that it could be. Each of us understood that this meant excellence in EACH of the mission areas as well as in the bonds that unite the missions.
- *Mutual respect:* The respect that each of us displayed for all others was both abundant and readily apparent. If this were not the case, it would have been easy for any of us to discount the opinions held by others. However, because the respect was sincere, we had to seriously consider positions that differed from our own. For me, this meant occasionally acknowledging that opinions held by others may have been more meritorious than my own.
- *Trust:* This turned out to be the most important element for me. I have worked in other circumstances where this element is missing. In the absence of trust, it can be unsafe to express a dissenting view and to truly and completely engage in candid dialogue. The trust among the EADs facilitated frank, sincere, truthful, and sometimes painful conversations.
- *Communication:* Open lines of communication were essential to our problem solving. We were each given ample opportunity to articulate our concerns as well as to rebut the positions taken by others. Though many of the discussions were heated, they took place in a safe and respectful manner; no one's views were dismissed by others and each one of us was encouraged to express and emphatically convey our positions.
- *Personal view:* I believe that occasional conflict and tension is an important attribute of productive, dynamic and successful institutions. In my view, institutions, like individuals, become complacent, unimaginative, insipid and content with the status quo if they do not seek and then tackle conflicts directly. Conflict avoidance results in institutional mediocrity rather than in a process of continuous progress, improvement and growth. In order to achieve excellence and persistently raise the bar of what is excellent, discord, friction, tension and debate are good things. Along these lines, I have coined the phrase: Creative Conflict for Productive Purposes.

However, conflict is only a good thing when it is used for productive purposes. This is only possible when healthy relationship-centeredness exists within an institution. The principles of RCCI are the enablers of cooperative, creative and constructive clashes and make it productive to engage in solving such conflicts if it is for the greater institutional good.

In the end, I am not sure whether the budget crisis of 2005 was good or bad for the IUSM. But, I do believe that the relationship-centered process we used to resolve the crisis has made us a far stronger institution. I feel proud and privileged to be a part of such a dynamic and unparalleled school of medicine.

Ora Pescovitz,

Executive Associate Dean, Research Affairs

Spreading culture change beyond IUSM

The original RCCI grant included funds for a conference on Relationship-centered Care in the 3rd year of the project; the specific agenda was not further specified. Over the first two years, as we learned in conversations with colleagues about other schools' efforts to address their informal curricula, our thinking about this conference coalesced around the idea of an "immersion conference." We invited interdisciplinary teams of clinical and administrative educational leaders from several medical schools to gather as a learning community to learn from each others' experiences. As the host school IUSM opened its doors to become a "living laboratory," with participants spending time conducting field observations out in the campus environment ("immersion"), giving special attention to the values expressed in and transmitted through everyday behavior. Twenty medical schools submitted applications. Teams from eight schools were selected: Baylor, Dartmouth, Drexel, McMaster, Missouri-Columbia, North Dakota, Southern Illinois, and University of Washington. These teams plus a team from Indiana came together in August 2005 for the Immersion Conference.

The conference design was itself relationship-centered, with daily attention to personal readiness, time for fostering and deepening relationships, and opportunities for reflection and exchanges within and between teams. After initial presentations about Relationship-centered Care, the informal curriculum, and approaches to organizational culture change, the participants spread out to observe a wide range of activities, including ward rounds, other teaching sessions, committee meetings, a Discovery Team meeting, EADs meetings, and others. Participants were also encouraged to make observations in informal venues such as cafeterias and hospital corridors. Teams from each medical school had opportunities to present their own culture-change innovations, to discuss what they were learning, and to formulate and present plans for their work back home. Throughout the conference, participants also experienced first hand a variety of relational meeting practices such as check-in, Appreciative

Inquiry, and reflective debriefing that enhanced the expression of professional values in daily work.

By the conclusion of the conference, participants had become an action-learning network. Each team created an initial road map to foster continuing culture change at their medical school. All were eager to continue meeting as an ongoing learning community. Subsequent to the conference, IUSM requested and received a grant to hold two additional annual immersion conferences. As another unplanned outcome, the members of the IUSM team, surprised to discover innovations and practices at IUSM that were new to them, suggested holding an "internal" immersion conference to form an action-learning network of interdisciplinary clinical teams at IUSM to disseminate mindfulness and practices that support relationship-centered culture. This idea evolved into a year-long Internal Immersion process on the hidden curriculum in clinical care venues where the majority of graduate medical education takes place.

Blind alleys and missteps

Emergent strategies did not always succeed and we did not always live up to our commitment to relationship-centered process.

Bringing the RCCI into departments

One member of the Discovery Team had the idea to create a culture-change initiative within his own department in parallel with and in support of our school-wide project. This stimulated the idea for us that a small number of "vanguard departments" might pioneer the development of approaches for bringing Relationship-centered Care and Administration further out into the organization and, more importantly, to the clinical sites where students were learning. We hoped that these departments could then help other departments follow the same path. This was clearly our idea, but turned out not to be that of the department leaders. Despite their initial enthusiasm and an effort on our part to help prepare an application for an intramural grant, our agenda never rose sufficiently high on their priority lists to gain their sustained commitment. After eight months of effort, we abandoned this strategy.

Overlooking relationship amidst the urgency of tasks

At the beginning of year three, we invited several additional people to join the Formation Team to create a more robust stewardship group. At the very first meeting attended by the new members, we reverted to old ways of behaving, focusing on task and neglecting relationship.

> We were involved in a dialogue of some time urgency about a prospective grant during the first meeting in which two of the new members were present. We jumped into a contentious conversation about how to conceptualize the grant, which somehow seemed

bumpier than our usual give and take. After the meeting, I realized that we had not taken the time to orient these new members to our intentions and ways of working together, nor did we integrate them by sharing stories about how we came to this work, a method we used to help form the team in the first place. We all had felt uncomfortable about this during the meeting, but not one of us said anything. We had let ourselves get too preoccupied with the tasks of the meeting and weren't mindful of the relationships. It felt terrible, and very different from our usual process. I realized afterwards that with our new members we were in fact a new group and needed to attend anew to our relationships as well as to individual and group expectations and processes. I sent out an email suggesting that we do so at the next meeting. That next conversation was seminal in (re)building trust and respect among the members of our newly enlarged group. I learned once again that investing in relationships is the sine qua non for successful work and that there are no short cuts.

Penny Williamson

The good news is that the practice of Relationship-centered Care does not require that we never stumble, only that we catch ourselves and respond to our missteps. Sometimes greater trust can be built by recognizing and repairing a breach in relationship than if the breach had never happened in the first place.

OUTCOMES
Organizational change
Participation in the RCCI

Several kinds of data offer a triangulated perspective on the impact of the RCCI to date. The first concerns the level of participation in RCCI activities. More than 900 faculty, students, residents, staff, allied health professionals and patients have been involved to date. Among the faculty, it's possible to identify those who are most active and influential based on their participation in committees. IUSM's 29 formal working committees are made up of 297 faculty members (9.3% of the total IUSM faculty), 96 (33%) of whom participated in RCCI activities. Of the 173 faculty who are more actively engaged, participating in two or more committees, 90 (52%) participated in RCCI activities. Among the 10 committees focused on education and student life, 71% of the committee members and 9 of 10 chairs have participated in the RCCI. A picture thus emerges of the RCCI having reached those faculty members who are most involved in governance, faculty affairs, education and student life at IUSM, and who are thus well positioned to further disseminate mindfulness of culture and new patterns of relating.

Observations by participants

The direct observations of participants constitute a second kind of data that bears out this image of changing patterns of relating. At every Discovery Team meeting, members described changes they observed or attempted to enact. Their reflections were recorded in the meeting minutes, and can be grouped into several categories.

➤ New meeting formats and practices: IUSM faculty, staff and students introduced new practices into standing meetings, teaching conferences and other activities to make them more relational and collaborative. For example, the Appreciative Inquiry-based practice of sharing success stories has spread widely in both administrative and educational contexts.

➤ New individual behaviors: Many individuals intentionally stepped outside the norm in the hope of instigating new patterns of interaction. For instance, a Discovery Team member described how she summoned the courage to make a positive suggestion in a committee meeting that was usually quite negative and at which she was the junior member. The Chair commended her for the idea and asked to meet with her after the meeting to follow up. Upon hearing this story another Discovery Team member exclaimed, "Your example has given me courage. I commit myself to speaking up next week at a meeting where I am usually silent, and where much could be done differently."

➤ New institutional procedures and programs: These ranged from faculty development programs for new hires to new student-leadership positions.

➤ Public communications about culture: Faculty, residents and students created new communications vehicles to raise awareness of the changing IUSM culture including an RCCI newsletter and monthly informational emails.

Observations by an independent evaluator

The observations of an independent evaluator constitute a third kind of outcome data. This individual, DeWitt (Bud) Baldwin MD, a senior educator, researcher and clinician administrator, was engaged by the Fetzer Institute to observe the work of the RCCI and make periodic reports. He made monthly visits to IUSM timed to coincide with those of the external consultants. In addition to observing RCCI activities, he conducted extensive interviews with a variety of informants. The following are examples of quotes that he recorded.

From the senior deans:

➤ "[The RCCI has been a] crucial enabler, providing a framework and a methodology for setting up and facilitating the conversations that have had and are having such a broad impact on the school."

➤ "We are infecting people, one at a time. There's a significant change from two years ago. People are talking and behaving differently."

➤ "The RCCI has helped me to be a more caring and thoughtful individual in the way I deal with other people than I otherwise would have been during this time."

➤ "Our level of professionalism is substantially higher—what we expect from each other and from ourselves, especially in our relationships with students. I'd like to think that professionalism in our relationships with patients has been there all along, but our relationships with students and with each other have changed. We show more respect for each other; we value each other and are more sensitive to each other's needs. These newer behaviors are becoming an expected norm."

➤ "I think my conversations with faculty are a little bit different. I go into them now having consciously decided not to have preformed opinions. I'm more of an active listener."

➤ "The previous sense of cynicism towards high-minded ideals is gone. Behaviors that are detrimental to relationships are much less evident than they were before at a faculty level. Expressions of anger and disrespect are less-acceptable parts of our culture."

From faculty members:
➤ "We feel we are changing the nature of our conversations [at committee meetings]."
➤ "We are learning to 'check in', to learn from each other."
➤ "[We are learning to] reframe from the usual crime and punishment scene to one of being more present, more respectful."
➤ "It's a wonderful idea and program, taking on organizational and cultural change in such a large and complex organization. Having been at some of the meetings, the thing I've been most impressed about is how the initiative has accomplished one of its goals, achieving effects at two levels, from the top down and bottom up. The effect as shown in the students' stories [in an online journal] has been amazing, and from being at meetings with the Deans, to have gotten their complete buy-in and support is nothing short of a huge success."

From medical students and residents:
➤ "At the Discovery Team meetings there were . . . all the 'relational tools' people brought in—ways of seeing things, understanding a different point of view, that I learned from. I'm trying to incorporate these into my ways of doing things and it has broadened my skills considerably."
➤ "I did notice that I said something to a resident recently and they said, 'Oooh, I like the words you used', and it was something someone said during the coaching sessions and I thought, 'Maybe I *am* learning something.'"
➤ "Before becoming aware of the RCCI, I'd look at things in the school and pick out all the bad things. I'd say, 'I don't like doing this exercise, I don't get anything out of it and I don't understand why I have to do it.' Now I realize that my complaining does no good. In general, I try to focus on

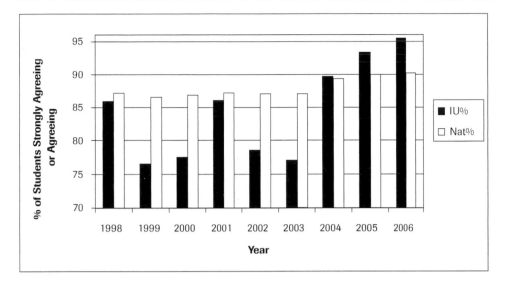

FIGURE 13.1 Trends in medical students' responses to the item "overall satisfaction with the quality of your medical education" on the AAMC Graduation Questionnaire.

more positive things. For example, I just had very positive autopsy exercise yesterday, so when I go to school today, I'll tell my friends how great it was—it was not easy and it took a long time, but it's what medicine is all about. So they'll go in with a good attitude. That's part of continuing the dialogue."

Student survey results

The fourth source of outcome data is the annual Graduation Questionnaire administered by the Association of American Medical Schools. One of the factors giving rise to the RCCI was the longstanding trend of below-average scores for students' overall satisfaction with the quality of their medical education. In 2004, the second year of the RCCI, that trend began to change. IUSM graduates' ratings were at the national average for the first time, and they continued to rise in 2005 and 2006 to levels well above the national mean (*see* Figure 13.1). This upward trend reflects many contemporaneous initiatives and circumstances at IUSM including a change in leadership, maturation of the new curriculum, and the creation of new courses, as well as the RCCI. While it's impossible to determine how much of this trend can be attributed specifically to the RCCI, it is clear that a substantial change in the learning environment has taken place.

Personal change

For most of us who were involved, the RCCI was anything but business as usual. It required us to "be the change" and it left us personally changed in some way. Here are stories from three senior project members.

> . . . the RCCI was anything but business as usual. It required us to "be the change" and it left us personally changed in some way

Deb Litzelman, a role model for many people, described her own stretching to live the principle of being fully present, and that enabled her to help others do likewise:

> With role models before me and coaches at my side, I looked inward to find MY capacity to contribute to the vision of a different kind of organization and community. Intensely private and introverted by nature, I tried sharing pieces of myself and my life with others so that we might better understand and appreciate our differences and recognize our similarities. Profoundly impacted by the death of my mother in 2003, I tried writing haiku—having never written a poem in my life—along with other reflections. My piece was included in the medical student booklet, "Reflections."
>
> During clinic one afternoon, a medical student shyly approached me and said, "I was touched by what you wrote about your mother." (My mother had donated her body to the cadaver lab at my alma mater.) The connection I felt with that medical student at that moment was unpredictably and intensely intimate.
>
> Several months later, following the futile [resuscitation] on the angiogram table in the radiology department of our 400 lb, 25-year-old patient with a huge saddle pulmonary embolus, I hugged my weeping resident as we unknowingly prepared ourselves for the next four hours of caring for the patient's estranged parents and his brothers' hysteria upon receipt of this bad news. I saw this resident just the other day—he is now a cardiology fellow—we chatted in the hallway together and re-experienced our special connection.
>
> Deb Litzelman

Bud Baldwin, the external evaluator for the RCCI, describes his initial skepticism and a seminal turning point in his understanding of how change happens.

> My story is one of doubt and skepticism, my own failure to believe in what I was seeing and hearing, my own lack of faith in the very process to which I had believed I was firmly committed, and yet, at the test, found myself wanting.
>
> It was the beginning of my second year with the project, as the project staff was beginning a purposeful, formal effort to become involved with graduate medical education. The Resident Engagement Team had come up with the idea of providing support

to residency program directors in meeting the ACGME's newly mandated Professionalism competency. From working at the ACGME, I was aware of the difficulty most programs across the country were experiencing in knowing what and how to teach this competency. I even possessed the informative PowerPoint presentations that the ACGME staff used when they visited various programs to explain "how to do it." I immediately fell back on my habitual dependence on "expertise," and prepared myself and the PowerPoint presentation, which I thought would assist the RCCI team (which I obviously had decided in advance would at least appreciate, if not require such help!).

On the day of the session, my confidence was not particularly buoyed up when I saw the loose agenda and the absence of printed material and electronic projection equipment, and further observed that the leaders for the session were not persons I knew to be centrally involved on the project staff, or whose qualifications I knew. I purposely sat at the back (after all, my "expertise" had not been requested), and waited for what I feared might be a debacle, especially since the session had been scheduled for more than two hours in the very heart of the working day with some extraordinarily busy people. Indeed, I observed the invited participants entering tentatively, looking uncertain, generally in supportive twos for the women and singles for the men. They all seemed somewhat disconcerted by the seating, small horseshoe arrangements of six chairs each, and again when they discovered there were no handouts. A number checked their cell phones and pagers. Ah ha, I thought, I'll bet they've all arranged to be paged in about 45 minutes, so they can leave in case they are bored.

To my surprise, the session began with an air of calm assurance on the part of the "unknown" leaders as they asked the participants how they were currently teaching professionalism. Bingo! In short order, there were nine different and creative approaches up on the board that were already in use. How powerful, I thought, and how competent—of both the leaders and the participants!

As the session progressed into rounds of Appreciative Inquiry about their personal experiences of professionalism, the energy in the room rose sharply, and smiles appeared on the participants' formerly expressionless faces. People relaxed and body language became more receptive.

Suddenly, as I had predicted, a succession of pagers and cell phones began to ring. One after another, people came to the back of the room (where I was sitting) to answer their pages and calls. Contrary to my earlier suspicions, I overheard them saying hurriedly that they did not want to be disturbed, then they rushed back to the discussion. To my knowledge, not a single person left the session early, and a number stayed afterward talking in small groups.

My hurt pride could find some small consolation in the fact that at least I had correctly read the initial reactions and defenses of the audience—after all, wasn't I just like them? But my overwhelming feeling was one of amazement and discovery. Not only that this stuff really does work if you give it a chance, but that the process of building relationships and releasing creativity is the most powerful force in the world—if we don't get in the way!

Bud Baldwin

Thomas Inui reflects on the impact of this project on his life-long stance of rational planning and top-down organizational oversight:

For most of my life in academe, I have been able to see the possibilities in "the dark side." Show me a failed grant and I'll be ready to work on a strategic re-submission; a stagnating career, and I'll be looking for experience and skills that others would find invaluable in other settings; a reduction in force in the teeth of shrinking core budgets, and I'll be trying to understand how program pruning might strengthen an institution's "root stock." In addition to being a durable optimist, I've been a constant planner, always wanting to know how my own choices and those of others fit (or didn't fit) into a complex web of organizational dynamics for change. The "rational man" in me never slept.

Others came to rely upon me for these traits. I rose in rank and responsibilities partly because of my research and success as an educator, but also because I found administrative responsibilities enticing—administration was not a dirty word, and administrative duties were not beneath me. From my first job on, I wanted to be a driver, not just a rider on the academic bus.

As a consequence, I became a designated problem solver. I was the go-to person for problems that wouldn't go away. My first chairman encouraged this trait, taught me "Murphy's Law" (if something can go wrong, it will), and suggested that leadership was the art of making policy that protected the institution/program from an inevitable march of bad choices that faculty members would make. Academe was Lord of the Flies incarnate. Trusting others did not become my strong suit.

At the outset of the Relationship-centered Care initiative, I was solidly in this career-long orientation. I loved the Appreciative Inquiry approach (it fed my optimism), but assumed that we would need to choose where to take it. I imagined a parallel set of change strategies would be required to enforce organizational standards and that top-down controls would be needed to bring about desired change. I expected these environments, and the people within them, to be refractory to change.

It was, then, somewhat astonishing when I began to see that AI could be counted upon to highlight negative behaviors and regrettable situations in organizational narratives with positive outcomes. In these AI narratives, people encountered challenges and found creative ways through (around, over, under) them. Wisdom triumphed over thoughtlessness; caring overcome carelessness; kindness trumped mean-spiritedness. The storytellers were not Pollyannas. Their stories revealed the "dark side" but also suggested how we all might do better.

I was not the only "listener" to these narratives who understood what they offered. Through the various RCCI dissemination activities (open forums, speaking, newsletter, reports, articles) many members of the academic community, including members of the faculty, staff, students, and administration, heard these stories and began to see a more value-coherent "way forward." Some of these listeners were among those who had taken actions that caused harm to others in the past—for various reasons. They had tantrums in the operating room, disparaged students, made cynical statements about patients because they had lost sight of other ways to seek what they most wanted—surgical excellence, ambitious learning, and adherence with medical recommendations. The stories reminded them, or perhaps in some instances taught them for the first time, that there are other approaches to these ends. These same individuals began to "experiment" with new approaches and were rewarded by those around them for doing so. No new policies were needed, no penalties, and no remediation mandated. Instead, hearing about an alternative model, they tried it and were reinforced. New behaviors became habits. Exceptional behaviors to inevitable challenges became "standard operating procedures."

The consummate planner, I could not predict where a positive action and innovative approach would emerge. To my surprise, people in high-risk environments were just as likely to take positive steps as others, perhaps because the felt need resided there. In spite of being one of the principal leaders for RCCI, the weight of responsibility for designing project plans was not upon my shoulders. I would take my initiatives within my own environment, but expect that institutional "emergence" would serve as the optimal intelligence for program activities institution-wide. As the RCCI leader, when asked what the RCCI would do in the next year, I would earnestly and honestly answer "I have no idea!" The next question was often "How can I get involved?"—to which I would respond, "Just show up and see what speaks to you." "What are my responsibilities if I join in?" "Whatever you choose to do." The astonished and pleased countenances that materialize in these exchanges revealed the scarcity of free choice in academe and just how refreshing and infectious the prospects of true community volunteerism can be. Even the designated problem solver could choose what he wanted to do.

Tom Inui

KEY RELATIONSHIPS AND RELATIONAL STRATEGIES

Relationship was at the very heart of the Relationship-centered Care Initiative. Its goals and methods involved paying attention to processes of relating as they were happening in the moment, and to enacting in every teaching and administrative interaction the same values of partnership and shared decision making that characterized the clinical practice of Relationship-centered Care. Our principal intervention was to invite storytelling about moments of exemplary relationship to foster greater mindfulness. We visited many committees and departments and invited them to reflect on their own relationship processes, prompting them to change those processes. We disseminated meeting formats and methods to make them more relational and less impersonal. Participants tended to like this new meeting environment better than the old one, and were inspired to bring the new methods to other meetings. And in the course of all this activity, those of us on the project team paid careful attention to our own relationship processes, trying to live the change as consistently as we could.

The selection of the original members of the Formation Team was based largely on relationships either between the team members and IUSM, or between team members themselves. Tom Inui, Rich Frankel, Penny Williamson and Tony Suchman had known each other for many years through their involvement in several national medical organizations. Only with such a deep degree of trust could the IUSM leaders open their organization to outsiders to instigate change. Deb Litzelman was chosen for her extensive network of relationships within IUSM.

The project grew as the Formation Team members formed relationships with a growing number of people at IUSM. We tried to identify "kindred spirits" and help them meet each other to form a "community of congruence," that is, people with a common vision and purpose. [7]

Another crucial set of relationships was between the Formation Team members and the Dean, Craig Brater. Each of these relationships formed under different circumstances, but the net result was the Dean's confidence in and public enthusiasm for the project. While there was an enormous amount of grassroots involvement—indeed, that's where the vast majority of the RCCI's work was done—it was greatly facilitated by the Dean's public support and commitment. The project was simultaneously bottom-up and top-down.

HOLDING THE PARADOX OF PLANNING AND EMERGENCE

It is easy to feel confident about emergent design in hindsight, now that we can see all that has happened, but for many members of the IUSM community it was a leap of faith to proceed with an emergent process, and far from effortless. A few months after the first Open Forum, a Discovery Team member reflected:

> No immediate plans appeared evident. I have worked with our unit and other IUSM groups in strategic planning. I was ready and eager to take the themes we had identified and move forward, perhaps helping to identify groups of interested individuals throughout IUSM to brainstorm how we could expand and cultivate more experiences that had the characteristics of the high-point experiences identified in the interviews. But this was not the plan. In fact, having any plan at all appeared to be thinking in the wrong direction. The Discovery Team continued to meet regularly. At each meeting Penny and Tony asked us what changes we were noticing in the IUSM culture, and what we were trying. I was not sure what new "things" I should be trying. I had always tried to be friendly and helpful to my colleagues, but I knew this wasn't enough. What else was I supposed to be doing? Without a new plan, the meetings began to feel somewhat unproductive.
>
> Ann Cottingham

> "Having any plan at all appeared to be thinking in the wrong direction."

As project manager for the RCCI, Dave Mossbarger, was the living interface between being true to the emergent design and doing the planning necessary to conduct this project in a large bureaucracy. He more than anyone else was the one to hold this paradox.

> While we appropriately tout the strategy of emergent design and the discipline of mindfulness as key elements of success for effecting culture change at the IU School of Medicine, we had to live in a money-conscious and time-conscious world. We dealt regularly with concrete issues that required structure and attention to finances and time limits. As project manager, I knew that whatever we did—regardless of how "unplanned"—the Fetzer grant set finite limits of time and budget. In addition, Fetzer required quarterly operational status reports and annual financial reports, and Indiana University required annual budgets up front, updated each year. These constituted real world "plans" which I had to provide somehow despite our "unplanned" design and desire to let activities

emerge. I found this quite challenging!

Other factors that demanded planning and structure were: Internal Review Board processing; scheduling the limited time when the external consultants were present on site with a growing number of recurring meetings; and following up on and documenting the project's many activities.

In practice, holding this paradox required a lot more coordination, creative development, and budget revising than would have occurred for the usual planned project. The administration and logistics included managing the funds, arranging lodging, reserving rooms and videoconferencing equipment for meetings, and arranging hospitality as needed, often on short notice. The follow-up for meeting actions required persistence and approaching folks in a positive, relational way while maintaining accountability.

So while the project was not "planned", neither was it left completely to chance. As stewards of the vision, the Formation Team was proactive, in the following ways.

- We informed, educated, invited, promoted, and publicized the RCCI to provide transparency and reach all levels of the community. (This included one-on-one meetings, presentations to groups, DT meetings, Open Forums, web site postings, student bulletin board, RCCI Newsletter, numerous emails, paired interviewing, Center visits, and newspaper articles. Our mantra was, "Hide nothing, because we have nothing to hide."
- We remained alert for and sought synergy with complementary programs and activities.
- We followed up on the "ripples" in myriad places, as described above.
- We "opened the space" for a safe haven in which people could address the current culture and the desired culture of the school, all in a positive light, across silos. While the Discovery Team was the primary venue for this, all our activities contributed.
- We made decisions, delegated, scheduled, monitored and gave feedback—all in service of keeping the initiative moving and on track. There was always deliberative work to be done, mostly behind the scenes.
- We persisted! We did all the above throughout the project, not just at the outset, emphasizing the positive while acknowledging the negative and maintaining accountability. Most of our communication was informal and horizontal throughout the organization.

Dave Mossbarger

> While we appropriately tout the strategy of emergent design . . . we had to live in a structured, money-conscious, and time-conscious world.

Ann and Dave weren't the only ones to be challenged by the paradox of planning and emergence. As the project entered its third year, the external consultants experienced a sense of rising anxiety and responsibility about whether the project would achieve sustainability. So they sought a way to build more momentum and participation.

In the course of the project, it was not unusual for either one of us to experience anxiety and feel tempted to try to steer the process in one direction or another. Usually, the other one of us would recognize this and help us stay on track, remaining open and curious and engaging the participants in the project in setting their own direction. But one time, caught in the grip of time running out, we both lapsed back into control mode. Noting how successful the first round of Discovery Interviews had been in raising awareness of culture and attracting volunteers, we envisioned a new round of interviews by the Discovery Team, which by then numbered more than 80 people.

We invited all the Discovery Team members to a special meeting that was billed as an opportunity to reflect on what had happened so far and to plan next steps together.

Over forty members attended and engaged enthusiastically in the first part of the meeting, conducting appreciative interviews about changes they had experienced in the school. But then, disregarding our deep conviction that ripples needed to emerge from within the group, we announced our intention of engaging them in a new round of interviews. This fell utterly flat. The participants felt misled about the purpose of the meeting: they had not signed up to be interviewers and were disappointed not to be having a more open and collaborative conversation to plan next steps. They felt—correctly—that we had preempted their process.

It was painful to recognize our error and the size of the opportunity we had just missed. We worried that trust and momentum would be lost. But instead of trying even harder to control the project, we initiated a reflective conversation on what had happened, how we screwed up, lessons learned and what we should do next. We wrote a letter to the Discovery Team apologizing for our meltdown and offering our lessons learned. We re-learned the difficult and humbling lesson that "you can't push the river," and felt grateful that the depth of relationships we had established with DT members helped us to repair this breach.

Penny Williamson and Tony Suchman

CONCLUSIONS/LESSONS LEARNED

Revealed in this storied description of the Relationship-centered Care Initiative are at least three important lessons. First, changing the global patterns of relating that we call "organizational culture" involves changes in the local patterns of everyday interaction. The work of changing the culture of medical education at IUSM was accomplished by a growing number of individuals "being the change," i.e., taking the social risk of acting outside of existing patterns, introducing new patterns of conversation at meetings, and offering new ways of being together. This was both a top-down and bottom-up process. It was important to have the participation of people in positions of formal leadership whose behavior is particularly visible and who could call attention to and provide support for the project. But the principal work was at the grassroots level as one person positively influenced another to be more mindful of their actions in the moment, then the second person catalyzed a third and so on in spreading ripples of change. These patterns were reinforced through circles of reciprocal influence. For example, students and residents were positively affected by faculty and faculty by senior mentors, as one might expect. However, the faculty and senior leaders were re-energized and inspired by students, too.

Second, the process of culture change involves changes in beliefs and expectations. The expectation that "this is just how things are and it will never change" is self-fulfilling, and constitutes one of the most powerful constraints holding existing patterns of relating in place, no matter how undesirable those patterns might be. People must experience new behaviors and outcomes to raise their expectations, but they will only engage in new behaviors to the extent that they are hopeful, that is, that their expectations are raised. As the preceding stories show, many of those involved in the RCCI began in a state of disbelief, anxiety, skepticism, and cynicism. This should not surprise us. Becoming a professional in healthcare has too often meant creating and abiding a division between one's soul and role, living in a world where showing one's heart is considered unprofessional and "leaving one's self at the door" is both expected and explicitly taught. And yet, as Parker Palmer writes, just below the surface is a yearning to be "divided no more" and to live and work in community. Given even a small bit of positive experience, people are willing, even eager, to regain their hope and to believe that change just might be possible.

The appreciative interviews and ongoing focus on the positive capacity within each person and within the organization allowed a new sense of hope to emerge, a new belief in the possibility of a relationship-centered culture at IUSM. Rising expectations made it easier to engage in new behaviors leading to more positive experiences, further enhancing expectations in a virtuous cycle. Thus, the change in educational culture at IUSM involved not only changes in patterns of relating but also in patterns of organizational identity—what the people at IUSM thought about their own organization.

Third, this project offers a "proof-of-concept" for emergent design:

Our willingness to "not know" helped make it all possible. Instead, we looked for kindred spirits to join us as partners and supported their ideas. One thing kept leading to another. We kept our eyes open for serendipitous opportunities and connections, and we kept on building relationships with more and more people. To look back on all the new projects and processes that emerged and continue to emerge—things we never could have dreamt of, let alone planned—is as meaningful a professional experience as I could ever ask for.

Tony Suchman

NOTES

1 The RCCI was funded by a 3-year grant from the John E Fetzer Institute.

2 Tressolini C and the Pew–Fetzer Task Force on Health Professions Education. *Health Professions Education and Relationship-Centered Care.* San Francisco, CA: Pew Health Professions Commission; 1994.

3 Palmer P. *A Hidden Wholeness: the journey toward an undivided life.* San Francisco: Jossey-Bass; 2004. pp. 57–8.

4 Stacey R. *Strategic Management and Organizational Dynamics: the challenge of complexity.* Harlow, England: Pearson Education Ltd; 2000.

5 Palmer P. *The Courage to Teach.* San Francisco, CA: Jossey-Bass; 1998. p. 10.

6 Batalden P, Leach D, Swing S, *et al.* General competencies and accreditation in graduate medical education. *Health Aff* (Millwood). 2002: **21**(5): 103–11.

7 Palmer P, op. cit. pp. 172–5.

8 Palmer P, op.cit.

Commentary: Indiana University School of Medicine

Can a large-scale change in the culture of an organization be realized without *a priori* grand plans and a timetable? The story of the Relationship-centered Care Initiative (RCCI) at the Indiana University School of Medicine (IUSM) tells the remarkable story of just such a major change in culture. The desired outcome was clear: to foster professionalism by creating a more relationship-centered culture in the entire medical school such that the lived experience of students was aligned with the formal curriculum. However, counter to traditional wisdom, the path to reaching this goal was emergent by design. The story of the RCCI is an account of how a deliberate plan of emergence held in balance with a desired outcome and combined with an appreciative, relational and mindful approach, led to ripples of change that transformed the culture of the second largest medical school in the United States.

This chapter provides proof of the concept that an emergent design is not only possible, but is a powerful and effective strategy for effecting culture change, even in a large, complex organization. Through providing rich details of the on-the-ground work including processes and numerous individual experiences, this case study offers myriad useful lessons for adopting an emergent approach to change.

IMPLEMENTING AN EMERGENT DESIGN

The core role of the RCCI leadership team at IUSM (named the Formation Team) was to hold a stance of "not knowing" all the steps for proceeding while being stewards of the culture-change process—requiring a very different set of responsibilities from guiding a pre-determined plan. Their role was "not to plan and implement, but to notice patterns of relating at IUSM, instigate what they hoped would be constructive disturbances in those patterns, observe the results, and discern the next steps. And . . . to engage a growing number of people in this same process." The Formation Team decided upon a single intervention and a light infrastructure to nurture what emerged. That first intervention was the collection of 80 interviews by a Discovery Team to uncover examples of the IUSM culture at its best.

A public forum was held to share these stories with the larger community. Embedding the sharing of stories in the admission of "not knowing" how things should or would continue to unfold had the effect of opening doors and hearts. Because most people weren't familiar with emergence as a strategy (likely holding the implicit idea of the machine model of change), being transparent and explaining this approach was a vital part of the RCCI, as was the consistent invitation for all interested persons to become involved. Interested members of the IUSM community joined the Discovery Team and found a trustworthy and growing community of support and authentic conversations. When they realized that ideas weren't going to originate from "the top" it unleashed their creativity, contributions, and commitment in a cascading ripple. New ideas were born, shared and took hold; possibilities for a desired future began to emerge. Involved people became ambassadors and invited other colleagues into the process.

This chapter offers important lessons for adopting an emergent approach to change. Such an approach takes as much effort as traditional top-down initiatives. Both planning and flexibility are required to provide the infrastructure for evolving processes. Because no blueprint is available, a stewardship group must develop core strategies as they proceed. These include fostering reflection (noticing pattern making in each moment—catching ourselves in the act of culture building) and being mindful of potential leverage opportunities for culture formation (such as how people are brought into the organization, how performance is assessed and rewarded, and how cultural breaches are addressed). Mindfulness in these arenas often leads to insights and changes in approach.

AN APPRECIATIVE APPROACH TO CULTURE CHANGE

In addition to the use of an emergent design, another distinguishing feature of the RCCI was the belief in an appreciative approach to change—helping people discover the positive core of their culture. The RCCI began at a demoralized time for the medical school: students felt unheard and unappreciated; faculty, overburdened; and leaders, distressed. A decade of dedicated work had led to the adoption of a competency-based curriculum. But, as in most other US medical schools, there was a mismatch between what students were taught formally and what many experienced day to day. Beginning this initiative with appreciative interviews did more than lift up powerful stories of relational and collaborative culture when IUSM was at its best. It raised morale and hopefulness among interviewers and those telling their stories. As energy shifted from demoralization and discouragement to what was working and what was possible, new members became engaged and innovative ideas were born and flourished across every sector of the school. In the face of some healthy skepticism that such an approach could not possibly work (including, at first, from members of the Formation Team and school leaders) an appreciative approach proved robust and effective and gained many converts along the way. Far from skimming over difficulties, it provided the means for exploring how individuals had successfully dealt with all manner of challenges in an effective, relational way.

The strengths-based focus of the original stories was supplemented by appreciative meeting practices introduced in the Discovery Team and carried to many other venues. Practices at meetings included regular sharing of appreciative observations (examples of relational culture building ideas that had been tried or witnessed) and appreciative debriefings at the ends of meetings (naming instances during the meeting that were particularly useful or engaging). In these ways the habit of looking for and celebrating what was working became a familiar context within which challenges could be explored without losing sight of desired gains, and members experienced giving and receiving affirmation for their efforts—an all too rare occurrence.

THE IMPORTANCE OF ATTENDING TO RELATIONSHIPS AND RELATIONAL PROCESSES

It should be no surprise that the Relationship-centered Care Initiative would include a primary focus on fostering and sustaining relationships. This chapter demonstrates the core importance of regular attention to the quality of relationships, helped immeasurably by the creation of trustworthy groups that are able to learn together, solve challenging issues, welcome and nurture innovations, and support each other through disheartening times.

It became commonplace in many groups for members to consider the question: "How can we attend to x (this issue, this person, the work of this committee, etc.) in a more relational way?" Introducing these sorts of conversations fostered reflection on the relational implications of personal and organizational behavior in all venues. This is abundantly described for the Formation Team, the Discovery Team, and the Dean and Executive Associate Deans (EADs), among others. From the start, the Formation Team recognized the importance of conducting their work in a relationship-centered manner, "fostering culture change in a way that modeled the new culture" including "setting aside ample time to reflect on our work together." In their work with the EADs the external consultants invited in-depth check-ins as well as regular reflections on how challenging issues could be handled in a relational manner. In many other groups as well, the adoption of relational meeting practices such as "check-ins" and respectful listening allowed colleagues to become known as persons, contributing to more robust relationships and more effective work.

SELF-AWARENESS, PERSONAL ENGAGEMENT AND COURAGE

Echoing the lessons from Chapter 5, this chapter illustrates powerfully the self-awareness, belief in self and others, and courage needed to attend consistently to a relationship-centered approach to the work, depending as it does on mindfulness "in the moment" and the use of self as the main instrument of change. There are countless heroes in this story—individuals who often reached beyond their comfort zone to try something new, name something that was not right and work to make it better (be not silent), affirm a colleague, speak their truth, and join in the ongoing efforts to create a more relationship-centered culture. These were "internal agents" in at least two senses: changing their environment from within the organization and changing internally in the process. (As one faculty member said, the consistent attention to Relationship-centered Care recalled him more often to mindfulness with profound results of feeling more connected more of the time.)

Not all efforts succeeded and some took a very long time to come to fruition (hence the need for courage and patience). Ripples of change happened because of the efforts of students, residents, physician and nurse faculty members, staff, and administrative leaders. Perhaps the most poignant examples of success were evident in the practice of Relationship-centered Care when it mattered most, in the midst of the most challenging times (such as layoffs necessitated by state budget cuts and a cheating scandal). Conventional wisdom might say, "this issue is too important to take time out for relationships," but the RCCI demonstrated many times over that this is actually the most crucial time. Individual courage and self-awareness were bolstered in trustworthy communities. The RCCI represents an interweaving of individual acts supported in communities of learning and support. It is an ongoing process that is repeated in every act. As in other stories (*see* Chapters 6, 7) one cannot put Relationship-centered Administrative practices into effect and then let them go. One must rather create an ongoing process which like any other type of administration requires nurture and attention.

CHAPTER 14

Conclusion

Leadership requires foresight—the ability to look towards the future, make plans, strategize and move an organization forward. The pantheon of popularly acknowledged leaders is filled with people who envisioned new products, services and business processes, so much so that one could easily get the idea that leadership is a matter of creating brilliant designs.

But the only place the future is ever constructed—and the only place a leader ever acts—is right here in the present, "in the moment." So effective leaders need not only to be forward thinking but also to be capable of noticing and participating mindfully in the continuous and emergent pattern-making of the organizational conversation. They must understand how profoundly their moment-to-moment behavior influences organizational culture. They must have the skills and the awareness of self and others to create a workplace environment that invites innovation and inspires people to give their best. They need a realistic understanding of how change happens—not by executive fiat but by many small, mindful disturbances in existing patterns that spread and grow. And they need to be authentically and courageously present to inspire trust and followership in others.

These qualities were present in the leaders described in the case studies. The result: transformational changes in organizational culture and performance, and ripples of positive change that spread to parent organizations and even to the larger community. The combination of relationship-centered leadership and openness to the emergence of new possibilities paid off in improvements in financial performance, staff morale, patient satisfaction, staff initiative, and team effectiveness and productivity. In short, Relationship-centered Administration works.

The case studies allow us to witness the creation of both physical and social spaces that promote teamwork, creativity and good workflow. They illustrate the application of various methods to foster environments that encourage open and honest expression of feelings, perceptions, and new ideas, even when they challenge the accepted standards of organizational culture and conventional wisdom. And they show that such relational environments can be created even in situations where staff members are initially discouraged, resistive, and distrustful.

We have also seen that the skills and techniques of Relationship-centered Administration can be learned; leaders don't have to be born that way. Skills and attitudes such as reflection, deep listening, attending to interpersonal process, and having the courage to let go of control can be cultivated and taught.

Beyond the theories, skills and methods of the case studies, there is an even more important underlying message, a message of hope. Many readers may be working in organizations with conventional approaches that will govern, to a large extent, their entire working lives. *Leading Change in Healthcare* demonstrates that these organizations can be transformed radically in a positive, relational direction. It is possible to systematically create better structures and processes that value people, encourage creativity, promote relationship, and foster authenticity; these organizations get better results. By paying constant attention to everyday encounters, fostering courage and authenticity in leaders and applying the lessons of complexity, positive psychology and Relationship-centered Care we can not only hope for but expect transformation in our organizations and perhaps eventually in our society.

A 4-step model of relationship-centered communication

Penelope R Williamson

In Chapter 4, we explored the concept of Relationship-centered Care—a clinical approach based on partnership and shared decision making at every level: between patient–clinician, between members of the healthcare team and between healthcare organizations and the community. In this book, we're extending the concept to include a similar partnership-based approach to organizational leadership and management, calling it Relationship-centered Administration. This chapter describes a 4 step model of specific communication and relationship techniques that can be used to build partnership. These are also the skills that promote the expression of diversity and responsiveness, the key factors that favor innovation and adaptability (the emergence of new patterns of thinking; *see* Chapter 2). Following the description of each step, we offer examples of communications exercises or illustrative teaching tools. Simply imagining these exercises can bring the abstract principles to life; actually trying them is even better. And, of course, these exercises are available to anyone attempting to teach these skills in the course of their work as an educator or organizational-development consultant.

STEP 1: BEING PERSONALLY PRESENT AND INVITING OTHERS TO DO LIKEWISE

The first step of relationship-centered process is to be fully present and to invite others to do likewise, or more simply, to "show up." We can only be present in a relationship to the extent that we make ourselves available to the other person and welcome and acknowledge his or her presence. This is not simply a matter of physical presence, although that is certainly a factor—not being physically present can constrain the potential of a relationship, as in not keeping an appointment or interacting only in cyberspace. But even when we are physically present, it is necessary to bring ourselves fully into the moment. Are we offering our genuine thoughts and feelings as they arise or are we holding parts of ourselves back behind a screen of stereotyped conversation? Are we authentic and do we invite the authenticity of the other? Do we behold with full attention the person before us, or are we distracted, with significant portions of our attention focused elsewhere? And if we do behold this person, how do we let that person know and feel that he or she is truly being seen, heard, and respected?

Reflective listening exercise: In a group of any size, ask participants to divide up into pairs. Invite partners to take turns describing to each other what it feels like to be in that moment, right there and then. The first speaker has an opportunity to reflect for a moment on the content of her consciousness—the physical sensations, anticipations, distractions, delights, fears, whatever. As she notices these, and to the degree that she is willing (always having the right to choose what she wishes to disclose), she describes them. A typical comment might be, "I'm aware of a slight tension in my stomach, like butterflies. This exercise is new to me, so it makes me a little nervous. But I'm also hopeful about working in this group and I think I will learn a lot." The role of the listener is to attend to the speaker, and to limit his responses to simply reflecting back what he understands his partner to be communicating. "So you're feeling a mix of things: eagerness about learning, but also a little apprehension, like being in slightly unfamiliar territory." It might be a mirroring back of the partner's actual words, or a summary or paraphrasing, and it might include a reflection of non-verbal cues, as well (e.g. "You smiled broadly as you were saying that.") After just a minute or two, the partners trade roles.

This very brief and simple exercise often provokes profound insights. Participants often discover how seldom they notice what's going on in the here-and-now of their own experience. Their attention is often away in the future or back in the past. For some people, even this limited self-disclosure may feel new and uncomfortable. But they also describe the joy at having the time to reflect, and to speak knowing that they will not be interrupted—they do not have to actively hold the floor—and they appreciate being heard. The experience of listening elicits strong responses, too. Many people are surprised how hard it is to restrain themselves from offering stories or reactions of their own, to simply be with and acknowledge the other person. But they also feel that their patience and restraint is rewarded: resisting the urge to ask directive or leading questions gives space to the speaker to introduce poignant themes that the listener could never have known to ask about; there can be a surprising efficiency in this strategy of restraint. Both speaker and listener are struck by the profound sense of contact or connection that can emerge in a very short time. Following this exercise, people often resolve to give more undivided attention to others and to be better listeners.

Reflective listening is one of the most powerful and efficient of all communication skills. It simultaneously accomplishes three tasks. First, it verifies the accuracy of what's being understood, preventing subsequent misunderstandings, errors and even conflicts and all the associated extra effort and potential harm. Second, it demonstrates to the interviewee that the interviewer not only understands but also cares enough to want to understand correctly. Third, it often encourages the interviewer to say more. Three tasks accomplished with one simple statement: it doesn't get more efficient than that.

STEP 2: SPEAKING YOUR TRUTH AND LISTENING TO UNDERSTAND THE TRUTHS OF OTHERS

This step builds upon the first one by calling attention to the interdependent disciplines of advocacy and inquiry. Skilled advocacy involves articulating our point of view and the reasoning behind it. When our opinions aren't fully formed, explaining our thinking to others gives us a chance to explore and better understand it ourselves.

Advocacy is greatly facilitated by inquiry, the offering of time, attention, and curious open questions to help someone develop and articulate his or her thinking. Inquiry begins with curiosity and a genuine wish to understand the other person's perspective. It involves temporarily putting aside our own ideas and agenda, letting the other person talk without interruption and without having to fight to keep the floor. It requires a discipline of silencing the inner voice in us that is already formulating a response (regardless of whether our intent is to agree or disagree) and thus distracts our attention from the other person. Inquiry also involves refraining from asking questions intended to lead the other person toward a particular point of view and instead asking straight-forward, non-leading questions that invite reflection and the further synthesis of ideas. And there is a continuing role for reflective listening to ensure that we have an accurate understanding and that the other person feels heard and understood.

Skillful inquiry and advocacy exercise: Invite participants to form pairs or triads. Each person takes about 10 minutes to respond to a thought-provoking question, explaining the basis for her response (skilled advocacy). Her partner(s) ask open, honest questions to explore her thoughts and feelings in greater depth and reflect back what they are understanding (skilled inquiry). They specifically refrain from commenting on the views being expressed or offering views of their own. Examples of open, honest questions include: "Tell me more about that," "What does ___ mean to you?" and "How did you come to hold this value?" but not "How could you possibly believe that?" or "Have you thought that [some other point of view] might be true?" Questions may widen the scope of the conversation, whether they are abstract and general (e.g. "What core values inform your work as a leader?") or highly specific (e.g. "What do you think of the new performance-based incentive plan?" or "What are you telling yourself about why the patient is acting this way?").

Skilled inquiry is epitomized in the image of a good newspaper reporter conducting an interview. The reporter's views are irrelevant in the conversation—the content of the interview is filled with thoughts of interviewee, and the reporter's role is to help the interviewee bring those thoughts forward.

In debriefing this exercise, participants report that just as in the first exercise, it takes discipline to hold back their own opinions when interviewing. They describe both the difficulty and value of quieting their "inner voice," but they find themselves able to listen better and to understand more deeply. As listeners, they appreciate the unusual and delightful experience of being able to thoughtfully explore and elaborate on their thinking without having to fight to keep the floor. And having felt fully heard and understood, they feel better able to hear the views of others.

At a typical hospital committee meeting, the usual pattern of conversation is one of escalating exchanges of interrupted advocacy as people attempt to prevail over one another in a contest of ideas, a battle over who's right and who's wrong. A more functional pattern would consist of successive rounds of advocacy supported by inquiry, with new understandings emerging from the interplay of diverse ideas. But this depends upon how well people manage the differences that are surfaced by effective inquiry and advocacy. This leads us directly to the third step of relationship-centered process.

STEP 3: VALUING AND HARNESSING DIFFERENCE AND DIVERSITY

If the participants in a relationship are practicing effective inquiry and advocacy, it will not take long for major differences to emerge. The way people perceive and respond to their differences may be the single most important factor that determines the quality of partnership. It is without doubt the greatest source of difficulty, frustration and wasted energy in relationships. So we can describe this third and arguably most critical step as valuing difference and diversity.

A group's differences and diversity are its most important natural resource. If there was no diversity—if everyone's thinking was exactly alike—there would be no source of novelty from which new ideas could emerge. There could be no creativity, learning, growth or adaptation. We can find a useful parallel in population biology: the less the variability within a population, the less capable it is of adapting to environmental changes and the closer it is to extinction.

To value difference and diversity as a resource, we must first overcome our habitual "either-or" and "right-wrong" ways of thinking and instead allow ourselves to recognize that multiple divergent perspectives can be true simultaneously. Most situations are so complex that no one can see every facet; each person holds some unique piece of the truth. If any person's perspective is excluded, everyone loses.

The cone in the box exercise: A simple drawing of a cone inside a box is a profound tool for demonstrating the need to value and explore diverse perspectives (*see* Figure A2.1).[1] Participants are asked to imagine that there is a cone (for example, one of the pylons used on highways to divert traffic or mark hazards) inside a dimly lit box with a peephole at the top of the box and another on the side. They are the asked to describe what Person A would see looking down from the peephole on top (a circle or a point) and then what Person B would see looking from the side (a triangle). We then let the participants "listen in" on a conversation between Persons A and B:

"What do you see in there?"

"Well, it's some kind of circle."

"What? That's no circle. It has three points. It's a triangle."

"A triangle? Are you crazy? It's smooth and round. It's obviously a circle. I can see it clearly."

"You need your eyes examined. It's a triangle, plain as the nose on my face."

And on it goes from there.

After acknowledging the familiarity of this kind of conversation, we explore why A and B get into an argument, and quickly identify two major causes: 1) the assumption that there is one right answer (an "either-or" perspective), and 2) an intense need to not be wrong—to avoid shame and maintain the integrity of one's identity. But as the figure shows so clearly, reality is more complex than either perspective alone. The As and Bs need each other's perspectives to gain a more complete and accurate understanding. The As may be supervisors and the Bs front-line workers. Or the As may be women and the Bs men; or clinicians and administrators. The A might be you and Bs might be everyone else. The point still holds: **if either side can successfully suppress the other's point of view, everyone loses.**

When explorations of difference are framed in terms of right and wrong, or winning and losing, they are destined to fail. Everyone is left with an incomplete and inadequate understanding. The Cone in the Box reminds us to take a "both-and" perspective, to recognize that seemingly contradictory perspectives can be simultaneously true, and to explore these perspectives with openness and curiosity. That brings us right back to Skilled Inquiry and Advocacy as essential skills for exploring and harnessing difference. To them we add two additional skills.

➤ Skilled Self-Monitoring—the capacity to notice what we are feeling—is a helpful precursor to Skilled Inquiry. It is this capacity to notice that we are starting to feel threatened by someone else's different perspective that gives us the chance to break out of the either-or habit, to remember that we are not necessarily wrong just because someone sees something differently, and to turn away from argument and toward wonder. ("I wonder why I'm feeling this way?" "I wonder what led him or her to that stance?") The discipline of shifting from needing to be right to curiosity allows us to move to inquiry.

➤ Relationship-building Statements, summarized by the acronym PEARLS (*see* Table A1.1).[2] Relationship-building statements are explicit affirmations of the other person and expressions of personal commitment to the relationship. They help to counter the potential of differences to disrupt relationships. When we express a point of view that differs from that of another person, that person may accept the difference at face value, or might begin to make inferences about the state of our relationship, perhaps interpreting the expression of difference as competition, disrespect or distrust. By using PEARLS to explicitly communicate our positive regard for that person and our commitment to maintaining a good relationship, it leaves less room for the more negative inferences to form.

TABLE A1.1 Types of relationship-building statements with illustrative examples. (Adapted from Clark W, Hewson M, Fry M, Shorey J. *Communication Skills Reference Card.* St Louis, MO: American Academy on Communication in Healthcare; 1998.)

Partnership	We'll see this through together
	I really want to work on this with you.
Empathy	It sounds like that was frightening for you.
	I can feel your sadness as you talk.
Acknowledgment	You put a lot of work into that project.
	You researched this proposal very thoroughly.
Respect	I so respect your commitment.
	I've always appreciated your creativity.
Legitimation	This would be hard for anyone.
	Who wouldn't be worried about something like this?
Support	I'd like to help you with this.
	I want to see you succeed.

PEARLS and inquiry exercise: To provide participants with first-hand experience of an alternative to the usual pattern when differences are encountered, namely advocacy and counter-advocacy, we use an exercise that involves the exploration of an actual controversial subject within the group. Each person has a chance to make a simple statement. The adjacent person in the circle offers a PEARL followed by an inquiry. The first person then responds to the inquiry with an elaboration of her initial opinion. Turn taking proceeds around the circle until each person has had a chance to practice offering a PEARL and an inquiry.

While it's not necessary (or even helpful) to adhere to such a rigid formula (PEARL followed by inquiry) in real-life conversations, this is such a powerful and underutilized combination that it bears rehearsing, making it easier to incorporate this method into actual conversations. Participants typically report gaining comfort and confidence during the course of this exercise.

Relationship statements help to weave a container that is capable of holding us together in the face of our differences so we can explore them and learn together. That container can also be strengthened by reminding everyone of our shared vision and purpose or other sources of common ground.

STEP 4: LETTING GO OF CONTROL AND TRUSTING THE PROCESS

We have now arrived at the fourth and last step of relationship-centered process, letting go of control and trusting the process. Rather than approaching a conversation with a predetermined outcome in mind and pushing relentlessly towards that outcome at every opportunity, we can approach it with a sense of curiosity and hopeful expectancy. We can trust that if we have helped to establish an excellent process—if people are being genuinely present to each other, practicing skilled listening, inquiry and advocacy, and welcoming of difference as a stimulus to creativity—then the conversation can scarcely fail to yield a constructive outcome, one that will be more creative, robust and well supported than anything we could have designed on our own or attempted to impose on the group. In a field as control oriented as healthcare, letting go of control is not easy, but it is important because, paradoxically, the effort to control only diminishes the result.

Dialogue exercise: We know of no better way to illustrate the creative and emergent potential of skilled conversation than to hold a dialogue. It's important that the topic be interesting and important to the participants. Just before beginning, it's helpful to invite them to make intentional use of the skills described above and to notice how others are using them. Twenty to thirty minutes into the dialogue, we call a "time out" and go around the circle inviting the participants to share their observations of how the conversation is going, what they are experiencing and what skills they've tried to use (always explicitly offering them the opportunity to pass). People often recognize the self-organizing nature of the conversation (*see* Chapter 3) and give and receive positive feedback for facilitative remarks. The time-out often intensifies everyone's sense of being present, thus deepening the subsequent conversation. In experiencing the method of taking a time-out to talk about the conversation, the participants are also experiencing first hand a powerful method that they can use to help groups free themselves when conversations become stuck.

Taken together, these four core steps of relationship-centered process allow people to work together more effectively across all levels of healthcare, whether they are patients, families and clinicians; professional colleagues; or clinicians, administrators and community members. They establish more trust, greater willingness to share diverse perspectives, greater ability to hear and be affected by each other's views, more resourceful ideas and plans, and more buy-in for whatever plans are ultimately chosen. And the experience of working together is likely to be more meaningful and satisfying to everyone.

NOTES

1 Brown J. *A Leader's Guide to Reflective Practice.* Victoria, BC: Trafford Publishing; 2006.

2 Clark W, Hewson M, Fry M, Shorey J. *Communication Skills Reference Card.* St Louis, MO: American Academy on Communication in Healthcare; 1998.

Principles and practices of relationship-centered meetings

Anthony L Suchman and Penelope R Williamson

The quality of relationships within a work team or committee has a profound effect on the group's results. It determines their willingness to bring forward their diversity and differences as a resource for creativity, their openness to change, their motivation and initiative, and their commitment to the group and its work. Many (if not most) meetings are conducted in a way that actually inhibits relationships and engaged conversation, resulting in meetings that feel dull and unproductive. Fortunately, there are some straightforward principles and simple meeting formats that can make meetings more relational and elicit high-quality participation. These methods require no additional time, only a little bit of courage to try something new. You can provide the leadership needed to suggest or implement these methods regardless of whether you are a team leader or a team member.

PRINCIPLE #1: INVEST TIME IN RELATIONSHIP BUILDING; IT WILL PAY LARGE DIVIDENDS IN EFFICIENCY AND PERFORMANCE

When members of a team know and trust each other, people can say what they think and explore each others' positions. Differences of opinion and perspective are a stimulus for creativity, not conflict (*see* Chapter 2 and Appendix 1). Meetings are enjoyable and the group makes rapid progress. Conversely, when people don't know each other, they get hung up on stereotypes ("What do you expect from an immunologist, or a social worker?"). They misinterpret each other's meanings and intentions and get mired in unnecessary conflict. They hold their ideas back for fear of ridicule and they waste a lot of time defending themselves and protecting their turf, time that could be better devoted to the work at hand. Often the urgency of the work makes it tempting to short-cut relationship building ("We don't have time for this 'soft stuff,' there's real work to do") but it is *always* a false economy. The more urgent the work, the greater the likelihood of inadvertent relational breaches that amplify over time, the more urgently good relationships are needed, and the poorer the efficiency and outcomes will be if they are lacking.

Methods

Initial meeting: There are many ways to help people get to know each other at the first meeting of a group. Participants can take turns introducing themselves, saying a bit about what they had to do or give up to attend the meeting and why it was important to do so. And/or they can tell a brief story about how they have come to be where they are at this point in their careers and lives. If the group numbers between 8 and 16, you might invite people to divide into pairs. People take turns interviewing each other for a few minutes using the questions above, then when the whole group reconvenes each person introduces her/his partner. If the group numbers eight or less, you might still use the paired interview approach or you can invite people to tell their stories directly to the whole group. In the latter case, it helps establish trust in the group to give people the option of passing if they'd rather not address the whole group (people rarely avail themselves of that option but it makes them comfortable to know they have it).

Subsequent meetings: At the start of each meeting, it's helpful to begin with a round of "checking-in," offering an invitation to each person (always with the option to pass) of reflecting on how they're doing at the moment or what might be going on for them outside of the meeting that might be diverting their attention. Often simply naming the distraction helps to ameliorate it, and if it is something truly difficult (a child's or parent's illness or a major home repair in progress, for instance), the team members can offer support and will know not to take it personally if that person is observed during the meeting to be staring off into space and scowling.

Another approach to check-in is to offer each person an opportunity to describe something that has gone well since the previous meeting.

PRINCIPLE #2: FOSTER HIGH-QUALITY CONVERSATION

The "free for all" conversational format at most meetings wastes time and potential. People have to fight to get the floor only to be interrupted before they can complete their thoughts; some people are not heard from at all. This leads to poor listening, ineffective articulation of ideas, a poor sense of teamwork and low commitment to any decisions that result. So instead of a free-for-all, use a little light structure in the service of better conversation.

Methods

Nominal group process: This is just a fancy term for giving each person in turn a specified amount of time without interruption to say what they think. You can allow a brief period of questioning before proceeding to the next person, or you can wait to hear from everyone before proceeding to questions and/ or freeform dialogue. In one variation, people suggest one idea at a time and keep going around the circle until there are no further ideas. Recording ideas on a board or flip chart can ensure that ideas are not lost. It's often useful to engage in another round of nominal group process after a discussion has been in progress for a while to see what level of consensus exists and what issues still need more attention.

Talking stick: This method involves using an object (traditionally a stick, but any object will do) to signify who has the floor. After finishing, a speaker passes the object to someone else who then has the floor. This method brings a little order to the conversation and helps people finish their thoughts without interruption.

PRINCIPLE #3: EXPLORE DIFFERENCE WITH OPENNESS AND CURIOSITY

When faced with a difference of opinion, people are all too easily hooked into a struggle over who's right and who's wrong. They fight as if their lives are at stake, and it's no wonder given all the humiliation associated with being wrong in traditional medical learning environments. The challenge here is to recognize that most situations are more complex than any one person can grasp, that everyone has a unique piece of the puzzle, and if anyone's piece is lost *everybody* loses (*see* Appendix 1). When people see things differently, most of the time they *both* are right.

Methods

The cone in the box: Figure A2.1 is a simple and effective graphic for helping people recognize that different perspectives are not mutually exclusive.[1] It shows a cone inside a box. People looking through a peephole at point A will see a circle, and at point B a triangle. Their observations may seem mutually incompatible and they will argue forever unless they can get past the belief that someone else's different perception invalidates their own and accept that reality is more complex than what they are seeing on their own.

Listen for internal reactions. A failsafe indicator that you have a difference of opinion is your internal reaction. The most useful thing you can do when you suddenly experience a strong feeling (e.g. anger, defensiveness, humiliation) in response to what someone else says or does is to pause for a moment and "turn to wonder"—"I wonder why I'm feeling this way?" "I wonder what led him or her to that stance?" The discipline of shifting from knowing that you are right to curiosity about your response allows you to move to inquiry.

Inquiry and advocacy: When encountering a difference of opinion, presume that the other person is competent and conscientious. Resist the initial temptation to argue, and instead use inquiry—exploratory questions—to better understand the other person's views and reasoning. If you can show that you understand his/her view by accurately reflecting it back, so much the better. Only then is it time to advocate your own perspective, clearly explaining your reasoning. And by then, you may have discovered there is in fact no difference, or that the heart of the difference is something other than what you thought at first, so you can respond more effectively. As a facilitator, you can help your group recognize when they are getting stuck in a right-wrong conversation and invite them to use more inquiry and less advocacy to find their way through.

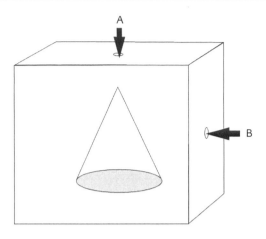

FIGURE A2.1 The Cone in the Box. (Adapted from Brown J. *A Leader's Guide to Reflective Practice.* Victoria, BC: Trafford Publishing; 2007.)

PRINCIPLE #4: IN PURSUING CHANGE, LEARN FROM SUCCESSES

Most groups working on organizational change focus on problems, trying to identify and fix the root causes. The major problem with this time-honored approach is that the problems are too often equated with people. No one likes to be a problem, so people divert a lot of energy into defending themselves to avoid shame; the conversation makes little headway. An effective and Zen-like alternative is to seek out and learn from instances in which the desired change is already present. They're almost always around if you look for them.

Method

Appreciative Inquiry: This philosophy and methodology for organizational change is based on discovering and building upon the existing capacity within an organization (*see* Chapter 3). For example, if we want to foster better interdisciplinary collaboration, we'll make more progress by learning from successful instances—what went right, what factors made it possible, and how we can do more of that—than discussing where things went wrong and why. Curiously, we'll end up talking about exactly the same issues, attitudes and behaviors in either conversation, but with very different emotional tones that profoundly influence people's openness to change. A typical AI process begins with people pairing up and taking turns telling each other stories of successful collaboration. The interviewer can explore the partner's experience in more detail using questions such as:

➤ What did you do or bring to the situation that contributed to the success?
➤ Who else was involved and what did they do that helped?
➤ What aspects of the setting or situation made a difference?
➤ What useful lessons can we take from this story?

Partners can then present each other's stories and lessons learned, to the whole group. This method is, in fact, a powerful form of participative inquiry. It invites people to step forward from a place of capacity rather than defensiveness, and helps people feel more hopeful and welcoming of change.

Appreciative debriefing: A similar approach can be applied in miniature at the close of each meeting. You can invite (with the option of passing, as always) each participant to reflect on moments during the meeting that they found particularly useful, important or engaging. This encourages people to become more aware of the process of their meetings and to discover how they can be helpful to each other. Positively reinforcing these helpful behaviors increases the likelihood of their use in future meetings and builds the sense of connection in the group, thus serving Principle #1.

PRINCIPLE #5: WHEN MEETINGS GET STUCK, INTERRUPT THE PATTERN

Sometimes meetings get stuck. You may find yourselves going around the same arguments again and again. Or one person may be dominating the conversation or holding fast to a point when the rest of the group is ready to move on. There may be rising emotions that are not being acknowledged. In such situations, the group can find itself caught in a pattern from which it is unable to extricate itself.

Method

Reflective time out: An effective way to help the group share responsibility for managing itself is to take a time out from the conversation to reflect together on the conversation itself. Questions like "How is the conversation going so far?" or "What are you experiencing at this moment?" invite people to notice what's happening and to learn from others' observations. Other questions can help the group think about how to move forward: "What would help us right now?" or "What might we try to do differently?" The conversation can sometimes be stuck because an important issue has not yet been explicitly named (there's an "elephant in the room"). A question like "What important topics are we not yet talking about?" can open the door. The meeting leader or a facilitative group member can offer answers to these questions and make suggestions about how to change the conversation (and may need to if the other group members are not forthcoming), but the group learns more and partnership is enhanced if the group can find its own solutions.

In a reflective time out, you can offer people a quiet moment for reflection and then hear from each person (a variation on the method of nominal group process described above). If there is not sufficient trust and safety for people to speak their concerns to each other directly, another variation is to ask people to write their comments down and hand them in to be read anonymously.

PRINCIPLE #6: TRUST THE PROCESS; DON'T TRY TO CONTROL THE OUTCOME

Good group process draws forth the best capacity of the group. You will no doubt find yourself heading into some meetings convinced that you already know what decision the group should make, and trying (subtly, or so you think) to steer the group towards your predetermined outcome. There are two major problems with this approach: 1) People don't like feeling manipulated; they will fight you and will be unmotivated to follow through; 2) The group is smarter than you are, so your solution is unlikely to be as good as what the group would come up with. Rather than focusing on the desired *outcome*, focus on maximizing the quality of the *process*—on the quality of relationships and trust, and on the quality of listening, exploring, advocating and understanding. If the process is as good as possible, the best possible outcome will result.

Methods
All of the above!
The relationship-centered principles outlined above rest on a strong body of evidence. Relationship quality is well associated with a wide variety of organizational outcomes in healthcare including quality and safety of care, cost, patient and staff satisfaction, and the capacity to learn new procedures (*see* Chapter 4). The principles and methods are also easy to apply. They may be unfamiliar and may feel a bit awkward at first. But if you share your awkwardness with the group and let them know what you're trying to do and why, they will support you. Just remember what you are trying to accomplish—creating a more relational environment in which to work and get care. Bold change is accomplished by people who are willing to risk something new. Using these simple principles and methods, you can help your teams reach a new level of performance and engagement. We create the new model by living it in each meeting, and it will grow in ways none of us can imagine. May you have courage and success!

NOTE
1 Brown J. *A Leader's Guide to Reflective Practice*. Victoria, BC: Trafford Publishing; 2007.

A relationship-centered approach to delegation and accountability

Anthony L Suchman and Penelope R Williamson

Effective delegation and accountability are core tasks of successful leadership and management. When done well, those with newly delegated responsibilities build their capacity, unleash their creativity and enhance their self-efficacy. Effective delegations also give leaders more time to mentor those in their charge and to focus on larger system issues. Too often, however, leaders do not effectively delegate tasks or ensure accountability for their implementation. The delegation may be too vague or there might be micromanaging instead of true delegation. Feedback may be impromptu and impressionistic if it is given at all. It may be focused more on the person than on the behavior, and does not lead to performance improvement. Ultimately, if performance levels are unacceptable, delegations are often withdrawn in a manner that is unnecessarily hurtful to the individual and harmful to the organizational culture. Worse yet, the unfulfilled delegation may *not* be withdrawn and the poor performance allowed to continue, to the detriment of customers, co-workers and the whole organization.

Fortunately, there are some straightforward principles and practices that can help you make effective delegations and maintain accountability, thus maximizing the performance of your team or organization. We offer these below, along with illustrative conversations showing what these principles might look like in action. We divide the presentation into three sections that correspond to three obligations we have to those to whom we make delegations: a well-conceived delegation (made to the right person with clear expectations and adequate support); honest assessment of progress with feedback and coaching as needed; and withdrawal of a delegation, role or position that isn't working.

MAKING A WELL-CONCEIVED DELEGATION

In making an effective delegation, your first and most important task is to **choose the right person**—to seek the best alignment between the task and the individual. While the selected individual must have sufficient skills and experience to take on the new role, (s)he doesn't necessarily have to be the most skilled or experienced person. Other factors are equally important in assessing best fit. People are most creative, committed and effective when their work holds personal interest and meaning. Perhaps the delegation represents a step up in responsibility, a chance to gain new knowledge and skills, or a chance to develop important new working relationships. Perhaps the work is in a domain for which an individual has a longstanding interest or passion. Or maybe the work will enhance the individual's visibility within the organization. It's helpful to exchange perspectives about fit with the person you've chosen. It reinforces a pattern of partnership from the outset and it can reveal important considerations of which you might not have been aware. Avoiding an unwise delegation is far more efficient than having to clean up afterwards.

Once you have chosen the right person, it is important that you **establish clear expectations** for the work you are delegating. This means not only naming the overall task or role to be delegated but also providing enough details to ensure that you and your employee share an accurate understanding of what is being asked: what is the desired outcome, what is the deadline, what resources are available (or must not be used), who else should or should not be involved, and any other parameters within which the delegation must be carried out. The amount of detail provided will depend on the nature of the work and the experience of the appointee. The simplest way to ascertain the level of detailed information an employee needs is to ask! It is often helpful for the boss to start this inquiry, as it may be difficult for an employee to do so. Negotiating clear, mutually understood expectations strengthens partnership by letting the employee know she is not in this alone, and has a supportive thinking partner. It is also the basis for reviewing performance and providing feedback along the way. Unambiguous expectations are the starting point for maintaining accountability.

It is also essential to **ensure adequate preparation and resources** for the person to do the job. As above, an open, transparent conversation can help you learn what an employee needs to perform the task well. Do they have or can they acquire the resources, knowledge and skills needed? These might include financial, educational or other resources; emotional support; and a constructive environment. Taking on a new role or task might necessitate prioritizing or giving up some current responsibilities. What help will you provide at the start and over time? Clear negotiation of these important variables will help pave the way for a successful delegation.

Finally, it is crucial to **arrange for a feedback session** at the time of the initial delegation. Delegation requires supervision; it is not a hand-off but rather a reapportioning of responsibilities. It is far more efficient and beneficial to all involved to have timely assessments of successes and needs along the way, making course corrections as appropriate, than to discover at some end point that expectations have not been met. It is helpful to arrive at an understanding ahead of time about when performance will be assessed and what criteria will be used. Here again, expectations can be mutually established. Involving the employee in each step of the delegation reinforces and models partnership and sets the stage for trust and mutual accountability.

To summarize, the four steps in making a well-conceived delegation are as follows.

➤ **Choose the right person.** Find alignment between the needs of the organization and the personal goals and interests of the person receiving the delegation.

➤ **Establish clear expectations.** Be sure expectations are shared by both the person in charge and the employee.

➤ **Ensure adequate preparation and resources.** Make sure people have or can acquire the resources, knowledge, and skills to do the job; including training, financial or other resources; emotional support; and a constructive environment.

➤ **Plan the assessment prospectively.** Arrive at an understanding ahead of time of how and when performance will be assessed; preferably mutually decided upon.

Delegation meeting

Here is how a delegation conversation might go:

Boss: Hi Rob. Is this a good time to meet? (Yes? Good) I'm very pleased to be talking with you today. I have heard you express an interest in taking on larger-scale projects and have observed your excellent way of relating with people, and we have a need that just might fit. I'd like you to coordinate our annual community-outreach meeting, which is set for June 7th, four months from now. I think you would do an outstanding job with this. I hope you'll agree to take this on.

Rob: I'm delighted you thought of me, and would like to consider it. What is involved?

Boss: We already have a venue and a date which is a good thing but it creates the need for efficient planning as it is only four months away. I'd expect you to coordinate the work of everyone who will be involved and to keep on top of the planning and implementation along the way. Let me ask you, have you done something like this before?

Rob: I've headed up some projects of a smaller scale.

Boss: The basics are likely familiar. Let's explore how you might take your experience to a larger scale! What would be helpful?

Rob: I'd appreciate knowing how you would approach this task.

Boss: I'd suggest that you begin by creating a timeline with all the major tasks so that you can pace yourself accordingly. Also, you'll probably want to gather a planning team to help you think of all the necessary steps and carry out all that will need to happen to bring about this important gathering. I'm available to meet with you weekly or at least bi-weekly over this time to be of help and to provide supervision since this is your first time with a project of this scope. How does that sound? What are your thoughts?

Rob: That all sounds good. I like the idea of a planning team and also that you'll be available for consultation and supervision. Will I have any other support (time freed up from my other roles, secretarial help)?

Boss: You bet. (Gives details of what will happen and support.) Is there any other help you need to get started?

Rob: I have to admit, I've never created a timeline before.

Boss: Thanks for being forthright. I can show you how I approach this. I'd start by drawing a line across a sheet of paper. The end point is the event. The beginning point is today. We've already agreed that you will form a planning team. If you can do that by next week, put an x there to mark the spot. Then think of all the tasks that will be involved (such as marketing, creating a schedule, lining up speakers or workshops, arranging for food and lodging, etc.) and in what order they need to be done, and list them on the line. Sometimes it's helpful to work backwards from the date of the event. You might take a first stab at this and then invite your planning team to help fill in and refine your draft. Does that help?

Rob: That is great. I have a good sense of what I need to do now and am pleased you thought of me for this project. I'm glad to accept.

Boss: Good. I'm delighted, and feel confident you'll do well. Time is of the essence, and everything that happens will depend on the timeline and the planning team. I'd like to meet again as soon as you have created a draft of the timeline and gathered the planning team. Is a week enough time for those two steps? (Rob—Yes; I think so). Good. Then let's meet next Friday at 2 pm and I'd like to see the timeline and know who's on the team by then.

ASSESSING PROGRESS AND GIVING FEEDBACK

Having made a well-conceived delegation with clear descriptions of expected outcomes and the parameters within which they must be achieved, the next step is to follow through with planned progress assessment. This step is much simpler for having defined the assessment criteria in advance: you both know what data to gather and there is less potential for misaligned expectations. The crucial success factors here are honest feedback, effective coaching and good partnership process.

➤ Use direct observations whenever possible.

➤ Celebrate and reinforce successes; reinforce positive expectations.

➤ Show genuine belief in the capacity of the other to grow and perform.

➤ Offer mentoring/guidance as appropriate; invite the other person to make his/her thinking process explicit.

➤ Point out errors and omissions, using them as learning opportunities for presenting alternative approaches.

➤ Use partnership and dialogue skills (PEARLS, skilled inner-listening, inquiry and advocacy) (*see* Appendix 1).

➤ Make a plan for the next timely cycle of performance review and evaluation: when it will take place, what specific performance expectations will be assessed, what data and criteria will be used.

Feedback meeting

Here is how a follow-up meeting might go:

Boss: Hi Rob, it's good to see you. How have you been doing since we met last week?

Rob: Very well. I have pulled together a six-person planning team and we had our first meeting, yesterday. I think they are a very good group, representing the spectrum of activities in our organization that will be needed for bringing about this community-outreach gathering. I emailed you the names yesterday. (Boss—Yes, I got them.) They are eager to be helpful and had some great ideas already; I felt good about our first meeting and about planning the event.

Boss: Terrific. I have already heard a buzz of excitement, and have observed that you've gone about pulling together your planning team in a relational and inclusive manner. I'm glad you included people with a broad range of responsibility and capabilities; it looks to be a great team. Now, what about the timeline?

Rob: I have started on it, but didn't get as far as I'd hoped. (Perhaps shows sketchy timeline with only a few points on it.)

Boss: I'm a little surprised that you have not done more on this, as we talked last week about how important the timeline is to all that follows, and that time is of the essence. Tell me, what has gotten in the way?

Rob: After our team met yesterday, I got slammed with two urgent deadlines from my regular "day job" and didn't want to let my colleagues down. I was up till midnight finishing that work, and just haven't had the time to sit down and put all the points on the timeline—from our conversation in the planning team and from my own thinking. I didn't want to present you with a half-baked product. I'll do it in the next few days.

Boss: I can see how that could happen. I can also see that this is an important learning opportunity for you. The annual meeting is very important to the whole organization and to our community. Your leadership will determine its success. Taking this on presents a chance for you to prioritize and to set limits on what you can and cannot do while you are coordinating this effort. How will you approach this now?

Rob: I think I just have to say no to some other "urgent" things that keep appearing on my plate, until this is done.

Boss: Yes, I agree. As you know, I arranged for you to be able to cut back on your regular work for these few months so I have your back on this.

We absolutely need this timeline in the next few days. I believe in your capacity to do both things: let your immediate supervisor know what you can and can't do in the short run, and put this timeline together by Tuesday. You've made a great start with the team. Now we need this organizational piece in order to ensure we can pull off the meeting. Can I count on you for that?

Rob: Yes, I'll get it done.

Boss: Good. Let's meet on Tuesday at 3 pm with the timeline. Please send me a draft in advance of the meeting so I can review it. See you then.

ENDING A DELEGATION, ROLE OR POSITION THAT ISN'T WORKING

Most of the time, when you have delegated a job or task thoughtfully, set clear expectations, given actionable feedback and offered timely coaching, things work out well. The delegation and feedback sessions provide opportunities for celebrations, course corrections and learning along the way. Occasionally, however, in spite of these steps and good intentions, things do not work out, and in service to patients/customers, co-workers, the organization (and its mission) and even in service to the underperforming employee, it falls to you to end a delegation, or even a job. It is important to learn the skills of ending a delegation well. Paradoxical as it may seem, it is possible to do this in a relational manner, preserving an employee's self-worth and a relational organization culture.

➤ Set the stage ("As we had planned, we're meeting to compare your actual progress with the goals and expectations we discussed previously.")

➤ Forecast the bad news ("I'm afraid the news isn't good.")

➤ Give the news, stating it clearly and unambiguously ("Your efforts haven't fulfilled our needs; I can't keep you in this role.")

➤ Characterize the problem as mismatch between the individual's strengths and what the role requires ("I've seen that you are good at x, y and z. This role requires a, b, and c. It's just not the right match and it's not good for you or for the organization for you to stay in this role.")

➤ Keep the focus on the behavior and not the person. ("Your work is not sufficiently organized and it's not completed on time."—rather than "You're no good.")

➤ Use empathy and other PEARLS (*see* Box A1.1) ("I imagine that this is pretty hard to hear . . .")

It is essential to emphasize that ending a delegation represents a mismatch between the strengths of the person and the role requirements of the job. This is not a bad person; rather, their behavior didn't meet agreed expectations. Even if this is not the right task for this person at this time, it is important to indicate that you still have belief in the capacity of the person. And it is helpful to be empathic to how hard it is to hear bad news (as well as to give it!)

We come back to our scenario with the Boss, and Rob. Rob has not sent a timeline in advance of the meeting as requested, and an email prompt has led to an incomplete timeline that does not meet the needs for the project. Rob has not been able to let go of the "urgent" tasks that are always present, in order to attend to what is most important. Here is how that meeting might go:

Meeting to end a delegation

Boss: Hello Rob. Our meeting today is to compare your actual progress with the goals and expectations we have discussed. I'm afraid the news isn't good. In spite of your best efforts, your work on the timeline has not been sufficiently organized or timely enough to meet the needs of this project. I have decided I cannot keep you in this role.

Rob: (hangs his head) I'm very disappointed. I know I can do it. I've been trying so hard and I'm getting better.

Boss: I can empathize. This must be hard to hear.

Rob: It is—I feel like I've failed.

Boss: I don't see it that way. I see it as more of a mismatch between your strengths at this time and what the role requires. You have great strengths with part of this role (gathering the right people and getting them involved) but the organizational aspects and efficiency are also vital to a time-sensitive initiative like the annual community-outreach meeting. You have not been able to manage your time efficiently and get the detailed timeline completed even with several extensions. I have to balance the needs of the organization with your learning needs.

I see this is my error, in part. I pushed you too fast into this role. You are on a learning curve regarding learning effective time management. I believe you can become good at this; but it will take more time than we have available right now. I'd like to help you continue to learn, but can't do it at the cost of this program's success.

Rob: You still believe I can learn this?

Boss: I do; if you're interested in making this a part of your repertoire.

Rob: I really am.

Boss: I'm glad to hear it. I'd like you to work closely with Dr X for the remainder of this project. I have asked her to take the lead on the meeting. You'll be her second-in-charge. She has great strengths in time management and you'll learn a lot from working with her. And you'll continue to bring your gifts in working with the team. How does that sound?

Rob: silence . . . It feels like a demotion; but I'm also glad I'm not off the project all together and that you believe I am not a lost cause. I want to lead projects like this in the future. I think it will be good to work with Dr X.

Boss: I admire your graciousness in handling this shift of responsibilities. I think this will be an important turning point for you, and I look forward to our continued work together.

Rob: Thank you.

Unclear delegations and inadequate processes of accountability are arguably the leading cause of yield-loss in organizations, and the most easily correctable. Using the principles described above you can improve the practice of delegation and accountability, which will improve organizational performance and at the same time foster a workplace culture of respect and partnership.

Index